Windows® CE For Dummies®

Cheat Sheet

Windows CE Keyboard Shortcuts

Press These Keys	To Do This
Alt+Tab	Display the Task Manager window
Alt+Esc	Switch between open windows
Alt+H	Display a Help window for the current program
Windows key*	Pop up the Start menu
Windows key+C	Open the Control Panel folder
Windows key+E	Open the My Handheld Explorer folder
Windows key+H	Display the Help window for Windows CE
Windows key+I	Open the Stylus Calibration option
Windows key+K	Open the Keyboard Properties option
Windows key+R	Open the Run window

** The Windows key resembles the Windows CE logo. It is usually located between the Ctrl and Alt keys on the keyboard of your handheld PC.*

Frequently Encountered Buttons

Tap on This Button	To Do This
	Remove, or *cut,* an item so that you can move it somewhere else by using the Paste command
	Copy the selected item so that you can insert a copy somewhere else by using the Paste command
	Paste the last thing you cut or copied into the current location of the cursor
	Save the current information
	Open a file
	Delete the selected item
	View the contents of the parent folder
	Create a new folder

Keyboard Editing Options

Press These Keys	To Do This
Ctrl+A	Select the entire document
Ctrl+C	Copy a block of information from a document
Ctrl+F	Locate information
Ctrl+V	Paste the last information that was copied or cut
Ctrl+X	Cut a block of information from a document
Ctrl+Z	Undo the last action you performed
Ctrl+S	Save the current document
Ctrl+N	Open a new document
Ctrl+O	Open an existing document

Cheat Sheet $2.95 value. Item 0260-3.
For more information about IDG Books, call 1-800-762-2974.

...For Dummies: #1 Computer Book Series for Beginners

Windows® CE For Dummies®

Cheat Sheet

Helpful Hints

- You can find hidden menus on your device by simply holding down the Alt key and tapping on a location with the stylus. For example, to access the hidden menu that provides options for organizing the layout of your desktop, hold down the Alt key and tap in the center of the desktop. To quickly empty the Recycle Bin, hold down the Alt key and tap on the Recycle Bin icon. On the menu that pops up, tap on the Empty Recycle Bin option.
- Press Shift+Caps Shift to turn on the All Caps option, which makes every letter you type appear as an uppercase letter. To turn off the All Caps option, press Shift+Caps Shift again.
- When you change the batteries in your device, make sure that you always change the main batteries before changing the backup battery. Never remove both the main and backup batteries at the same time — doing so erases everything on your device.
- To move icons around on your desktop, simply tap on the desired icon and drag the stylus across the screen to the desired location.
- To minimize a window on your device, simply tap on the button for that window on the taskbar. When you want to open the window again, tap on the same button on the taskbar.
- If an OK button appears in the upper-right corner of a window, you need to click on that button to save any changes you make in the window. If you click on the X button to close the window, the changes you make may not be saved.

Navigating Documents

Press These Keys	*To Do This*
Alt+Up Arrow key	Move up one page in the document
Alt+Down Arrow key	Move down one page in the document
Alt+Left Arrow key	Move to the left side of a document
Alt+Right Arrow key	Move to the right side of a document
Ctrl+Alt+Left Arrow key	Move to the top of a document
Ctrl+Alt+Right Arrow key	Move to the bottom of a document

WINDOWS® CE FOR DUMMIES®

WINDOWS® CE FOR DUMMIES®

by Jinjer Simon

IDG BOOKS WORLDWIDE

IDG Books Worldwide, Inc.
An International Data Group Company

Foster City, CA ♦ Chicago, IL ♦ Indianapolis, IN ♦ Southlake, TX

Windows® CE For Dummies®

Published by
IDG Books Worldwide, Inc.
An International Data Group Company
919 E. Hillsdale Blvd.
Suite 400
Foster City, CA 94404
http://www.idgbooks.com (IDG Books Worldwide Web site)
http://www.dummies.com (Dummies Press Web site)

Library of Congress Catalog Card No.: 97-72412

ISBN: 0-7645-0260-3

Printed in the United States of America

10 9 8 7 6 5 4 3 2 1

1E/ST/QW/ZX/IN

Distributed in the United States by IDG Books Worldwide, Inc.

Distributed by Macmillan Canada for Canada; by Transworld Publishers Limited in the United Kingdom; by IDG Norge Books for Norway; by IDG Sweden Books for Sweden; by Woodslane Pty. Ltd. for Australia; by Woodslane Enterprises Ltd. for New Zealand; by Longman Singapore Publishers Ltd. for Singapore, Malaysia, Thailand, and Indonesia; by Simron Pty. Ltd. for South Africa; by Toppan Company Ltd. for Japan; by Distribuidora Cuspide for Argentina; by Livraria Cultura for Brazil; by Ediciencia S.A. for Ecuador; by Addison-Wesley Publishing Company for Korea; by Ediciones ZETA S.C.R. Ltda. for Peru; by WS Computer Publishing Corporation, Inc., for the Philippines; by Unalis Corporation for Taiwan; by Contemporanea de Ediciones for Venezuela; by Computer Book & Magazine Store for Puerto Rico; by Express Computer Distributors for the Caribbean and West Indies. Authorized Sales Agent: Anthony Rudkin Associates for the Middle East and North Africa.

For general information on IDG Books Worldwide's books in the U.S., please call our Consumer Customer Service department at 800-762-2974. For reseller information, including discounts and premium sales, please call our Reseller Customer Service department at 800-434-3422.

For information on where to purchase IDG Books Worldwide's books outside the U.S., please contact our International Sales department at 415-655-3200 or fax 415-655-3295.

For information on foreign language translations, please contact our Foreign & Subsidiary Rights department at 415-655-3021 or fax 415-655-3281.

For sales inquiries and special prices for bulk quantities, please contact our Sales department at 415-655-3200 or write to the address above.

For information on using IDG Books Worldwide's books in the classroom or for ordering examination copies, please contact our Educational Sales department at 800-434-2086 or fax 817-251-8174.

For press review copies, author interviews, or other publicity information, please contact our Public Relations department at 415-655-3000 or fax 415-655-3299.

For authorization to photocopy items for corporate, personal, or educational use, please contact Copyright Clearance Center, 222 Rosewood Drive, Danvers, MA 01923, or fax 508-750-4470.

About the Author

Jinjer Simon started her computer career in 1984 when she entered college and took her first computer programming class. Since that time, it seems that very little transpires in her life without somehow being associated with a computer. She rarely ventures far without a computer of some type — which makes her handheld PC a welcome addition to her life, because it now gives her the freedom to take a computer everywhere.

Jinjer has worn several hats in the computer industry, ranging from computer programmer to end-user support and documentation development. She currently works as a consultant designing online computer documentation for Microsoft Windows software, writing user manuals, creating software training guides, and developing Internet Web sites.

Jinjer lives in Carrollton, Texas, a suburb of Dallas, with her husband Richard, and their two children, Alex and Ashley. In her spare time, when she is not writing books, or playing mom, she enjoys traveling with her family and finding new hobbies, such as her most recent interest in scuba diving.

ABOUT IDG BOOKS WORLDWIDE

Welcome to the world of IDG Books Worldwide.

IDG Books Worldwide, Inc., is a subsidiary of International Data Group, the world's largest publisher of computer-related information and the leading global provider of information services on information technology. IDG was founded more than 25 years ago and now employs more than 8,500 people worldwide. IDG publishes more than 275 computer publications in over 75 countries (see listing below). More than 60 million people read one or more IDG publications each month.

Launched in 1990, IDG Books Worldwide is today the #1 publisher of best-selling computer books in the United States. We are proud to have received eight awards from the Computer Press Association in recognition of editorial excellence and three from *Computer Currents*' First Annual Readers' Choice Awards. Our best-selling *...For Dummies*® series has more than 30 million copies in print with translations in 30 languages. IDG Books Worldwide, through a joint venture with IDG's Hi-Tech Beijing, became the first U.S. publisher to publish a computer book in the People's Republic of China. In record time, IDG Books Worldwide has become the first choice for millions of readers around the world who want to learn how to better manage their businesses.

Our mission is simple: Every one of our books is designed to bring extra value and skill-building instructions to the reader. Our books are written by experts who understand and care about our readers. The knowledge base of our editorial staff comes from years of experience in publishing, education, and journalism — experience we use to produce books for the '90s. In short, we care about books, so we attract the best people. We devote special attention to details such as audience, interior design, use of icons, and illustrations. And because we use an efficient process of authoring, editing, and desktop publishing our books electronically, we can spend more time ensuring superior content and spend less time on the technicalities of making books.

You can count on our commitment to deliver high-quality books at competitive prices on topics you want to read about. At IDG Books Worldwide, we continue in the IDG tradition of delivering quality for more than 25 years. You'll find no better book on a subject than one from IDG Books Worldwide.

John Kilcullen
CEO
IDG Books Worldwide, Inc.

Steven Berkowitz
President and Publisher
IDG Books Worldwide, Inc.

Eighth Annual Computer Press Awards 1992

Ninth Annual Computer Press Awards 1993

Tenth Annual Computer Press Awards 1994

Eleventh Annual Computer Press Awards 1995

IDG Books Worldwide, Inc., is a subsidiary of International Data Group, the world's largest publisher of computer-related information and the leading global provider of information services on information technology. International Data Group publishes over 275 computer publications in over 75 countries. Sixty million people read one or more International Data Group publications each month. International Data Group's publications include: **ARGENTINA:** Buyer's Guide, Computerworld Argentina, PC World Argentina; **AUSTRALIA:** Australian Macworld, Australian PC World, Australian Reseller News, Computerworld, IT Casebook, Network World, Publish, Webmaster; **AUSTRIA:** Computerwelt Osterreich, Networks Austria, PC Tip Austria; **BANGLADESH:** PC World Bangladesh; **BELARUS:** PC World Belarus; **BELGIUM:** Data News; **BRAZIL:** Annuário de Informática, Computerworld, Connections, Macworld, PC Player, PC World, Publish, Reseller News, Supergamepower; **BULGARIA:** Computerworld Bulgaria, Network World Bulgaria, PC & MacWorld Bulgaria; **CANADA:** CIO Canada, Client/Server World, ComputerWorld Canada, InfoWorld Canada, NetworkWorld Canada, WebWorld; **CHILE:** Computerworld Chile, PC World Chile; **COLOMBIA:** Computerworld Colombia, PC World Colombia; **COSTA RICA:** PC World Centro America; **THE CZECH AND SLOVAK REPUBLICS:** Computerworld Czechoslovakia, Macworld Czech Republic, PC World Czechoslovakia; **DENMARK:** Communications World Danmark, Computerworld Danmark, Macworld Danmark, PC World Danmark, Techworld Denmark; **DOMINICAN REPUBLIC:** PC World Republica Dominicana; **ECUADOR:** PC World Ecuador; **EGYPT:** Computerworld Middle East, PC World Middle East; **EL SALVADOR:** PC World Centro America; **FINLAND:** MikroPC, Tietoverkko, Tietoviikko; **FRANCE:** Distributique, Hebdo, Info PC, Le Monde Informatique, Macworld, Reseaux & Telecoms, WebMaster France; **GERMANY:** Computer Partner, Computerwoche, Computerwoche Extra, Computerwoche FOCUS, Global Online, Macwelt, PC Welt; **GREECE:** Amiga Computing, GamePro Greece, Multimedia World; **GUATEMALA:** PC World Centro America; **HONDURAS:** PC World Centro America; **HONG KONG:** Computerworld Hong Kong, PC World Hong Kong, Publish in Asia; **HUNGARY:** ABCD CD-ROM, Computerworld Szamitastechnika, Internetto online Magazine, PC World Hungary, PC-X Magazin Hungary; **ICELAND:** Tolvuheimur PC World Island; **INDIA:** Information Communications World, Information Systems Computerworld, PC World India, Publish in Asia; **INDONESIA:** InfoKomputer PC World, Komputek Computerworld, Publish in Asia; **IRELAND:** ComputerScope, PC Live!; **ISRAEL:** Macworld Israel, People & Computers/Computerworld; **ITALY:** Computerworld Italia, Macworld Italia, Networking Italia, PC World Italia; **JAPAN:** DTP World, Macworld Japan, Nikkei Personal Computing, OS/2 World Japan, SunWorld Japan, Windows NT World, Windows World Japan; **KENYA:** PC World East African; **KOREA:** Hi-Tech Information, Macworld Korea, PC World Korea; **MACEDONIA:** PC World Macedonia; **MALAYSIA:** Computerworld Malaysia, PC World Malaysia, Publish in Asia; **MALTA:** PC World Malta; **MEXICO:** Computerworld Mexico, PC World Mexico; **MYANMAR:** PC World Myanmar; **NETHERLANDS:** Computer! Totaal, LAN Internetworking Magazine, LAN World Buyers Guide, Macworld Netherlands, Net, WebWereld; **NEW ZEALAND:** Absolute Beginners Guide and Plain & Simple Series, Computer Buyer, Computer Industry Directory, Computerworld New Zealand, MTB, Network World, PC World New Zealand; **NICARAGUA:** PC World Centro America; **NORWAY:** Computerworld Norge, CW Rapport, Datamagasinet, Financial Rapport, Kursguide Norge, Macworld Norge, Multimediaworld Norge, PC World Ekspress Norge, PC World Nettverk, PC World Norge, PC World ProduktGuide Norge; **PAKISTAN:** Computerworld Pakistan; **PANAMA:** PC World Panama; **PEOPLE'S REPUBLIC OF CHINA:** China Computer Users, China Computerworld, China InfoWorld, China Telecom World Weekly, Computer & Communication, Electronic Design China, Electronics Today, Electronics Weekly, Game Software, PC World China, Popular Computer Week, Software Weekly, Software World, Telecom World; **PERU:** Computerworld Peru, PC World Profesional Peru, PC World SoHo Peru; **PHILIPPINES:** Click!, Computerworld Philippines, PC World Philippines, Publish in Asia; **POLAND:** Computerworld Poland, Computerworld Special Report Poland, Cyber, Macworld Poland, Networld Poland, PC World Komputer; **PORTUGAL:** Cerebro/PC World, Computerworld/Correio Informático, Dealer World Portugal, Mac*In/PC*In Portugal, Multimedia World; **PUERTO RICO:** PC World Puerto Rico; **ROMANIA:** Computerworld Romania, PC World Romania, Telecom Romania; **RUSSIA:** Computerworld Russia, Mir PK, Publish, Seti; **SINGAPORE:** Computerworld Singapore, PC World Singapore, Publish in Asia; **SLOVENIA:** Monitor; **SOUTH AFRICA:** Computing SA, Network World SA, Software World SA; **SPAIN:** Communicaciones World España, Computerworld España, Dealer World España, Macworld España, PC World España; **SRI LANKA:** Infolink PC World; **SWEDEN:** CAP&Design, Computer Sweden, Corporate Computing Sweden, Internetworld Sweden, it.branschen, Macworld Sweden, MaxiData Sweden, MikroDatorn, Nätverk & Kommunikation, PC World Sweden, PCaktiv, Windows World Sweden; **SWITZERLAND:** Computerworld Schweiz, Macworld Schweiz, PCtip; **TAIWAN:** Computerworld Taiwan, Macworld Taiwan, NEW ViSiON/Publish, PC World Taiwan, Windows World Taiwan; **THAILAND:** Publish in Asia, Thai Computerworld; **TURKEY:** Computerworld Turkiye, Macworld Turkiye, Network World Turkiye, PC World Turkiye; **UKRAINE:** Computerworld Kiev, Multimedia World Ukraine, PC World Ukraine; **UNITED KINGDOM:** Acorn User UK, Amiga Action UK, Amiga Computing UK, Apple Talk UK, Computing, Macworld, Parents and Computers UK, PC Advisor, PC Home, PSX Pro, The WEB; **UNITED STATES:** Cable in the Classroom, CIO Magazine, Computerworld, DOS World, Federal Computer Week, GamePro Magazine, InfoWorld, I-Way, Macworld, Network World, PC Games, PC World, Publish, Video Event, THE WEB Magazine, and WebMaster; online webzines: JavaWorld, NetscapeWorld, and SunWorld Online; **URUGUAY:** InfoWorld Uruguay; **VENEZUELA:** Computerworld Venezuela, PC World Venezuela; and **VIETNAM:** PC World Vietnam. 3/24/97

Dedication

This book is dedicated to my husband and best friend, Richard, for all his love and support over the past ten years.

Author's Acknowledgments

I want to thank Colleen Rainsberger for the fantastic job she did making sure that everything came together on this book, and the other editorial people, Pat O'Brien, Tammy Castleman, Michael Simsic, Patricia Pan, and Jennifer Davies, who worked with Colleen to make sure that everything made sense in the book. I would also like to thank Jill Pisoni for providing me the opportunity to get involved with IDG Books.

I would like to thank my technical editor, David Libby, who helped make sure that the information covered in this book was accurate.

Finally, I would like to acknowledge the efforts of all the other production people at IDG who were involved in making this book a success by doing everything from page layout and proofreading to indexing.

Publisher's Acknowledgments

We're proud of this book; please send us your comments about it by using the Reader Response Card at the back of the book or by e-mailing us at feedback/dummies@idgbooks.com. Some of the people who helped bring this book to market include the following:

Acquisitions, Development, and Editorial

Senior Project Editor: Colleen Rainsberger

Senior Acquisitions Editor: Jill Pisoni

Product Development Director: Mary Bednarek

Copy Editors: Tammy Castleman, Jennifer Davies, Pat O'Brien, Patricia Pan, Michael Simsic, Susan Diane Smith

Technical Editor: David B. Libby

Editorial Manager: Seta K. Frantz

Editorial Assistant: Chris H. Collins

Production

Project Coordinator: Debbie Stailey

Layout and Graphics: Cameron Booker, Angela F. Hunckler, Todd Klemme, Kate Snell

Proofreaders: Sharon Duffy, Joel K. Draper, Karen York

Indexer: Joan Griffits

Special Help

Stephanie Koutek, Proof Editor

General and Administrative

IDG Books Worldwide, Inc.: John Kilcullen, CEO; Steven Berkowitz, President and Publisher

IDG Books Technology Publishing: Brenda McLaughlin, Senior Vice President and Group Publisher

Dummies Technology Press and Dummies Editorial: Diane Graves Steele, Vice President and Associate Publisher; Judith A. Taylor, Product Marketing Manager; Kristin A. Cocks, Editorial Director

Dummies Trade Press: Kathleen A. Welton, Vice President and Publisher; Stacy S. Collins, Product Marketing Manager

IDG Books Production for Dummies Press: Beth Jenkins, Production Director; Cindy L. Phipps, Supervisor of Project Coordination, Production Proofreading, and Indexing; Kathie S. Schutte, Supervisor of Page Layout; Shelley Lea, Supervisor of Graphics and Design; Debbie J. Gates, Production Systems Specialist; Tony Augsburger, Supervisor of Reprints and Bluelines; Leslie Popplewell, Media Archive Coordinator

Dummies Packaging and Book Design: Patti Sandez, Packaging Specialist; Lance Kayser, Packaging Assistant; Kavish + Kavish, Cover Design

♦

The publisher would like to give special thanks to Patrick J. McGovern, without whom this book would not have been possible.

♦

Contents at a Glance

Cartoons at a Glance

By Rich Tennant

"I find it so obnoxious when people use their cellular phone in public that I'm making notes about it on my handheld PC for a future opinion piece."

page 55

"GATHER AROUND, KIDS. YOUR MOTHER'S WINDOWING!"

page 305

"OK—ANTIDOTE, ANTIDOTE, WHAT WOULD AN ANTIDOTE ICON LOOK LIKE? YOU KNOW, I STILL HAVEN'T GOT THIS DESKTOP THE WAY I WANT IT."

page 7

"OK, SO MAYBE COMDEX WASN'T READY FOR OUR MICROWAVE SLOW-COOKER THIS YEAR, BUT I STILL THINK WE SHOULD GO AHEAD WITH THE TRACKBALL GARAGE DOOR OPENER."

page 229

"OH, WELL SHOOT! MUST BE THAT NEW PAINT PROGRAM ON MY HANDHELD PC."

page 173

IN A STROKE OF SELF RELIANCE, RAY EXTENDS THE POWER ON HIS LAPTOP BY TAPPING INTO THE BATTERY ON HIS SLEEPING NEIGHBOR'S HEARING AID.

page 283

Fax: 508-546-7747 • E-mail: the5wave@tiac.net

Table of Contents

Introduction

You are about to embark on quite an adventure as you explore one of Microsoft's newest creations, the Windows CE operating system. *Windows CE For Dummies* introduces you to the world of Windows CE in a very friendly manner, by providing examples that are easy to relate to your everyday life.

Windows CE was designed to be a user-friendly operating system, not some complicated thing for all of the self-proclaimed computer nerds. On that basis, this book illustrates the simplicity of using Windows CE, leaving the technical jargon for those who really thrive on it. Although I do occasionally offer you a few bits of Windows CE trivia, you can simply ignore this information as you use this book.

About This Book

Windows CE For Dummies provides you with an in-depth reference for answering all your questions when working with Windows CE. Don't feel pressured to read this book from cover to cover. All you need to read is the information that explains the features you want to understand.

This book's design makes it easy to use. Whenever you come across something in Windows CE that you don't understand, simply flip to either the table of contents or the index in this book to locate the topic you want to read about. You find that you can quickly gather the information you need and be back to work in no time.

Conventions Used in This Book

To help you quickly spot the information you need, I use consistant terminology when I refer to actions that you can perform.

If you've used any other Windows operating system, or even a Macintosh, you're probably familiar with the terminology of *clicking* on an item by using your mouse. Because Windows CE runs on devices that have a touch screen and stylus, you encounter the terms *tap, double-tap,* and *drag and drop* in this book. Here's how to tap dance:

- **Tap.** If instructions tell you to tap on an item, you need to take the stylus (the funny little pencil that came with your handheld PC) and use it to tap on the item on the screen.
- **Double-tap.** When I tell you to double-tap on a specific location, you simply take your stylus and tap on the item twice in a fairly short amount of time. I also show you how you can customize your handheld PC's settings based on the speed you tap.
- **Drag and drop.** One more new thing you get to try out is how to perform a drag and drop operation under Windows CE. It probably makes more sense to call this the tap, drag, and release operation, but to maintain the common computer lingo, I still refer to it as *drag and drop* in this book. To do this, touch the desired item with your stylus, drag the stylus across the screen to the new location, and then pick up the stylus to release the item.

Of course, because you read about connecting to your desktop computer in some of the chapters in this book, be prepared to click on an item with your mouse.

I occasionally instruct you to press certain keys simultaneously on the keyboard — both your handheld PC and desktop computer keyboards. Instead of always saying "simultaneously press both the Alt and R keys on the keyboard," I say something like:

Press Alt+R

You will also want to make sure that you understand the shorthand that I use to tell you to select an option on a menu on your handheld PC or desktop computer. Instead of saying something long like "select the Copy option on the Edit menu," I tell you to perform the task in the following manner:

Choose Edit⇨Copy

By using this method to express menu selections, you should be able to quickly look at a description and spot the options you need to select.

What You're Not to Read

As you may have already noticed, this book contains sections labeled with the Technical Stuff icon. Anytime you see this icon, feel free to ignore the information contained in that section. I include this technical information for computer-nerd-wannabes. You don't need to read these sections if you are simply trying to figure out how to perform a specific task.

On the other hand, if you are aspiring to impress some friends, you can always thumb through the book and read one of the sections with the Technical Stuff icon. You are sure to impress even the nerdiest of computer nerds with this information.

Foolish Assumptions

I have foolishly assumed that you're reading this book because you either recently purchased or will soon purchase a handheld PC or another device running Windows CE. I also assume that you are looking for pointers on how to make this handheld PC become a useful tool and not just another one of those must-have gadgets that are now collecting dust on a shelf in the office.

You are probably someone who is frequently on the go and requires the ability to take important information with you, such as information about appointments, copies of proposals and budgets, and even important contacts.

You may even be looking for a good communication device that enables you to not only keep up with e-mail messages from the office, but also to dive into the vast world of the Internet without hauling around a big computer.

How This Book Is Organized

I divided the information in this book into six parts. Each part provides chapters that relate to the topic of the part. Grouping related information in the book makes for an easy search when you try to locate information about the topic that interests you.

Part I: Windows CE Basics

Before diving into the middle of Windows CE, this part provides some of the basic information about Windows CE, such as how to set up your handheld PC and how to work with your Windows CE desktop. You also figure out the importance of the taskbar and how to monitor your Recycle Bin.

Part II: What Can I Do with My Handheld PC?

Now that you've spent all that money on this new little gadget, learn to perform various tasks on it, such as maintaining your daily schedule, keeping track of tasks, maintaining a current list of contacts, and even creating different documents. This part covers most of the free programs that come already installed on your handheld PC.

By exploring the information in this part, you quickly learn how to make your new handheld PC a useful tool. You won't find it sitting on some shelf collecting dust like other gadgets you may have purchased.

Part III: Interfacing with Your Desktop Computer

Do you have Microsoft Word documents that you want to take to a meeting with you? Or perhaps you want to work on your budget at home. You can connect your handheld PC to a desktop computer to copy files; load new programs onto your handheld PC, and even back up the information on your device.

This part covers the various tasks that you can perform by simply connecting your handheld PC to a desktop computer that runs the handheld PC Explorer program.

Part IV: Getting Online with Windows CE

Probably one of the most fascinating uses for a handheld PC is the ability to connect to the Internet from this small device. With the aid of a modem, you can quickly connect to the Internet and send e-mail messages from anywhere as long as you have access to a phone line.

You can also use your handheld PC to connect to other locations, such as a company server, where you can send and receive e-mail messages.

Part V: Personalizing Your Handheld PC

Find out how to quickly personalize your handheld PC by displaying your personal information when you turn on your device. You can also password-protect your handheld PC to eliminate the possibility of someone else's gaining access to your information.

Part VI: The Part of Tens

Based on the title of this part, it is probably fairly easy to guess that this part has something to do with the number 10. This part provides lists of useful information, such as the ten most popular Windows CE devices and ten common problems you may encounter with Windows CE.

Icons Used in This Book

If you have taken the time to thumb through this book, you have probably noticed the little pictures that frequently appear in the margins of the book. You use these little pictures (commonly referred to as *icons*) as guides when you explore the information contained in this book. If you have read other *...For Dummies* books, you are probably already familiar with these icons.

Nerd alert! This icon immediately signals you that the information in the section targets aspiring computer nerds. You can feel free to avoid this information. However, if you are bored and looking for a way to impress your friends, you may want to take a small peek at the information in this section.

When you're reading a section in the book, make sure that you look at the information covered here. You find handy pointers that simplify using Windows CE.

Don't forget about these pointers when you use Windows CE.

Make sure that you carefully follow any of the information that the Warning icon highlights. By paying close attention to this advice, you can avoid pitfalls that you may encounter when working with Windows CE.

Where to Go from Here

Well, you are ready to start exploring the world of Windows CE. Remember, this book is your reference. Feel free to mark commonly used pages, highlight useful paragraphs, and even make notes in the margins. The more you personalize this book, the more useful it will be.

Remember to use the table of contents and index when you're looking for information about a specific topic. By using these simple tools, you can quickly locate what you need, without spending hours thumbing through the book page by page.

And don't forget about the Cheat Sheet at the beginning of the book. You can remove this card from the book and place it in a location where you can quickly refer to it while working in Windows CE.

Part I
Windows CE Basics

The 5th Wave By Rich Tennant

"OKAY—ANTIDOTE, ANTIDOTE, WHAT WOULD AN ANTIDOTE ICON LOOK LIKE? YOU KNOW, I STILL HAVEN'T GOT THIS DESKTOP THE WAY I WANT IT."

In this part . . .

This part explains the basics of Windows CE, one of the newest operating systems to hit the market. No matter what your background may be, you will find it helpful to understand some of the basic features of Windows CE before you attempt to do much with your handheld PC.

This part also looks at handheld PCs, the devices that currently run Windows CE. You get a tour of the basic features of the handheld PC, as well as advice regarding what to look for if you are thinking of purchasing one. Most important, you find out all you need to know about working with the Windows CE desktop and navigating the world of Windows CE.

Chapter 1

What Is Windows CE?

In This Chapter

- Understanding Windows CE and comparing it to Windows 95
- Figuring out the capabilities of Windows CE
- Looking at the features of a handheld PC
- Selecting a handheld PC
- Turning on your handheld PC for the first time

Handheld PCs have invaded the computing market. You can find them not only in large computer stores, but also in almost any store that sells computers or handheld organizers. One thing these new handheld PCs have in common is that they all run Windows CE, a new operating system from Microsoft.

Handheld PCs are meant to be used by the everyday person, such as the real estate agent who needs to keep track of her appointments, the salesperson who would like to quickly check his e-mail, and even the casual user who would like to play a game of Solitaire while waiting to see the dentist. If these new devices create the type of excitement that the developers anticipate, distinguishing the computer nerd from the everyday person will be difficult, because everyone will be carrying one of these little gizmos.

This chapter hopefully eases some of the confusion about this surge of excitement by providing a brief overview of Windows CE and the new handheld PCs, including an explanation for each of the parts on the device. The chapter also walks you through setting up your handheld PC for the first time.

Understanding Windows CE

Windows CE is essentially a scaled-down version of Microsoft's popular Windows 95 operating system. Microsoft created Windows CE so that it would have an operating system that could be used on a hardware system with very little memory requirements, such as a handheld PC. (An *operating system* is a program that controls all the stuff that occurs on a computer.)

Handheld PCs (handheld personal computers, often called *handhelds*) were designed to be small enough to carry in your front pocket yet powerful enough to be useful. Wow, these things almost sound like something you have seen on all those space movies, right? I like to describe a handheld PC as a laptop that is about the same size as a checkbook (assuming that your checkbook is roughly the same size as mine). The dimensions of the units are approximately 7 inches long by 3 inches wide and about 1 inch thick (unopened). Of course, when you open the device to use it, it measures about 7 inches square, and about 1/2 inch thick.

Because the unit is so small, you can easily carry it with you. Think of all the places you have hauled — or should have hauled — a laptop just to finish a proposal or adjust the budget figures. Now you can carry one of these small devices and work on your documents at your leisure.

Each handheld PC comes with the monitor and keyboard built-in. The major downside is that the keyboard is much smaller than a normal keyboard and, therefore, more difficult to use.

Windows CE controls all the events that occur on the handheld PC that is running it. In other words, Windows CE keeps track of the location of each program, determines where to store a document, knows which programs you are currently using, and keeps track of the current date and time. All the stuff that occurs from the time you turn on the handheld PC until you turn it off again is managed and controlled by Windows CE. (Remind you of anyone you know?)

Windows CE provides all the essential elements of Windows 95 and allows you to add only the extra bells and whistles that are relevant to your situation. In fact, Windows CE looks a lot like Windows 95, (see Figure 1-1). A good comparison of the two operating systems would be looking at the menu in a pizza parlor: Windows 95 is a combination pizza; Windows CE is a cheese pizza.

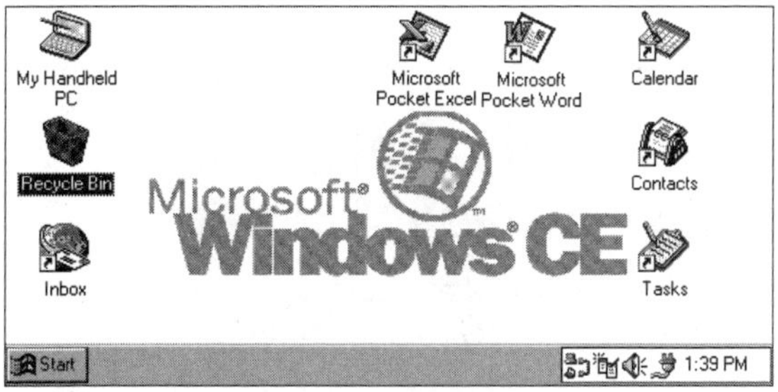

Figure 1-1: Windows CE looks a lot like Windows 95.

One frequently mentioned feature of Windows CE is its capability to *interface* with Windows 95 or Windows NT. (That is, you can connect your Windows CE device to a desktop computer running either Windows 95 or Windows NT.) This way, you can take important information from your desktop computer and carry it with you on your handheld PC. For example, you can copy your appointments off your desktop computer and place them on your handheld PC. Then you can carry your schedule home or into a meeting. In fact, you can even take a spreadsheet or a word-processing document into a meeting and make changes to it on your handheld PC as decisions are made.

With Windows CE, you also have the capability of moving information from your handheld PC onto your desktop computer so that you can access the same information under Windows 95 or Windows NT. The chapters in Part III explain how to transfer your data, load new software onto your handheld PC, synchronize your Calendar and Tasks with your desktop computer, and more.

Currently, the only use of Windows CE is on the handheld PCs. Several vendors have developed handheld PCs that run Windows CE. Microsoft plans that Windows CE will eventually be found on other common household products, such as the menu on your television, your VCR, or even on your telephone.

REMEMBER

You can aquire Windows CE only by purchasing a handheld PC. Handheld PCs resemble laptop computers, but they are small enough to fit in the palm of your hand.

Handheld PCs appear on store shelves next to other well-known handheld devices. To make a handheld PC easy to spot, the Microsoft Windows CE logo appears on the box. This logo identifies the handheld PC as a device that runs Windows CE. The Windows CE logo looks like a small window pane and is basically the same logo that Microsoft uses for Windows 95; the main difference is that you'll see *Microsoft Windows CE* under the logo. The logo can also be found on most of the handheld PCs. Windows CE comes already installed on each of these devices. Therefore, by purchasing a Windows CE device, you do not have to concern yourself with the hours of frustration caused by installing a new operating system; it has been done for you.

TECHNICAL STUFF

Windows CE trivia that you can use to impress your friends

Windows CE is a true 32-bit operating system just like Windows 95 and Windows NT 4.0. But unlike these other memory-intensive operating systems, Windows CE requires a relatively small amount of memory to run. Windows CE comes installed on each handheld PC and takes up only about 4MB of *ROM* (read-only memory). Most handheld PCs run Windows CE with only another 2MB of *RAM* (random-access memory). This 2MB of RAM is where you can load and store additional programs and files for your handheld PC.

Because Microsoft was able to remove much of the fluff from the operating system, Windows CE can run on devices that have little memory. Because Windows CE is a scaled-down version, however, it lacks some of the fancy features available in Windows 95.

On the other hand, a typical Windows 95 installation requires a minimum of 40MB of hard disk storage for the operating system. On top of that, Windows 95 will not even run without at least 4MB of RAM.

Another important thing to note is that Windows CE uses a form of disk compression that allows you to store a large file without using too much disk space.

You will not be able to replace your Windows 95 operating system on your desktop computer, or even your laptop, with Windows CE just yet, but it is interesting to note the difference in memory requirements for an operating system that looks and feels almost the same.

Because Windows CE brings to the table an extremely powerful operating system that has very limited hardware requirements, it is the perfect operating system for small electronic devices. Windows CE will soon be available on several different types of devices that do not have the resources to run a memory-intensive operating system like Windows 95.

Locating Installed Windows CE Programs

Windows CE comes with several useful programs, which are already installed on your handheld PC. You will soon notice that most of the programs that come with Windows CE resemble the programs that are available for use on other versions of Windows.

Keep in mind that these are not the only programs you can use with Windows CE. One of the major advantages of owning a handheld PC that runs Windows CE is that the Windows CE operating system provides the ability to add new software to your handheld PC more easily than to other types of handheld devices.

Table 1-1 provides a list of the programs that you will find already installed on your Windows CE handheld PC. Icons for most of these programs are already sitting on the desktop of your handheld PC. (Don't despair if you are unable to immediately locate the program you want; each of these programs is discussed in detail in the appropriate chapter in this book.)

Table 1-1 Windows CE Programs (The Freebie Stuff)

Program	*Description*
Microsoft Pocket Word	This word processing program very closely resembles the much acclaimed Microsoft Word. With this program you can create and review memos, letters, reports, and so on. For more information about Microsoft Pocket Word, see Chapter 6.
Microsoft Pocket Excel	This spreadsheet program is a scaled-down version of Microsoft Excel. You can use this program to create spreadsheets to keep track of expenses, manipulate data, and so on. For more information about Microsoft Pocket Excel, see Chapter 7.
Calculator	This little program allows you to perform calculations. It keeps track of the last calculation performed on an on-screen paper tape, similar to an adding machine. This program very closely resembles the Calculator program in other Windows operating systems.
Tasks	This program resembles an electronic to-do list. It allows you to create and keep track of tasks that you need to perform. For more information, see Chapter 4.
Calendar	You can use this program to keep track of appointments and events. Your current tasks can also be viewed from within the Calendar program. For more information about using Calendar, see Chapter 3.
Contacts	You can create an electronic address book of all your important contacts. For more information, see Chapter 5.
Clock	You can keep track of not only the current time, but also simultaneously track the time in another location. This feature allows you to quickly switch your handheld PC to the current time as you travel into a different time zone.

(continued)

Table 1-1 *(continued)*

Program	*Description*
Pocket Internet Explorer	With many handheld PCs, this program comes on a CD-ROM and is not yet installed on the device. This program enables you to use your handheld to surf the Net. For more information, see Chapter 15.
Solitaire	Of course, no Windows operating system would be complete without a version of Solitaire. You will find that the Windows CE version closely resembles other Windows versions of the popular game, as shown in Figure 1-2.
Inbox	With the use of a modem, you can use the Inbox program to send and receive e-mail messages from any location. For more information, see Chapter 16.

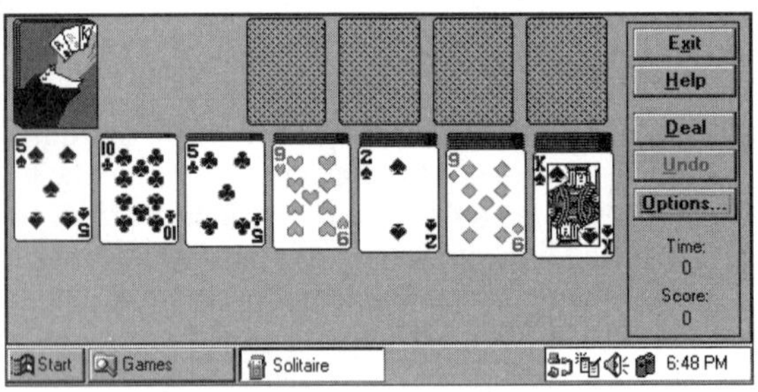

Figure 1-2: No version of Windows would be complete without a version of Solitaire.

Examining a Handheld PC

Each handheld PC comes equipped with its own unique set of bells and whistles. These added features, such as modems and extra memory, are designed to influence you to select one handheld PC over another one. Some basic items, however, are common to all handheld PCs. This section looks at each of these items and describes how each one was designed specifically for use with Windows CE.

The touch screen and stylus

Your handheld PC comes equipped with a *touch screen,* meaning that to make a selection on your handheld PC, you simply touch, or *tap,* the option you want to select. Windows CE offers touch-screen capabilities for all programs that run on your handheld PC.

Handheld PCs come with a stylus to make tapping on-screen items an easy task. The *stylus,* which looks like a little pencil, replaces the mouse used with other Windows operating systems. Anytime you want to make a selection on your device, simply use the stylus to tap on the option you want to select.

Depending on the item you are selecting (an icon, button, menu option, and so on), you may need to tap twice on the item, called *double-tapping.* For example, you need to double-tap on an icon to start the corresponding program. Unfortunately, no exact science exists for determining when to tap or double-tap; the best recommendation is to first tap on the item, and if you don't get the results you want, try double-tapping.

With touch-screen capabilities, you can even drag items across the screen. Simply place the stylus on the item you want to select and then "drag" by moving the stylus across the screen to where you want to place the item.

REMEMBER

You can tap on the screen with anything, including your finger. Keep in mind, though, that fingers do leave fingerprints on the screen, so this method may not be the best one.

The size of most screens is approximately $4^{1}/_{2}$ inches by $2^{1}/_{2}$ inches, and each one has a monochrome display, although some handheld PCs have hit the market with larger screens. A *monochrome* display means that everything appears in shades of gray on the screen. So looking at a monochrome monitor is like looking at a black-and-white photo of an item, rather than a color photograph.

If you ever lose your stylus, you can purchase a replacement. Be sure to locate a stylus that will fit in the stylus storage location on your device. Several styles of styluses are available, most of them much fancier looking than the one that comes with the handheld PC. The only problem is that the fancier ones probably will not fit the location where your original stylus was stored — if you purchase one of these, you will have to find another place to keep it.

The keyboard

I am sure that you will be pleased to note that each Windows CE device comes with a fully functional keyboard. Unlike the standard 101-key keyboards that come with most desktop computers, the handheld PC keyboard has only 61 keys. The handheld PC does not have all the weird function keys and the extra set of numbers (affectionately referred to as the numeric keypad) that clutter up standard desktop computer keyboards. But you will still find all the other standard keys.

The screen is hard to read

Depending on the lighting conditions, you may find that reading the screen of the handheld PC is difficult. This problem usually occurs when the display is either too dark or everything displayed on-screen is too light. You can't see the screen because the contrast setting is not appropriate for the current lighting conditions.

Each handheld PC provides a way to adjust the contrast settings of the screen. This adjustment may be either a dial or a specific key combination on the keyboard. By changing the contrast settings, you can adjust the brightness of the items on-screen. You will probably need to adjust this setting frequently as you move from one location to another, depending on the lighting conditions.

If you have adjusted the contrast and the screen is still blank, your batteries may be dead. Try changing the main batteries, or if you are using a rechargeable battery, recharge it. If you are still unable to see anything on-screen, you may need to press the Reset button. Occasionally, just like a desktop computer, the handheld PC locks up and needs to be reset. If this still does not solve the problem, contact the manufacturer.

Okay, so you have a standard keyboard, but look at how small those keys are! Obviously, the keyboard has been condensed so that more keys could be placed in a smaller amount of space. So unless you have extremely small fingers, you will probably find typing on the keyboard somewhat cumbersome. Don't despair — as you've heard a thousand times, "practice makes perfect" — so the more you use the keyboard, the faster and more comfortable you will become with it. Okay, I know that was no help, but what else can I say? You just can't use a small keyboard easily. But look on the bright side: You can use the stylus to accomplish many of the tasks you want to perform on your handheld PC, although you will find the keyboard valuable whenever you want to create an e-mail message or modify a spreadsheet.

TIP

If you are really having a difficult time pressing the keys on the keyboard, try pressing the keys with the back of your stylus. This may become tedious if you have a great deal of text that you need to type, however.

If you are accustomed to using a keyboard with your desktop computer, you probably understand the function of most of the keys on your handheld PC. They all have the same functionality as the keys with the same name on the keyboard for your desktop computer. Just in case you want a refresher, Table 1-2 provides a quick overview of the major keys on the keyboard of your handheld PC.

Table 1-2	When Should I Press that Key?
Key	***Description***
Shift	The Shift key has the same functionality it had on the old typewriters. If you hold down this key while you type a letter, you get the uppercase version of the letter. The Shift key is also used to access the characters that sit above the numbers on the top row, as well as other characters that are sitting on keys with two characters.
Caps Shift	Pressing both the Shift+Caps Shift turns on the All Caps option, so that every letter you type is an uppercase letter. To turn off the All Caps option, press the two keys again. Pressing the Caps Shift key by itself provides exactly the same results as the Shift key.
Tab	The Tab key allows you to jump from one location to another on a screen where you are entering information. For example, if you are typing contact information in the Contacts program, you can use the Tab key to move from the Name field to the Title field. You can also use this key in word processing programs, such as Pocket Word, to indent text a specified amount of space. You can press Alt+Tab to pop up the Task Manager window, which shows which programs are currently running on your handheld PC. You can use this window to quickly jump to a program in the list or to close a program. This key combination can be especially useful if a program locks up on your handheld PC. You can simply open the Task Manager window and then tap on the End Task button to close the task.
Alt	The Alt key allows you to perform alternative functions with certain keys on the keyboard. On some handheld PCs, the text on the Alt key is a different color, such as pink. All of the functions that you can use the Alt key to perform are listed in the same color on the corresponding keys. For example, to move the cursor up one page, you hold down the Alt key and press the key with the pink label *PgUp*. On other handheld PC keyboards, the Alt key functions are simply listed on the keyboard above the corresponding keys. You can also use the Alt key open the first pop-down menu at the top of a screen. As a Windows standard, this menu option is usually called *File*. This feature is a useful way to access the menus at the top of the screen, but with the touch-screen capability of your handheld PC, it is probably something you will rarely use.

(continued)

Table 1-2 *(continued)*

Key	*Description*
Ctrl	You use this key, normally referred to as the Control key, similarly to the way you use the Alt key. For example, in Microsoft Pocket Word, you can press Ctrl+F to pop up the Find window so that you can locate text within your document. Again, with the addition of the touch screen, you will probably rarely use this key.
Esc	This key, normally called the Escape key, is basically what its name implies — a way to cancel an operation in progress.
Enter	In a word processor, such as Microsoft Pocket Word, you use the Enter key to move the cursor to the beginning of the next line and create a new paragraph in your document. Remember, if you are typing a paragraph, the word processor will automatically move the text to the next line when you get to the end of the current line. It will also move the cursor to the beginning of the next page when you get to the end of the page. This feature is commonly referred to as *word wrap.* Therefore, you only need to press the Enter key when you want to create a new paragraph. You also use this key to accept data or an option on the screen. By pressing the Enter key, you inform Windows CE that you agree with the stuff and want to continue.
Delete/Backspace	When you press the Delete/Backspace key, the character to the left of the cursor is removed from the screen. To remove characters on the other side of the cursor, hold down the Shift key and then press this key.

Turning on your night-light

Most handheld PCs come with a backlight. A *backlight* illuminates the display so that you can read your handheld PC in dimly lit conditions. This feature is very useful if you want to use your handheld PC in places such as your car, at a restaurant, or even in bed at night. The backlight is quite valuable — look for this feature when you purchase your handheld PC.

That mysterious Windows key

One of the newest keys to appear on a keyboard is the Windows key. The key is so named because it looks exactly like the logo that Microsoft uses to represent the Windows operating systems. This key was added to several new keyboards when Windows 95 was introduced to the market. Unless you ran out and bought a new keyboard after Windows 95 was released, you may not have seen this key yet.

Many of the new handheld PCs come equipped with this key. If your handheld PC has this key, it is probably located on the left side of the Alt key. You can use the Windows key can be used by itself or in conjunction with other keys on the keyboard, as outlined in the following table:

Combination	Description
Windows key	Opens the Start menu.
Windows key+C	Opens the Control Panel, which allows you to change your handheld PC's settings.
Windows key+E	Opens the My handheld PC folder on your handheld PC. This key combination has the same result as selecting the My handheld PC icon on the desktop.
Windows key+H	Opens the Windows CE Help file.
Windows key+K	Runs the Keyboard Properties program so that you can set or modify specific keyboard settings.
Windows key+I	Runs the Stylus Properties program so that you can recalibrate the way the stylus selects stuff on-screen.
Windows key+R	Displays the Run window, in which you can type the name of a specific program that you would like to use. If you don't know the name of the program you want to use, you can select the Browse button and search for the program that you want to run.

If your unit has a backlight, you'll find a switch on the handheld PC, probably near the display. For the exact location of the button, refer to the manufacturer's documentation.

On most handheld PCs, the backlight stays on for only a short amount of time. Because the backlight uses extra battery power, it turns off to make sure that you don't accidentally forget and leave it on. If you need to use it for a longer amount of time, simply press the backlight button again. If your handheld PC is plugged in to an electrical outlet or connected to your desktop computer, the backlight may stay on indefinitely.

If you use your backlight extensively, your batteries will run down more quickly, because of the battery power the backlight requires. If you intend to use your handheld PC for an extended amount of time, try to find a location with an adequate amount of light so that you don't need to use the backlight at all.

On some handheld PCs, you can modify the amount of time that the backlight stays on. Check the hardware documentation that came with your handheld to see if you have this option.

Battery power — How long does it last?

All handheld PCs are designed to run on battery power. Handheld PCs usually have two types of battery power: the main batteries and the backup battery.

Most handheld PCs use standard AA-size batteries as the main batteries; you simply replace them when they are no longer working. Some handheld PCs provide the option of purchasing a rechargeable battery which was designed to replace the AA-size batteries. Most of them also either come with, or provide the ability to, add an AC adapter that can be used to plug in the handheld PC into an outlet, thus conserving battery power and renewing the rechargeable battery if installed.

The backup battery is found in another location on the device. This battery is a longer-lasting one that is used to maintain the computer's memory when the main batteries are run down or removed from the unit. Because this battery is only used when the main batteries are no good, it should last much longer than the main batteries. Some manufacturers speculate that the backup battery has a life of about five years, but this information is all based on your usage of the unit and how quickly you replace the main batteries when they are run down.

When the time comes to replace either the main or backup batteries, make sure that you verify the battery size required by your handheld PC. Each handheld PC has its own unique battery requirements. For more information, refer to the hardware documentation that came with your device.

Replacing the batteries

Never remove both the main batteries and the backup battery from your unit at the same time. Without some type of battery in your unit, you will probably lose most of the stuff you have stored on the handheld PC.

If you determine that both the main and backup batteries need to be replaced at the same time, make sure that you replace the main batteries first, and then replace the backup battery. You need to ensure that the unit has enough battery power to maintain the storage before replacing the backup battery.

Whenever you replace the main batteries, make sure that you use all new batteries. Do not replace them with a mixture of old and new batteries.

The battery storage location on each handheld PC is different. To determine the exact location of the batteries on your device, refer to the manufacturer's documentation.

What is my battery status?

To ensure that you do not run out of batteries during an important meeting or during a game of Solitaire on a flight to New York, you should periodically check the battery status for your unit. To do so, you use the Windows CE program called *Power Properties.*

To start the Power Properties program, you double-tap on its icon in the Control Panel folder. To open the Control Panel folder, select the Setting option from the Start menu. In the Control Panel folder, tap on the Power icon. The icon resembles a battery with a power plug sitting next to it.

The Power Properties program provides two tab options. The first tab option, Battery, indicates the status of the main and backup batteries (see Figure 1-3). This tab also tells you when the main batteries were last replaced and the amount of time that your handheld PC has been turned on since the batteries were last replaced. If the status of both types of batteries is Good, you do not need to worry too much. If either battery type has a status of Very Low, that battery should be changed immediately.

Windows CE is designed to help you conserve the life of your batteries. Based upon a predetermined setting, Windows CE automatically turns off when the specified amount of time elapses without the handheld PC being used. The options in the Power Off tab allow you to specify the amount of time that your handheld should remain on without activity, as shown in Figure 1-4. The default time is 3 minutes. To change this time frame, tap on the Down Arrow button and then highlight the amount of time you want. You can also change the amount of time by typing the numeric value on the keyboard; however, keep in mind that the maximum value you can select or type for this field is 5 minutes.

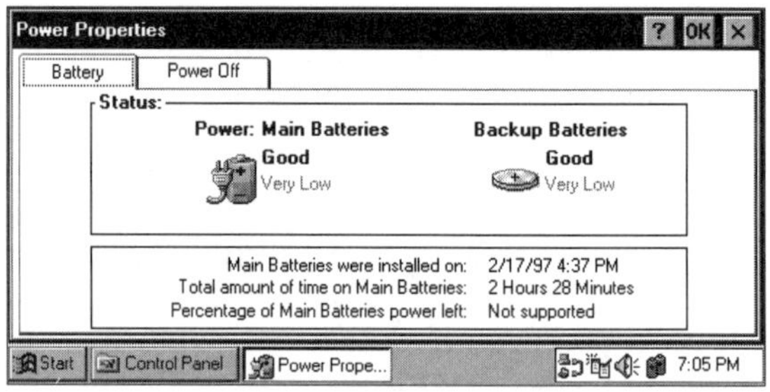

Figure 1-3: The Power Properties program indicates the power status for the main and backup batteries.

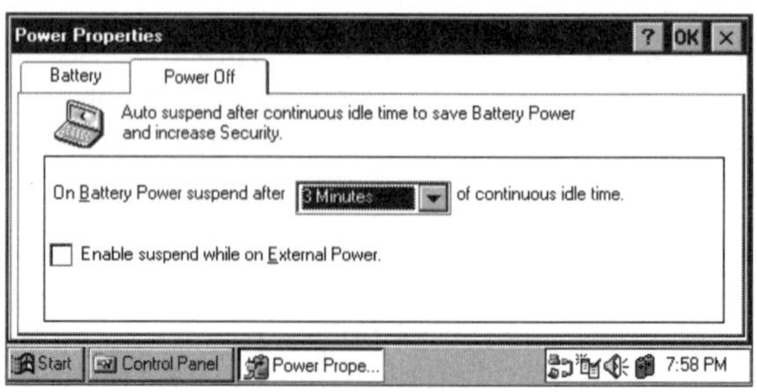

Figure 1-4: Specify the amount of time the handheld PC should remain idle.

Most people do not care if the handheld PC turns off when it is plugged into an AC outlet. If you still want your handheld to turn off in the amount of time specified on the Power Off tab option, tap on the box next to the Enable suspend while on External Power field. A check mark in the box indicates that you want the device to turn off within the specified amount of time, even if the device is plugged in.

What is this cable for?

When you unpacked your handheld PC, you probably noticed that at least one cable had been placed in your box. Three types of cables may be in the box with your device. With some handheld PCs, you may find all three, but most of the units come with only one standard cable. The other cables as accessories.

So what is each cable and how do you use it? Unfortunately, manufacturers seem to assume that you can read their minds and determine which cable is used where, so they rarely label the cables. Table 1-3 describes each of the three types of cables that come with most handheld PCs and describes how to determine which cable is which.

Table 1-3 Figuring Out HPC Device Cables

Cable	Description
Data Interface	This cable should come with each device. Without this cable, you cannot interface with a PC, making transferring information between your PC and your handheld PC impossible. This cable plugs into a 9-pin serial port on the back of your PC and then into the data port on your handheld.
Power	If this cable did not come with your handheld PC, you should be able to purchase it as an extra accessory, either from the manufacturer or at the store where you bought your handheld PC. This cable allows you to plug your handheld PC into an AC outlet, a good investment if you use your device in one location for an extended amount of time. This cable should have the standard two prongs, like anything you plug into the wall, and the other end plugs into the external power port on your device.
Battery Charger	You probably have this cable only if you also purchased a rechargeable battery for your handheld PC. This cable allows you to charge the rechargeable battery while the battery is still in the handheld PC. With many handheld PCs, the same cable is used for both connecting to an AC outlet and recharging the rechargeable battery.

Understanding storage capabilities

One issue that will probably haunt you is determining whether you have enough memory. Although all handheld PCs come with Windows CE already installed, Windows CE is installed in ROM (Read-Only Memory), meaning that it does not take up any of the space you use to store data files and extra programs. On most handheld PCs, this memory is approximately 4MB. (The size of this memory is not really that important, however, because you cannot add any programs or files to it.)

The area where you store all of your extra stuff is commonly referred to as *RAM* (Random-Access Memory). This memory is what you need to compare when looking for a handheld PC. All handheld PCs come with at least 2MB of RAM memory, but several of them come with much more than 2MB.

If you plan to load several extra programs, think about buying a handheld PC with a larger amount of RAM. If your device comes with a PC Card slot, you can also look at purchasing a storage card to plug into your handheld PC and add additional memory. The PC Card slot is available on most handheld PCs. It provides a location where you can add new options to your handheld PC, such as a modem or extra storage. So in reality, the options are limitless when it comes to storage capabilities of a handheld PC.

Another thing to keep in mind when you look at storage for Windows CE handheld PCs is that Windows CE uses a compression method for storing all files. Windows CE is able to shrink the size of everything it saves on your handheld PC. Therefore, a file that takes 2MB to store on your PC will be considerably smaller on your handheld PC.

Before you load new items onto your device, you should know how much memory you have available. You can use the System Properties program to determine the amount of available memory on your device. This program is available on the Control Panel.

What goes in that slot?

So you found the perfect handheld PC, or at least you thought you did, but now you discover that it doesn't have enough memory or that you really could use a modem. Well don't despair, you can have those added features in another way.

Most handheld PCs come with a *PC Slot,* usually located on the side of the handheld. This slot allows you to add additional options to your handheld PC. These options include memory cards, modems, serial ports, and so on. This slot is the standard size for normal PCMCIA cards, commonly referred to as PC Cards. PCMCIA, which stands for *Personal Computer Memory Card Interface Adapter,* cards are about the size of a credit card. They are used to add additional options to a handheld PC or desktop computer, such as a modem, extra storage, or even an extra serial port.

On some handheld PCs, the slot comes with a plastic card inserted in it. This card helps keep the handheld PC clean. Your handheld PC will probably not function properly without something in the slot, so don't remove the card unless you have something to replace it with.

Placing a card in this slot does have one drawback: All of the cards cause the handheld PC to use more battery power. Also, some modem cards require too much memory to work properly on these devices. Your best bet is to find a card that the manufacturer states has a low power consumption. This rating is typically indicated on the box when you buy the modem card.

Infrared port

You should find a little, black, shiny window on the side of your handheld PC, which is commonly referred to as the *infrared port.* An infrared port allows you to send data to another handheld PC thast has infrared port. For example, you can send a document to another handheld PC, or you can play a game with another handheld PC.

Storage memory versus disk memory

If you have stumbled across the System Properties program and looked at the Memory tab option, you have probably noticed that it talks about the Storage memory and the Program memory. Just when you had the RAM and ROM memory types under control, Windows CE throws in two new types.

Actually the difference between the two types is fairly simple. Both types of memory deal with the RAM memory that is in your handheld PC. Basically, a certain amount of the memory is used to run programs — this is the *Program memory.* The other portion of memory, *Storage memory,* is where programs and data files are actually stored.

Here's where confusion sets in: Windows CE already has its own memory location and now it needs to use some of your storage, too. The reason is that the RAM memory where the Windows CE operating system is stored does not allow anything to be written in it. When Windows CE runs, it is just like other operating systems and requires memory space where it can keep track of all the programs you are currently running. Because this information is temporarily written into memory, it requires some memory that can be written to — the *Program memory.*

Most handheld PCs come with the RAM divided between the Program memory and the Storage memory. The more Storage memory you allocate, the more programs and documents you can actually place on your handheld PC. On the other hand, the more Program memory that you allocate, the more programs you can run simultaneously.

If at all possible, leave this screen set to the default settings. If you find that you do not have the amount of memory you need, try adding a PC Card for additional storage.

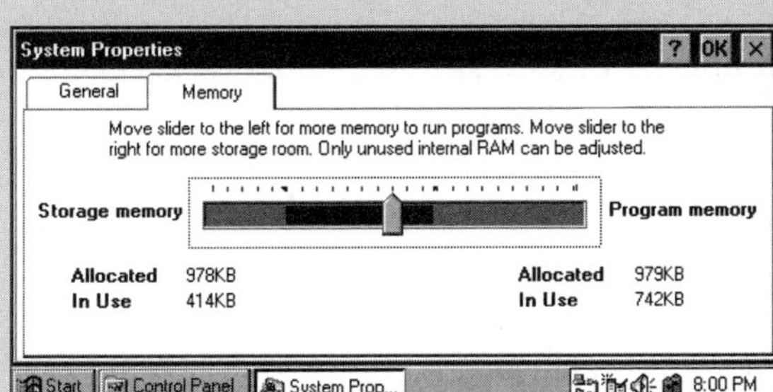

When you transfer data between two handheld PCs, you can send only one file at a time. The infrared ports on each handheld PC need to be lined up so that they can see each other, and nothing should be blocking either port. To ensure that the files transfer properly, the infrared ports need to be within about three feet of each other.

Because the infrared ports use a light beam to send information back and forth, some types of fluorescent lights may interfere with the data transfer. If you find that you are having problems interacting with the other handheld PC, try moving to another location.

Besides transferring files between handheld PCs, another popular use of the infrared port is to play games with users of other handheld PCs. If you decide to play a game with another person who owns a handheld PC, the game you select must be designed to work with the infrared port. For more information, refer to the documentation that came with the software game.

With some handheld PCs, you can send a document to print by using the infrared port. To find out if you have one of these devices, check the hardware documentation that came with your handheld PC. Even if your handheld PC has the capability of printing documents, however, you need to locate a printer that has an infrared port to receive the document. If you have both the handheld PC that can print and the printer that can receive, you are in great shape because you have eliminated the need to transfer the document to your desktop computer before printing it.

What is that flashing light?

If you have added any appointments to your Calendar program in Windows CE, you may have noticed a little light flashing on the top of your handheld PC while it was turned off. If the light is flashing, the device is trying to remind you of something. You may have an appointment at the dentist's office, or it may be time to start cleaning the garage.

You can specify when you want a reminder based on your selection in either the Calendar program or the Tasks program. When you select a reminder, you can also indicate whether you want a flashing light, beep, or both. This information is specified on the Notification Options dialog box, shown in Figure 1-5.

When you turn on your handheld PC, the flashing light turns off and you get a reminder message of the appointment or task, as shown in Figure 1-6. For more information about setting reminders, see Chapters 3 and 4.

Most handheld PCs also have a button you can press to turn off the flashing light without first turning on the unit. This feature is useful because turning your handheld PC on and looking at the scheduled event may not always be convenient. For more information, refer to the hardware documentation that came with your handheld PC.

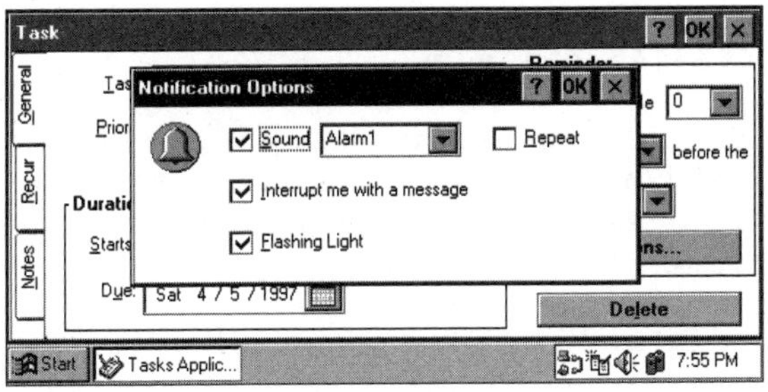

Figure 1-5: The Notification Options dialog box.

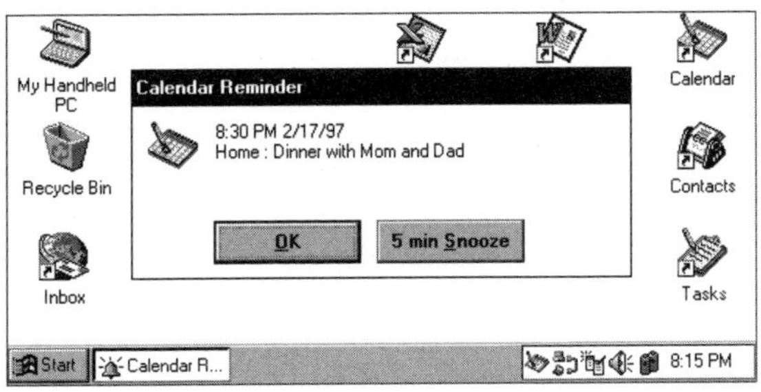

Figure 1-6: A friendly reminder of an appointment that is currently scheduled.

Should I press the Reset button?

Just like a desktop computer, each handheld PC has a Reset button. This button is not intended to be used on a regular basis, but some situations require you to use it. For example, some software demands that the handheld PC be restarted in order to install the information the program needs to run. The button is recessed and requires extra effort to push it, eliminating the chance of someone accidentally pressing it.

When you press the Reset button, the handheld PC totally shuts down so that when you turn it back on you are essentially rebooting it. (*Rebooting* is a term commonly used when talking about desktop computers; it refers to the process of totally restarting a machine.) If a program instructs you to press the Reset button, go ahead and do so, but first make sure that all other programs are closed.

TIP

Occasionally, for one reason or another, your handheld PC may not turn on when you press the On button. Should this problem occur, try pressing the Reset button and then pressing the On button again.

Selecting a Handheld PC

Buying a handheld PC can be almost as confusing as determining which desktop computer you should purchase. You need to look at these devices for only a few minutes to determine that each one is different and comes with its own unique features.

You will find handheld PCs with built-in modems, others with extra memory, different processors, and so on. I cannot, actually I will not, try to guess which handheld PC is best for you, but Table 1-4 explains these added features and indicates why you may want to consider locating a handheld PC with them.

Table 1-4 Added Features on Handheld PCs

Feature	*Description*
RAM	The more memory that your device comes with, the more programs and data that you can store without adding some type of external card. Obviously, the more memory, the more desirable the handheld PC. Keep in mind, though, that the more memory you want, the more money you're going to pay for the handheld PC. A handheld PC is capable of storing only a few different programs on 2MB of RAM. Another thing to keep in mind is the fact that the RAM on most of the handheld PCs can be upgraded; although, you should check to see if this option exists before buying the handheld PC.
Modem	Some handheld PCs offer a built-in modem. This feature is definitely worth consideration if you intend to use your handheld PC to send and receive a great deal of e-mail or connect to the Internet. A built-in modem frees up the PC-Card port for other types of PCMCIA cards that can be added to your handheld PC, such as extra storage.
Rechargeable Batteries	You can go through a bunch of batteries by using the handheld PC on a regular basis. One nice feature to consider is a handheld PC with rechargeable batteries. Most handheld PCs do have the option of purchasing rechargeable batteries as an added accessory.

Selecting the processor type

If you spend much time looking at handheld PCs, you may notice that several different types of processors are available. The processor is often referred to as the *CPU* (central processing unit). This little chip is the brains of your device. If you were to talk about a desktop computer, the CPU is either a Pentium or 486.

Many of the handheld PC processors are basically the same speed, although several types of processors exist. Some of them may claim to be slightly faster, which is definitely a good feature to look at. But with the design of Windows CE, everything runs fairly quickly already on all of the processors. Because the list of processors available for the devices is constantly changing, I am not going to specify any of the processors by name. But keep in mind that any processor that runs Windows CE must first have Microsoft's blessing. Therefore, if you trust Microsoft, the processor must be fairly reliable.

The only drawback about the different processors is the fact that each Windows CE software program has to be compiled by the software vendor so it will run on the specific processor type. Make sure that you know what type of processor the handheld PC that you buy has so that when you purchase additional software, you can verify that the software is designed to run on your handheld PC.

Don't make this distinction a major concern, however. Software vendors can easily make software for different processors, so most software can be found for several different processor versions. Also, most installation programs automatically determine which procesor is on your handheld PC, so you don't have to worry about indicating which version to install.

REMEMBER

Let me ease some fears here by pointing out that all of these handheld PCs have been designed specifically to run Windows CE; therefore, you cannot make a wrong decision, as long as you buy a box with the Windows CE logo on it. If all of this mention of added-feature stuff causes frustration, forget about it and just buy the one you think looks the nicest. After all, they all run Windows CE.

Turning on Your Handheld PC for the First Time

Like most new computers, your handheld PC presents you with some strange screens the first time you turn it on. These screens help you set up your device so that you can use it properly. After you set up the handheld PC, you won't see most of these screens again.

When you turn on your handheld PC for the first time, assuming that it has never been turned on before, the HPC Setup Wizard appears, as shown in Figure 1-7.

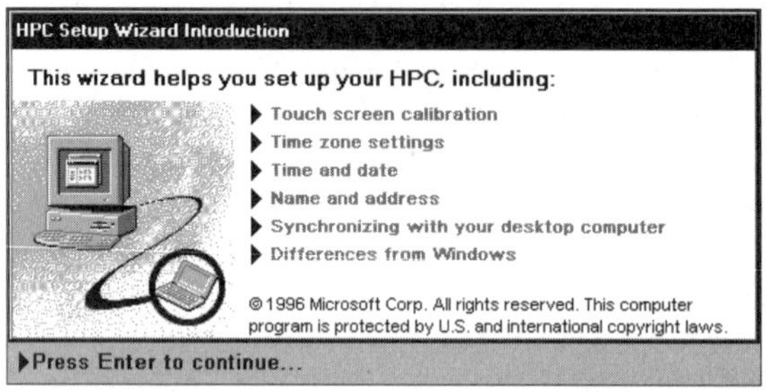

Figure 1-7: The HPC Setup Wizard helps you set up your handheld PC.

Setting up your handheld PC

The HPC Setup Wizard provides a brief introduction to Windows CE by explaining the touch-screen capabilities, helping you set up your time zone information, allowing you to set up personal information, and explaining some differences between Windows CE and other versions of Windows. When you start the HPC Setup Wizard, the first screen that appears provides an overview of the setup process.

The sooner you set up your handheld PC, the sooner you can get on to more exciting things, like setting up your calendar. So grab your handheld PC and follow these steps:

1. **On the HPC Setup Wizard Introduction screen, press the Enter key to start the setup process.**

   This screen is the first screen displayed when you run the HPC Setup Wizard (refer to Figure 1-7).

2. **Review the information about the stylus on the next screen, and press the Enter key to continue.**

3. **On the Calibration screen, shown in Figure 1-8, tap on the large + (plus sign) in the middle of the screen.**

   After you tap, the + will move to another location on the screen. Continue chasing the + around the screen by tapping with the stylus.

   You may feel like you're playing cat and mouse, but actually, your handheld PC is adjusting itself to ensure that your taps are recognized. This process of setting the tapping action is referred to as *calibrating the touch screen.*

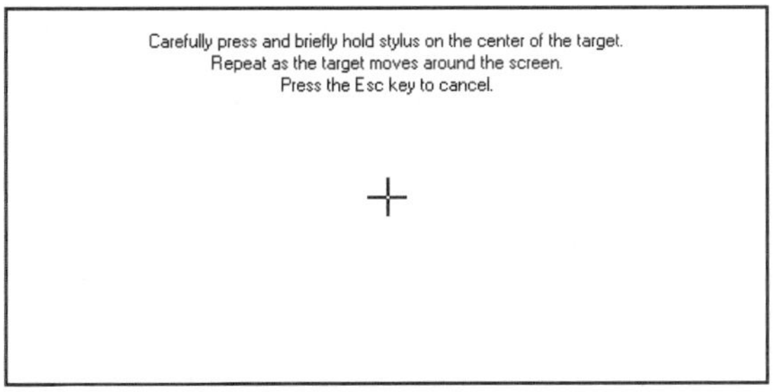

Figure 1-8: To calibrate your touch screen, use the stylus to touch the + in the center of the screen.

If you think that you have made a mistake, don't despair, simply press the Esc key and the calibration process restarts by placing the + in the center of the screen again.

4. **After you calibrate the screen, tap on the Next button at the bottom of the screen to display the Set Time Zone screen.**

   You use this screen to indicate your time zone so that your handheld PC can adjust your appointments accordingly. You can also set up the time zone for a city that you visit frequently so that you can quickly change the time on your handheld PC to match your current location.

5. **To set the time zone for the location where you spend the most time, either tap on the correct location on the map, or tap on the Down Arrow button next to the City field and then tap on the closest city to your location.**

   To set the time zone for a city that you travel to often, or intend to spend some time in, tap on the Visiting tab on the left side of the screen and select the time zone. Figure 1-9 shows the screen with the two time zone options.

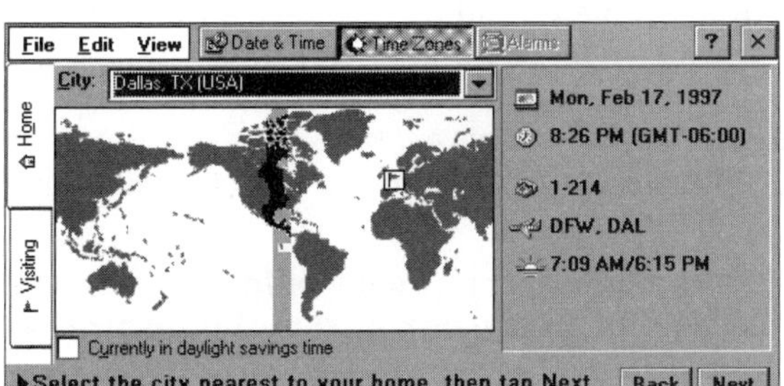

Figure 1-9: You can set up your handheld PC to keep track of two time zones simultaneously.

6. **After specifying the time zone information, tap on the Next button at the bottom of the screen to display the Set Date and Time screen.**

   Here is where you make sure that the date and time settings are correct for your time zone. To select the date, you can either select the date on the calendar or type the date in the field beneath the calendar.

7. **To select a date on the calendar, tap on the arrows at the top of the calendar to move from one month to the next. When you locate the correct month, tap on the day you want to select.**

8. **To adjust the time, either tap on the hand on the clock and drag it to the location you want to select, or type the time in the field beneath the clock.**

   Figure 1-10 shows the date and time settings for someone who lives in Dallas, Texas, with visiting times set for Paris, France.

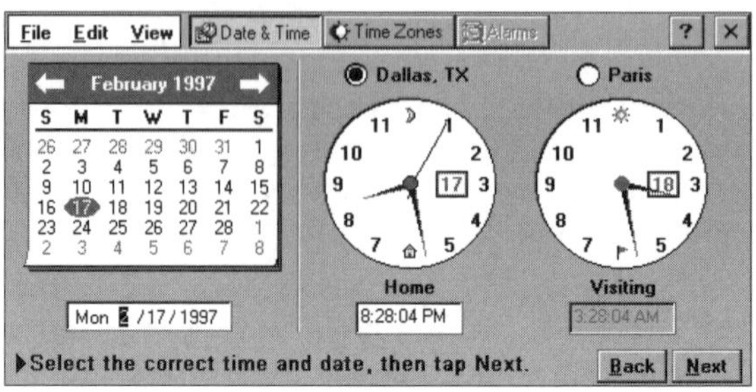

Figure 1-10: Setting the current date and time.

9. **After you specify the time and date information, tap on the Next button at the bottom of the screen to display the Owner Information screen.**

   This screen allows you to enter your personal information on the handheld PC. Much like a name tag, this information allows someone to figure out to whom the handheld PC belongs, should you misplace it.

10. **Type your information in each of the fields on this screen.**

    Make sure that you at least enter a name and phone number so that someone can contact you. You never know when you may accidentally misplace your unit.

11. **If you would like to display your owner information each time the device is turned on, tap on the box next to the Display Owner Identification field.**

    A check mark in the field indicates that option is selected, as shown in Figure 1-11. With this option selected, when someone turns on your handheld PC, he will immediately see who the owner is. Using this feature is particularly important if your handheld PC is password protected. Without knowing your password, no one who finds your handheld PC can see any information that points to the rightful owner.

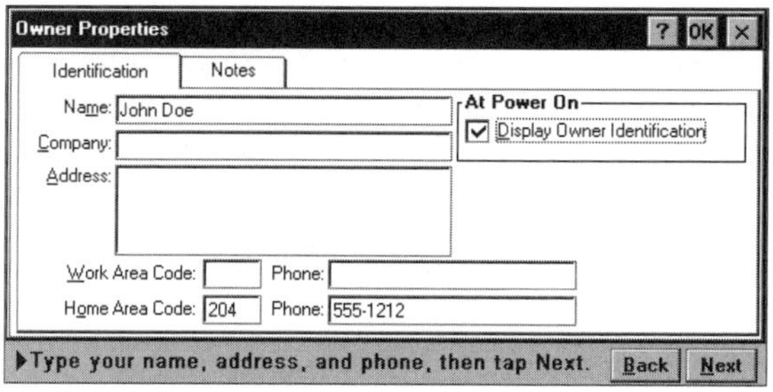

Figure 1-11: The Display Owner Identification field.

12. **Click on the Notes tab to add any additional personal information that you want displayed when the device is turned on.**

    Again, make sure that you tap on the box next to the Display Owner Notes at Power on field if you want the information to display when the unit is turned on.

13. **When you finish setting up your personal information, tap on the Next button to complete the setup program.**

    The HPC Setup Wizard provides three more screens that provide additional pointers about Windows CE.

14. **When you get to the last screen, tap on the Done button to close the HPC Setup Wizard and save the settings.**

    Congratulations! You have successfully set up Windows CE. You are now ready to start exploring your device.

TIP: As you move through the setup process for your handheld, if at anytime you want to return to a specific screen during the setup process, tap on the Back button until the screen you want to view appears.

TIP: After you use your handheld PC for a while, you may find that it does not seem to respond to your taps as well as it did when you first set it up. Do not despair; all you have to do is to recalibrate the touch screen. To load the Calibration screen, simply hold down Alt+Ctrl+= (the equal sign) on the keyboard.

Rerunning the Setup Wizard

You can rerun the HPC Setup Wizard at any time. Although you will rarely come across an occasion when you will want to do so, the option is available. The only time I would run the Setup Wizard again is if I knew I wanted to modify most of the setup information; otherwise, all of this information can be modified in the Control Panel folder by selecting each individual icon.

To run the HPC Setup Wizard you need to select the Welcome icon. This icon resembles a light bulb and is located in the Accessories folder, which you can access by choosing Programs from the Start menu. When you double-tap on the Welcome icon, the HPC Setup Wizard appears, as discussed in the preceding section.

Chapter 2

Working with Your Windows CE Desktop

In This Chapter

- Organizing your desktop
- Recycling unwanted files and programs
- Using the loyal taskbar
- Navigating around the windows

Before you embark on an exciting new adventure, you need to organize your equipment. You need to make sure that you have a map, for example, so that you don't set off in the wrong direction. Similarly, before you use your Windows CE handheld PC, organize the items on your Windows CE desktop so that you can easily locate them when you need them. In this chapter, you explore some of the basic elements of Windows CE and discover the role these items play in the use of Windows CE. You find out all about the Windows CE desktop and the items that are placed on the desktop when you first set up your handheld PC. This chapter also covers other extremely useful items that you encounter on your desktop, such as the Recycle Bin, the taskbar, and the Start menu. Finally, this chapter familiarizes you with the elements of a window.

What Are All Those Pictures on the Desktop?

When you run Windows CE, the first thing you see is a screen covered with a bunch of little pictures, as shown in Figure 2-1. If you have used Windows 95, this arrangement probably looks familiar to you. This initial screen is commonly referred to as the *desktop,* and the little pictures are called *icons.* These little icons represent programs that are stored on your handheld PC. Whenever you want to run the program that is associated with an icon, all you have to do is double-tap on the icon with the stylus.

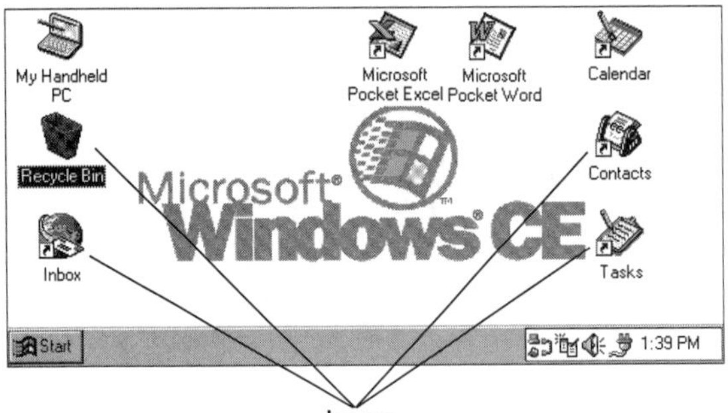

Figure 2-1: The desktop displays the items that you use most often.

As shown in Figure 2-1, Windows CE comes with many unique icons. Table 2-1 outlines the icons that are installed on your desktop when you first run Windows CE. These icons are not the only ones that you can place on your desktop; just as with your desk at home or at work, you have the freedom to reorganize the items on your desktop to suit your needs (see the next section).

Table 2-1 Deciphering the Icons

Icon	*Purpose*
	If you tap on this icon, you see everything that exists on your handheld PC. Tapping on this icon is equivalent to choosing Start⇨Explore.
	The Recycle Bin stores all your deleted files until you empty it. ***Note:*** The fastest way to empty the Recycle Bin is to hold down the Alt key while you tap on the Recycle Bin. When the pop-up menu appears, tap on the Empty Recycle Bin command.
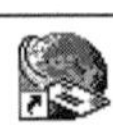	This icon represents the Inbox. If you use your handheld PC to send and receive e-mail, you will become very familiar with this icon.
	Tap here to create spreadsheets (called *workbooks* in Windows CE lingo) by using Microsoft Pocket Excel.
	Tapping on this icon displays Microsoft Pocket Word, which allows you to create a new document.
	This icon starts the Calendar program. You can keep track of where you need to be and when you need to be there simply by using this program.
	Tapping on this little rolodex icon allows you to keep track of your personal contacts.
	Use this icon to list tasks you need to complete, such as cleaning the garage or checking out the . . .*For Dummies* home page. After you list the tasks, you can view them by using the Calendar program.

TIP

Don't bother memorizing the icon for every program. Each icon is labeled with the name of the program or file to which it corresponds.

Organizing Your Desktop

The Windows CE desktop is kind of like the top of your desk at work or home. Normally, people try to keep the items they use most often on top of their desks — a phone, stapler, Rolodex, calendar, and so on. You use the Windows CE desktop the same way: You set up your desktop so that you can easily access the items you use most often when you work with your Windows CE handheld PC. For example, you may choose to keep your word processor, the Calendar program, your contact list, and the Recycle Bin within easy reach.

REMEMBER

If you think of your Windows CE desktop as the place where you want to keep only the things you use most, it should not become too cluttered. If your desktop does become messy, however, you can always use your handy Recycle Bin to do some spring cleaning.

Arranging your icons

You can arrange the icons on your desktop in many ways. The easiest way is to place the stylus on the icon you want to move and drag the icon across the screen, just like picking up the phone and putting it on the other side of your desk. Of course, moving items around one by one can become a little tedious. Have you ever wanted to wiggle your nose and have everything move to an appropriate location? With Windows CE, you have almost the next best thing. The desktop menu provides several options for organizing your desktop.

The desktop menu, shown in Figure 2-2, appears when you hold down the Alt key and tap on an icon (any icon) on the desktop. The menu options enable you to have Windows CE automatically arrange and sort your icons in several ways:

- If you want to make sure that your icons are always in neat little rows and columns on the desktop, be sure to tap on the Auto Arrange option. If you select this option, no matter what you add to your desktop, the icon is placed in the next row or column on the screen. To cancel the automatic arrangement of icons, you need to tap on this option again.
- When you move icons around on the screen, you can select the Line Up Icons option to ensure that the icons look uniform in the new layout.

- If you have different types of icons on your desktop, such as Pocket Word files, programs, and even worksheets, you may want to sort them so that icons of the same type are placed together. This grouping is often referred to as *sorting items based upon their type*. To do this, tap on the Arrange By Type option on the desktop menu.
- You can arrange all the icons on the desktop in alphabetical order, as shown in Figure 2-3. This way, as long as you know your alphabet, you can quickly locate the icon for a program. To arrange the icons alphabetically, tap on the Arrange By Name option on the desktop menu.

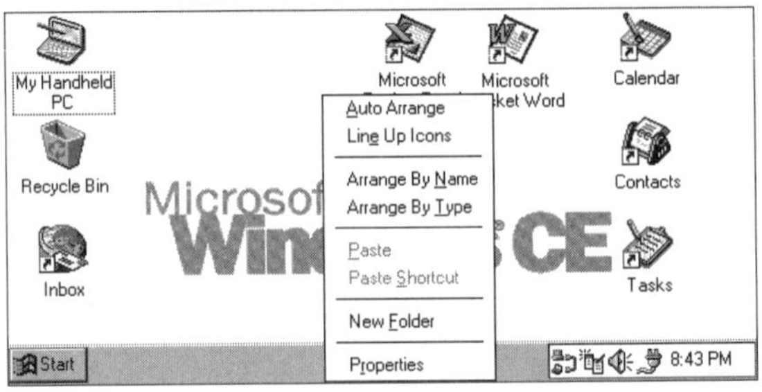

Figure 2-2: To display the desktop menu, hold down the Alt key and tap on the desktop.

Note: When Windows CE sorts the icons, it places the My Handheld PC and the Recycle Bin icons in the same location, on the left side of the screen. For some unknown reason — well, the reason is unknown to most of us — these two stubborn icons have decided that they are not going to budge from those locations.

TIP

You can create a new folder and place it on the desktop by selecting the New Folder option on the desktop menu. I find this feature is useful for keeping track of documents that I use most often.

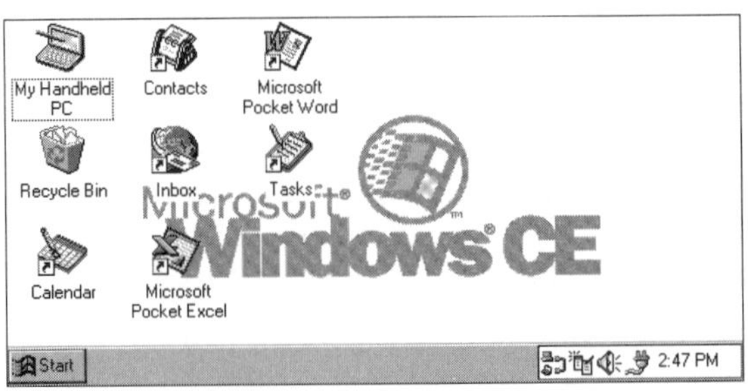

Figure 2-3: The Arrange By Name option arranges most of the icons alphabetically.

What about the right mouse button?

If you have ever used Windows 95 or Windows NT 4.0, you are probably used to pressing the right mouse button, or *right-clicking,* when you want to display additional menu options for any option on the screen. Unfortunately, Windows CE does not come with a mouse, so using the right mouse button commands is impossible — right?

Wrong. You can access the menus that you are used to getting by right-clicking by simply holding down the Alt key before tapping on an item with the stylus.

If you are looking for an option but can't find it on the menus that are currently displayed, try holding down the Alt key and tapping. In many places within Windows CE, you can find new menus.

Adding a new program to the desktop

You can add any new program to your Windows CE desktop. When you add items to the desktop, you are really adding a shortcut to the desktop. A *shortcut* is a link to the actual program or file. The really cool thing about shortcuts is that you can remove the shortcut from your desktop without removing the program from your handheld PC.

You can add a shortcut to the desktop in many ways. The easiest method is to use the Desktop Shortcut option on the program's menu:

1. **Hold down the Alt key and tap on the Calculator icon.**

   This icon looks like a miniature calculator. You can find it in the Accessories folder. When you hold Alt and tap on it, a menu appears onscreen, as shown in Figure 2-4.

The Desktop Shortcut option

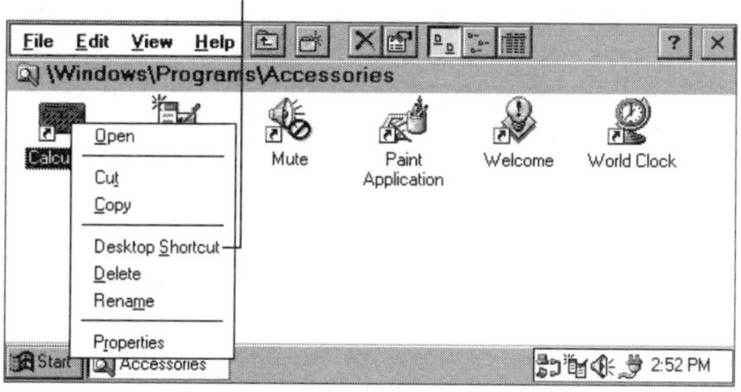

Figure 2-4: To add the Calculator program, tap on the Desktop Shortcut option.

2. Tap on the Desktop Shortcut option.

The next time you view the desktop, the Calculator option appears, as shown in Figure 2-5. The little arrow in the lower-left corner of the icon indicates that the icon represents a shortcut to the program.

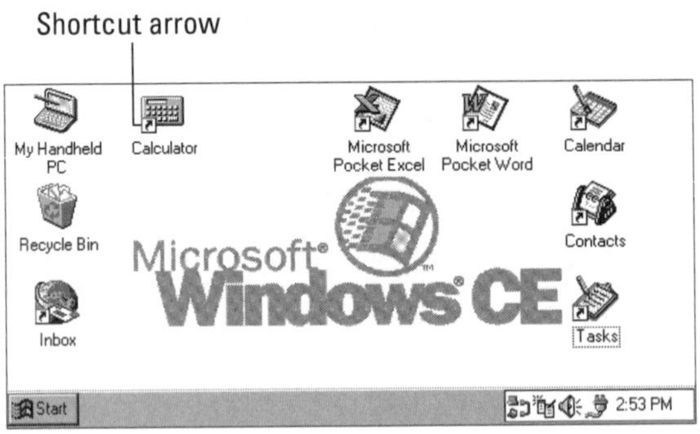

Figure 2-5: The little arrow identifies a shortcut icon.

WARNING!

Use caution when you delete icons from your handheld PC. If you remove an icon that does not have a little arrow in the lower-left corner, you remove the actual program.

Recycling Unwanted Items

Everyone has been taught, some better than others, to use a recycle bin when he or she throws things away. So you may not have been too shocked to find the Recycle Bin icon sitting in the upper-left corner of your screen.

The Recycle Bin is a folder on your system that contains all the items that you have deleted, as shown in Figure 2-6. It works in the same fashion as a real recycle bin. When you delete a file or a program, Windows CE places the specified item in the Recycle Bin. Deleted items remain in the Recycle Bin until you "empty" the bin or retrieve the item. By using the Recycle Bin, you can recover deleted files as easily as you might salvage the sports section from the household recycle bin.

TIP

You can drag items from your desktop into the Recycle Bin by tapping on the item you want to delete and dragging it onto the Recycle Bin icon. Anything that is dragged onto the Recycle Bin icon is removed from its location on the desktop.

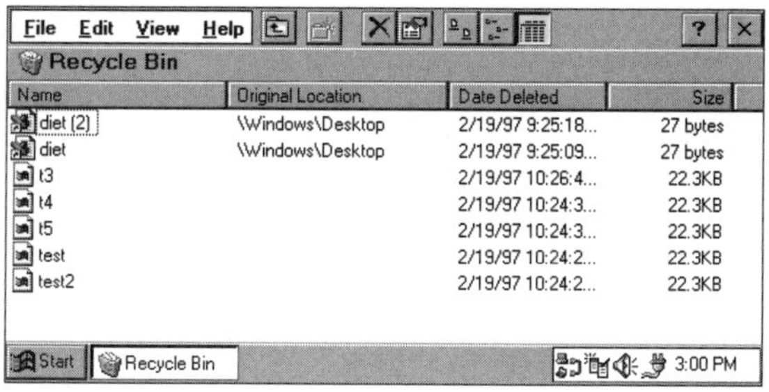

Figure 2-6: Double-tap on the Recycle Bin to see the items that you have deleted.

TECHNICAL STUFF

Keeping tabs on the Recycle Bin

Windows CE comes with the default amount of storage for the Recycle Bin set at 10 percent of the storage memory for storing deleted files. You can adjust the amount of storage by using the Recycle Bin Properties dialog box. This screen appears when you choose Edit⇨Properties.

The dialog box indicates the maximum amount of memory available for deleted files. To adjust the percentage of memory that should be used for deleted files, place the stylus on the slider and drag it to the appropriate amount.

If the number of items in the Recycle Bin exceeds the allotted amount of storage, a message appears, indicating that you need to remove some of the files from the Recycle Bin before you can add more.

Unless you have a specific reason for changing the size of the Recycle Bin, such as a sudden urge to do some extensive spring cleaning, I suggest leaving the memory setting at the default setting of 10 percent.

In this dialog box, you can also specify that no files are ever placed in the Recycle Bin. If you select this option, you will not be able to recover an item after you delete it. I do not recommend selecting this option.

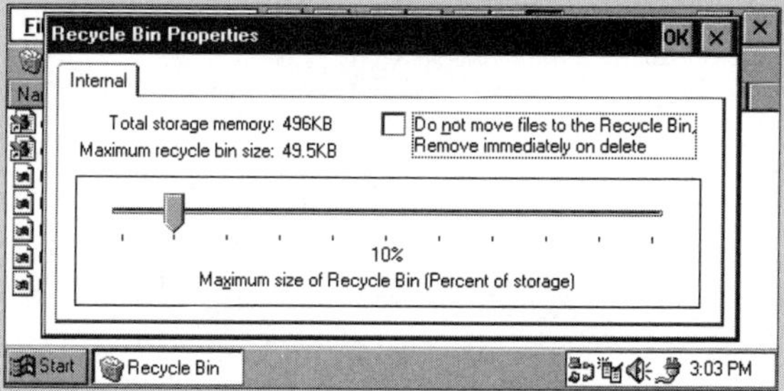

As soon as you add an item to the Recycle Bin, the Recycle Bin icon changes from an empty bin to one that is full of papers. This change is a notification to you that you have trash to empty. The quick and easy way to empty the Recycle Bin is to hold down the Alt key and tap on the Recycle Bin icon, and then tap on the Empty Recycle Bin option. However, you may want to check the Recycle Bin before emptying it. You never know what you may have hiding in there. Follow these steps:

1. **Open the Recycle Bin by double-tapping on its icon.**
2. **Choose Edit⇨Empty Recycle Bin.**

   If you want to remove a single item from the bin, tap on the item in the list and then choose Edit⇨Delete.

TIP: You can return items in the Recycle Bin to their original location. Open the Recycle Bin, highlight the item you want to retrieve, and choose Edit⇨Restore. The item is returned to its original location.

Giving the Taskbar Something to Do

If you have played around with Windows CE at all, you have probably noticed the horizontal bar across the bottom of the screen. This bar, shown in Figure 2-7, is commonly referred to as the *taskbar.* The taskbar creates a button for each window that you have open. The button that appears to be "pressed down" is the window that is currently displayed on-screen. In Figure 2-7, for example, the Calendar program is displayed. To switch to another open window, tap on the window's button on the taskbar.

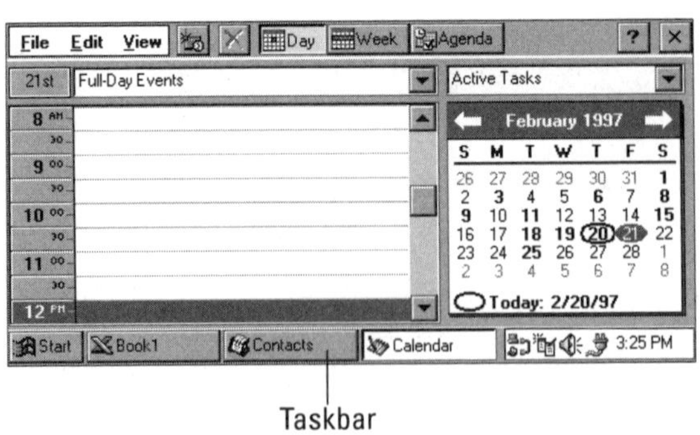

Figure 2-7: The taskbar monitors your activity within Windows CE.

Closing programs that won't respond

Sooner or later, a program on your handheld PC will stop working, and no matter what button you tap on, it won't do a thing. This experience can be rather frustrating, but luckily, Windows CE provides an option for solving this dilemma.

You can force the program to close by using the Task Manager window. To display this window, press Alt+Tab.

You can highlight a specific program by tapping on it and then select the End Task option to close the selected program.

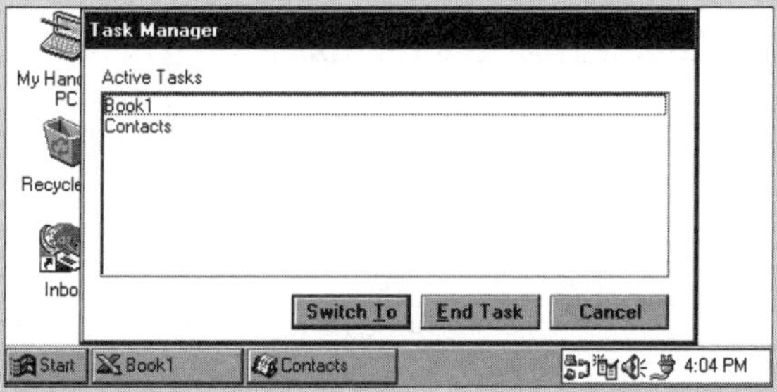

To minimize an open window, tap on the window's button on the taskbar. You can reopen the window by tapping on the button a second time. When you *minimize* a window, you are making it invisible so that you can see your desktop; the window remains that way until you tap on its button again. Boy, don't you wish you could make things invisible on your real desktop?

TIP: The right side of the taskbar is the *status area.* You find the clock in this area. Depending on your settings, you may also find other icons, including an icon that indicates the current battery status and one that shows whether the handheld PC is connected to a desktop computer.

The left corner of the taskbar is where the Start button resides. When you press this button, a menu of seven options appears. These options help you find different information contained on your handheld PC. The Start menu is discussed in the section, "Unveiling the Start Menu," later in this chapter.

Doing Windows

Each time you run a program, it opens on-screen in a *window.* A window is a box on the screen where each program runs. Actually, I think it looks more like a new page, but I guess it would have sounded kind of strange to name an operating system *Pages.*

All windows have a standard look and feel. This design provides consistency between programs. In other words, a standard blueprint, created by some nerdy computer programmer, is used to design all the windows that appear in Windows CE. After you understand how to locate information on the blueprint, you can quickly familiarize yourself with a new program. Figure 2-8 shows the parts of a typical Windows CE window.

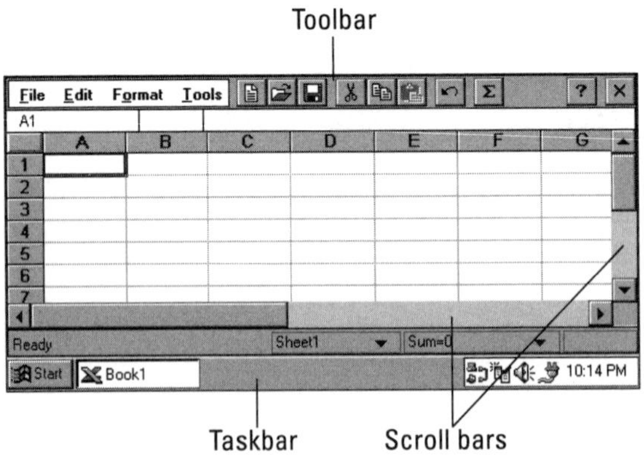

Figure 2-8: Each part of the window has a unique name and function.

When you open a new window, any other windows that are currently open stay open. You can figure out which windows are open by looking at the buttons on the taskbar. The button that appears to be pressed down is the window that is currently displayed. To switch to another window, tap on its button. Or you can switch between windows by pressing Alt+Esc. Windows CE scrolls through the windows that you have open in the order that they are listed on the taskbar.

The toolbar

The toolbar provides the commands you use to do most of the stuff in Windows CE. Notice that the toolbar contains several words, such as *File* and *Edit*. When you tap on one of these words, a menu containing a series of options appears. For example, you can tap on the word *Edit* to open the Edit menu, and then tap on the command you want to use. The toolbar also contains several buttons. You tap on a button to choose its corresponding command. The exact menu options and buttons displayed on the toolbar vary depending on the program you're running. Figure 2-9 shows the window for Pocket Excel with the Edit menu selected.

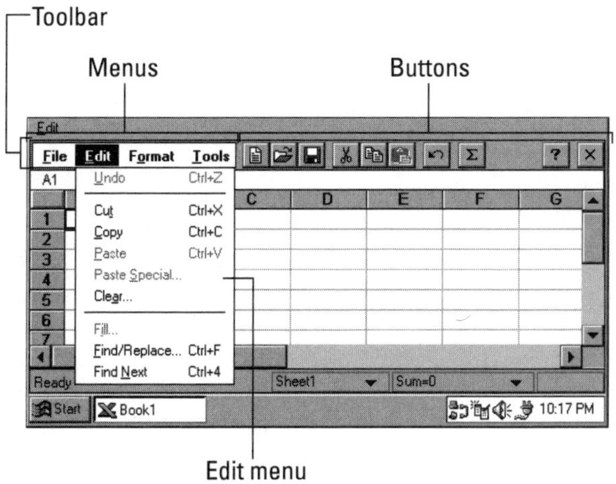

Figure 2-9: Tapping on a word on the toolbar displays a menu of options for the program running in the window.

Sometimes, options appear on a menu in a light gray color. This *grayed-out option* cannot currently be used. If you are using Pocket Word, for example, the Paste option on the Edit menu remains grayed out until you have copied or cut some text.

To close a menu without choosing an option, tap the stylus anywhere else on the screen.

If you misplace your stylus, you can use the keyboard to access the menus on the toolbar. Press the Alt key to open the first menu on the menu bar, which is usually the File menu. After you open the menu, you can use the arrow keys to scroll up and down and from one menu to the other. After you decide which option you want, press the Enter key to choose it.

The left side of the toolbar normally contains buttons. Each of these buttons performs a different task. Three standard buttons appear in the left corner of most windows, as discussed in Table 2-2.

Table 2-2 Those Little Buttons

Tap on This Button	*To Do This*
	Close the window. If the OK button is also displayed in the left-hand corner, the window is closed without saving the changes you have made.
	Display the online help file for the program that is running in the window.

The toolbar may contain other buttons between the menu options and the three buttons outlined in Table 2-2. These buttons are specific to the program you are running. For example, Pocket Excel has a button (which looks like a pair of scissors) that you can use to cut text. If you are not sure what other buttons do on the toolbar, refer to the chapter in this book that provides information about the specific program you are running.

The scroll bars

If the stuff that you are trying to view on your handheld PC will not all fit on-screen, Windows CE provides a funny-looking bar on the right side of the screen, as shown in Figure 2-10. If the information is too wide to display on-screen, Windows CE places a similar bar at the bottom of the window. These bars are affectionately known as *scroll bars*. If you tap on the Up Arrow button, the screen moves up one line at a time each time you tap. Tapping on the Down Arrow button moves the screen down one line at a time. The overall effect is that of "rolling" through the document.

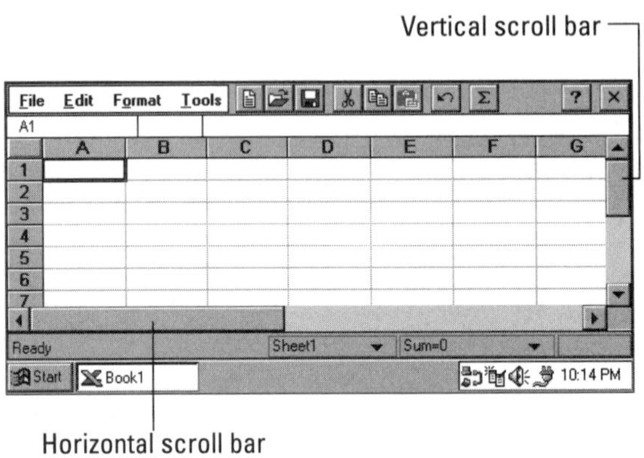

Figure 2-10: The scroll bars allow you to slide information up and down or left and right on the screen.

Windows CE also places scroll bars at the bottom of the window when the information is too wide to display on the screen. Scroll bars do not always behave the way you want them to. Depending where you tap on the scroll bar, the screen either scrolls up or down a line at a time, or all the text on the screen may change. Table 2-3 attempts to ease the confusion by explaining the results when you tap on various parts of the scroll bar.

Table 2-3 Taming the Scroll Bar

Tap on This Part	*To Do This*
Above the box	Display a screen-full of information prior to the first line currently displayed on the screen.
Below the box	Display the next screen-full of information below the last line displayed on the screen.

Tap on This Part	*To Do This*
Down Arrow	Scroll the display down one line. When you tap on this button, the line that is currently at the top of the screen is no longer visible.
Up Arrow	Scroll the display up one line. When you tap on this button, the last line on the screen is no longer visible.

TIP

You can place the stylus on the box in the scroll bar and drag the box up and down to view the information you want.

Doing Dialog Boxes

When you use Windows CE, you frequently encounter windows that appear after you choose an option in a program. You use these windows, commonly referred to as *dialog boxes,* to communicate with Windows CE. Dialog boxes come in all shapes and sizes, and the type of information that they contain varies. They may simply request that you type a simple numeric value in one field, or you may need to specify values for several different fields. For example, you use the dialog box shown in Figure 2-11 to indicate the height you want a row to appear in a worksheet in Pocket Excel.

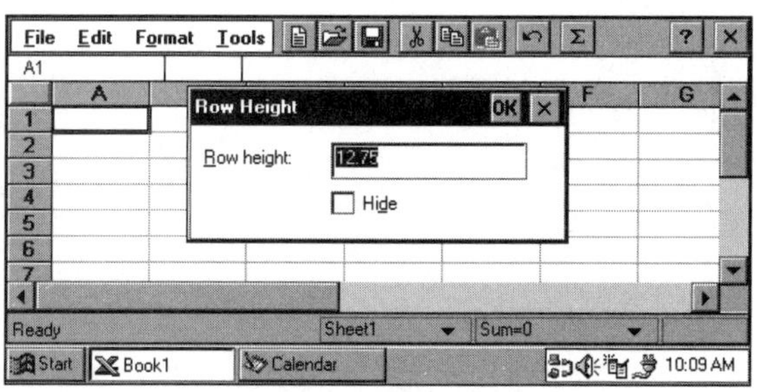

Figure 2-11: Dialog boxes request certain types of information.

Windows CE also uses dialog boxes to inform you of something, such as the fact that it cannot locate the program you requested or your batteries are running low. Dialog boxes that are used for this purpose are called *alert boxes.*

A couple of things are standard on all dialog boxes in Windows CE, however:

- You will always find the name of the dialog box in the upper-left corner of the window.
- Windows CE always provides a way for you to close the window. Each dialog box has at least two buttons in its upper-right corner. Table 2-4 describes these buttons.

Table 2-4	Buttons for Closing Dialog Boxes
Tap on This Button	*If You Want To*
OK	Close the window and save all the changes you have made
×	Close the dialog box without saving the changes you have made

Unveiling the Start Menu

When you tap on the Start button, located at the bottom-left corner of your screen (on the taskbar), you unveil the Start menu. This menu contains seven options, as shown in Figure 2-12. Each option in the Start menu takes you to a different type of information contained on your handheld PC, as outlined in Table 2-5.

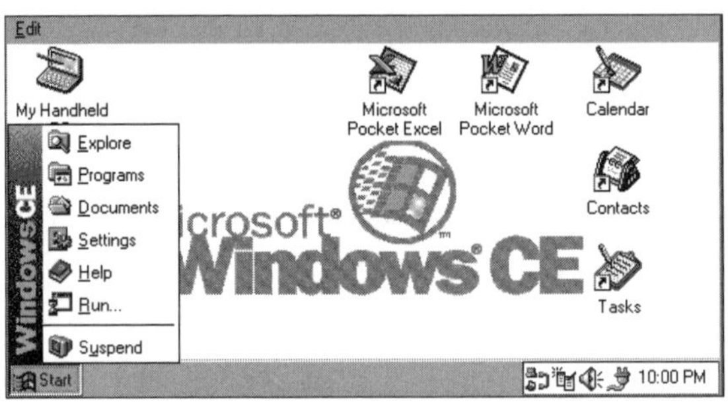

Figure 2-12: The Start menu provides tools you can use to search out different types of information.

Table 2-5	The Start Menu
Tap on This Option	*To Do This*
Explore	Use Windows CE Explorer to look at the files contained on your handheld PC. You can see all types of files, including programs, Word documents, and spreadsheets. You can find more details on file management and working with Windows CE Explorer in Chapter 9.
Programs	Locate and run a program residing on your handheld PC.

Tap on This Option	*To Do This*
Documents	See the most recent documents that you created and quickly open a document by tapping on the associated icon.
Settings	Adjust system settings for your handheld PC, such as changing the wallpaper on your desktop, or setting a password for your handheld PC.
Help	Access the Windows CE online help system, where you can find some quick pointers on using Windows CE. Find more information about Windows CE online help later in this chapter.
Run	Quickly run a program, as long as you know the name of the program.
Suspend	Safely shut down your handheld PC. For details, check out the "Shutting down for the day" section in this chapter.

Unlike Windows 95 and Windows NT, Windows CE does not allow you to add items to the Start menu. You can only add items to the windows that appear when you select either the Explore or Programs options.

Exploring your handheld PC

Not everything that you want to access on your handheld PC is available on the Windows CE desktop. Windows CE comes with a program called *Windows CE Explorer* that you can use to locate and organize all the files on your handheld PC. Windows CE Explorer appears when you tap on the Explore option on the Start menu.

Windows CE uses files and folders to deal with everything that is stored on your handheld PC. A *folder* is a place to store related files, just like you store related pieces of paper in a folder on your desk. The word *file* is a general term that refers to each item on your handheld PC, such as programs, word processing documents, spreadsheets, and so on. The Windows CE Explorer is your tool for working with the different files and folders stored on your handheld PC.

For more details about working with files and folders in the Windows CE Explorer, refer to Chapter 9.

Searching for programs to run

If you are looking for a specific program file, you probably don't want to be bothered with all the other types of files that are stored on your handheld PC. Fortunately, Windows CE provides an option that allows you to look only at the program files in each folder.

To view the program files on your handheld PC, use the Programs option in the Start menu. Tapping on this option opens Windows CE Explorer in the Programs folder, as shown in Figure 2-13.

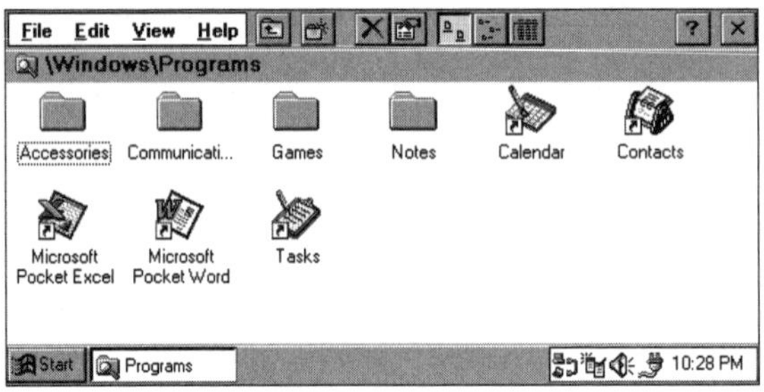

Figure 2-13: The Programs folder can help you find a specific program.

You can double-tap on a folder to open it, or you can tap the Previous Folder button to close a folder and view the contents of the parent folder. The Previous Folder button looks like a folder with an arrow pointed up on the front of it.

REMEMBER

Only program files are displayed in the Programs folder, so don't be concerned if you can't find other files that you added to that folder. You can verify the complete contents of the folder by choosing the Explore option from the Start menu.

Finding the most recent documents

Have you ever sat down at your computer to work on a proposal you started the previous day but then couldn't remember what you named the proposal when you saved it? Windows CE can tell you the name of the most recent documents that you created, regardless of the program you used to create the document.

To see the most recent documents that you worked with on your handheld PC, choose the Documents option from the Start menu. The Documents option opens the Recent folder in Windows CE Explorer, as shown in Figure 2-14. In the Recent folder, Windows CE maintains shortcuts to the documents you created or modified most recently.

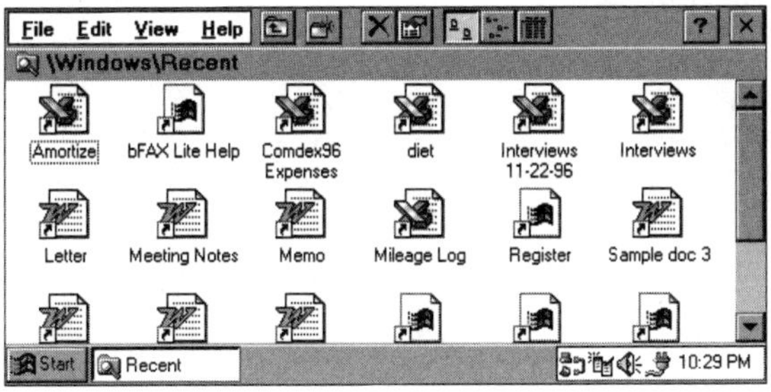

Figure 2-14: The Recent folder contains shortcuts to the documents you created or modified most recently.

To open a document from the Recent folder, double-tap the corresponding icon. Windows CE automatically knows which program created the document and opens the document in that program.

To determine which document you modified most recently, tap the View Details button on the toolbar. Then tap on the Modified column to have the list sorted in order based on the date they were last modified. The most recently modified documents are at the bottom of the list.

You can tap on a folder to open it or tap on the Previous Folder button to close a folder and view the contents of the parent folder.

Finding some extra help

You may find yourself in a situation where you need help with your handheld PC, and this book is not sitting by your side. Of course, I can't imagine ever going anywhere without *Windows CE For Dummies,* but the day may come when that is the case.

Fortunately, Windows CE does provide some limited pointers in a Help file installed on your handheld PC. This help file, shown in Figure 2-15, appears when you select the Help option from the Start menu.

When you first open the Help file, you see a list of underlined options. Each underlined option is called a *link.* If you tap an underlined option, the help file jumps to the specified location, and the corresponding information appears.

The Help file contains five buttons, as described in Table 2-6.

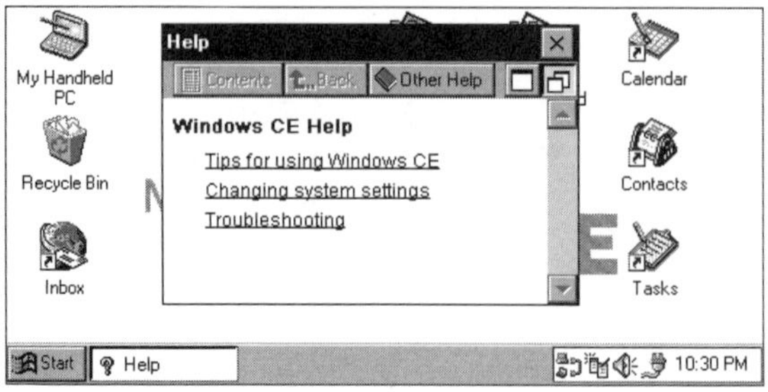

Figure 2-15: The Windows CE Help window provides tips for using your handheld PC.

Table 2-6 Help File Buttons

Tap This Button	*To Do This*
Contents	Return to the main screen. You can use this button to "return home" if you get lost in the Help file.
Back	Display the Help screen you viewed prior to the current one. Tapping on this button is like turning to the previous page in a book.
Other Help	Display a list of the Help files that are available on your handheld PC for the other programs you have installed. To select a Help file, tap its title.
	View the Help file on the full screen. This button provides a better view of the information.
	View the Help file in a window.

TIP

Most Windows CE programs also come with their own unique Help file. To open the Help file for a program that you are currently running, tap on the question mark button in the left corner of the screen.

Running a program

The easiest way to run a program on your handheld PC is to locate the icon that represents the program. However, if you don't want to search for the icon, you can quickly run a program, as long as you know its name.

To run a program, choose the Run option from the Start menu. The Run dialog box appears, as shown in Figure 2-16. Type the program name in the Open text box and tap on the OK button. The program runs when you tap the OK button, as long as Windows CE can locate a program with the name you typed.

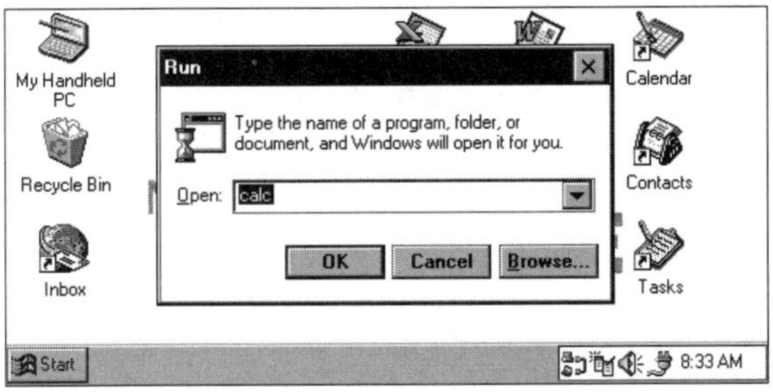

Figure 2-16: The Run program provides another option for running a program.

If you don't remember the exact name of the program, you can tap on the Browse button and search for the program on your handheld PC. But if you don't know the program's name, I suggest just using the Programs option or the Explore option to locate the program.

When you open the Run dialog box, the Open text box contains the name of the last program that you ran using the Run option. You can tap on the Down Arrow button to display a list of programs that you have run in the past by using the Run option. To run one of the programs in the list, tap on the name of the program and then tap on the OK button.

Shutting down for the day

Probably one of the more confusing issues with a handheld PC is figuring out the best way to shut it off. All handheld PCs come with an Off button on the keyboard, so of course, your first instinct is to press the Off button when you are ready to shut down. Unfortunately, pressing the Off button is not the best shutdown option for some handheld PCs. If you have not saved the information in your open files, you could lose this information.

The best way to turn off your handheld PC is to choose the Suspend option from the Start menu. When you choose this option, Windows CE makes sure that all open files have been saved properly and then turns off the handheld PC.

When you use the Suspend option, Windows CE remembers what you were working on and opens those programs and documents the next time you turn on your handheld PC. If you have any unsaved documents, Windows CE saves the documents and opens them the next time you use your handheld. Windows CE does not prompt you for a filename before shutting off your handheld PC, however. After you save the file, Windows CE gets rid of the unnamed version that it saved when you suspended your handheld PC.

On many handheld PCs, the Off button performs the same function as the Suspend option. The best way to determine if your Off button works like the Suspend option is to run a program, such as the Calculator program, and then press the Off button. If the Calculator program is still running when you turn your handheld PC back on, the Off button on your handheld PC is really a suspend button.

TIP

If your Off button produces the same results as the Suspend option, the only way to totally reboot your handheld PC is to press the Reset button. This action is rarely necessary, but you may have a program that instructs you to press this button to reboot your handheld PC.

Part II

What Can I Do with My Handheld PC?

"I find it so obnoxious when people use their cellular phone in public that I'm making notes about it on my handheld PC for a future opinion piece."

In this part . . .

Now that you have spent all of that money for that new fancy handheld PC, probably the last thing you intend to do is to have it sit on some shelf and collect dust. To help you put your new toy to good use, this part shows you how to use many of the free programs that you have received with Windows CE. In this part, you find answers to the following questions:

- How do I remember all my appointments before I get a phone call telling me that I am late?
- How do I make sure that I never forget mom's phone number?
- How do I make sure that I remember our anniversary?
- How do I work on that proposal without hauling home a big laptop?
- How do I adjust the budget figures while dining with a customer?

You can find the answers to these questions and more, all within this part of the book.

Chapter 3

Organizing Your Time

In This Chapter

- Opening the Calendar program
- Creating appointments and events
- Figuring out your agenda for the day
- Synchronizing Calendar with Schedule+ 7.0 or Microsoft Outlook

Windows CE provides a full-blown calendar program, called *Calendar,* that you can use to schedule all the important stuff in your life. After you set up an appointment, your handheld PC reminds you when it is time for the appointment with a friendly beep, a flashing light, or both. (When you create the appointment, you decide how you want to be reminded.) Of course, that may ruin some of those good excuses we all have for missing a meeting or a dentist appointment. But at least you can be reminded of the appointment and then decide whether you want to remember it. After all, no one else has to know that you have such a powerful device at your disposal.

This chapter leads you through the process of creating appointments and events for all of the important — and not-so important — things you have to get done.

Locating Your Calendar

The Calendar program is usually fairly easy to locate. Because Calendar is such an important program, most handheld PCs are set up by the manufacturer so that the icon is sitting on your Windows CE desktop. The icon should be located on the right side of your desktop (unless, of course, you have reorganized your desktop). The icon resembles a pencil writing something on a desktop calendar. To start Calendar, you simply use the stylus to double-tap on the Calendar icon.

If you cannot find the Calendar icon on your desktop, don't despair; you can locate it by following these simple steps:

1. **Use the stylus to tap on the Start button (located in the bottom-left corner of the screen).**

   A pop-up menu containing various selections appears.

2. **Tap on the Programs option.**

   Windows CE Explorer opens the Programs folder. Assuming that the Calendar icon was not moved by the icon gremlin, it appears in the Programs folder (see Figure 3-1).

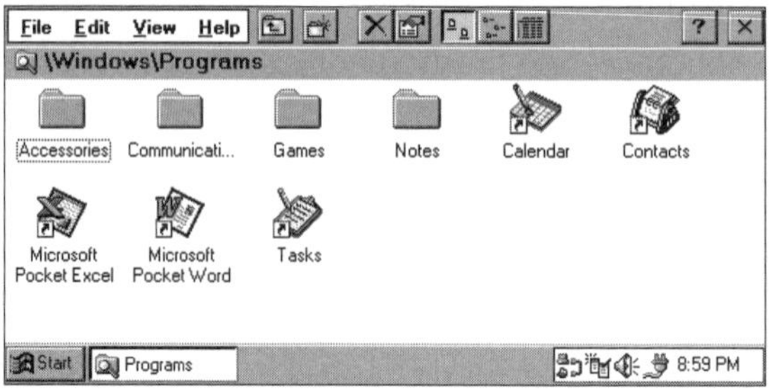

Figure 3-1: You can use Explorer to locate the icon in the Programs folder.

3. **Double-tap on the Calendar icon to display the Calendar program, shown in Figure 3-2.**

   You use this view of the Calendar program to set up all the important stuff you have to do, such as appointments and special events.

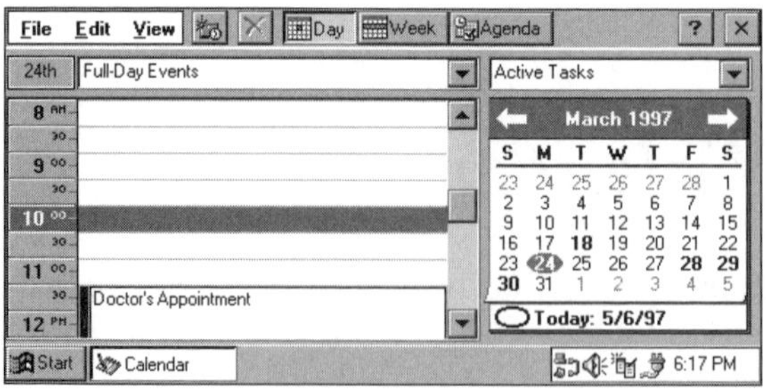

Figure 3-2: The Calendar program displays the appointments you have scheduled.

TIP: If you have been using Schedule+ 7.0 on your PC to keep track of your appointments, you can transfer those appointments to your handheld PC. I discuss this topic in more detail in the section, "Synchronizing Calendar with Schedule+ 7.0," later in this chapter.

Changing Your Frame of View

All right, I realize that I probably can't change your opinion about life on Mars, but at least I can show you how to look at your calendar information in a different way. Windows CE provides several ways to look at the information in the Calendar program; you can view the agenda for a day or you can view a week's worth of information on-screen, as shown in Figure 3-3.

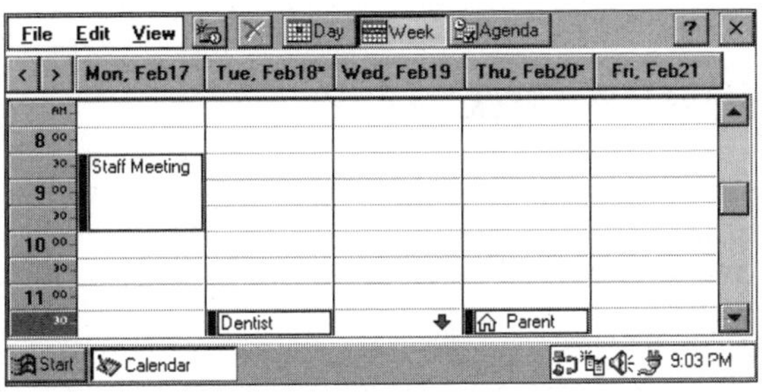

Figure 3-3: Week view displays either a five-or a seven-day week.

To view the week's appointments, you simply tap on the Week button on the toolbar at the top of the screen. When you view Calendar in Week view, only the usual five working days (Monday through Friday) are displayed. To see the entire week, choose View⇨5 Day Week View, removing the check mark from the 5 Day Week View option.

Each appointment appears on the calendar at the specified time. If you look closely, you may see one or more symbols next to each appointment. Each of these little pictures serves a purpose. Table 3-1 provides a description of the four symbols that may be displayed next to an appointment in either Day or Week mode.

Table 3-1 Deciphering the Symbols of an Appointment

Symbol	*Description*
	You set a reminder for the appointment.
	You added additional information about the appointment on the Notes tab.

(continued)

Table 3-1 *(continued)*

Symbol	*Description*
	The appointment is a *recurring appointment,* meaning that it occurs on a regular basis.
	You set a location for the appointment.

Creating an Appointment

An *appointment* is something that is scheduled to occur within a specific timeframe on a specific date. For example, you might use an appointment to represent the time when you need to be at Mom's house for Sunday dinner.

Before Windows CE can keep track of your appointments, you need to enter them into the Calendar program. Now, if you want to conveniently forget to attend something without feeling guilty about it, you probably don't want to add that appointment to Calendar. Or if you do, make sure that your handheld PC doesn't remind you of the appointment, and as long as you remember to forget to check your handheld PC at that time, you will still forget the appointment.

TECHNICAL STUFF

Did someone say *Information Manager?*

If you have read magazine articles about Windows CE or looked at other information from Microsoft, you may have heard about the Information Manager. If you look on your handheld PC, however, you won't find the Information Manager program anywhere. Why? Because *Information Manager* is a term that some computer nerd came up with to refer to the way the Calendar, Tasks, and Contacts programs all work together. For example, after you create a task in the Task program, you view the task in the Calendar program. Pretty cool, huh?

Don't be concerned that your device is lacking some valuable piece of software; you have the Information Manager programs, but they are named for their own unique functions: Calendar, Tasks, and Contacts.

That said, suppose that you need to create a dental appointment for next Thursday, April 10, at 3:30 p.m. You decide to create this appointment in Day view, because using this view is the easiest way to view the stuff going on each day. To create the appointment, simply follow these steps:

1. **On the small calendar in the bottom-right corner of the screen, tap on the date of the appointment. For example, locate April 10 for the dental appointment, as shown in Figure 3-4.**

   When you tap on a date, a black circle appears around it, indicating that the due date is selected.

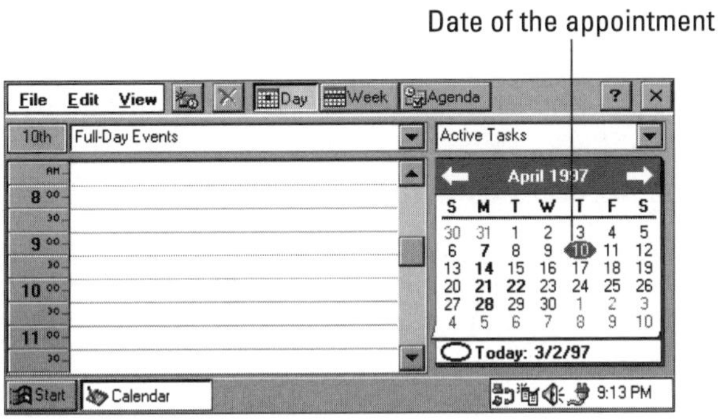

Figure 3-4: When you create an appointment, first locate the date of the appointment on the calendar.

2. **In the time section on the left side of the screen, use the scroll bars to locate the time of the appointment.**

   For the dental appointment example, the time is 3:30 p.m.

3. **Tap on the time of your appointment (for example, 3:30 p.m.) and drag the stylus down the screen to the time when the appointment should be over (for example, 5:00 p.m.).**

   If you draw a line from one time to another, that time frame appears highlighted on-screen, as shown in Figure 3-5.

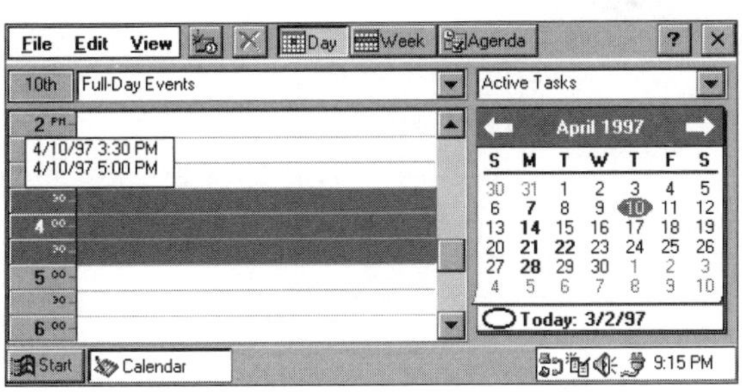

Figure 3-5: Highlight the time frame of the new appointment.

4. **Tap on the New Appointment button on the toolbar at the top of the screen.**

   The New Appointment button is the button on the left, next to the View menu. It looks like a small calendar with a clock on top of it. You can also display the Appointment card by choosing File⇨New Appointment.

   After you choose the New Appointment button or command, an Appointment card appears.

5. **In the Desc field, type the description for your appointment.**

   If you are adding a dental appointment, for example, type something as simple as **Dentist**.

   In Day view, you can highlight a time on the calendar for a new appointment and start typing. Windows CE recognizes the fact that you want to create a new appointment and opens a new Appointment card. Whatever you type appears in the Desc field for the appointment.

6. **In the Location field, indicate the location of the appointment.**

   If you have had an appointment at this location previously, you can tap on the Down Arrow button next to the field and then tap on the location in the drop-down list that appears; otherwise, type the desired location in the field.

7. **In the Duration section, make sure that the Starts fields contain the correct date (for example,** `Thu 4/10/97`**) and the correct time (for example,** `3:30 PM`**). Also, make sure that the Ends fields contain the correct date (for example,** `Thu 4/10/97`**) and the correct time (for example,** `5:00 PM`**).**

   If you need to change the date, tap on the Calendar button next to each field to display the Date Picker dialog box, as shown in Figure 3-6. Double-tap on the date you want to add to the Appointment card. To correct the time, tap on the Down Arrow button and then tap on the correct time.

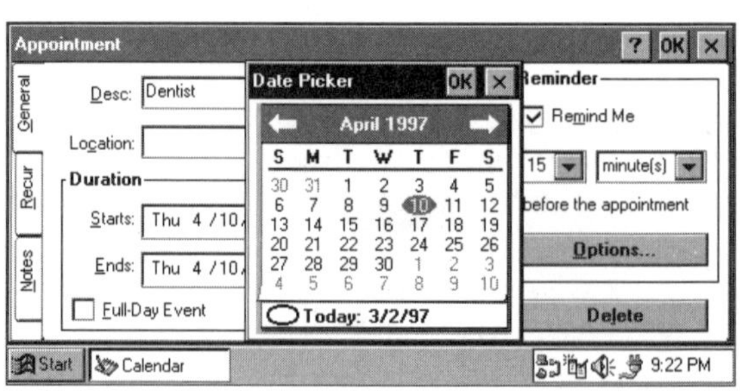

Figure 3-6: To adjust the date in the Starts or Ends fields, use the Date Picker dialog box.

When you select a date in the Starts field, Windows CE places the same date in the Ends field. By the same token, if you set the date in the Ends field without setting the date in the Starts field, Windows CE places the same date in the Starts field. Windows CE assumes that you intend to start and complete the appointment on the same date.

8. **Tap on the OK button in the top right corner of the screen to save the appointment.**

Windows CE reminds you of an appointment 15 minutes prior to the appointment. You can adjust this setting in the Reminder section of the Appointment card. For more information, see the next section, "Settting a reminder for your appointment."

Setting a reminder for your appointment

You don't do any good if you set up an appointment and then forget to show up for it. This is where Windows CE really shines. Windows CE can remind you of an appointment, even when your handheld PC is turned off. How your handheld PC reminds you depends the settings you specify. If you have your handheld set up so that the light flashes and the unit beeps 15 minutes prior to an appointment, for example, the unit beeps to get your attention, and the light flashes until you turn on your handheld PC and view the Calendar Reminder message. Figure 3-7 shows a sample Calendar Reminder message.

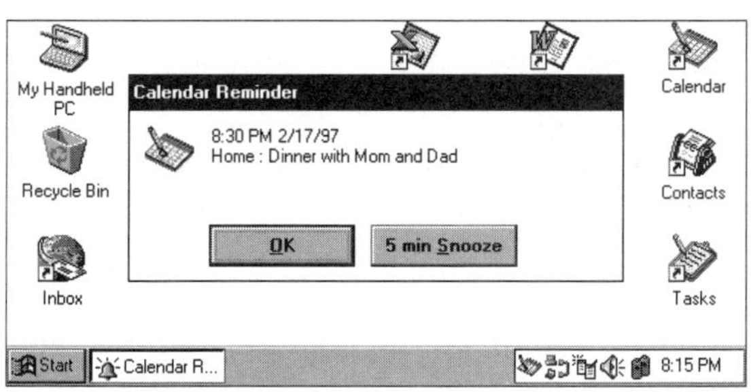

Figure 3-7: If you have a scheduled appointment, a message appears on-screen to remind you of the appointment.

You set the reminder information in the Reminder section of the Appointment card. You can set the reminder information when you create the new appointment or after the appointment has been created. Simply follow these steps:

1. **Double-tap on the appointment to display its Appointment card, as shown in Figure 3-8.**

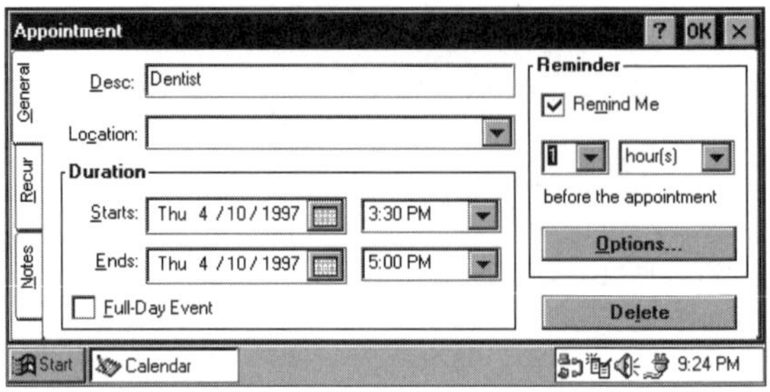

Figure 3-8: The Appointment card.

2. **Make sure that a check mark appears in the check box next to the Remind Me field.**

   Windows CE reminds you of an appointment only if you have selected the Remind Me check box.

3. **In the first selection list field, under the Remind Me field, tap on the Down Arrow button and tap on the amount of time you want.**

   You can select a value of 1, 5, 10, 15, 30, or 45 in this field. If you want to set a reminder for an hour prior to the appointment, for example, tap on 1.

   If you want your reminder to be at a time interval that is not available in the list, such as 20 minutes before the meeting, type a value in this field by highlighting the value that is currently in the field and typing a new value.

4. **In the next selection list field, you can choose minutes, hours, days, or weeks. Simply tap on the Down Arrow button and then tap on the option you want to select. To set the option to hours, tap on the hour(s) option.**

5. **Tap on the Options button to set the type of reminder you want for this appointment.**

   When you tap on the Options button, the Notification Options dialog box appears (see Figure 3-9).

6. **Tap on the reminders you want.**

   When you select a reminder, a check mark appears in the box next to the option.

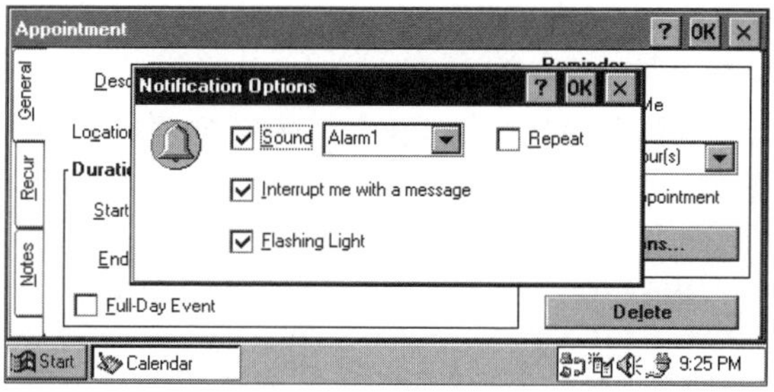

Figure 3-9: The Notification Options dialog box.

If you select the Sound option or the Flashing Light option, Windows CE reminds you of the appointment even when you've turned off your handheld.

Windows CE comes with sounds you can select for the Sound option in the Notification Options dialog box. The easiest way to determine the sound you want is to test each one until you find one that you like. The only way to test a sound is to use the Volume & Sounds option in the Control Panel folder. For more information on this option, see Chapter 18.

Making an appointment recurring

Most people have appointments they need to attend on a regular basis, such as weekly staff meetings or workouts at the gym. These types of appointments are called *recurring appointments.* With Windows CE, if you set up an appointment as an recurring appointment, it continues to appear on your calendar. You don't need to add a new appointment each time.

To set up the information about a recurring appointment, you use the Recur tab on the Appointment card, as shown in Figure 3-10. You can set the information for an appointment when you create the appointment or after you create the appointment. Simply follow these steps:

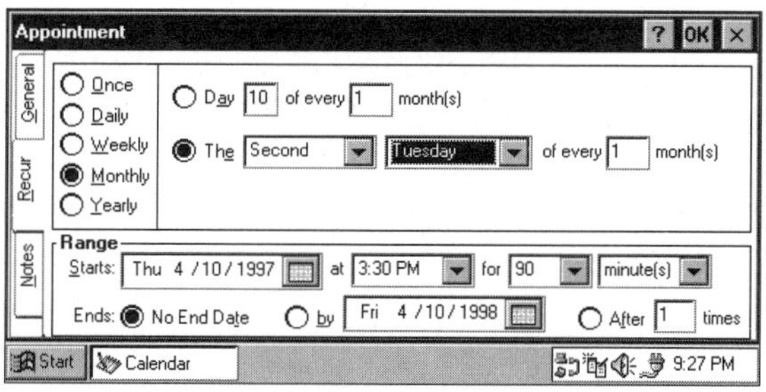

Figure 3-10: Use the Recur tab to set the time frame for a recurring appointment.

1. **Locate the appointment you want to set as recurring and double-tap on it to display the Appointment card.**
2. **Tap on the Recur tab, located on the left side of the screen.**

   You use the options that appear to indicate how often the appointment recurs.
3. **In the column on the left side, tap on the radio button that indicates the frequency with which you want the appointment to occur. If you want to create a task that occurs every month, for example, select the Monthly option.**

   The options that appear differ depending on the option you select in this column. If you select Monthly, for example, the center of the screen contains options to specify the day of the month or a specific week.
4. **Indicate the time at which you want the appointment to reoccur. If you have a monthly appointment, for example, you can indicate that you want it to always occur on the second Tuesday of the month, as shown in Figure 3-10.**

   If you want to specify that a monthly appointment should occur on a specific day of the week, for example, you tap on the second radio button, next to the word *The.* Next, tap on the Down Arrow button and highlight the word *Second* in the drop-down list, tap on the Down Arrow button next to the second field, and highlight the word *Tuesday* in the drop-down list. Finally, type the number **1** in the last field.
5. **In the Range section of the screen, indicate when the appointment begins and ends in the Starts fields.**

   The Starts fields information varies depending on the information you entered on the General tab. If the information is not correct, you can change it here, and the updated information will be reflected on the General tab. To change each field, tap on the button next to the field and make the selections you want.
6. **In the Ends fields, you indicate when you no longer intend to have this recurring appointment. If you are setting an appointment to occur indefinitely, select the No End Date option.**

   You can modify the Ends fields at any time. So if you determine that you no longer want to have the appointment after next month, you simply return to this option and set the date for when the last appointment should occur.
7. **Tap on the OK button to save the information on the Recur tab.**

   REMEMBER: The default information that appears in the Range section comes from the information set up for the first appointment on the General tab.

Creating a full-day event

An *event* is something that is taking place on a specific date but lasts for an indefinite amount of time. If you are like me, you have several events, such as birthdays and vacations, that you need to add to your calendar so that you don't forget them. You add these types of events to the Calendar program in basically the same fashion that you create an appointment.

When you add an all-day event to your calendar, the event appears above the list of appointments (in Day view). If you have multiple full-day events scheduled for that day, you simply select the Down Arrow button to view a list of the events.

To add a Full Day event in Day view, simply follow these steps:

1. **Tap on the Down Arrow button next to the Full-Day Events field and then tap on the New Full Day Event option.**

   A new Appointment card with the Full-Day Event check box selected appears as shown in Figure 3-11. Because the Full-Day option is selected, the Start and Ends fields do not contain time fields.

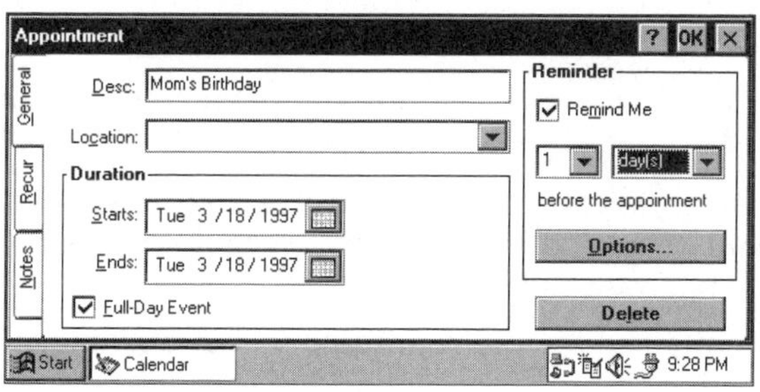

Figure 3-11: You add a full-day event by selecting the Full-Day Event check box.

2. **In the Desc field, type a description for the event. If you are scheduling a family vacation, for example, you might type** Family Vacation.

   Be sure to use a description that allows you to easily recognize the event you have scheduled.

3. **In the Location field, type a location for the event —** Cancun, Mexico, **for example.**

   If you have had another event or appointment previously at a location, you can tap on the Down Arrow button and select the location from the list of other locations.

4. **Make sure that the Starts field contains the date the event starts — for example,** 6/1/1997.

   If the date is not correct, tap on the Calendar button next to the field. The Date Picker dialog box appears (see Figure 3-12). Tap on the correct date. If you need to move to the previous or next month on the calendar, tap on the arrows next to the month name.

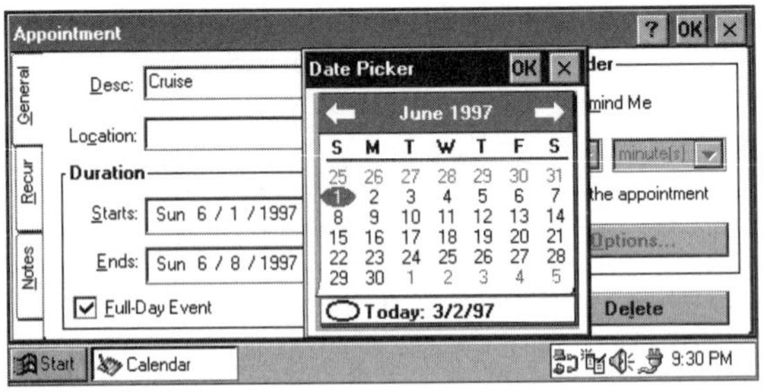

Figure 3-12: The Date Picker dialog box.

5. **Make sure that the Ends field contains the date the event ends — for example,** 6/8/1997.

   If the date is not correct, tap on the Calendar button next to the field and tap on the correct date in the Date Picker dialog box.

6. **If you want your handheld to remind you prior to your vacation, tap on the Remind Me check box so that a check mark appears in the box.**

   As with appointments, you are adding events so that you will remember them. Unless you check your calendar on a regular basis, I recommend always having a reminder for an event.

7. **Select the time interval for the reminder — for example,** 1 day.

   To select the time interval, tap on the Down Arrow button and then tap on a number in the list. Then tap on the Down Arrow button for the next field and tap on Day(s).

8. **Tap on the OK button to save the new event to your calendar.**

Here are a few things to keep in mind when dealing with full-day events on the calendar:

- The days of your scheduled event appear bold on the calendar, just as with an appointment.
- Full-day events do not appear on the calendar when you view it in Week view. An asterisk appears next to the date if you have scheduled an event for the specified date, however.

- If you view the calendar in Agenda view, Calendar lists the full-day events at the top of the summary list of appointments and events.

Adding additional information to an appointment

Have you ever showed up at an appointment and forgotten to bring along some information that you needed, or perhaps, remembered that you had an appointment but misplaced the directions to get there? Well, Windows CE provides a solution to all these dilemmas. The Calendar program provides a page where you can include additional information about an appointment. In fact, if you make an appointment to go grocery shopping, you could type your entire grocery list on this page.

So where is this page? To view it, all you have to do is display an Appointment card (either a new or existing card) and then tap on the Notes tab. A blank page appears where you can place information about the appointment, as shown in Figure 3-13. Windows CE creates a separate Notes tab for each appointment.

Figure 3-13: Type any additional information, such as the address for the appointment, on the Notes tab.

Removing Unwanted Appointments and Events

The time will come when you'll want to remove an appointment or event from your calendar. Of course, it would be too simple to be able to use the same steps to delete both appointments and full-day events, so you've got to remember different steps for each process.

Keep in mind that Windows CE does not remove appointments from your calendar. This way, you can review the previous months and determine what you were doing on a specific date. The drawback is that each appointment and full-day event that is stored uses some of your handheld's memory. If you are running low on memory, you may want to consider removing some of the old appointments.

Deleting an appointment

To delete an appointment, all you need to do is follow these simple steps:

1. **Open either Day or Week view, and locate the appointment you want to delete.**

   Make sure that you tap on the appointment so that it is highlighted on-screen.

   To use Day or Week view, you must have selected one of those buttons in the toolbar. If you are in Agenda view, you cannot delete appointments.

2. **Tap on the delete button at the top of the screen in the Toolbar.**

   The delete button resembles a giant X. When you tap on it, a message box appears to verify your selection (see Figure 3-14).

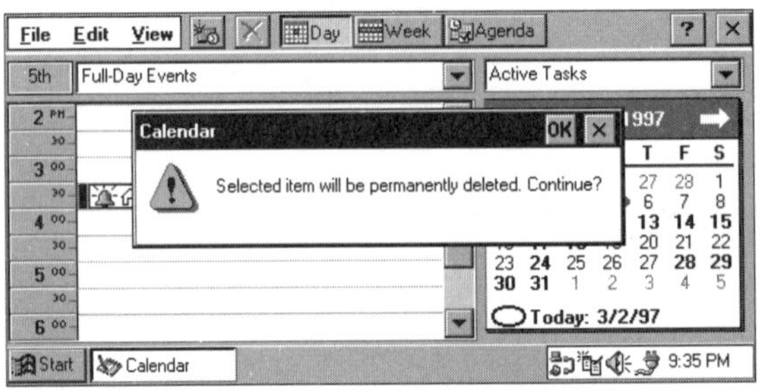

Figure 3-14: To delete the selected appointment, tap on the OK button; otherwise, tap on the X button.

Deleting a full-day event

To delete a full-day event, all you need to do is follow these simple steps. You can use these same steps to remove an appointment.

1. **In either the Day or Week view, locate the full-day event you want to delete.**

   After you locate the date, tap on the Down Arrow button to view a list of the full-day events for that date and then tap on the one you want to delete. When you tap on the event, the Appointment card appears for that event.

2. **Tap on the Delete button in the bottom-right corner of the Appointment card.**

   A message box appears to verify your selection (refer to Figure 3-14).

Viewing Today's Agenda

You can view all the appointments, events, and tasks you have scheduled for the day by using Agenda view, shown in Figure 3-15. By viewing the agenda, you are able to see a list of all the stuff you have scheduled for the selected day. To open Agenda view, tap on the Agenda button in the toolbar.

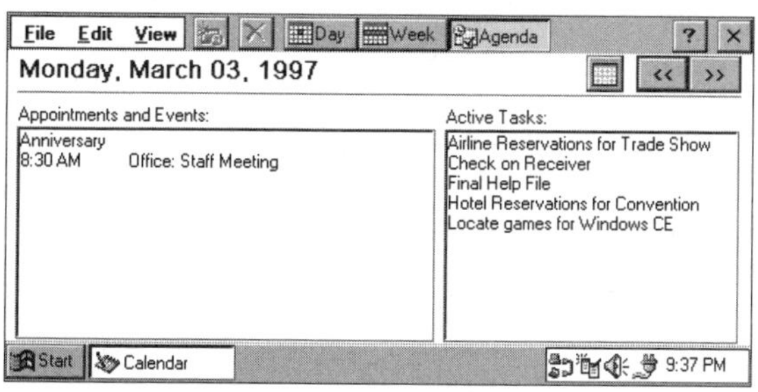

Figure 3-15: Agenda view summarizes everything you have scheduled for the selected day.

REMEMBER

You cannot add or modify appointments or events while viewing the agenda. If you want to make modifications, you must first select either Day or Week view.

Full-day events appear at the top of the appointments list. The list provides only the start time for each appointment.

The Active Tasks section contains the tasks that were either scheduled to be started today or have not yet been completed. Remember, you create the tasks by using the Tasks program discussed in Chapter 4.

To view the agenda for a different date, you can either tap on the Calendar button to display the Date Picker dialog box, tap on the >> button to display the next date after the current one, or tap on the << button to display the previous.

Synchronizing Your Calendar with Schedule+ 7.0 or Microsoft Outlook

If you are currently using your desktop computer to maintain your calendar, you probably do not want to retype everything onto your new handheld PC. If you are using Microsoft Schedule+ 7.0 under Windows 95 or Microsoft Outlook on your desktop computer, you are in luck.

REMEMBER

Windows CE lets you copy all the calendar information from Schedule+ or Microsoft Outlook onto your handheld PC. By the same token, you copy the calendar information on your handheld back into Schedule+ or Microsoft Outlook. This process of making sure that both your handheld PC and desktop computer contain the same personal calendar information is called *synchronizing*.

To synchronize your device with your desktop computer, a few things are required:

- A data cable connected between your device and desktop computer
- H/PC Explorer running on your desktop computer
- Microsoft Schedule+ 7.0 or Microsoft Outlook on your desktop computer

For more detailed information about synchronizing your device and desktop computer, see Chapter 11.

Chapter 4

Keeping Track of Everyday Tasks

In This Chapter

- Figuring out when to create a task
- Locating the Tasks program
- Creating a new task
- Creating recurring tasks
- Adding notes to a task
- Downloading tasks from your desktop computer
- Sorting your tasks
- Indicating that a task is completed
- Modifying tasks
- Checking today's tasks in the Calendar program

With the Tasks program, you can quickly create your own personal to-do lists. After you add tasks to your handheld PC, you can view the current tasks on your personal calendar, and your handheld PC reminds you to either start or complete a task.

This chapter shows you how to set up all your tasks by using the Tasks program that comes with Windows CE. You also see how to use the Calendar application to view all of the tasks that need to be worked on for a particular day. Most important, you see how to set your handheld PC to remind you to perform a task.

Is It Really a Task?

The difference between a task and an appointment (or a recurring appointment or a full-day event) can be confusing until you get the hang of thinking in Windows CE-speak. You create a *task* for something that you need to accomplish but not necessarily at a specific time; you create an *appointment* for an event that occurs at a set time. If you have a doctor's appointment tomorrow at 2:00 p.m., for example, you should create an appointment. If you intend to clean the garage sometime this weekend, you should create a task — perhaps called *clean the garage* — and assign a time frame of Friday through Sunday.

You create tasks by using the Tasks program, which is discussed in this chapter. You create appointments, recurring appointments, and all-day events by using the Calendar program, which is discussed in Chapter 3.

Create a task if you know you need to do something but don't intend to start at a specific time.

Locating the Tasks Program

Before you can create a task, you need to locate the Tasks program on your handheld PC. The Tasks program provides a central location where you can keep track of all your individual tasks. This program is fairly easy to find.

The Tasks program is probably sitting on the desktop of your handheld PC. The icon for the Tasks program looks like a pencil making a list of items on a clipboard. When you locate the icon, double-tap on it to open the Tasks program.

If you cannot find the Tasks program icon on your desktop, you should be able to locate it by following these simple steps:

1. **Use your stylus to tap the Start button (in the bottom-left corner of the screen).**
2. **Tap on the Programs option on the Start menu.**

   Windows CE Explorer opens the folder on your handheld PC called *Programs*. You should be able to locate the Tasks icon in the Programs folder, as shown in Figure 4-1.

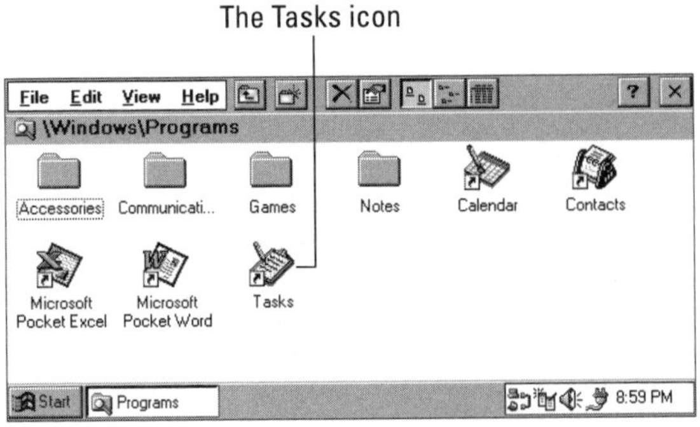

Figure 4-1: Tap on the Tasks icon to open the Tasks program.

3. **Tap on the Tasks icon to open the Tasks program, shown in Figure 4-2.**

   You use this program to create, modify, and view your list of tasks. Remember, the Tasks icon resembles a pencil making a list on a clipboard.

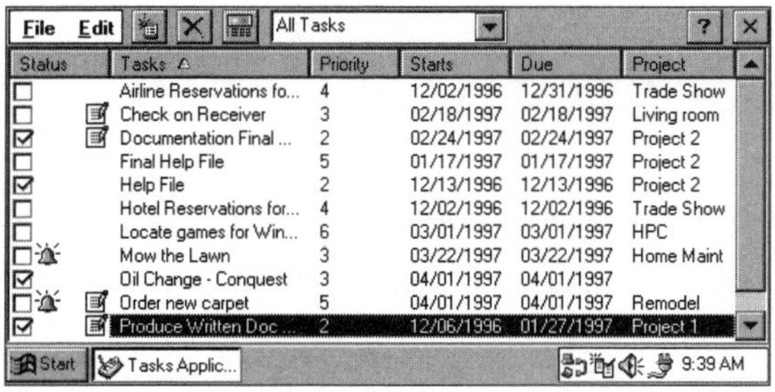

Figure 4-2: The Tasks program displays a list of the existing tasks on your handheld PC.

TIP: If you use Schedule+ 7.0 or Outlook on your desktop computer to keep track of your tasks, you can transfer those tasks to your handheld PC. You can even transfer tasks from your handheld PC to your personal computer. I discuss these topics in more detail later in this chapter.

A check mark in the box in the Status column indicates that you have completed the corresponding task. You can add and remove check marks by simply tapping on the box.

Creating a New Task

You can use the Tasks program to create your own electronic to-do lists. You do not need to be concerned about the order in which you add your tasks to the Tasks program. After you add tasks to your handheld PC, you can sort them anyway you want. Simply follow these steps:

1. **Open a new Task card, as shown in Figure 4-3, by tapping on the New Task button, located on the toolbar at the top of the screen.**

   The New Task button is the button on the left next to the Edit menu option. It looks like a list of items with a light in the top-left corner.

   You can also open a new Task card by selecting File⇨New Task.

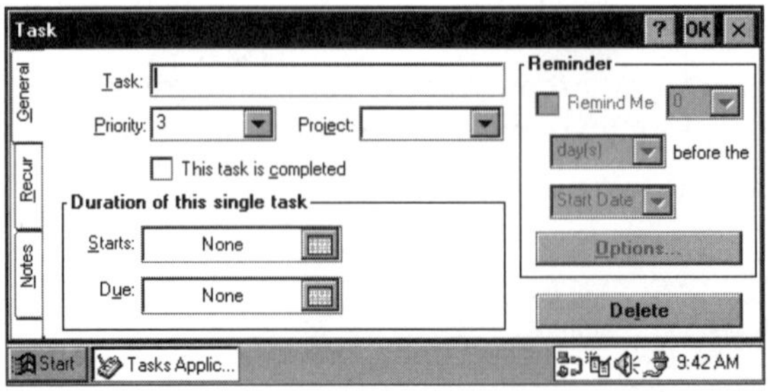

Figure 4-3: Use the Task card to create a new task.

2. **Type the description for your new task in the Task field.**

   Although you can enter an indefinite number of characters, Windows CE only saves the first 36 characters of the description. You can enter 36 characters in the Task field without scrolling any characters out of the field. If you can read the entire description without scrolling the text, you have fewer than 36 characters and will have no problem saving your description. If you want a more detailed description of the task, you need to enter this information on the Notes tab. (See "Adding Notes to a Task" later in this chapter.)

3. **Tap on the Down Arrow button in the Priority field and assign a priority to this task.**

   If you do not select the priority value, Windows CE assigns 3 to the task. You can use the Priority field to sort out the most important tasks. For example, if you assign a priority value of 1 to the most important tasks, all the priority 1 tasks appear first on the Tasks screen.

   TIP: Technically, you don't have to prioritize your tasks. If you don't want to prioritize the tasks, simply maintain a consistent value in the Priority field for all tasks that you create. You can just leave the default value of 3 in the field.

4. **Type the name of the project in the Project field or tap the Down Arrow button next to the field and highlight the name of the project you want to assign for this task.**

   If you have previously created a task for the project, you will find its name in the list when you tap the Down Arrow button. If the task is not in the list, enter the project name in the Project field; the next time you create a task for this same project, you will be able to select the Down Arrow button and highlight the project name.

   If you don't want to assign a project to the task, leave the Project field blank.

TIP: You can use the Project field to group related tasks. If you have a project called *Kitchen Upgrade,* for example, you can assign the Kitchen Upgrade to the Project field each time you create a task that deals with upgrading the kitchen. Later, you can view only the tasks that relate to that project in the Tasks window.

5. **Tap on the Calendar button next to Starts field to open the Date Picker dialog box, as shown in Figure 4-4, and then double-tap on the date you want to add to the Task card.**

   The Calendar button resembles a page of the calendar and is located on the right side of each date field. When the Date Picker window first appears, it contains either today's date or the last date selected on the current Task card. You can scroll to a different month by tapping on the left and right arrows that appear next to the name of the month.

   You can manually type the date in both the Starts and Due fields, although this is probably not the best way to enter the dates. You cannot just type **2/14/97**. If you type the **2,** the application automatically fills in the rest of the date, based on today's date. (For example, if today is the 18th of December 1996, the date would be 2/18/1996.) To change the day, you need to either click on that portion with the stylus and then type over it or use the arrow keys on the keyboard to move to that portion of the date.

   When you select a date in the Starts field, the same date is automatically placed in the Due field. If you want the task to be completed by a different date, you need to select a date for the Due field.

   Likewise, if you set the date in the Due field without setting the date in the Starts field, Windows CE places the same date in the Starts field. Windows CE assumes that you intend to start and complete the task on the same date.

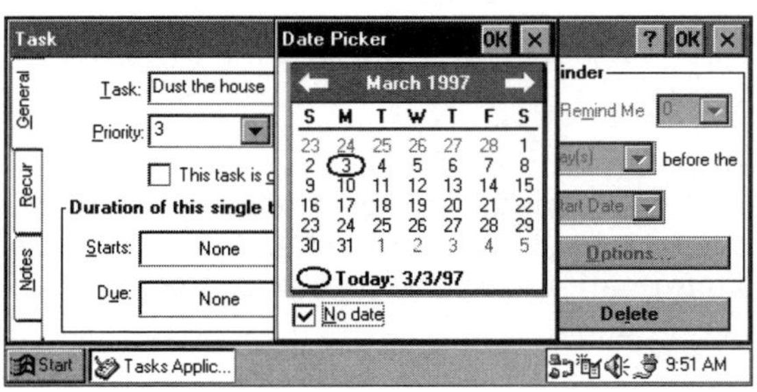

Figure 4-4: The Date Picker dialog box allows you to easily locate the date.

6. **Tap on the Calendar button next to Due field to open the Date Picker dialog box and then double-tap on the approximate date when the task should be complete.**
7. **Tap on the OK button to save the new task.**

Select the This task is completed check box only if you have finished the task. When you select this box, a check mark appears in the box, and a message appears in the Duration of this single task section, indicating the date the task was completed. A check mark also appears next to the task in the Tasks window.

Setting task reminders

How many times have you made a list of things you need to do and then forgotten to look at your list? If you use the Tasks program to create your list, your handheld PC can remind you when you need to complete a task. How your handheld PC reminds you depends on the settings you specify. If you set your handheld PC to flash its light and beep 0 days prior to the start date for the task, your handheld PC will beep to get your attention and then flash its light until you turn on the handheld and see the reminder message, shown in Figure 4-5.

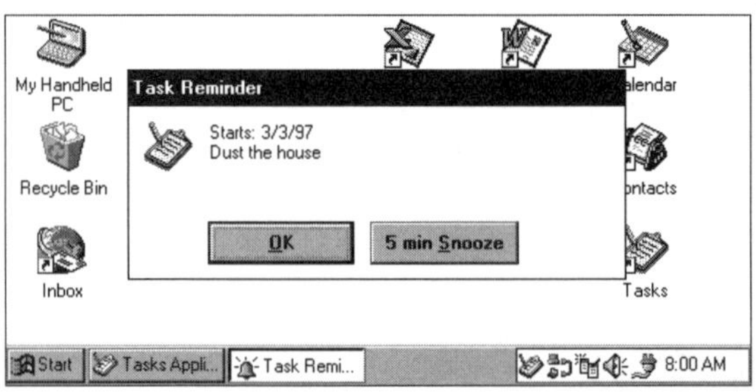

Figure 4-5: A friendly reminder to complete a task.

You set the reminder information on the Task card in the Reminder section. You can set the reminder information either when you create the new task or after you create the task by simply double-tapping on the selected task. You can modify this information anytime after you create the task. Here's how to set a reminder for a task:

1. **Open the Task card for a task in your list.**

   To open the Task card, locate the task you want to open and double-tap on it with the stylus.

2. **Make sure that a check mark appears in the check box next to the Remind Me field as shown in Figure 4-6.**

   Windows CE reminds you of an appointment only if you select the Remind Me check box.

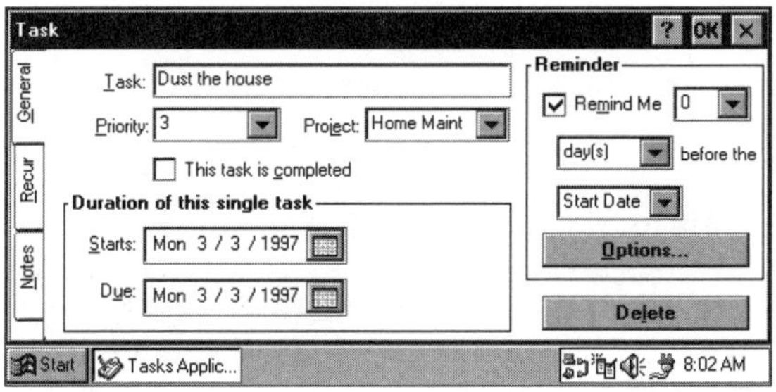

Figure 4-6: Setting a reminder for a task.

3. **In the field with the first Down Arrow button, tap on the Down Arrow button and select a value.**

   You can manually type a value in this field by simply highlighting the value that is currently in the field and typing a new value.

   If you want to be reminded on the day that you need to start a task, set the reminder for zero days, as crazy as that seems, and the alarm will sound promptly at 8:00 a.m. that morning.

4. **In the next field, tap on the down arrow button and select the day(s) option.**

5. **In the final field, tap on the down arrow button and select the Start Date option.**

   You can also have Windows CE remind you prior to the due date instead of the start date.

6. **Tap on the Options button to set the type of reminder you want for this task.**

   When you tap on the Options button, the Notification Options dialog box appears (see Figure 4-7). You use this dialog box to specify the way you want to be notified of a start date for a task.

7. **Tap on the reminders you want for the task.**

   Check marks appear in the boxes next to each option you select.

If you select either the Sound option or the Flashing Light option, your handheld PC reminds you of the task even when it is turned off.

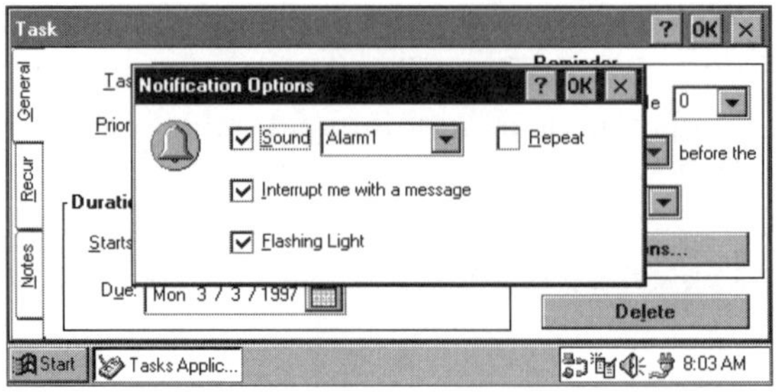

Figure 4-7: The Notification Options dialog box.

Windows CE comes with sounds you can select for the Sound option on the Notification Options dialog box. The easiest way to determine which sound you want is to test each one until you find one that you like. To test a sound, you use the Volume & Sounds option in the Control Panel folder. For more information, see Chapter 18.

Creating recurring tasks

We all have different tasks, such as washing the car, mowing the lawn, or even taking a bath, that need to be done on a regular basis. Instead of creating a new task each time you need to get the oil changed in the car, you can create one task that reminds you to do it every three months.

To set up the information about the recurring task, you use the Recur tab on the Task card, as shown in Figure 4-8. You can set this information when you create the task or after you have created the task.

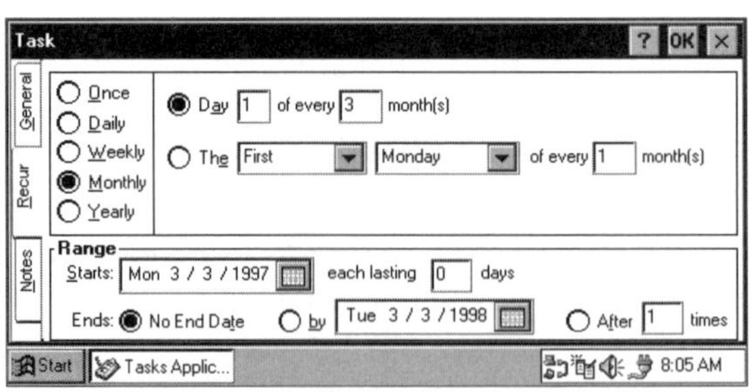

Figure 4-8: Use the Recur tab to set the time frame for a recurring task.

To create a task that repeats on a monthly basis, follow these steps:

1. **Open the Task card for the task you want to make recurring.**

   To open the Task card, use the stylus to double-tap on the task.

2. **Tap on the Recur tab on the left side of the screen.**

   This displays new options for setting the time interval of the recurring task.

3. **In the column on the left side, tap on the option that indicates how frequently you want the task to repeat.**

   The option you select in this column determines which options appear in the center of the screen. If you select the Monthly option, for example, the center of the screen contains options to either specify the day of the month or a specific week.

4. **Indicate the time when you want the task to reoccur. Tap on the first radio button, next to the word Day.**

   If you have a monthly appointment, for example, indicate that you want it to always occur on the second Tuesday of the month.

5. **Check the values in the Starts fields of the Range section of the screen.**

   The Starts field information comes from the information you set on the General tab. If the information is not correct, you can change it here, and it will be reflected on the General tab. To change each field, simply tap on the button next to the field and make your changes.

6. **In the Ends fields, indicate when you no longer intend to have this recurring task.**

   If you want the task to occur indefinitely, select the No End Date option. You can modify the Ends fields at any time.

7. **Tap on the OK button to save the information on the Recur tab.**

Adding notes to a task

If you are like me, most of your tasks probably need more information than you can enter in the Task field on the General tab. One of my most frequent tasks is grocery shopping, and it doesn't do any good to go shopping without a list, does it? Well, those wise little computer programmers thought of that when they designed the Tasks program. You can enter all the information that you want about each task on the Notes tab. It is available when you view the Tasks card, shown in Figure 4-9.

You can enter an unlimited amount of information on the Notes tab. You can format the information any way you want, but you can't use different fonts.

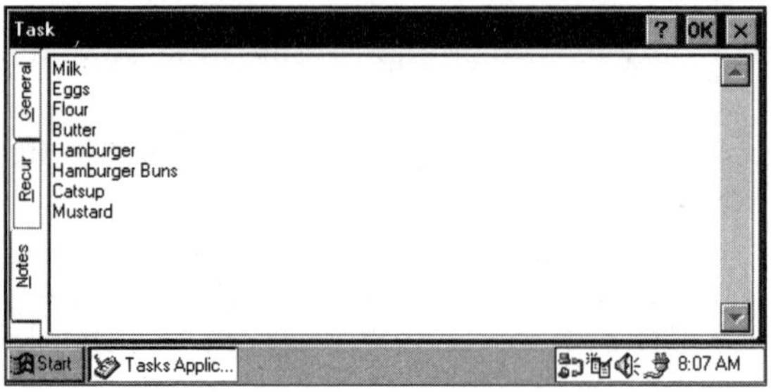

Figure 4-9: Enter any additional information, such as your grocery list, on the Notes tab.

Removing Tasks

The time will come when you'll want to remove a task from the list. No matter what your reasoning, deleting a task is rather easy.

Keep in mind that Windows CE does not remove tasks that have been completed so that you can look back and see when you finished a particular task. You may want to remove old tasks, however, because each task hogs some of your handheld PC's memory. You also may want to delete some old tasks because the more tasks you have in your list, the more difficult it is to see what tasks you have yet to complete.

To delete a task, follow these simple steps:

1. **In the tasks list, locate the task you want to delete.**

   Make sure that you tap on the task so that it is highlighted on-screen.

2. **Tap on the Delete button at the top of the screen in the toolbar.**

   The Delete button resembles a giant X. When you tap on the Delete button, a message box appears to verify your selection, as shown in Figure 4-10.

3. **Tap on the OK button to delete the task.**

   You can also delete a task by opening the Task card and then tapping on the Delete button.

TIP: In case you are really in a spring-cleaning mood, you can quickly remove all the tasks that you completed by selecting Edit⇨Delete Completed Tasks.

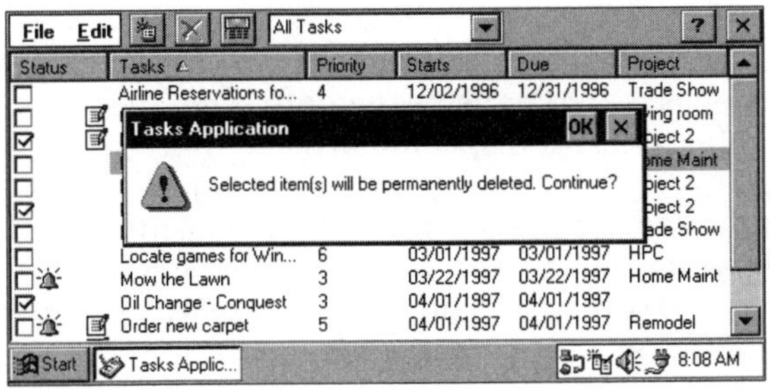

Figure 4-10: To delete the selected task, tap on the OK button; otherwise, tap on the X button.

Examining Your List of Tasks

As you add more and more tasks to the task list, the list becomes increasingly difficult to read. Fortunately, you can change the way the list appears so that it is easier to read. You can sort the list by any of the columns of information, or you can even indicate that you want to see only the tasks related to a specific project.

Sorting the tasks

On your mark, get set, alphabetize your list of tasks. Okay, I am just joking — Windows CE can alphabetize the list of tasks probably before you can figure out what comes after A.

You can sort the list of tasks based on any of the columns of information that appear in the Tasks program. Simply tap on the column's name, and Windows CE sorts the tasks by the information in that column. For example, simply tap on the word *Project* at the top of the column to sort the list of tasks based on the project name. Windows CE sorts the items alphabetically based on their project name (see Figure 4-11).

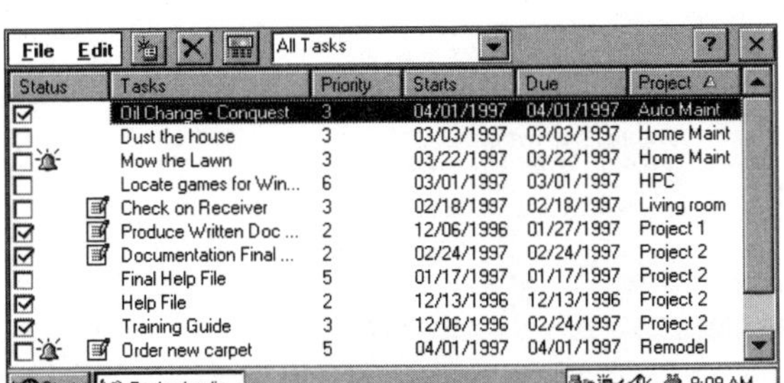

Figure 4-11: To sort the list of tasks based on the value in a column, simply tap on the column name.

Viewing only specific tasks

You also can view only the tasks that meet specific criteria. For example, you can view only the tasks that have been completed, the tasks that need to be completed, or the tasks for a specific project.

You use the field in the toolbar, with the Down Arrow button next to it, to indicate which tasks you want to view. If you want to see only the completed tasks, tap on the Down Arrow button and then tap on the Completed Tasks option, in the drop-down list (see Figure 4-12).

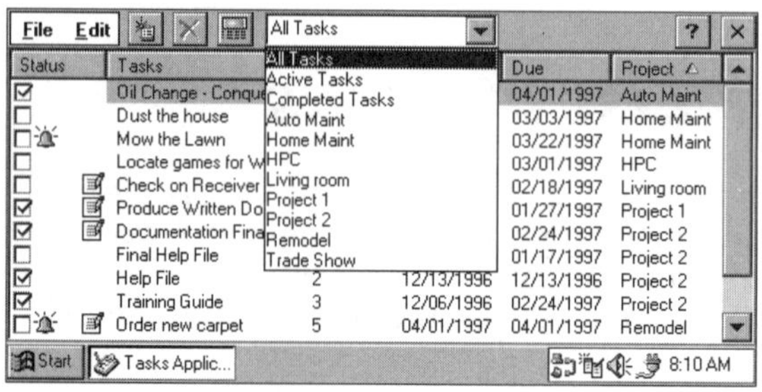

Figure 4-12: You can use this drop-down list to indicate which tasks you want to view.

Indicating That a Task Is Completed

The most exciting part of having a list of things to do is crossing items off of the list as you finish them. Windows CE makes it quite simple to indicate that an item has been completed.

You use the Status column in the Tasks program to indicate whether or not a task has been completed (see Figure 4-13). If the check box in the Status column is empty, you still need to complete the task. If the check box contains a check mark, Windows CE knows that you have completed the task. To place a check mark in the check box, simply tap on the box next to the task.

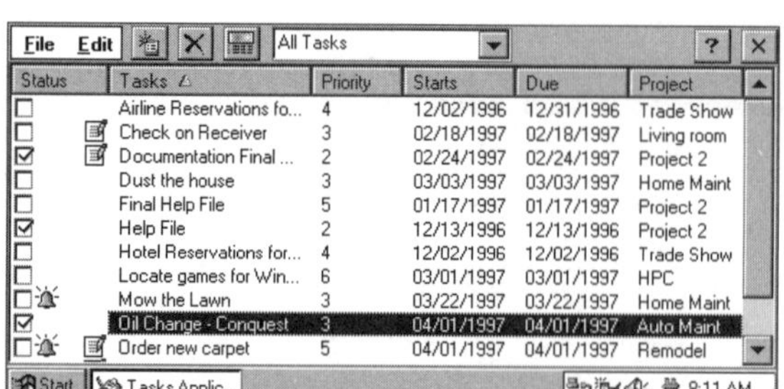

Figure 4-13: The Status column indicates exactly which tasks you have completed.

When you mark a task as completed, Windows CE inserts a message into the Duration of this single task section of the Task card for the task to indicate the date the task has been completed (see Figure 4-14). Windows CE also removes the task from the Active Tasks field on your calendar.

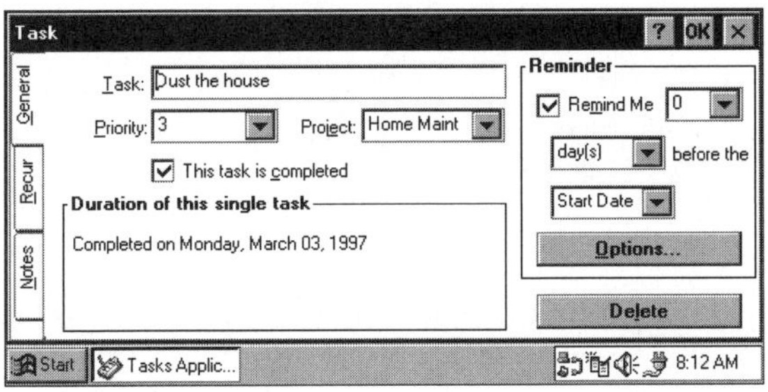

Figure 4-14: Windows CE indicates when you complete the task.

I am sure that you would be disappointed if I didn't tell you that Windows CE provides another way to indicate that the task is completed. If you select the Task card for the task, you can tap on the check box next to the This task is completed field. This method is useful when you want to view the Task card before you mark it as complete.

Modifying Tasks

For some reason, few of us can create tasks without having to modify them. Of course, you can always double-tap on the task in the list and make modifications to the Task card. In my opinion, this is the easiest way to modify a task because you can edit everything about the task in one location. But if you do that all the time, you will never get to use the other button on the toolbar, the Edit Panel button. This button is designed to look like the Edit Panel opened above the list of tasks.

In Edit Panel view, you can change the task name, priority, project, and start and end dates of the highlighted task (see Figure 4-15). You must change any other information about a task on its Task card.

This view is useful if you want to change something, such as the Priority, in several tasks. You can simply scroll down the list to display one task after another in the Edit Panel.

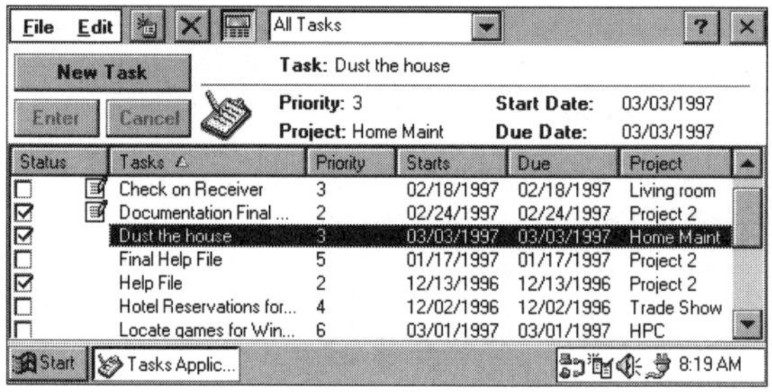

Figure 4-15: Tap on the Edit Panel button to quickly view basic information about each task.

You can create a new task in the Edit Panel mode by tapping on the New Task button and then entering the information identifying the task. If you create a task in this mode, you can only specify information for the fields that are displayed. If you want to add additional information, you need to open the Task card for the task.

Checking Today's Tasks in the Calendar Program

One cool thing about Windows CE is how programs seem to all work together. If you create tasks by using the Tasks program, for example, you can view the tasks that you need to do on a particular day by tapping on the Down Arrow button above the calendar in the Calendar program (see Figure 4-16). You can also view your daily tasks by tapping on the Agenda button (see Figure 4-17).

The scheduled task continues to show up in Calendar for each day, until you indicate that the task has been completed.

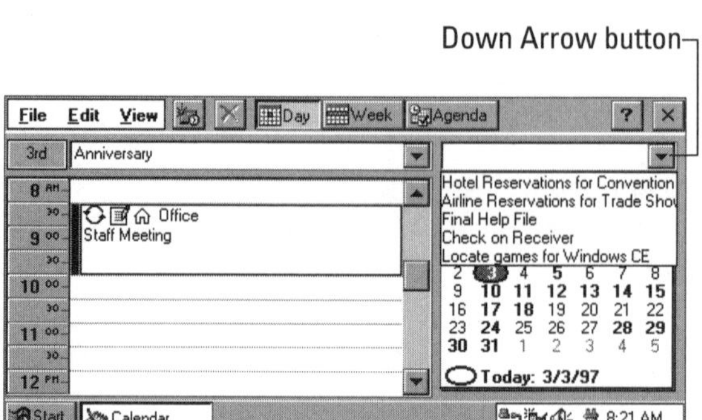

Figure 4-16: You can check your tasks for the day by selecting the Down Arrow button above the calendar.

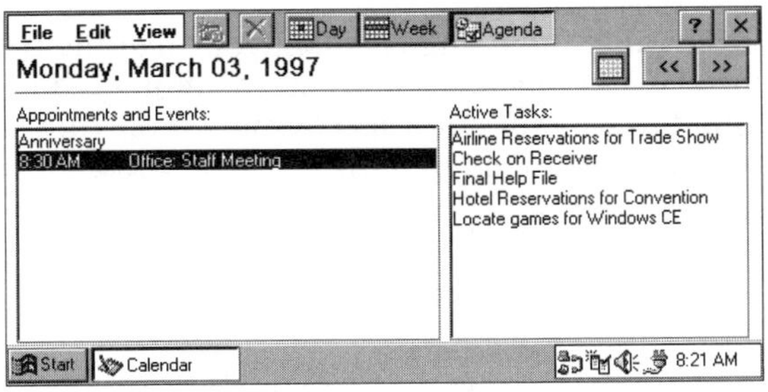

Figure 4-17: When you view the calendar in Agenda view, scheduled tasks appear on the right side of the screen.

From the Calendar program, you can view the details of a task by double-tapping on the task name in the list. When you double-tap on the task, the Task card for the selected task appears.

Synchronizing Tasks with Your Desktop Computer

If you use your desktop computer to maintain your tasks, you probably do not want to re-enter everything onto your new handheld PC. If you are using Microsoft Schedule+ 7.0 or Microsoft Outlook under either Windows 95 or Windows NT 4.0, you don't have to.

With Windows CE, you can copy all of the to-do information from your desktop computer onto your handheld PC. You also can turn around and copy the task information on your handheld PC back to your desktop computer. This process of making sure that the handheld PC and desktop computer contain the same personal calendar information is called *synchronizing*.

In order to synchronize your handheld PC with your desktop computer, you need a few things:

- A data cable connected between your handheld PC and desktop computer
- Handheld PC Explorer running on your desktop computer
- Microsoft Schedule+ 7.0 or Microsoft Outlook on your desktop computer

For more detailed information about synchronizing your handheld PC and your desktop computer, see Chapter 12.

You should create and modify recurring tasks on your handheld PC — not your desktop computer. Recurring tasks marked as completed in Schedule+, on your desktop computer, will not show as completed on your handheld PC. Recurring tasks marked as completed on your handheld PC, however, will show up as completed in Schedule+.

Chapter 5

Maintaining an Electronic Address Book

In This Chapter

- Locating the Contacts program
- Creating a new contact
- Locating a contact in the list
- Sharing contact lists with other handheld PCs
- Adjusting the display options for the contact list
- Backing up and restoring a contact list

Unless you are a hermit, you probably have a list of people with which you correspond on a regular basis. To help you keep track of these people, Windows CE provides a program called *Contacts* that resembles an electronic address book. You can store all kinds of information about the people and businesses that you contact regularly, and you can find the person you are looking for without manually flipping through a "real" address book or card file.

This chapter discusses the various ways you can use the Contacts program to create, view, and modify your contacts' information. It also discusses how you can obtain data from other sources, such as your desktop computer or another handheld PC.

Finding the Contacts Program

Before you can keep track of information about different people and companies, you first must decide where you want to store this information. If you write it down in an address book, you'll probably have to get out the correction fluid to correct an entry when someone moves. If you store the information on your handheld PC, however, you can simply retype the new information in the appropriate location.

Usually, the Contacts program is fairly easy to locate. Even though the program is called *Contacts,* not Address Book, its icon resembles a desktop address organizer. The icon should be sitting on the right side of your desktop (unless you have reorganized your desktop). After you locate the icon, double-tap on it to display the Contacts program.

If you cannot find the Contacts program icon sitting on your desktop, don't despair. You should be able to locate it by following these simple steps:

1. **Use your stylus to tap the Start button (in the bottom-left corner of the screen) to open the Start menu.**
2. **Tap on the Programs option on the Start menu.**

   Windows CE Explorer opens the Programs folder. You should be able to locate the Contacts icon, as shown in Figure 5-1.

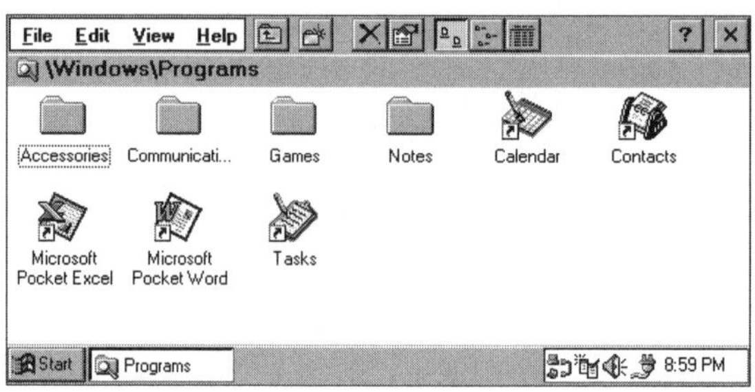

Figure 5-1: You can use Windows CE Explorer to find the Contacts icon in the Programs folder.

3. **Double-tap on the Contacts icon to display the Contacts program, as shown in Figure 5-2.**

   This program is where you set up all of the important information about the different people and businesses that you need to contact in the future.

TIP

If you use Schedule+ 7.0 or Microsoft Outlook on your PC to keep track of your contacts, you can transfer those contacts to your handheld PC. I discuss this topic in more detail later in this chapter in the "Transferring Information Between Your Handheld PC and a Desktop Computer" section. See the "Sharing Contacts with Other Handheld PCs" section, later in this chapter, to find out how to share contacts with other Windows CE users.

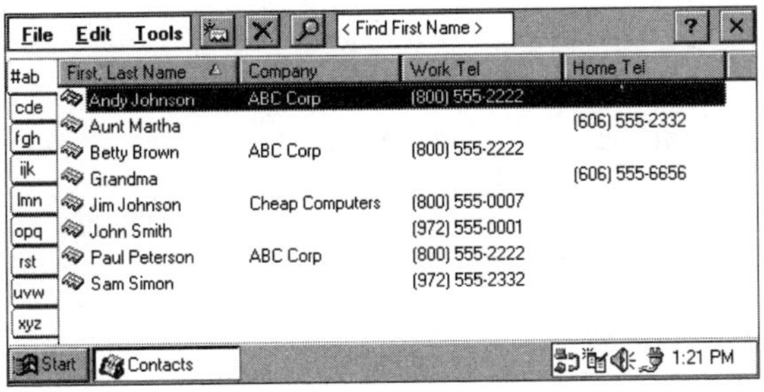

Figure 5-2: The Contacts program displays an alphabetical list of all your contacts.

Creating a New Contact

You can add any type of contact to your contact list. You may want to add the phone number of your favorite pizza delivery location, keep track of extensions for your coworkers, or maintain a Christmas card list. The Contact list can store anything and everything you want to know about each person. If you cannot find an appropriate field in which to add the information you want, you can enter the information on the Notes tab for the specific contact card.

To create a new contact, follow these steps:

1. **Tap on the New Contact icon on the toolbar at the top of the screen.**

   The icon resembles an address card with a star above it. You can also add a new contact by selecting File⇨New.

   The Contact card that appears contains three tabs. The sections that follow describe each of these tabs in detail.

2. **Enter information about the new contact on any or all of the tabs and then tap on the OK button to save the card.**

   In order to save a Contact card, either the Name field or the Company Name field must contain a value. If you try to save the card without filling in one of these fields, you receive an error message.

TIP

If you are fortunate enough to have already set up all this information in Schedule+ 7.0 or Microsoft Outlook on your desktop computer, you can copy the information to your handheld PC. For more information, refer to the "Transferring Information Between Your Handheld PC and a Desktop Computer" section, later in this chapter.

Free-form information?

Each contact card has an open block of space in which you can enter the contact's name and address. Windows CE automatically separates the name into first, middle, and last name segments. It also separates the address into components by street address, city, state, zip code, and country.

If you want to ensure that you enter names and addresses in the correct format, you can open the Confirm screen and specify each individual piece of the address or name. To display the Confirm screen, tap on either the Name or Address field to highlight it, and then tap on the Confirm button that appears next to the field. This button resembles one large field being divided into smaller fields.

When you tap on the Confirm button, either the Confirm Address screen, or Confirm Name screen appears so that you can enter the appropriate information. Simply type the appropriate information in each field and then tap on the OK button.

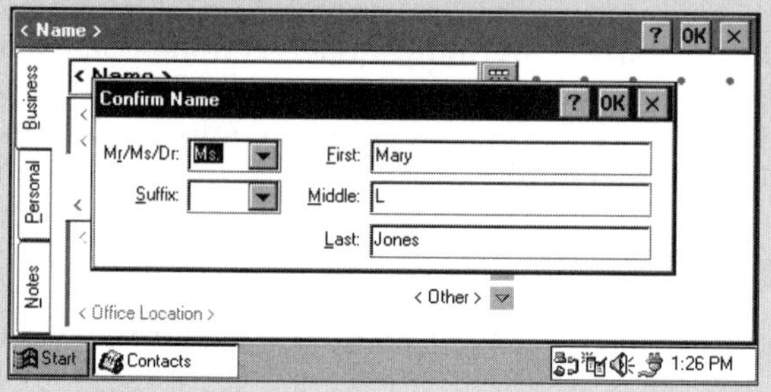

Business tab

You use the Business tab, shown in Figure 5-3, to add business information about a contact. For example, you can enter your favorite computer sales person or movie theater, or information about your coworkers, such as their phone extensions.

Type the information you want in each field on the Business tab. To move the cursor between fields, you can either tap in the field or use the Tab key.

The Business tab has two fields labeled Other. In these fields, you can enter some kinds of information, such as the name of the person's assistant or the assistant's phone number, that does not belong in any of the other fields. To add information into an Other field, tap on either the field name or the Down Arrow button next to the field to display a list of the kind of information that you can enter (see Figure 5-4). Highlight the kind of information that you want to enter and then enter the information in the field next to the name.

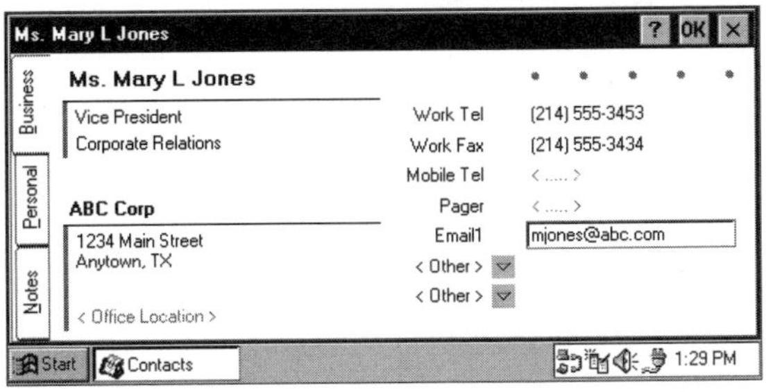

Figure 5-3: Use the Business tab for the pertinent business information about a contact.

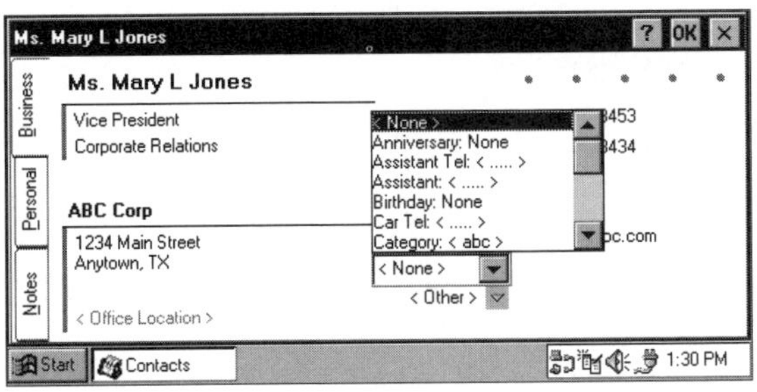

Figure 5-4: Enter additional business information in the Other fields.

Windows CE remembers the values that you enter in each option of the Other list. Therefore, you can store a value for each option, even though you can display only one option at a time in each of the Other fields.

Personal tab

You enter personal information about a contact in the Personal tab, shown in Figure 5-5. Simply type the information in each field. To move the cursor between fields, you can either tap in the field or use the Tab key.

The Personal tab also has two fields labeled Other. You can use these fields to enter personal information about the contact, such as the person's car telephone number or children's names, that does not belong in another field. To add information in this field, tap on either the field name or the Down Arrow button next to the field to display a list of the kinds of information that you can add (see Figure 5-6). Tap on the kind of information you want to enter and then enter the information in the field next to the name.

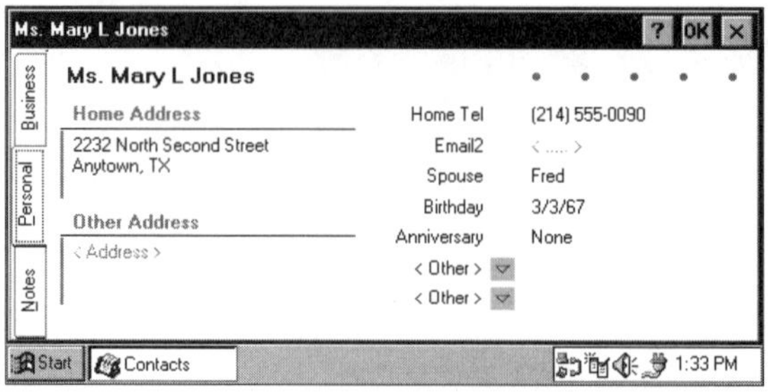

Figure 5-5: Use the Personal tab for a contact's personal information.

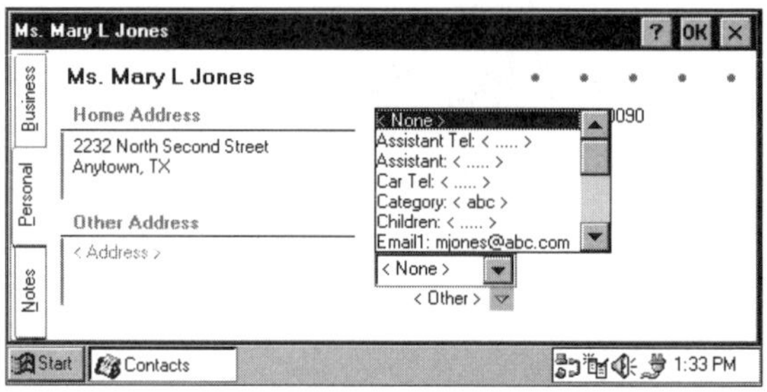

Figure 5-6: Enter additional personal information in the Other fields.

Windows CE remembers what you enter for each option in the Other list. Therefore, you can store a value for each option, even though you can see only one option at a time in each of the Other fields.

Notes tab

You can enter any information that doesn't belong in either the Business or Personal tabs in the Notes tab (see Figure 5-7).

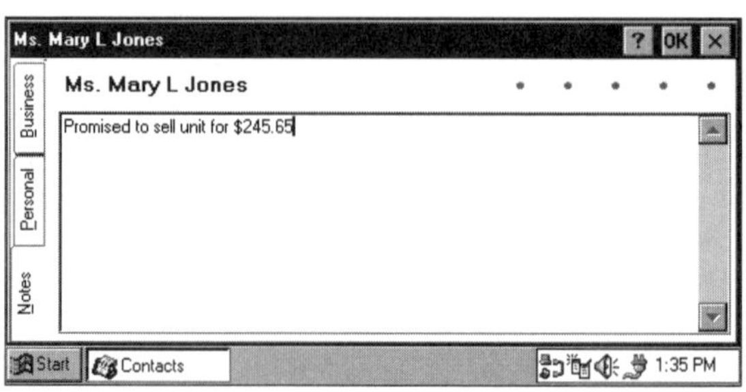

Figure 5-7: Type any additional information, such as the price the salesman quoted you, on the Notes tab.

You can enter an unlimited amount of information on the Notes tab using whatever type of formatting you desire. Unfortunately, no special fonts are available, so you can't be too fancy.

Locating Contacts

As you add more and more names to the contact list, the list gets longer and more difficult to read. Fortunately, you can view the information in several ways. You can sort the list by any of the columns of information, jump to the contacts that begin with a specific letter of the alphabet (if you know what you are searching for), or use the Find command to locate a contact.

Looking at the list alphabetically

You may have noticed the various tabs along the left side of the list that have the letters of the alphabet on them. You can use these tabs to jump to the contacts that start with specific letters of the alphabet. If you want to view the contacts that start with the letter T, for example, tap on the tab labeled *rst.* Windows CE highlights the first contact that begins with either the letters R, S, or T (see Figure 5-8).

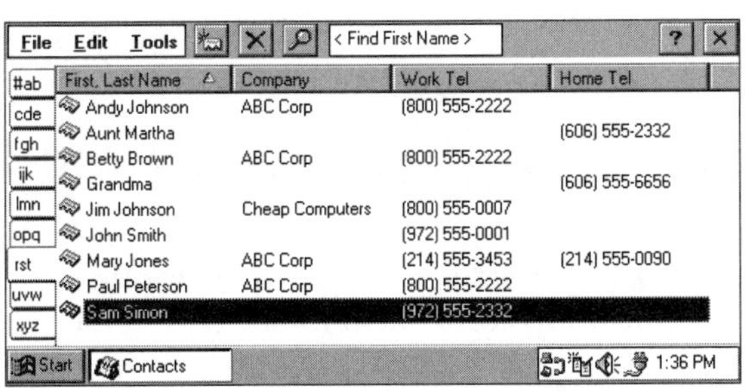

Figure 5-8: Tap on the tabs on the left side of the screen to jump alphabetically through the list.

If you tap on a tab that doesn't have any matches, Windows CE highlights the next closest match. For example, if you tap on *cde* and no contact starts with C, D, or E, Windows CE jumps to the next name after the letter E.

Sorting the contacts

Windows CE automatically sorts the list of contacts alphabetically based on the values in the first column, which is normally the Name column. You can, however, sort the list by another column, such as the Company Name column, if you want.

To sort the list of contacts by another column, tap on the column name. When you tap on a column, a triangle marker moves into the title of the column to indicate which column you are using to sort the list of names, as shown in Figure 5-9.

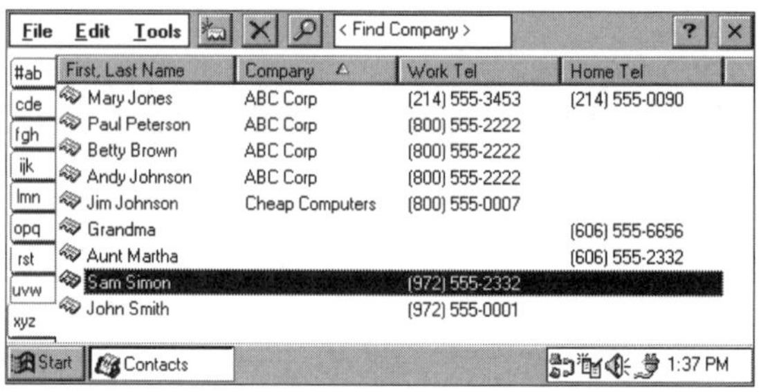

Figure 5-9: To sort the list based on the value in a column, tap on the column name.

You can resize the columns so that more information appears on-screen by tapping on the bar between the column names and dragging it left or right.

Quickly locating information in the list

You can use the Quick Find field to find a specific word or name in the sorted column. The Quick Find field is located on the toolbar at the top of the screen, next to the button with the magnifying glass on it.

To locate a contact, type the name or word you are looking for in the Quick Find field, as shown in Figure 5-10. As you type each character, Windows CE scrolls down the list to find the closest match.

You can use the Quick Find field only to search the column that is currently being used as the sort column. If you are sorting the list by the Name column, for example, you can use Quick Find to find a specific name.

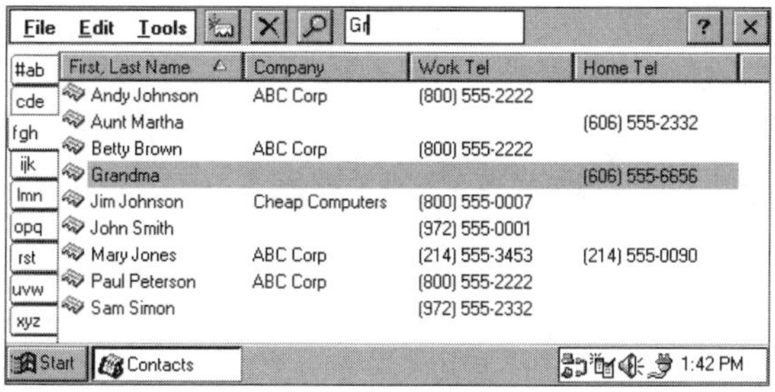

Figure 5-10: As you enter a value in the Quick Find field, Windows CE finds the closest match.

Finding information on a contact card

You can locate a contact card by using the Find button. The Find button resembles a magnifying glass and is located on the toolbar at the top of the screen.

When you tap on the Find button, the Find window appears (see Figure 5-11). In the Find window, type the text you are looking for and then tap on the Find Next button. Windows CE searches all of the contact cards until it locates the text you specified.

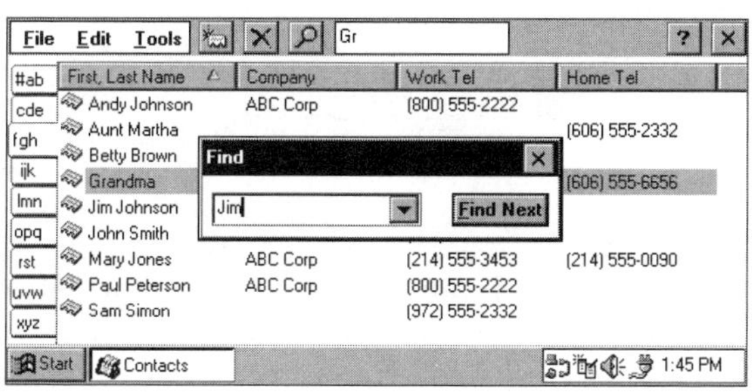

Figure 5-11: Type the information you are searching for in the field on the Find window.

You can also open the Find window by selecting Tools⇨Find. And if you have previously searched for a word, you can tap on the Down Arrow button and select the word rather than enter it again.

More than likely, the first card that appears will not be the card you are looking for. You can search again for the specified text by tapping on the Find Next button. You can continue to tap on the Find Next button until Windows CE locates the card you want to find or is unable to locate another match.

To make finding a contact card easier, search for text that is specific to the contact card you are looking for.

Changing the Display Options

You may find that the columns that appear in the Contacts window are not exactly the ones you want. If your list contains mostly personal addresses, for example, you probably don't care for the Company name and Work Tel columns.

To specify which columns appear in the Contacts window, choose Tools⇨Options. The Options dialog box appears (see Figure 5-12). The Options dialog box allows you to not only specify which columns appear in the Contacts window but also the default country and area code to be used when adding contacts.

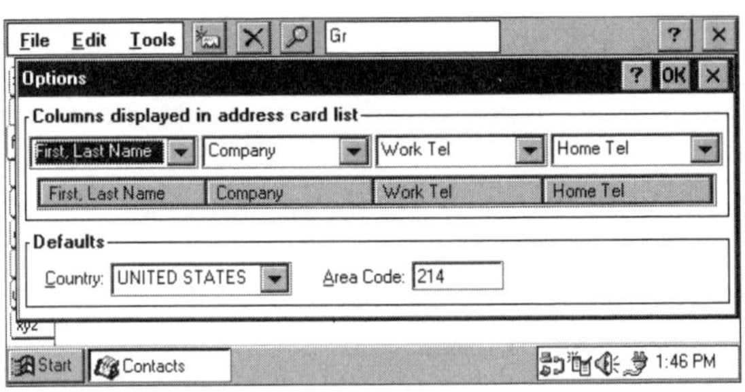

Figure 5-12: You can specify which columns appear in the Contacts window.

To change the information that appears in a particular column, tap on the Down Arrow button next to the column and select the information. You can select any of the fields that appear on the contact card.

The contacts' names always appear in the first column. You can specify only whether you want the first names or last names to appear first. Windows CE sorts the column alphabetically based on which names come first. In other words, if the first names appear first, Windows CE sorts the names in the column alphabetically by first names.

The default country that is displayed when you create a contact card is the United States. If most of the contacts are outside the United States, tap on the Down Arrow button next to the Country field and select the appropriate country.

The default area code that displays each time you type a phone number is the same as the area code you set up for your personal information. If you want to change the area code, type the area code in the Area Code field. Doing so changes the default area code for the Contacts program and leaves the system information alone.

Removing a Contact

You don't have to purchase a new address book to revise your contacts. Windows CE makes removing unwanted contacts from your Contact list quite simple.

To delete a contact, follow these simple steps:

1. **Locate the contact in the contact list.**
2. **Tap on the contact to highlight it.**
3. **Tap on the Delete button at the top of the screen in the toolbar.**

   The Delete button resembles a giant X. When you select it, a message box appears to ask you to verify your selection (see Figure 5-13).

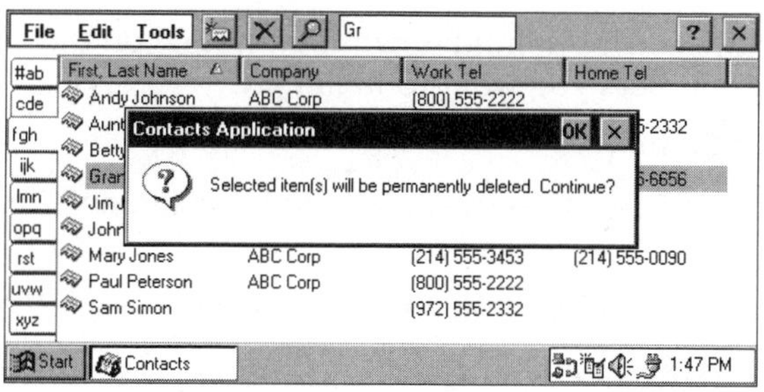

Figure 5-13: To delete the selected contact, tap on the OK button.

TIP

You can also delete a contact by choosing Edit⇨Delete Item. Or you can press Ctrl+D to delete the selected contact, in case you prefer to use the keyboard.

Sharing Contacts with Other Handheld PCs

You can use the Contacts program to share contacts with another handheld PC, as long as both handheld PCs have an infrared port.

The infrared port looks sort of like a black mirror on your handheld PC. If you are unsure whether your handheld PC has an infrared port, refer to the hardware documentation that came with the handheld PC.

To share contacts with another handheld PC, follow these steps:

1. **Make sure that both handheld PCs are turned on and the Contacts program is running on each handheld PC.**
2. **Place the handheld PCs so that the infrared ports line up.**

   The ports need to be within about three feet of each other, with nothing blocking the view. Because infrared ports use light beams to transfer data, they can't transfer information unless they have a good view of each other.
3. **On the first handheld PC (the one with the information), highlight the contacts you want to send to the other handheld PC.**

   To select multiple contacts, hold down the Ctrl key on the keyboard and tap on the contacts you want to highlight.
4. **Select the File⇨Send.**

   A message box indicates that the handheld PC is looking for another handheld.
5. **On the other handheld PC, select File⇨Receive.**

   When the handheld PCs make contact with each other, the information is transferred from the first handheld PC to the second handheld PC.

TIP: Some types of fluorescent lighting can interfere with the data transfer. If you have problems transferring data, try moving the handheld PCs to another location.

REMEMBER: Make sure that the infrared ports are not blocked by anything. If they cannot see each other, the handheld PCs can't transfer data.

Transferring Information Between Your Handheld PC and a Desktop Computer

If you currently use your desktop computer to maintain your contact list, you probably do not want to retype everything onto your new handheld PC. If you use Microsoft Schedule+ 7.0 or Microsoft Outlook under either Windows 95 or Windows NT 4.0, you don't have to.

Windows CE has been designed so that you can copy all of the contact information from your desktop computer onto your handheld PC. You can also turn around and copy the contact information on your handheld PC back into Schedule+. This process of making sure that both the handheld PC and desktop computer contain the same personal contact information is called *synchronizing.*

In order to synchronize your handheld PC with your desktop computer, you need to have a few things:

- A data cable connected between your handheld PC and desktop computer
- Handheld PC Explorer running on your desktop computer
- Microsoft Schedule+ 7.0 or Microsoft Outlook on your desktop computer

For more detailed information about synchronizing your handheld PC and desktop computer, see Chapter 11.

You need to keep a few things in mind when you transfer contact information between your handheld PC and Microsoft Schedule+.

- Unfortunately, Schedule+ does not offer all the information fields that are available in the Contacts program on your handheld PC. You cannot transfer the following fields of information into Schedule+: Middle, Mr/Mrs/Dr, Suffix, Car Tel, Children, Email2, Email3, Home Fax, and Web Page.
- A few information fields in Schedule+ are not available in the Contacts program. You cannot copy the information in these fields to your handheld PC: User2, User3, and User4.
- Two fields change names when you transfer from a handheld PC to a desktop computer. The Email1 field on your handheld PC becomes the User1 field in Schedule+, and the Work Fax field on your handheld PC becomes the Fax field in Schedule+.

Chapter 6

Working with Documents in Pocket Word

In This Chapter

- Locating Pocket Word
- Creating a new document
- Opening an existing document
- Locating text
- Formatting text
- Creating an outline
- Opening a Microsoft Word document
- Printing documents

Have you ever dreamed of being able to take minutes at a meeting and instantly have the minutes transferred to your desktop computer without totally retyping them? Or maybe, you are like me and have sat in the waiting room at a doctor's office wishing you could be working on the proposal for the presentation you are to give the next day.

Windows CE handhelds save precious time with a standard feature that sets them off from the competition: word processing capabilities. The word processing program available on your Windows CE handheld PC, called *Microsoft Pocket Word,* very closely resembles other versions of Microsoft Word. If you're an avid Microsoft Word user, however, you quickly find that Pocket Word lacks several of the bells and whistles that come with Microsoft Word.

In this chapter, you discover how to unleash the powers of Pocket Word. You create new documents, work with documents that you've created on your handheld PC, and transfer documents back to your desktop computer. Pocket Word provides various formatting options that you can use to add some pizzazz to each document.

Locating Pocket Word

Before you can create memos, work on a proposal, or type your sister a letter, you need to locate Pocket Word on your handheld. On most handheld PCs, you can find the Pocket Word icon on your Windows CE desktop. The icon looks like a piece of paper with a large W sitting on top of it. Double-tap on the icon to display Pocket Word.

If you cannot find the Pocket Word program icon on your desktop, don't despair. You can locate it by following these simple steps:

1. **Tap on the Start button (in the bottom-left corner of the screen).**

   When you tap on the Start button, a pop-up menu that contains various options appears.

2. **Tap on the Programs option.**

   Windows CE Explorer opens the Programs folder. You can find the Pocket Word program icon in this folder, as shown in Figure 6-1.

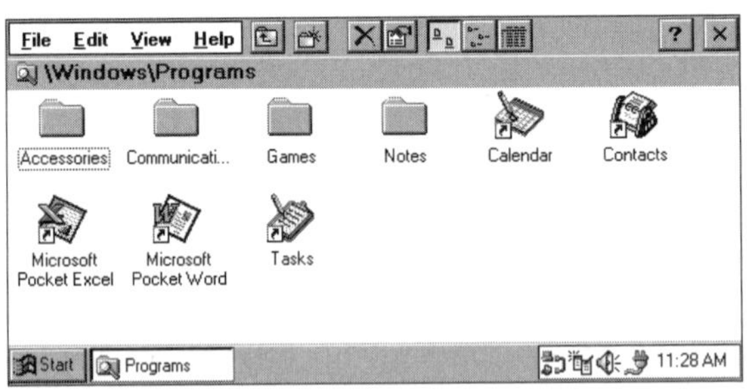

Figure 6-1: You can find the Pocket Word icon in the Programs folder by using Windows CE Explorer.

3. **Double-tap on the Pocket Word icon to display the Microsoft Pocket Word program, as shown in Figure 6-2.**

TIP: You can work on Microsoft Word documents that you copy to your handheld PC from your desktop computer. You find out more later in this chapter, in the section, "Opening a Microsoft Word Document."

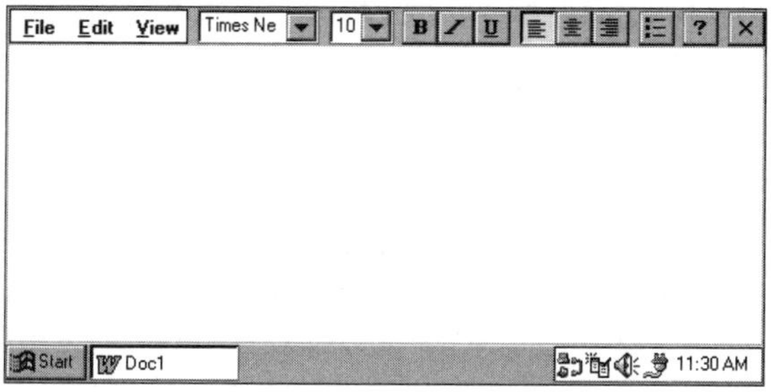

Figure 6-2: You can use Pocket Word to create memos, notes, reports, and more.

Creating a New Document

When you start Pocket Word, the program automatically opens a new, blank document. You can begin to create your document and then save it when you're finished.

If you've already opened a document and want to create a new document, choose File⇨New. A blank, unnamed document appears, ready for your information.

Saving Your Document

When you create a new document or modify an existing document, you need to save it so that you can access it again at another time. When you save a document that you created by using Microsoft Pocket Word, Windows CE places a copy of the document in the folder that you specify. This process is essentially the same as placing a copy of a memo in your file cabinet at your office. You locate the file where you want to store the document and then you place the file in the folder.

WARNING! If a document is very large, save it often as you work on it. An unexpected dead battery or wrong key combination can wipe out your efforts. By saving your document often, you ensure that you do not lose your work or most recent changes if something goes wrong.

Depending on the document that you have open, the process that occurs when you save the document varies. In other words, if you have never saved the document, Windows CE needs to gather some information from you before you save the document. On the other hand, if you've worked on the document in the past, you hardly even notice Windows CE doing anything when you save the document.

Saving a document for the first time

When you save a document for the first time, Pocket Word needs to know the name that you want to assign to the document and the location where you would like to place the document.

You must name the document so that Windows CE can distinguish among the different documents on your handheld PC. The document name must identify the information it contains so that you can quickly locate it later.

To save a document for the first time, you need to specify information describing the document on the Save As window. To do so, follow these steps:

1. **Choose File⇨Save.**

   When you select the Save option, the Save As dialog box appears, as shown in Figure 6-3.

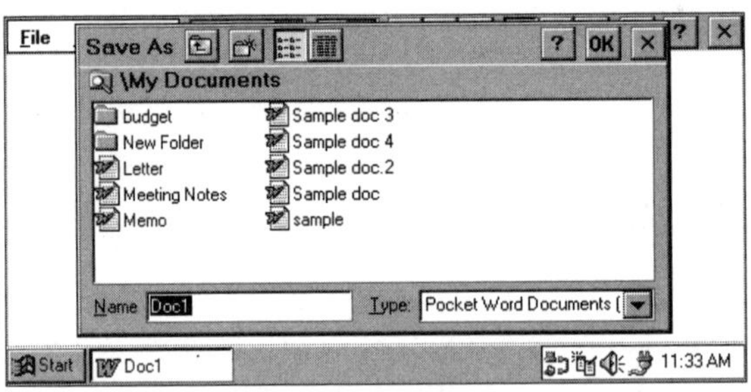

Figure 6-3: Use the Save As dialog box to name your document and specify a location for it.

   If you have not previously saved a document, the Save As dialog box appears when you select the Save option.

2. **In the folder list, tap on the folder in which you want to save your document.**

   When you save a document using Pocket Word, Windows CE assumes that you want to place it in the My Documents folder. This may not always be the location where you want to place it, however. If the icon for the folder you want is sitting in the folder list, double-tap on the folder to open it.

   If an icon is not displayed for the folder in which you want to save your document, you can tap on the Previous Folder button. The Previous Folder button looks like a folder with an up arrow on it.

3. **Type a name for the document in the Name field.**

   Use a name that indicates what the document is about. For example, **Memo1.**

4. **In the Type field, tap on the Down Arrow button and highlight the Pocket Word Documents type.**

   Save all documents that have any type of formatting as Pocket Word documents. When you save a document as a Pocket Word document, Windows CE automatically adds a three-character extension at the end of the document name — *.pwd.* (An *extension* tells Windows CE what type of file a document is.) Saving your document this way maintains all the formatting that you applied to the document. If you transfer the document to your desktop computer, the Handheld PC Explorer converts it to a Microsoft Word file. (The extension for a Microsoft Word File is *.doc.*)

5. **Tap on the OK button to save the new document.**

TIP

If you select the Plain Text Documents for the value in the Type field, you save only the text of the document. (The extension for a text file is *.txt.*) Any formatting that you may have applied to the document, such as special fonts, is not saved. Select this file type only when you want to use the document with a program that cannot read a .pwd file.

You can save a document in another way: Press the Ctrl key and the S key simultaneously on the keyboard. Just another pointer for all you keyboard fanatics.

TECHNICAL STUFF

Windows CE allows each filename to be a total of 255 characters long. This length includes the period and the three-character extension that is added to each Pocket Word document to identify its file type. So basically, each filename can be 251 characters long. The filename can include any characters and numbers, with the exception of these: /, ?, : *, “, < >, and |.

You may find that the folder in which you want to store your document does not exist on your handheld PC. Fortunately, Pocket Word lets you quickly create the folder while you are saving the document. To create a new folder for a document, open the folder where you want to place the new folder. Then tap on the New Folder button in the toolbar at the top of the Save As dialog box. The New Folder button looks like a folder with a starburst behind it.

When you tap on the New folder button, a folder icon appears in the folder listing with the name New Folder highlighted, as shown in Figure 6-4. To name the folder, simply type a name for the folder, and then press the Enter key. After you create the folder, you can specify the name for the document and then tap on the OK button.

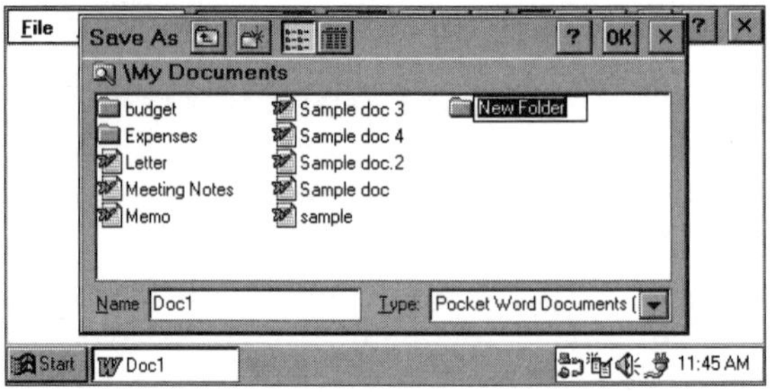

Figure 6-4: Type the name of the new folder in the box.

Saving a document that you previously saved

As I said earlier in the chapter, you should save your documents often. If you've saved your document previously, saving the document again and again is really quite easy. Simply choose File➪Save. As long as the document you are saving has been previously saved, Windows CE saves the document so that you can continue to work.

Saving a document with a new name

How often have you placed a document in one folder, and later decided to clean house and moved it to another folder? Pocket Word allows you to do the same thing. You may find that after you have saved a document, you want to save it in another location or give it another name. You can accomplish all of this stuff by choosing File➪Save As.

When you select the Save As option, the Save As dialog box appears onscreen (refer to Figure 6-3). The current name of the document appears in the Name field. To change the name, simply type a new name in the Name field and tap on the OK button.

To save the document with the same name but in a different folder, locate the folder in which you want to save the document and double-tap on the associated icon to open it. If the folder is not listed in the listing, tap on the Previous Folder icon to close the current folder and open the folder above it.

When you use the Save As option, the previous document remains with the same name and in the same location. The Save As option creates a new copy of the original document that contains any new changes that you have made.

You can also use the Save As option to save the document with a new file format, by selecting a different option in the Type field.

Remember — if you want to get rid of the original document, you need to use the Windows CE Explorer to delete the document. For more information, see Chapter 8.

Keep in mind that Windows CE allows you to have multiple documents with the same name in a folder, as long as they each have a three-character extension.

Closing a Document

Windows CE allows you to open several documents at a time. For each document you open, a button appears on the taskbar. The number you can open varies based on the amount of memory you have available and the size of each document. For convenience sake, I suggest not opening more than three documents at a time. Having too many windows open all at the same time can be cumbersome.

When you get tired of working on a document, you can close it so that it does not remain open and use up memory on your handheld PC. To close a document, simply tap on the X button in the upper-right corner of the screen. If you only have one document open in Pocket Word, the Pocket Word program also closes when you tap on the X button. If you still have other documents open, the current document closes, and Pocket Word displays the last document that you worked on.

You can also close a document by choosing File⇨Close. The Close option produces exactly the same results as the X button.

If you have not previously saved the document, a message window asks if you want to save the document before closing. To save it, tap on the Yes button. If you messed up the document, or just decided you don't want it, simply tap on the No button, and Windows CE trashes the document.

Opening an Existing Document

After you save a document in a folder under Windows CE, you can open it again at any time. You may want to open and revise it, or just read it again. To open a document, you need to choose File⇨Open. When you select the Open option, the Open dialog box appears, as shown in Figure 6-5.

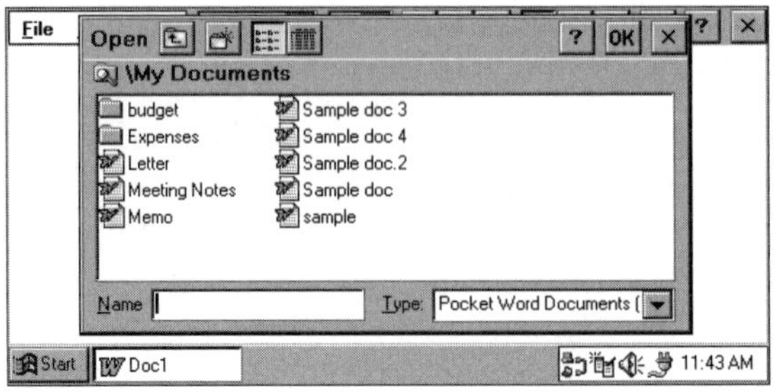

Figure 6-5: Use the Open dialog box to open document in Pocket Word.

Pocket Word assumes that you want to open a file from the My Documents folder. If the document you want to open is located in another folder, tap on the Previous Folder button to close the My Documents folder and open the folder above it. When you find the folder that contains the document you want to open, tap on the folder.

TIP

You can also open a document from Windows CE Explorer by double-tapping on the document's icon. If you double-tap on an icon for a Pocket Word document, the document is automatically opened in Pocket Word.

Opening the document you worked on last

You have probably at one time or another forgotten the name of the document you worked on just the day before. Luckily, Pocket Word remembers the last three documents that you worked on.

To see what you last worked on, or last opened and viewed, open the File menu, as shown in Figure 6-6. Between the Save As and Close options on the menu, you see the last three Pocket Word documents that you opened. Use the stylus to tap on the document you want to select or type the number next to document name.

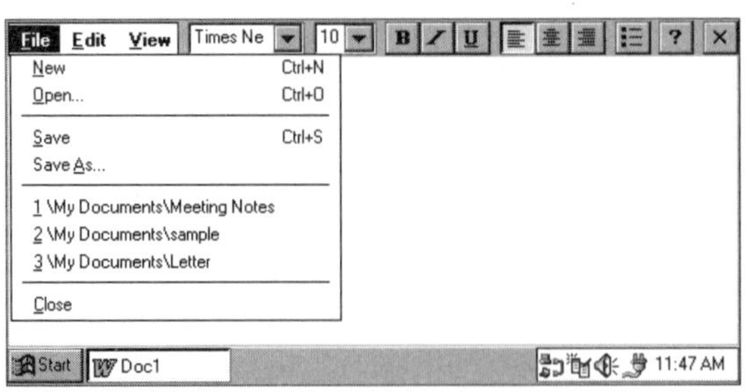

Figure 6-6: Pocket Word helps you remember what you did yesterday.

TIP: If you still cannot locate the document you are looking for, try checking the Recent folder. This folder appears when you select the Documents option on the Start menu. For more information, refer to Chapter 2.

Using a sample document

Have you ever needed to create a letter but forgotten how to format one? If so, you are in luck. Pocket Word comes with three sample documents — a memo, a letter, and a meeting notes document — that you can use to create a document. You can find these documents in the My Documents folder under these names: Memo, Letter, and Meeting Notes.

For those of you who are experienced Microsoft Word users, using a sample document is similar to using a template.

Follow these steps to open the Letter sample and create your own letter:

1. **Choose File⇨Open.**

   Pocket Word normally opens the My Documents folder, in which you can find the three sample documents. If you have a different folder open, use the Previous Folder button to move to the My Documents folder.

2. **Tap on the Letter document.**

   The Letter sample document opens within Pocket Word, as shown in Figure 6-7.

Figure 6-7: You can use a sample document to create a memo, letter, or meeting notes.

3. **Choose File⇨Save As.**

   Before you make changes to the sample letter, save it with a name to ensure that all of the changes you make are applied to the new letter and not saved in the sample letter.

4. **Enter a new name for the letter in the Save As window.**
5. **Select the folder in which you want to store the letter and then tap on the OK button.**
6. **Enter the appropriate information on the letter.**

You should replace almost all the text of the letter, especially the places where you see the < and > characters. These characters indicate the type of information that you should type in the field. To replace the information, highlight it and type the correct information.

REMEMBER: If you select the Save option instead of selecting the Save As option, you overwrite the sample document with the new information that you enter on-screen.

Locating Text

Sooner or later, you will want to locate a specific word or phrase within a document. You may just want to read the text surrounding a word or phrase, or you may need to correct a misspelled word.

You can use either the Find or the Replace option to locate text within your document. The Find option searches for the text and then highlights the text when it locates it. The Replace option searches for the specified text and then replaces it with the text in the Replace With field.

Finding specific text

Follow these steps to search for specific text in your document:

1. **Choose Edit➪Find or press Ctrl+F.**

   The Find dialog box appears, as shown in Figure 6-8.

2. **Type the text you want to look for in the Find what field.**

   You can type more than one word or only a portion of a word in the field.

   Select the Match whole words option to have Pocket Word find only whole occurrences of the text you enter in the Find what field. For example, if you enter **is** in the Find what field and select the Match whole words option, Pocket Word does not stop on words that contain *is,* such as th*is* and M*iss*.

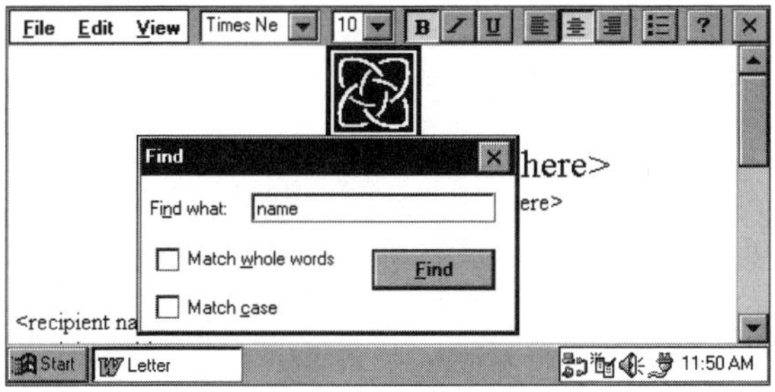

Figure 6-8: Use the Find dialog box to locate specific text within your document.

Select the Match case option to have Pocket Word find only words that match both the characters and the case of the text you enter in the Find what field. For example, if you enter **Is** in the Find what field and select the Match case words option, Pocket Word stops on *Is* but does not stop on *is*.

3. **Tap on the Find button.**

   Pocket Word searches the document from the current cursor location to the end of the document. It stops when it locates the first occurrence of the text that you entered in the Find what field. When Pocket Word locates the matching text, it highlights the text (see Figure 6-9).

Figure 6-9: Pocket Word locates the specified text and highlights it.

To have Pocket Word find another occurrence of the text that you typed in the Find what field, tap on the Find Next option. Or, if you have closed the dialog box, you can simply press Ctrl+F4.

Replacing text

Have you ever misspelled the same word again and again throughout a document? You could use the Find option to search for the word you want to modify and then manually enter the correct spelling. But that is the long and tedious method.

Looking for a diversion?

Very few of us can go through the day without some kind of diversion to break up the monotony. You may call mom on the phone, jog three miles, or take a long lunch and go shopping.

For those of you that have used previous versions of Windows, you have probably, on at least one occasion, found your escape in a game of Solitaire. Well I have good news: Windows CE also comes with a version of Solitaire.

You can find the Solitaire program in the Games folder on your handheld PC. You can find this folder by using Windows CE Explorer. The Solitaire program icon resembles a box of cards.

The game of Solitaire follows the age-old rules of Solitaire, except that since Windows CE deals the cards, you will find it difficult to cheat. The object of the game is for you to get all the cards stacked into four suit piles in order from Ace to King.

To move cards on-screen, simply touch the stylus to a card and drag the card across the screen to the location where you want it to appear. To deal the cards from the deck, you just need to double-tap on the top of the deck.

Just remember, if you are playing Solitaire during a business presentation, simply tap on the Solitaire button on the taskbar if the boss walks by. That will minimize Solitaire so that you look like you are hard at work.

When you need to replace text, you should use the Replace option. To search for and replace a word or phrase, follow these steps:

1. **Choose Edit⇨Replace or press Ctrl+H.**

   The Replace dialog box appears, as shown in Figure 6-10.

2. **Type the text that you want to replace in the Find what field.**

   You can type more than one word or only a portion of a word.

3. **Type the text with which you want to replace the specified text with in the Replace with field.**

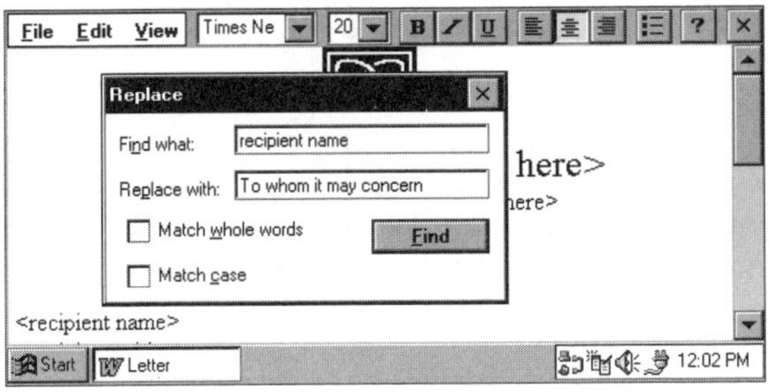

Figure 6-10: Use the Replace dialog box to locate and replace a specific word or phrase.

4. **Tap on the Find button.**

   Pocket Word searches the document from the current cursor location to the end of the document. It stops when it locates the first occurrence of the text that you typed in the Find what field. When Pocket Word locates the matching text, it highlights the text, and the Find/Replace dialog box appears, as shown in Figure 6-11.

Figure 6-11: Pocket Word verifies that you really want to replace the text.

5. **To replace the highlighted text, tap on the Replace button.**

   If you don't want to replace this text, tap on the Find button, and Pocket Word searches through the document for the next occurrence of the text.

TIP: If you are confident that you want to change every location of the text specified in the Find what field, you can tap on the Replace All button. Pocket Word replaces all of the remaining locations of the text without prompting you first.

Selecting Text with Windows CE

If you have used a previous version of Windows, you probably know that you can *select,* or highlight, text in many ways. In previous versions of Windows, one of the easiest ways to select text is to use your faithful mouse. Well, as I am sure you have figured out, Windows CE does not come equipped with a mouse. You have a stylus instead. Table 6-1 describes the easiest ways to select text in Windows CE.

Table 6-1 The Secrets of Selecting Text

To Select This Item	*Do This*
Any amount of adjacent text	Drag the stylus across the text
A word	Double-tap on the word
A paragraph	Tap three times somewhere in the middle of the paragraph
The whole document	Choose Edit⇨Select All

TIP

You can select pictures that may appear in your Pocket Word documents by tapping on the picture.

Moving Text

After you finish writing a letter to Grandma, you may decide that you want to move the paragraph asking her for a loan after the paragraph telling her how much you enjoyed snuggling with that quilt she spent six months knitting. This task is a piece of cake if you write the letter in Pocket Word.

To move items around in a document in Pocket Word, you use the Cut and Paste options, located on the Edit menu.

To move text, simply highlight the text on the screen and choose Edit⇨Cut. Then move the cursor to the location within the document where you want to move the text and choose Edit⇨Paste.

You can cut and paste any portion of a document, even pictures. You can even paste the text into another document, as long as you open that document and then find the desired location for the text before pasting.

You can also paste the text into another Windows CE program, as long as that program has a Paste option. Simply open the program in which you want to paste the text and use the Paste option.

Whenever you cut or copy something within Pocket Word, or any other Windows CE program, Windows CE places the information in an invisible location called the *Clipboard*. The Clipboard can contain only one selection at a time. So if you cut something that you want to paste somewhere else, be sure to paste it before copying or cutting anything else.

Copying Text

Have you ever typed a line of text that was so profound that you wanted to repeat it again in your document? Okay, maybe you're not a poet, but I am sure that you have written or will someday write something that you would like to copy and use in another location.

You copy text in Pocket Word just about the same way that you move text. To copy the selected text in Pocket Word, you choose Edit⇨Copy to copy text to the Clipboard, and then choose Edit⇨Paste to place the text in its new location.

You can copy and paste any portion of a document, even pictures. You can paste into the current document, another document, or even in the middle of another program (as long as that program has a Paste option).

The Clipboard can contain only one selection at a time. So make sure that you paste whatever you copy before you cut or copy something else; otherwise, you lose the information that you first copied.

Formatting Text

Unless you have been hiding in some dark room for the last few years, you have probably noticed that almost every type of document you see — memos, letters, reports, notes, and so on — different fonts, font sizes, and styles.

Using a variety of font types, sizes, and styles helps to make a document more appealing to its readers. For example, if you look at the layout of this book, you will notice that the main headings for each section are in a larger and bolder font than the subordinate headings so that the main headings are easy to spot as you thumb through the book.

With Windows CE, you can change the text formatting while you are creating a document. You can select a new font type, change the size of the current font, or apply font styles such as bold and italic.

Selecting a different font

You can add variety to your documents by using more than one font. For example, you may want to use a different font for the headings or the address information at the top of a letter.

To change the font you are using in a document, you use the Font drop-down list box, which is located at the top of the screen between the View menu and Font Size drop-down list box (see Figure 6-12).

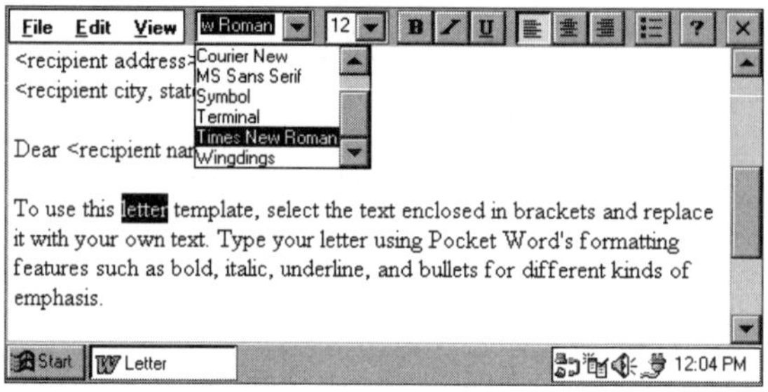

Figure 6-12: The Font drop-down list box displays the fonts you can select.

To format text with a different font as you enter the text into a document, tap on the Down Arrow button next to the Font drop-down list box and then tap on the name of the font you want to use. Any text that you type from that location on appears in the new font, until you change the font selection again.

To change the font of a block of text that you have already entered into a document, select the text and then tap on a font in the Font drop-down list box.

All Pocket Word documents use the same font when you first open them. To change the font throughout an entire document, choose Edit⇨Select All. Then select a font from the Font drop-down list box. All text you enter into the document uses the font you select.

TIP: Windows CE comes with only a few fonts. You can, however, copy fonts from your desktop computer to Windows CE by using the Handheld PC Explorer program under Windows 95 or Windows NT 4.0. For more infomration, see Chapter 8. ***Remember:*** Each font that you add to your handheld PC takes up some of your handheld's memory.

Changing the font size

One way to make something stand out in your document is to change the size of the font. For example, you should normally use a larger font for the headings in a document than you use for the text so that readers can quickly spot the headings.

To change the size of a font, tap on the Down Arrow button next to the Font Size drop-down list box and highlight the number that corresponds to the appropriate font size. The Font Size drop-down list box is located at the top of the screen between the Font Type drop-down list box and the Bold button, as shown in Figure 6-13.

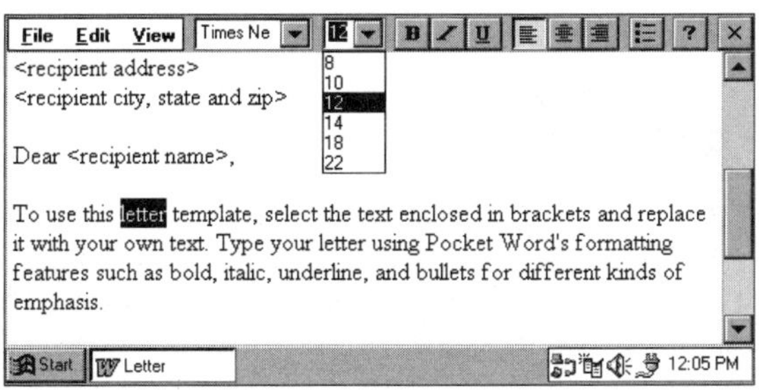

Figure 6-13: The drop-down list box displays the font sizes you can select for the current font.

When you change the font size in the middle of a document, any text that you type from that location on appears in the new font size. You can change the font size for a block of text by highlighting the text and then selecting the new font size in the Font drop-down list box.

Modifying the font style

Probably the easiest way to make text stand out in a document is to change the font style. See Table 6-2 for a description of each of the three font style buttons.

Table 6-2 Font Style Buttons

Button	Description
B	Makes the text appear in a bold font

(continued)

Table 6-2 *(continued)*

Button	*Description*
	Makes the text appear in an italicized font
	Underlines the text

To change the style of a font, tap one of more of the font style buttons and start typing. All the text you type appears in the selected font style until you unselect the style by again tapping on the corresponding button or buttons.

To change the font style for a block of text that you have already entered into a document, select the text and then tap on the appropriate font style buttons.

Creating a Bulleted List

Do you have a list of items that you want to add to your document? People commonly refer to a list of items as a *bulleted list.* A *bullet* is a small circle that is placed on the left side of each item in the list. The circle informs readers that the items are listed in no particular order.

Creating bulleted lists is quite simple in Pocket Word. Follow these steps:

1. **To start a bulleted list, tap on the Bullets button.**

   A bullet appears on the left side of the screen, and the paragraph is indented, as indicated by the position of the cursor.

2. **Type a word, such as** Apple**, and press the Enter key.**

   A bullet appears in the left margin for the next item.

3. **Now type another word, such as** Banana**, and press the Enter key.**

   Again, another bullet appears at the beginning of the next line of text.

4. **Type another word, such as** Orange**, and press the Enter key.**

   You now have a list of three bulleted items, with a bullet on the next blank line of text, as shown in Figure 6-14.

5. **Tap on the Bullets button again.**

   The Bullets button no longer looks like it is pressed down. The fourth bullet is removed, and now the text that you type will have normal formatting.

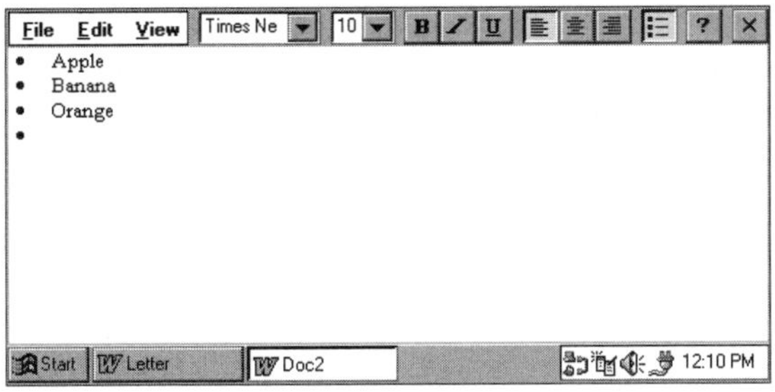

Figure 6-14: When you turn on the Bullets option, a new bullet appears each time you press the Enter key.

To place bullets next to a block of paragraphs, select the block of text and then tap on the Bullets button.

Outlining Your Document

You may have created a few outlines back in high school. If you remember, you are supposed to list the topics that you want to discuss and then take each topic and write a series of paragraphs that covers that information.

You can view your documents in Outline view in Pocket Word. You may find this view handy to view long documents. If you open a document in Outline view, you see only the headings. You can then locate and open the section of the document that contains the information you want to view.

You can also use the Outline view to take notes for a meeting. In fact, the sample Meeting Notes document that comes with Pocket Word is designed to be used in Outline view.

Viewing the outline of a document

Pocket Word usually displays documents in Normal view. To switch to Outline view, choose View⇨Outline. The text appears indented based on its heading level (see Figure 6-15).

When you look at your document in Outline view, you will find a small symbol in the left margin next to each paragraph. These symbols can provide you valuable information if you know how to interpret them. Table 6-3 provides an overview of each symbol used by Pocket Word.

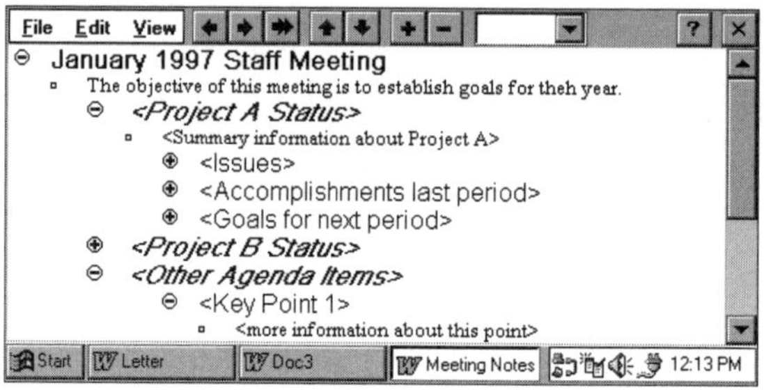

Figure 6-15: The Outline view is a good way to view a large document.

Table 6-3 Interpreting the Outline Symbols

This Symbol	*Indicates That*
○	This text is a heading, but it does not have any body text or subheadings under it.
⊖	This text is a heading and the corresponding body text and subheadings are currently displayed on-screen. A heading with this symbol is considered to be expanded because you can read the associated body text. Tap on this symbol to collapse the text.
⊕	This text is a heading but the corresponding body text and subheadings do not appear on the screen. A heading with this symbol is considered to be collapsed because you cannot read the associated body text. Tap on this symbol to expand the text.
□	This text is body text.

Working in Outline view

For some types of documents, you may find that it is easier to work in Outline view than in Normal view. If, for example, you want to write the main topics of a proposal first and then go back and expand on each topic later, you should use Outline view.

If you have worked in Outline view before, you may have noticed a bunch of funny arrow buttons on a toolbar near the top of the screen. You can use these buttons to help you move information around easily while in Outline view. See Table 6-4 for a brief description of each button. To use any of the buttons, you need to select the text that you want to change prior to tapping on the button.

Where does Pocket Word find the heading levels?

If you have ever used Outline view in Word for Windows, you may be aware that the heading levels used with Outline view correspond to the styles you use in your document. If you create a document in Outline view, Pocket Word uses nine heading level styles and one body text style. If you view a document that was created in Normal view in Outline view, Pocket Word assumes that the parts of the text that use a font size or style that is different than the font size or style used by the rest of the text are headings. So these lines of text appear at a higher level than the rest of the text in the document.

Table 6-4 Outline Buttons on the Toolbar

Button	*Purpose*
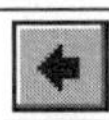	Moves the current text up one heading level
	Moves the current text down one heading level
	Changes the current text to the body text level
	Moves the currently selected text and all of the body text and subheadings under it, in front of the heading that proceeds it
	Moves the currently selected text and all of the body text and subheadings under it, after the heading that follows it
	Displays the body text and subheadings for the currently selected heading
	Hides the body text and subheadings for the currently selected heading

You use the drop-down list box that sits between the – button and the ? button to indicate which heading levels you want to view (see Figure 6-16). To view the entire document, you need to select the All Levels option. If you only want to view a portion of the document, such as the headers, select a heading level, such as Level 2.

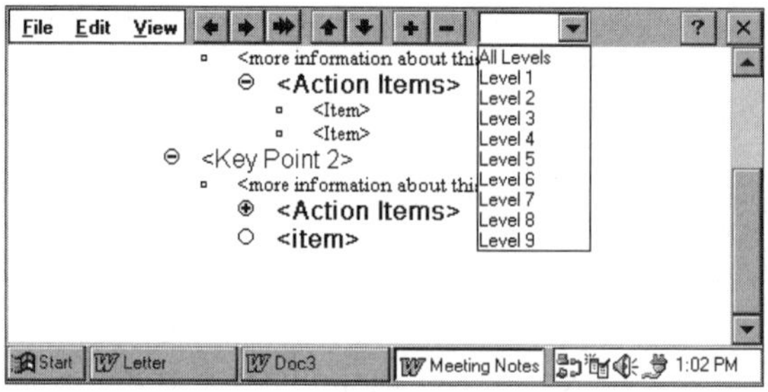

Figure 6-16: Use the drop-down list box to specify the amount of information you want to see on-screen.

Opening a Microsoft Word Document

The fact that you can transfer most Microsoft Word documents to a handheld PC that runs Windows CE is reason enough to use Windows CE. But, unfortunately, the more complex the formatting is in your Microsoft Word document, the more you lose during the conversion.

Because Pocket Word is a scaled-down version of Word for Windows, it doesn't provide many of the fancy formatting features that you often use in Word for Windows. Table 6-5 outlines some of the common formatting features and explains what happens when you convert the document to Windows CE.

Table 6-5 Lost Formatting for Pocket Word

Word for Windows Formatting Option	*Result in Pocket Word*
Fonts	Text appears in the closest font available in Pocket Word.
Font Color of gray	Text appears in the closest shade.
Tabs, alignment, bullets, numbering, and indentation	Text appears as in Word for Windows.
Paragraph spacing	Paragraph spacing is ignored. This feature is not supported by Pocket Word.
OLE Objects	If possible, OLE objects are converted to pictures and left in the document.
Tables	Because Pocket Word does not support tables, the cells are separated by tabs.

Word for Windows Formatting Option	*Result in Pocket Word*
Columns, index, table of contents	The text appears in the document, but some of the formatting is usually lost.
Numbering and fields	The text appears in the document, but some of the formatting is usually lost.
Headers, footers, footnotes, annotations, revisions, style sheets, borders, and shading	All these items are removed from the document.

Keep in mind that when these formatting options are removed from the document during the conversion to Windows CE, they are not added back when you convert the document back to Windows 95. Therefore, if you copy the same document back to your desktop computer, you may want to place it in a different location so that you do not overwrite the original; otherwise, you may find yourself forced to do a lot of reformatting.

Printing Documents

Unfortunately, you can't print a document directly from most handheld PCs. Check the documentation that came with the handheld PC to see whether you can print from it.

If you can't print from your handheld PC, you need to use the H/PC Explorer program on your desktop computer to print a file. To do so, choose File⇨Print, as shown in Figure 6-17.

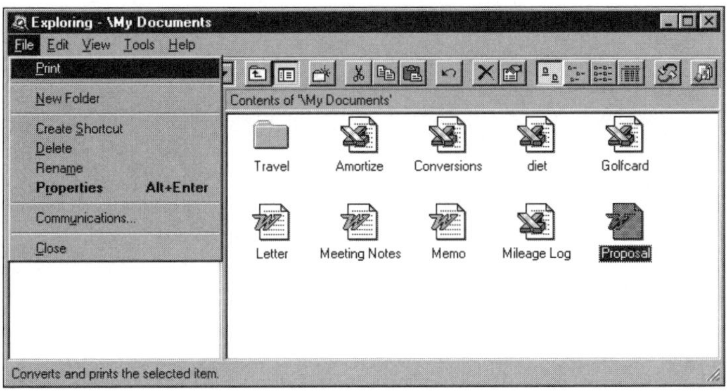

Figure 6-17: With H/PC Explorer, you can quickly select a file and send it to a printer.

When you select the Print option, the H/PC Explorer program automatically performs the following steps on your desktop computer:

1. **Temporarily copies the selected Pocket Word document to your computer. After the document is printed, H/PC Explorer removes the document from your computer.**
2. **Converts the Pocket Word document to a Microsoft Word document.**
3. **Opens the converted document within Microsoft Word.**
4. **Sends the word document to the printer that is set up as the primary printer for your computer.**
5. **Closes Microsoft Word.**

TIP

For more information about working with the H/PC Explorer on your desktop computer, see Part III.

Chapter 7

Crunching Numbers in Pocket Excel

In This Chapter

- Locating Pocket Excel
- Creating a new workbook
- Opening an existing workbook
- Selecting cells
- Adding data to a worksheet
- Using formulas
- Formatting a worksheet
- Opening an Excel workbook in Pocket Excel
- Printing a worksheet

Spreadsheets are one of the most popular types of programs used on PCs. You can use a spreadsheet to keep track of all types of data, such as hours worked, travel expenses, and monthly budgets. And by placing the data in a series of rows and columns, you can easily manipulate the data in various ways.

To keep up with the popular trend, Windows CE provides Pocket Excel, a scaled-down version of Microsoft Excel that runs on PCs. Pocket Excel provides many of the same capabilities found in its bigger brother. You can even open an Excel spreadsheet in Pocket Excel.

This chapter explains how to use Pocket Excel. I tell you how to create worksheets, use formulas, and format your worksheets.

Locating Pocket Excel

To calculate expenses, create a timesheet, or manage other types of data, you must first locate Pocket Excel. The icon for Pocket Excel sits on the Windows CE desktop on most handheld PCs. The icon looks like a piece of paper with a large X on top of it. To display Pocket Excel, locate the Pocket Excel icon and then use your stylus to double-tap on it.

If you can't find the Pocket Excel icon sitting on your desktop, don't despair; you should be able to locate it by following these simple steps:

1. **Use your stylus to tap the Start button (in the bottom-left corner of the screen).**
2. **Tap on the Programs option on the Start menu.**

   Windows CE Explorer opens the Programs folder on your handheld PC. You should be able to locate the Pocket Excel program icon in the Programs folder, as shown in Figure 7-1.

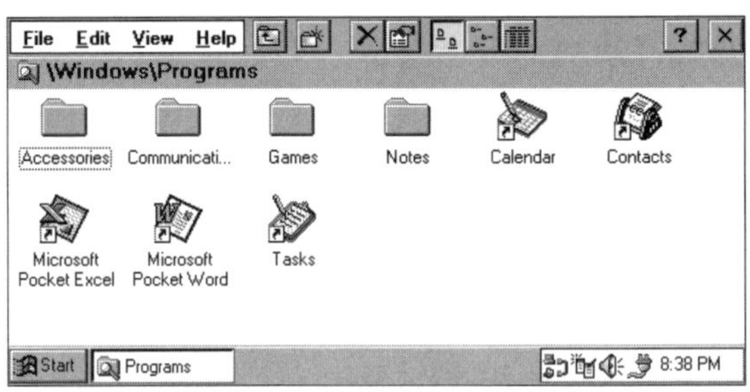

Figure 7-1: You can find the Pocket Excel icon in the Programs folder.

3. **Double-tap on the Pocket Excel icon in the folder to display the Microsoft Pocket Excel program, as shown in Figure 7-2.**

If you have used other spreadsheet programs, you will probably quickly notice that Pocket Excel uses two terms not found in many spreadsheet programs: *workbook* and *worksheet.* The *workbook* is what Pocket Excel calls the file where you store your data. Within each workbook, you can have several related pages called *worksheets.* You place the data on a worksheet. In other words, you lay out your spreadsheet on a worksheet. If you have a complex spreadsheet, you may use multiple worksheets to create it. After you have created all your worksheets, the workbook is the location where you store them. In other words, the workbook is the container for the individual worksheets; and the worksheet is where you create your spreadsheet.

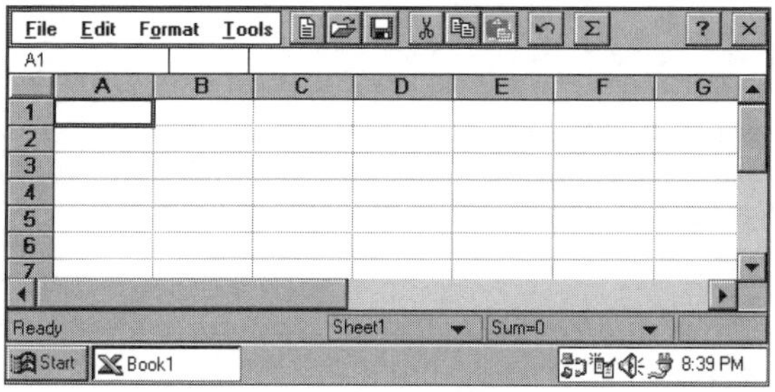

Figure 7-2: Use Pocket Excel to create worksheets.

See "Opening a Microsoft Excel Workbook" to find out how you can use Pocket Excel to work on Excel documents from your PC.

Creating a New Workbook

When you first open Pocket Excel, a new, blank workbook appears. If you are ready to create a new spreadsheet, you can enter your information and then save the workbook after you are finished.

If you already have one workbook open, you can create a new workbook by tapping on the New button on the toolbar. The New button resembles a sheet of paper. When you tap on the New button, a blank, unnamed workbook appears. You can see a button on the taskbar for the new worksheet you just opened.

You can also create a new workbook by choosing File⇨New or pressing Ctrl+N.

You have probably noticed by now that each worksheet in Pocket Excel looks like a big grid. Series of horizontal and vertical lines divide the screen, and small little boxes, or *cells,* appear between all these lines.

If you look closely, you can see that the cells are lined up in rows and columns on-screen. Pocket Excel provides labels for each row so that you can easily identify individual cells. The first cell on the spreadsheet is in column A and row 1, so it is called cell A1. The cell under it is cell A2, and the cell on the right side of it is cell B1.

By using this type of grid system to keep track of cells, you can easily manipulate the data in a worksheet by stating that you want to add all of the values in column A or row 2.

Opening an Existing Workbook

After you save a workbook, you may need to open and revise it, or just read it again. To open a workbook, choose File⇨Open. The Open dialog box appears (see Figure 7-3).

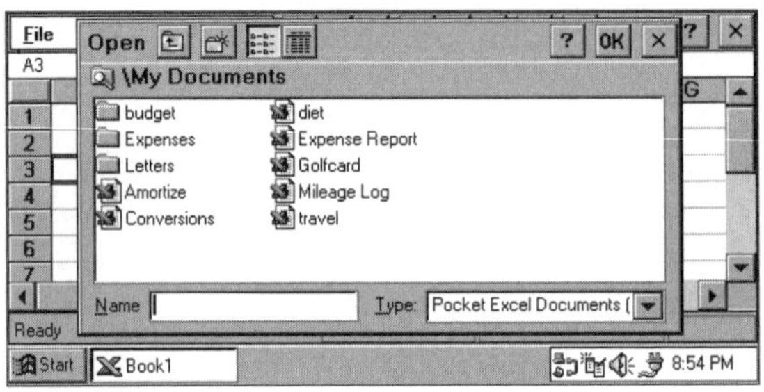

Figure 7-3: Use the Open dialog box to locate a workbook that you want to open.

Pocket Excel assumes that you want to open a workbook from the My Documents folder. If the workbook is located in another folder, tap on the Previous Folder button and open the folder above the My Documents folder. After you find the correct workbook, tap on it to open it.

TIP: You can also open a workbook from the Windows CE Explorer or from anywhere you see an icon for a Pocket Excel workbook. If you double-tap on an icon for a Pocket Excel workbook, Pocket Excel automatically opens that workbook.

Opening the workbook that you worked on last

What happens if you forget the name of the workbook that you worked on yesterday? If that hasn't happened to you yet, don't worry — it will. Fortunately, Pocket Excel remembers the last three workbooks that you worked on.

To see what you last worked on, or at least opened and viewed last, open the File menu (see Figure 7-4). Between the Save As and Close options, you see the last three workbooks that were opened on your handheld PC using Pocket Excel. To select one of these workbooks, tap on the workbook with the stylus, type the number next to the workbook name, or press the number corresponding to the file.

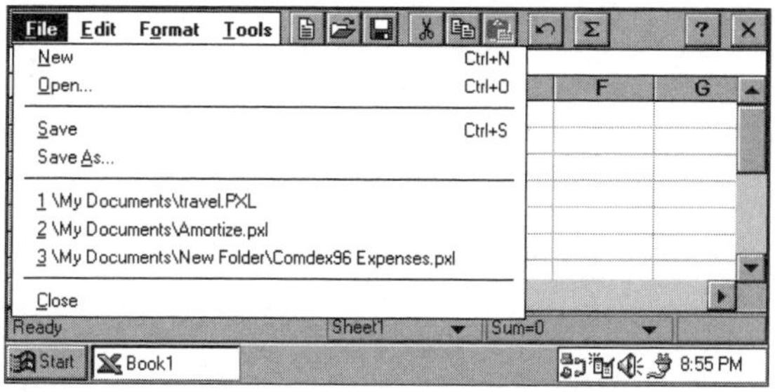

Figure 7-4: Pocket Excel keeps track of the last three workbooks you have used.

If you still can't locate the workbook you are looking for, try checking the Recent folder on your handheld PC. This folder appears when you choose the Documents option on the Start menu. For more information, refer to Chapter 2.

Using a sample workbook

Pocket Excel comes with five different sample workbooks that illustrate how you can use workbooks. You can modify these sample documents to fit your own purposes. Check out the My Documents folder to see these sample workbooks. Table 7-1 lists each workbook and describes how you can use them.

Table 7-1 The Pocket Excel Sample Workbooks

Workbook	*Use It To*
Amortize	Determine the monthly payments on a specific loan amount.
Conversions	Calculate the difference between the currency of two different countries. For example, if you are traveling in Mexico, you can determine the actual cost of an item in United States dollars if you know the current exchange rate and the price of the item in pesos.
Expense report	Create an expense report.
Golfcard	Keep track of golf scores.
Mileage log	Keep a mileage log for a trip.

Before you make changes to a sample workbook, save the workbook under a new name by choosing File➪Save As. Saving it before you make changes ensures that all of the changes you make are not saved in the original sample workbook.

Adding Data to a Worksheet

Opening a workbook doesn't do you much good if you don't know how to add data to it. Although you can add multiple types of data, such as dates, percentages, and fractions, to a worksheet, data comes in just two different categories: constants and formulas.

Working with constants

In Pocket Excel, all text, numbers, dates, times, currency, and percentages are considered to be *constants* (values that remain unchanged on the worksheet). When you enter a constant into a cell, it remains there until you replace it.

Pocket Word does recognize the difference between certain kinds of data. Therefore, you must use specific rules to enter specific kinds of values.

Adding text

To ensure that Pocket Excel treats text as text, format the cell as text. See "Formatting Cells" later in this chapter to see how to format cells. You can enter up to 255 characters in one cell. Although you normally see only the number of characters that fits in that cell's on-screen width, you may see more if the cell to the right is empty. Pocket Excel automatically left-justifies text within the cells.

Entering numbers

Pocket Excel assumes that all of the numeric values are positive, unless you indicate that they aren't. To indicate that a value is negative, type a minus sign in front of the number or place the entire number within parentheses.

Pocket Excel right-justifies numbers in the cells. Pocket Excel stores the numeric values with up to 15 digits of precision, even if fewer than 15 appear on-screen. This arrangement means that Pocket Excel keeps track of a total 15 digits on the left and right side of the decimal point.

Adding dates and times

You can enter times by a 12-hour or 24-hour (commonly referred to as military time) clock. If you enter time by the 12-hour clock, type **am** or **pm** after the time. For example, type **4:00 pm** to represent 4:00 in the afternoon.

You can enter dates by using either the / or the - (hyphen) character to separate the date. For example, you can type either **4/14/97** or **4-14-97** for April 14, 1997. You can also use three character abbreviations, such as **Apr,** to represent the months. You can also enter a date and time in the same cell by placing a space between the two values.

Dealing with currency

When you add currency values, you need to type the symbol for the currency before typing the number value. For example, to represent five dollars, you enter **$5.00**.

The default number of decimal places for currency values is 2, but you can reformat the cell to display up to 15 decimal values. Pocket Excel assumes that all the currency values are positive, unless you indicate otherwise. To indicate that a value is negative, type a minus sign in front of the currency value or place the entire value within parentheses.

Just like numeric values, currency values are right-justified within the cell.

Inserting percentages

You can enter a percentage in a cell in many different ways. The most common way to enter a percentage is to type a numeric value followed by the percent sign, such as **4%**. If you format the cell as a percentage, you can also enter the value as a decimal value, such as **0.67**, or as a formula that represents the percentage, such as $^{3}/_{4}$. For more information about formatting the cell, refer to "Formatting Cells" later in this chapter.

Using formulas

Formulas are basically any combination of operators, cell references, Pocket Excel functions, and names. For example, `5+6` is a formula, as is `=SUM(A3:A7)`. You can use formulas to manipulate and analyze the data that you add to the worksheet.

You can use the normal mathematical operators, as well as approximately 100 functions that come with Pocket Excel, to create formulas.

To insert a function in a cell, you need to select it in the Insert Function dialog box, shown in Figure 7-5. The Insert Function window appears when you choose Tools➪Insert Function.

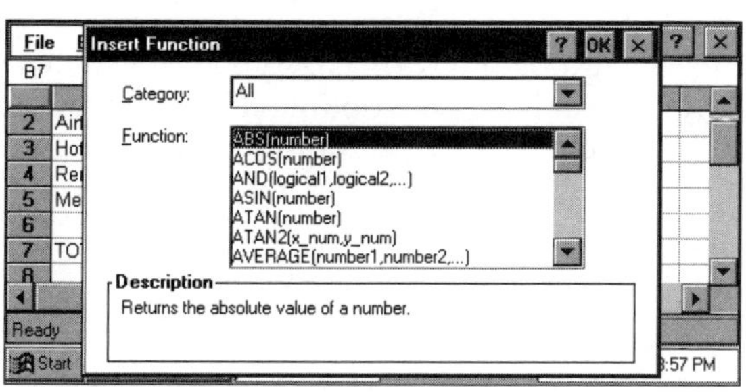

Figure 7-5: The Insert Function dialog box provides approximately 100 functions.

Highlight the function you want in the Function drop-down list box. Then tap on the OK button to paste the function into the Formula Bar.

TIP

To limit the list of functions in the Function drop-down list box, you can specify that only a specific type of function appears in the box by using the Category field. Tap on the Down Arrow button next to the Category field to display the Category drop-down list box and then select the type of function you are looking for.

Resizing Rows and Columns

When you look at a worksheet, you notice that all the cells on the sheet are evenly sized. This consistency is okay for some worksheets, but quite often you will probably want to resize the cells on the screen so you can read the contents of the cells better. For example, you may have one column that contains the descriptions for another column of numeric values. You can size the description column to be wider so you can see the contents of each cell, as shown in Figure 7-6.

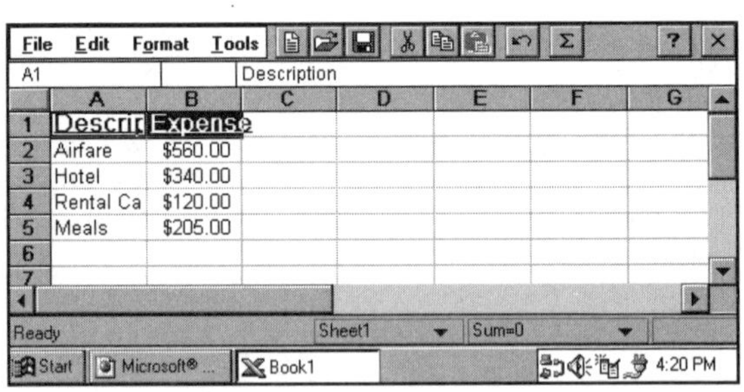

Figure 7-6: Resize rows and columns, so that all the information is easy to read.

Dragging rows and columns

The quick and easy way to resize a row or column is to tap on one of the lines that separate the column and row headings, hold the stylus down, and drag the line until the row or column is the size you want. When you tap on one of the lines, your cursor turns into a double-headed arrow indicating that you can now drag the line to the size you want, as shown in Figure 7-7.

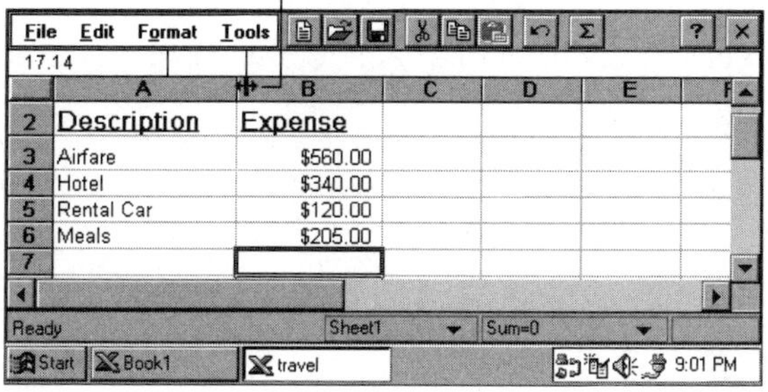

Figure 7-7: The double-headed arrow indicates that you can change the size of the row or column.

Using the formatting options

If you want to be more exact about the sizing that you use for a column or row, you can use either the Row Height or the Column Width option on the Format menu to specify the exact size for the column or row.

You can even hide a row or column that you don't want to appear on the worksheet. If you need to compute the results of some data but don't want the results to appear on the worksheet, you can hide the row or column in which the results lie.

The default size of each cell in the worksheet is about 9 characters wide and 12.75 points high. A *point* is a unit of measurement that describes the height of characters.

To change either the row height or the column width, choose the corresponding option on the Format menu. Enter the size in the Column Width dialog box that appears and then tap on the OK button (see Figure 7-8).

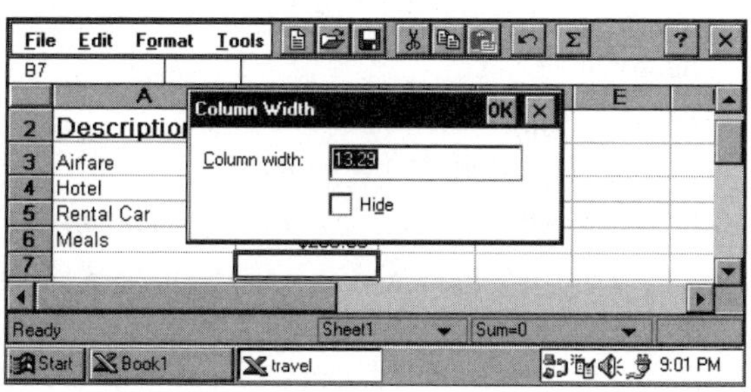

Figure 7-8: In the Column Width dialog box, type the column width you want.

Adding and Removing Cells

It may sound a little crazy to add more cells to a worksheet; after all, the worksheet appears to have an endless number of rows and columns. Sometimes, however, you may want to add another value or row of values, or remove some values out of the middle of the worksheet after you have already added data to the worksheet.

Adding cells

You can insert new cells into a worksheet at any location by using the Insert Cells dialog box, shown in Figure 7-9. When new cells are added, the surrounding cells move to make room for the new cells. Before you insert the cells, you need to determine what you want to be done with the other cells on the worksheet when you add the new cells. For example, if you select the Shift cells right option on the Insert Cells window, all the cells in the row to the right of the new cell move over one column. So if you add a new cell at location B2, the cell labeled B2 becomes C2, and C2 becomes D2, and so on. Table 7-2 describes the options available in the Insert Cells dialog box.

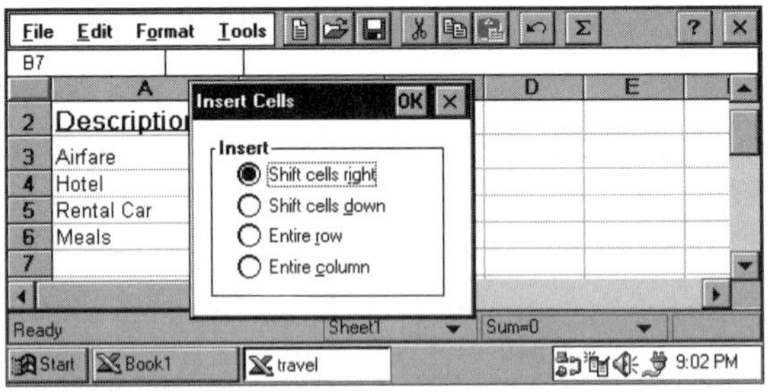

Figure 7-9: Use the Insert Cells window to add new cells to your worksheet.

Table 7-2 Inserting Cells

Option	*Result*
Shift cells right	All other cells in the row to the right of the new cell are shifted to the right one column.
Shift cells down	All other cells in the column are shifted down one row.
Entire row	A new row is added, and all rows below are shifted down one row.
Entire column	A new column is added, and all columns to the right are shifted over one column.

Removing cells

You can remove cells from any location in a worksheet by using the Delete Cells dialog box, shown in Figure 7-10. Before you delete the cells, you need to determine what will happen to the cells around the one you will remove. If you select the Shift cells left option in the Delete Cells dialog box, all the cells in the row to the right of the deleted cell move left one column. So if you delete the cell at location B2, then the cell labeled C2 becomes B2, and the cell labeled D2 becomes C2, and so on. Table 7-3 describes the options on the Delete Cells window.

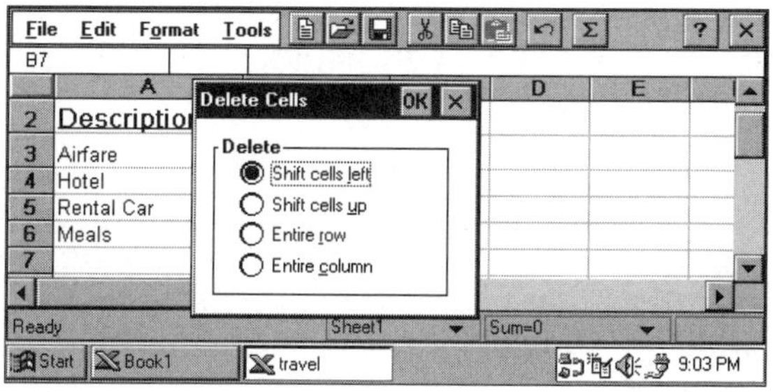

Figure 7-10: Use the Delete Cells dialog box to remove individual cells or entire rows and columns.

Table 7-3 Deleting Cells

Option	*Result*
Shift cells left	All other cells in the row to the right of the deleted cell are shifted to the left one column.
Shift cells up	All other cells in the column are shifted up one row.
Entire row	The current row is deleted, and all rows below are shifted up one row.
Entire column	The current column is deleted, and all columns to the right are shifted over to the left one column.

Moving Data on the Worksheet

You may find that you want to reorganize data after you place the data on the worksheet. Pocket Excel allows you to copy the data from one or more cells and place it in another location within the worksheet. You can even place it in another worksheet or workbook.

To move data around in a worksheet, you need to use the Cut and Paste buttons on the Standard toolbar. The Cut button resembles a pair of scissors, and the Paste button looks like a sheet of paper being placed on a clipboard.

To move the data, highlight the cells on the screen and tap on the Cut button. Then move the cursor to the location within the worksheet where you want to place the data and tap on the Paste button. If you are pasting multiple cells of data, you need to place the cursor in the first upper-left cell in which you want to paste the data.

Instead of moving the data within the worksheet, you may want to copy the data and paste a copy of it in another location. To copy the data, select the cells you want to copy on the screen and tap on the Copy button. Then select the cell where you want to paste the copied cells and tap on the Paste button.

TIP

Whenever you cut or copy something within Pocket Excel, or any other Windows CE program, the copied information is placed in an invisible location called the Clipboard. The Clipboard can hold only one selection at a time. So if you cut something that you want to paste somewhere else, make sure that you paste it before copying or cutting something else; otherwise, you may lose the information.

You can also use the Cut and Paste options that are available on the Edit menu. If you really like to do tasks with the keyboard, try pressing Ctrl+X to cut the data, or Ctrl+C to copy, and then Ctrl+V to paste the data in the desired location.

Formatting Cells

In Pocket Excel, you can apply different types of formatting to each cell. By formatting values in cells, you can ensure, for example, that Pocket Excel always treats the values in a particular cell as a percentage.

You can also specify how the data appears in the cell by selecting the desired font characteristics, such as font size and font style. Or you can add borders to the cell to make it stand out on the worksheet.

All of these cell formatting options are available in the Format Cells dialog box. The Format Cells window appears when you choose Format⇨Cells.

Indicating the category of data

You use the Number tab of the Format Cells dialog box, shown in Figure 7-11, to indicate the type of data that is contained in the selected cell. For example, if you assign a category of Percentage to a cell, Pocket Excel always treats the value in that cell as a percentage.

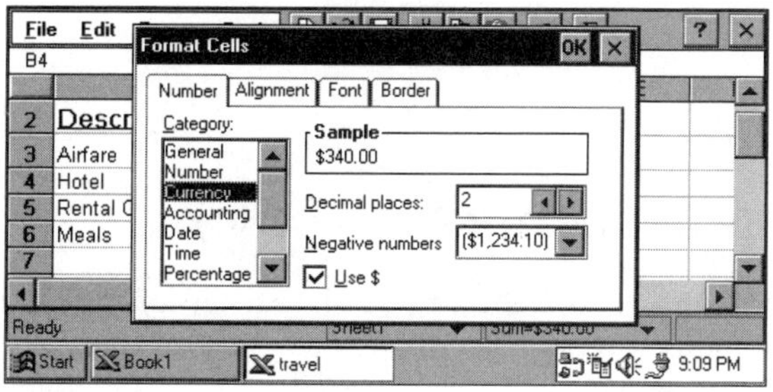

Figure 7-11: Use the Number tab to specify the type of value in the cell.

To specify the category for the cell, highlight the desired value in the Category list box. When you select the category, a sample of the selected category appears in the Sample section.

Each category type offers different options that appear on the right side of the dialog box. For example, if you select Number, you can select three more options. In the Decimal places field, use the Left and Right arrow buttons to specify the number of decimal places that you want to display. Then in the Negative numbers field, select either the value with the minus sign or the value surrounded with parentheses to indicate how negative values should be displayed. Finally, if you want a comma to separate every three digits of a number, such as 5,434, select the box next to the Use 1000 separator field. Look at the Sample section to see how the cell will look as you change the options for the cell.

Specifying cell alignment

Pocket Excel always formats certain types of data in certain ways. For example, text is always left justified in the cell, and numeric values are right justified.

You may decide that you want to specify your own alignment for the data in cells. To do this, you use the Alignment tab on the Format Cells dialog box, as shown in Figure 7-12. You can select the horizontal and vertical alignment of the data in the cell by tapping on the desired options.

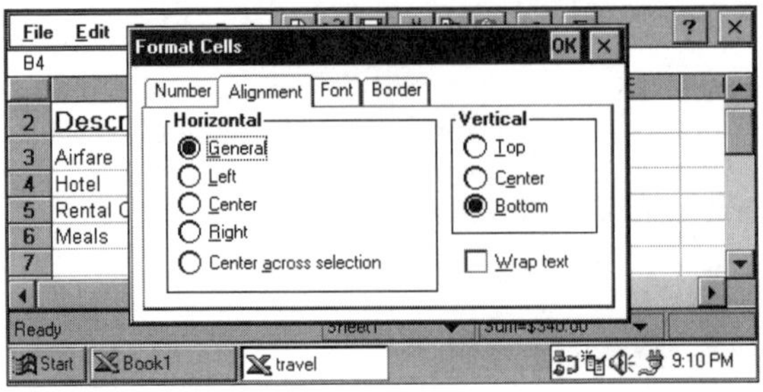

Figure 7-12: Use the Alignment tab to specify the horizontal and vertical spacing of cell data.

Indicating font values

You can make text in certain cells stand out on the screen by changing the font values for those cells. To change font values, tap on the Font tab on the Format Cells dialog box, as shown in Figure 7-13.

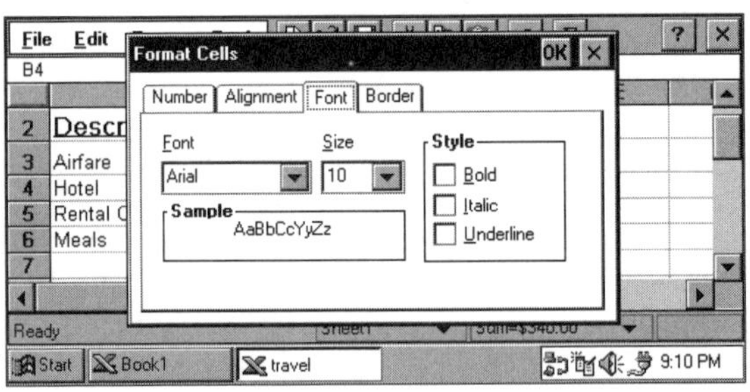

Figure 7-13: Use the Font tab to select the font type, size, and style for the cell.

As you make selections on this tab, the Sample section illustrates how the font selections will look in the cell. For the Font and Size drop-down list boxes, tap on the Down Arrow button and highlight the desired selections. In the Style section, tap on the box next to the desired font styles.

Selecting borders

Of course, no worksheet would be complete without some borders. You can select the borders on the Border tab of the Format Cells dialog box, as shown in Figure 7-14. Tap on the boxes for the types of borders you want.

TIP

Selecting the Outline option is the same as selecting all four of the other options (Left, Right, Top, Bottom). So if you want borders around the entire cell, select the Outline option.

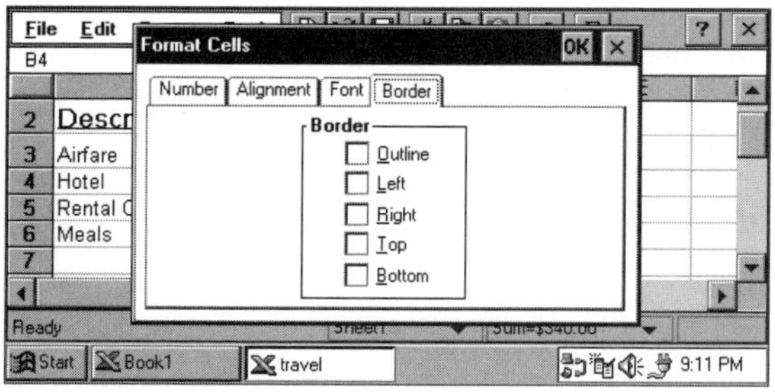

Figure 7-14: You can create borders around the selected cells with the Border tab.

Quickly Summing Data

The AutoSum button allows you to quickly sum the numeric values in a row, column, or even a series of rows and columns. The following steps show how you can easily sum numeric values within your worksheet:

1. **In the first cell of the worksheet, enter a numeric value, such as** 3.

   The first cell in a worksheet is always labeled A1. To place a value in that cell, tap on the cell with the stylus and then type the desired value. Whatever you enter appears in the Formula Bar under the Standard toolbar, as shown in Figure 7-15. To move the value to the cell, press Enter or tap on the check mark button next to the Formula Bar.

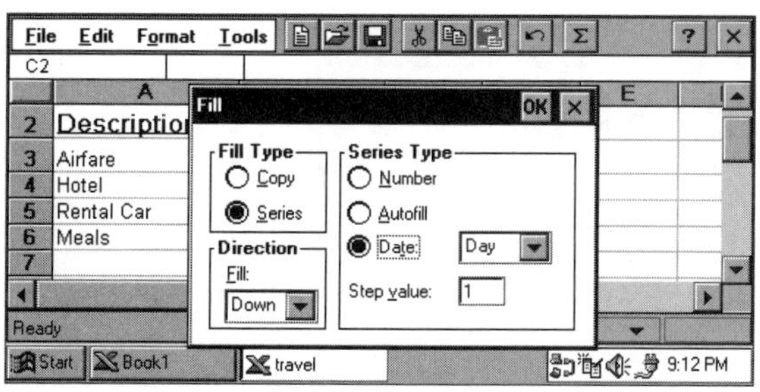

Figure 7-15: The Formula Bar is where all data entry occurs for the worksheet.

2. **In the cell labeled A2, enter a numeric value, such as** 4.

   Cell A2 is located directly under the first cell.

3. **In the cell labeled A3, enter a numeric value, such as** 5.

4. **Tap on the cell labeled A4 to select it.**

   The cell should be highlighted on-screen.

5. **Tap on the AutoSum button.**

   When you tap on the AutoSum button, the formula `=SUM(A1:A3)` appears in the Formula Bar. Tap on the check mark button to place the formula in cell A4.

TIP

The following tips are important to keep in mind when you work with formulas and the AutoSum button:

- Whenever a cell contains a formula, the results of the formula appear in the cell while you view the worksheet. To see the actual formula in the Formula Bar, tap on the cell to select it.
- If you tap on the AutoSum button, and it doesn't display the desired range of cells, you can drag the stylus across the cells to select them. Or you can enter the appropriate cells in the Formula Bar.
- You can use a colon in the formula to indicate a range of cells. For example, both a formula that says `=SUM(A1:A3)` and one that says `=SUM(A1, A2, A3)` adds cells A1 through A3.

Automatically Filling Cells with Data

If you want to copy data from some cells to other cells or insert a series of data in certain cells, you can use the Fill dialog box, shown in Figure 7-16. The Fill window appears when you choose Edit➪Fill.

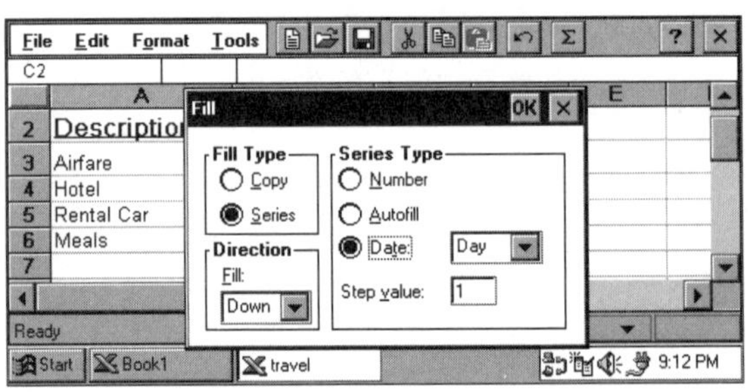

Figure 7-16: Add related data to a series of cells in the Fill dialog box.

Copying data

Copying data from cells within a worksheet is one of the most common uses for the Fill option. The following steps illustrate how to copy data from cells.

1. **Highlight the cells that contain the data you want to copy.**

   You cannot select more than one row or one column. To select a row or a column, tap on its heading.

2. **Extend the selected cells to include the location where you want the cells to be copied.**

   To select more cells, hold down the Shift key and select the new cells. If you are moving the data to a new row or column, tap on the heading.

3. **Select Edit⇨Fill.**

   The Fill screen appears.

4. **Select the Copy option in the Fill Type section.**

5. **Tap on the OK button to copy the data.**

   Pocket Excel copies the selected data into the specified cells.

Inserting a series of data

You can use the Fill option to add a series of data to the selected cells of your worksheet. A *series* is data that is arranged in some logical order. For example, the days in the week, when listed in order, are a series. In Pocket Excel you can have a series of numbers, a series of text that is followed by a number (such as session1), or a series of dates. The following steps illustrate how to create a series of data.

1. **Type the first value of the desired series in a cell.**

   Make sure that the cell is at the beginning of where you want your series to be located.

2. **Highlight the cell where you typed the data.**

   You can select one cell or an entire row or column. To select a row or a column, tap on its heading.

3. **Extend the selected cells to include the cells where you want the series to be located.**

   To select more cells, hold down the Shift key and select the new cells. If you are inserting the series into a new row or column, tap on the row or column heading.

4. **Choose Edit⇨Fill.**

   The Fill screen appears.

5. **Select the Series option in the Fill Type section.**

6. **In the Series Type section, select the type of series that you want to create.**

   Select Number to create a series of numbers. Enter the amount that the number should be incremented by in the Step value field. For example, to display every other number, enter **2**.

Select Autofill to create a series of values that is based on the contents of the first cell. The first cell must contain a day of the week, a month (you can use a three character abbreviation or spell it out), or text followed by a number, such as **Session1**.

Select Date to create a series of dates. Select a value in the drop-down list box indicating whether you want a day, month, or year for the date. Remember to type a value in the Step value field that indicates the increment value for the date. For example, to increase by 1 day, enter **1**.

7. **Tap on the OK button to create the series.**

   The selected series is created in the specified cells.

Locating Desired Data

You can use two different tools to locate data within your workbook. The Find option searches for the data and then highlights the data. The Replace option searches for the specified data and then replaces it with the data in the Replace With field.

Finding text

If you want to search for specific data, you can use the Find option. Follow these steps to look for some data in a worksheet using the Find option.

1. **Choose Edit⇨Find/Replace.**

   The Find dialog box appears, as shown in Figure 7-17.

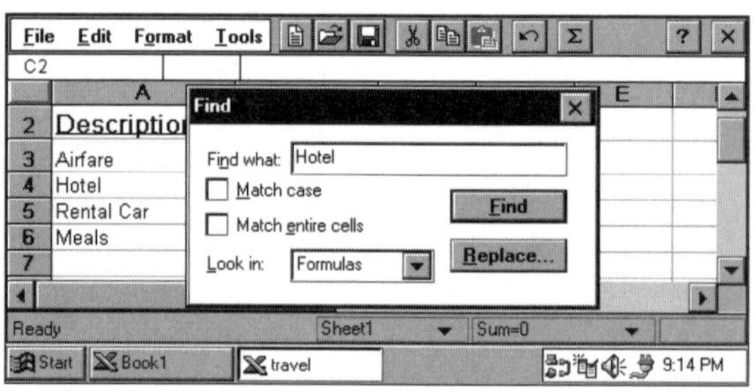

Figure 7-17: Locate specific data with the Find dialog box.

2. **Type the data that you want to look for in the Find what field.**

   You can type either all the data or just a portion of it, up to a maximum of 255 characters.

3. **Tap on the Find button.**

   Pocket Excel searches the document from the current cursor location to the end of the worksheet. It stops when it locates the first occurrence of the text that you entered in the Find what field. When Pocket Excel locates the matching data, it highlights the data on the screen, as shown in Figure 7-18.

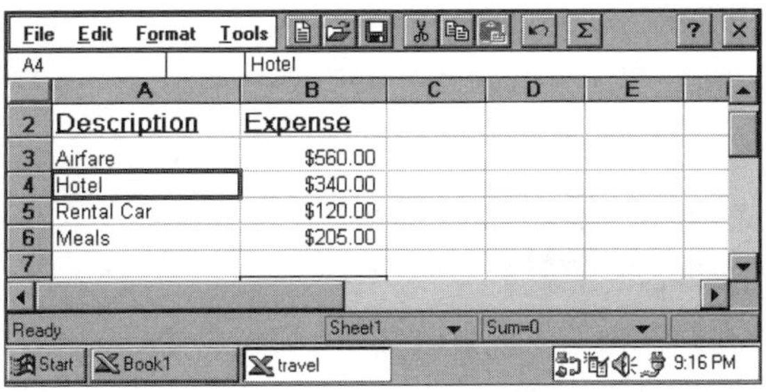

Figure 7-18: Pocket Excel locates the specified data and highlights it on the screen.

TIP

When you work with the Find/Replace option, these three tips help simplify the process of locating information, especially when you're searching a large document:

- To have Pocket Excel find another occurrence of the data that you typed in the Find what field, choose Edit⇨Find Next.
- Select the Match entire cells option to have Pocket Excel locate only the cells that contain an exact match to the text you enter in the Find what field. If you enter **153.34** in the Find what field and select the Match entire cells option, Pocket Excel does not stop at cells that contain any characters in addition to the ones in the Find what field. Pocket Excel, for example, does not match a cell that contains `2153.34`.
- If you select the Match case option, Pocket Excel locates only cells that match both the characters and the case of the text you enter in the Find what field. For example, if you enter **Is** in the Find what field and select the Match case words option, Pocket Word stops on the word *Is* but not the word *is*.

TIP

You can also use the keyboard for the Find/Replace and Find Next options. To display the Find dialog box, press the Ctrl and F keys simultaneously. To perform a Find Next option, press the Ctrl and 4 keys simultaneously. The keyboard options are useful when you don't have your stylus in your hand.

Replacing text

Have you ever misspelled a word throughout a spreadsheet? You can use the Find/Replace option to search for a misspelled word and replace it with the correctly spelled word. To replace text in a worksheet, follow these steps:

1. **Choose Edit⇨Find/Replace.**
2. **Tap on the Replace button to display the Replace dialog box.**

   The Replace dialog box, shown in Figure 7-19, allows you to specify the data to be placed in the location where Pocket Excel finds the data.

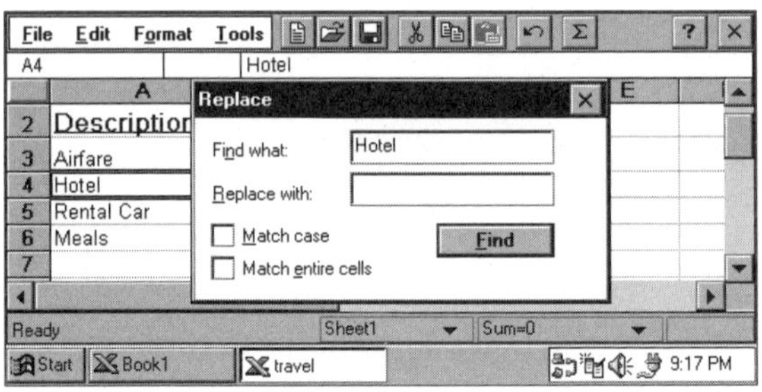

Figure 7-19: Use the Replace dialog box to replace data within your worksheet.

3. **In the Find what field, type the data that you want to replace.**
4. **Type the data that you want to replace the specified data with in the Replace with field.**

   Type the desired replacement data in this field. Pocket Excel places the exact text that you type in the location that you specified.

5. **Tap on the Find button.**

   Pocket Excel searches the worksheet from the current cursor location to the end of the document. It stops when it locates the first occurrence of the data that you entered in the Find what field. When Pocket Excel locates the matching text, it highlights the text, and the Find/Replace dialog box appears, as shown in Figure 7-20.

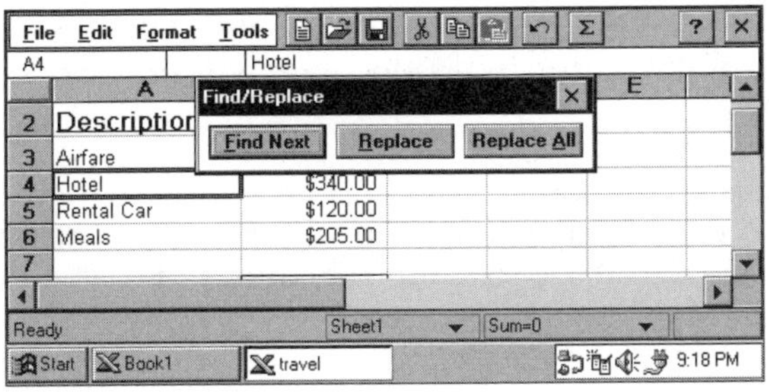

Figure 7-20: Pocket Excel locates the data and confirms that you really want to replace it.

Performing quick calculations

Obviously, worksheets serve a valuable function, but sometimes you just yearn for a calculator.

Well, you are in luck. You don't need to dig through those drawers to locate your trusty calculator; Windows CE provides one for you. Now you can have the best of both worlds — create elaborate spreadsheets and figure out the cost of two gallons of milk.

The Calculator program is normally located in the Accessories folder on your handheld PC. The icon for the Calculator program resembles a miniature calculator.

The Calculator program is similar to an adding machine; on the left side of the screen, it keeps a running total of the calculations that you have performed. The totals remain in the list box until you choose Edit⇨Clear Paper Tape.

To use the Calculator program, you can enter the values on the keyboard or tap on the desired buttons on the screen. Obviously, not all the buttons on the display are available on the keyboard, but you can find the buttons you use most often.

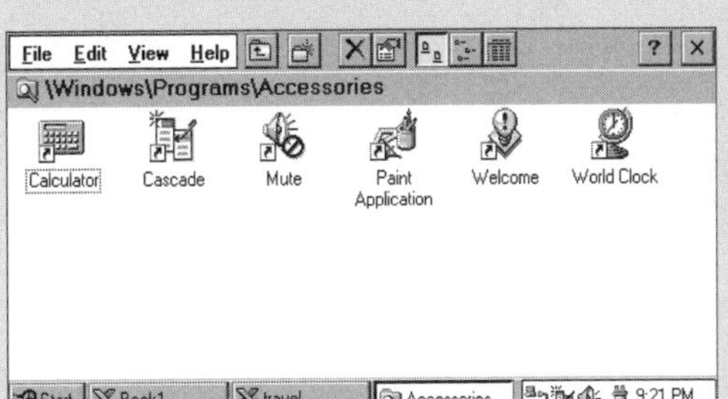

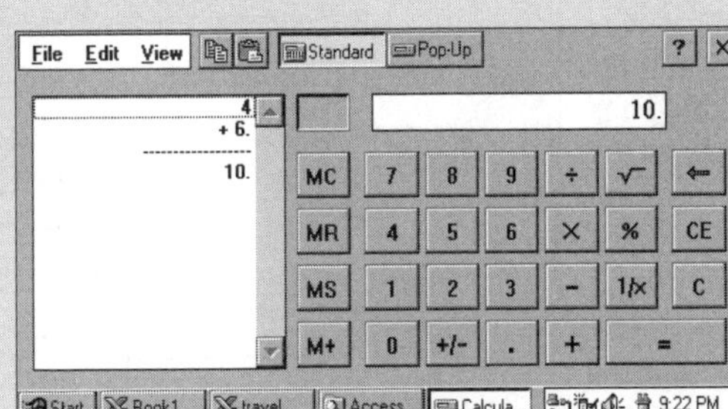

6. **To replace the highlighted data, tap on the Replace button.**

   If you don't want to replace the data, tap on the Find button, and Pocket Excel searches through the document for the next appearance of the data.

If you are confident that you want to change every location of the data specified in the Find what field, you can tap on the Replace All button and have Pocket Excel replace all the remaining locations of the text without prompting you first.

Working with Different Worksheets

Microsoft created workbooks to provide a more convenient way of linking together different worksheets. In Pocket Excel, each workbook can contain several related worksheets. For example, within a workbook titled Budget, you can have a separate budget worksheet for each month of the year.

When you open a specific workbook, Pocket Excel opens all the worksheets contained in the workbook. The worksheets are initially arranged in the order that they were added to the workbook. You can, however, rearrange them, as well as rename, remove, and add additional worksheets.

Most of the different options for worksheets are available in the Modify Sheets dialog box, shown in Figure 7-21. This dialog box appears when you choose Tools⇨Modify Sheets.

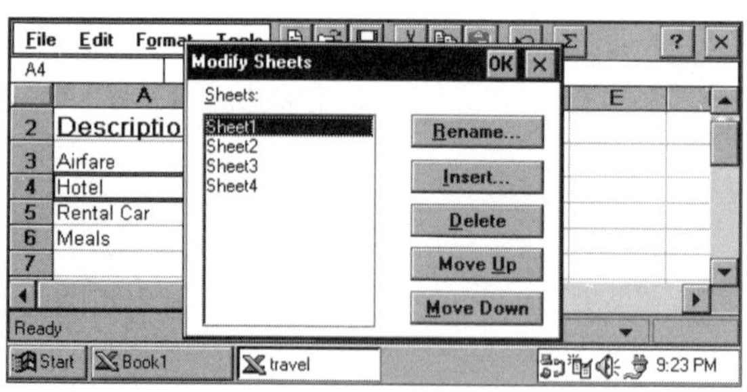

Figure 7-21: The Modify Sheets dialog box lists all the current worksheets in your workbook.

Viewing a different worksheet

Having access to different worksheets doesn't do you much good if you can view only the first one that appears. To view another worksheet within the currently displayed workbook, choose Tools⇨Modify Sheets to display the Modify Sheet window. Then highlight the desired worksheet and tap on the OK button in the right corner of the window.

You can also view a different worksheet by tapping on the Down Arrow button next to the worksheet name at the bottom of the screen. On the menu that appears (see Figure 7-22), tap on the name of the desired worksheet.

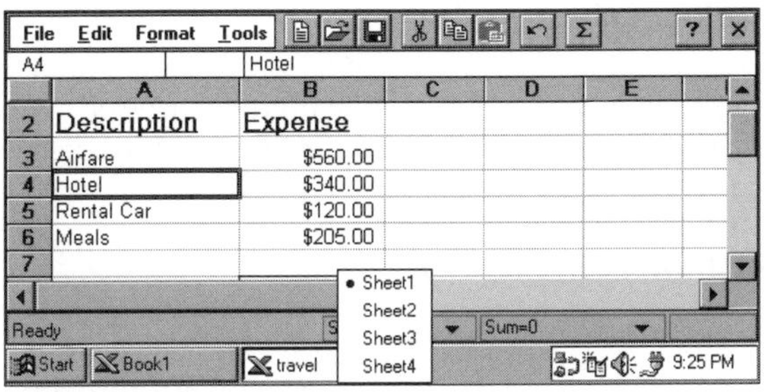

Figure 7-22: Use the menu to select the worksheet you want to view.

Changing the name of a worksheet

You may want to apply more creative names to each worksheet than those assigned by Pocket Excel. Pocket Excel, after all, uses such lifeless names as Sheet1, Sheet2, and Sheet3. Modifying the name of a worksheet is easy. Just follow these steps:

1. **Choose Tools⇨Modify Sheets.**

   The Modify Sheets window appears.

2. **Highlight the name of the worksheet that you want to rename.**

   Tap on the name with the stylus.

3. **Tap on the Rename button.**

   The Rename Sheet dialog box appears as shown in Figure 7-23.

4. **Type the new name for the worksheet in the Sheet name field.**

   You can assign a name of up to 31 characters in length.

5. **Tap on the OK button at the top of the Rename Sheet dialog box to change the name.**

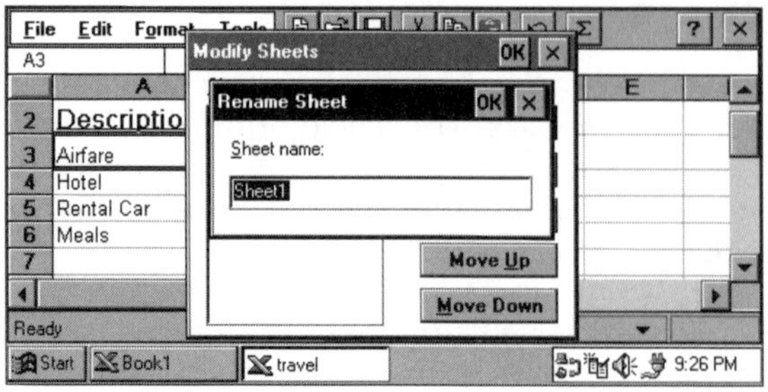

Figure 7-23: Enter the new name for a worksheet in the Rename Sheet dialog box.

Adding a new worksheet

Pocket Excel automatically creates four worksheets for each workbook. You can follow these steps when you want to add additional worksheets to a workbook:

1. **Choose Tools⇨Modify Sheets.**

   The Modify Sheets window appears.

2. **In the Modify Sheets dialog box, tap on the Insert button.**

   The Insert Sheet dialog box appears as shown in Figure 7-24.

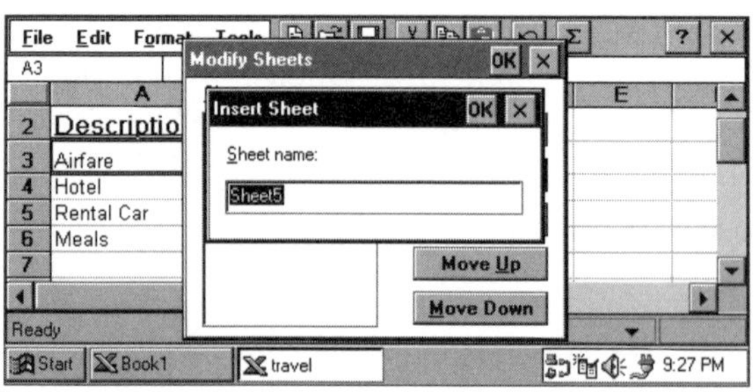

Figure 7-24: Name the new worksheet before it is added to the workbook.

3. **Enter a name for the worksheet in the Sheet name field.**

   You don't have to name the worksheet; if you don't enter a name, Pocket Excel uses the name that appears in the field. You can assign a name to the worksheet of up to 31 characters in length.

4. **Tap on the OK button at the top of the Insert Sheet window to add the sheet to the list in the Modify Sheets dialog box.**

Getting rid of a worksheet

You can remove a worksheet by using the Modify Sheets dialog box. Highlight the desired screen and tap on the Delete button. A confirmation message appears, asking you to verify your selection (see Figure 7-25). To remove the worksheet, tap on the Yes button; to keep it, tap on the No button.

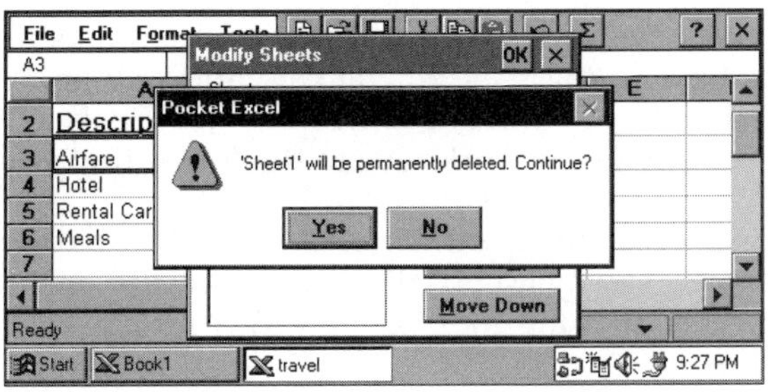

Figure 7-25: Pocket Excel verifies your selection before removing a worksheet.

Reordering the worksheets

You can also use the Modify Sheets dialog box to change the order of the worksheets within the workbook. To move a worksheet, highlight the worksheet and tap on either the Move Up button or the Move Down button. Repeat the process until the worksheets are listed in the order you want.

Closing a Workbook

You can have several Pocket Excel workbooks open at the same time. The number you can open varies based on the amount of memory you have available and the size of each workbook. I suggest that you don't open more than three workbooks at a time. Having too much stuff open makes working difficult.

When you get tired of working on a workbook, you can close it so that it does not eat your handheld PC's memory. To close a workbook, tap on the X button in the top-right corner of the screen. If you have only one workbook open in Pocket Excel, Pocket Excel also closes itself when you tap on the X button. If you still have other workbooks open, the current workbook closes, and Pocket Excel displays the last workbook that you worked on.

You can also close a workbook by choosing File⇨Close.

If you have not previously saved the document, a message window asks you whether you want to save the workbook before closing it. To save it, tap on the Yes button. If you messed up the workbook or just decide that you don't want it, tap on the No button to have Pocket Excel trash the workbook.

Saving a Workbook

Whenever you create a new workbook or modify an existing one, you need to save it in order to be able to access it again at another time. When you save a workbook that you have created using Microsoft Pocket Excel, Windows CE places a copy of the workbook in the folder that you specify.

Save the workbook not only when you finish working on it but also while you are working on it. By saving it periodically, you help to ensure that you don't lose your work if something goes wrong with your handheld PC.

Saving a workbook for the first time

When you save a workbook for the first time, you need to name the workbook and specify the location where you want to store it in the Save As dialog box. The Save As dialog box appears when you tap on the Save button in the Standard toolbar at the top of the screen. The Save button looks like a floppy diskette for a desktop computer.

To save a workbook for the first time, follow these steps:

1. **Tap on the Save button on the Standard toolbar.**

   The Save As dialog box appears (see Figure 7-26). The Save As dialog box appears only if you have not previously saved the workbook. You can also choose File⇨Save.

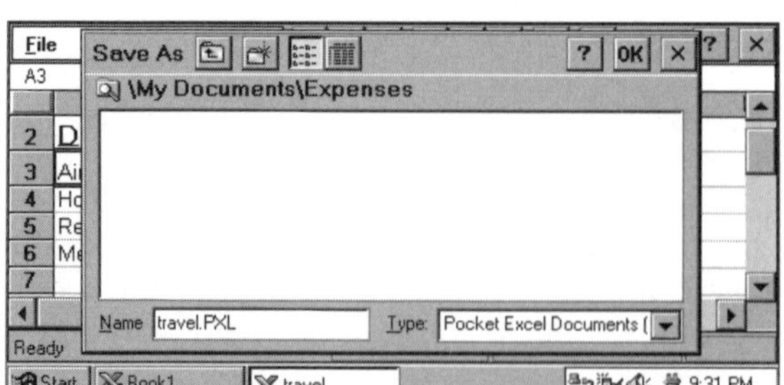

Figure 7-26: Indicate the name of your workbook and its location in the Save As dialog box.

2. **Tap the folder in which you want to save the workbook.**

   Whenever you save a workbook using Pocket Excel, Windows CE assumes that you want to place it in the My Documents folder.

   If you can't find an icon for the folder where you want to store the workbook, tap on the Previous Folder button. The Previous Folder button looks like a folder with an up arrow on it. When you tap on the icon, the current folder is closed and the parent folder, or the folder above the current folder, is opened.

3. **Enter a name for the document in the Name field.**

   You can assign any name to the workbook. Just remember to use a name that indicates the kind of information that the workbook contains.

4. **In the Type field, tap on the Down Arrow button and highlight the Pocket Excel Documents type.**

   You want to save all workbooks as Pocket Excel Documents (*.pxl). If you transfer the document to your PC, Handheld PC Explorer converts it to a file with an .xls extension so that you can open it in Microsoft Excel.

5. **Tap on the OK button to save the new workbook.**

TIP

You can also save a document by pressing the Ctrl and S keys simultaneously. Just another pointer for all of you keyboard fanatics.

TECHNICAL STUFF

A filename can be 255 characters long. This length includes the period and three character extension that is added to each Pocket Word document to identify its file type. So basically, each filename can be 251 characters long. These characters don't count as part of the 251: / ? : * “ < > |, and they can't be used to name a workbook..

Saving a workbook that you previously saved

You should periodically save a workbook that you are working on. You never know when you may run out of battery power or some other unplanned event may occur that causes you to lose power.

If you have already saved the workbook once, tap on the Save button in the Standard toolbar.

Quickly creating a new folder

You may find that the folder where you want to store your document does not exist on your handheld PC. If so, you can create the folder while you are saving the document.

To create a new folder for a document, open the folder where you want to place the new folder.

Then tap on the New Folder button in the toolbar at the top of the Save As dialog box. The New Folder button looks like a folder with a starburst behind it.

When you tap on the New folder button, a folder icon appears in the folder listing with the name New Folder highlighted. To name the folder, enter a name for the folder and then press the Enter key. After you create the folder, you can specify the name for the document and then tap on the OK button.

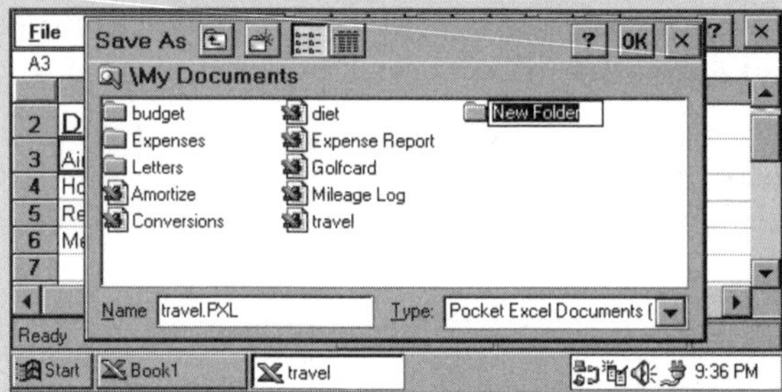

Saving a workbook with a new name

After you save a workbook, you may want to save it in another location or give it another name by choosing File⇨Save As.

When you choose the Save As option, the Save As dialog box appears on the screen, as shown in Figure 7-27. The current name of the workbook appears in the Name field. To change the name, type a new name in the Name field and tap on the OK button.

To save the workbook with the same name but in a different folder, locate the desired folder in the folder listing and double-tap on its icon to open it. If the folder does not appear in the listing, tap on the Previous Folder icon to close the current folder and open the folder above it.

When you use the Save As option, the original workbook remains with the same name and in the same location.

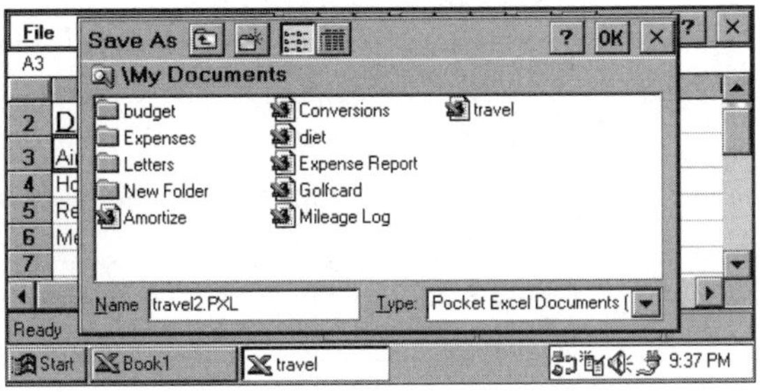

Figure 7-27: Use the Save As dialog box to change the name of your document and/or specify a new location.

You can also use the Save As option to save the workbook with a new file format by selecting a different option in the Type field.

REMEMBER

Remember, if you want to get rid of the original workbook, you need to use the Windows CE Explorer and delete it. For more information, see Chapter 8.

Opening a Microsoft Excel Workbook

One of the big advantages of owning a handheld PC that runs Windows CE is the fact that you can transfer most Microsoft Excel workbooks to your handheld PC. But, unfortunately, the more complex the formatting is in your Microsoft Excel workbook, the more you lose during the conversion.

When you convert a Microsoft Excel workbook to a Pocket Excel workbook, the file extension changes from .xls to .pxl. When you convert the workbook back to your PC, the extension changes back to .xls.

Because Pocket Excel is a scaled-down version of Microsoft Excel, several of the fancy formatting features in Windows 95 are not available on Pocket Excel. Table 7-4 outlines some of the common formatting features and explains what happens when you copy a spreadsheet to Pocket Excel.

Don't be too concerned with the information presented in Table 7-4. Use it as a reference if you want to determine why something was not converted in your workbook. Just keep in mind that most of the fancy features that are used in Microsoft Excel to make your spreadsheet more appealing can't be converted to Pocket Excel.

Table 7-4 Lost Formatting when Converting from Excel to Pocket Excel

Excel Formatting Option	*Result under Pocket Excel*
Alignment	All vertical text appears as horizontal text.
Borders	All border types appear as a single line and all patterns are removed.
Fonts	All fonts that are not available on your handheld PC are matched to the closest available font.
Font Color	Any colored fonts are converted to the closest shade of gray.
Formats	Custom number formats are displayed using the closest number format that is supported by Pocket Excel.
Formula	All formulas that are not supported by Pocket Excel are removed from the spreadsheet. If your Microsoft Excel spreadsheet contains a formula that is an array of values or contains an array argument, the formula is converted to a value.
Functions	All functions that are not supported by Pocket Excel are removed from the spreadsheet, and the value of the function appears in the corresponding cell.
Names	All names that reference other workbooks, arrays, formulas, or intersection ranges are replaced with the value `#NAME?`, indicating that the name could not be converted.
Objects	All types of objects are removed.
Pictures	All pictures are removed during conversion.
Pivot table data	All data is converted to values.
Sheets	All chart sheets, dialog sheets, and Excel 4.0 macro sheets are replaced with a blank worksheet.
Text boxes	All text boxes are removed.
VBA modules	All VBA modules are replaced with a blank worksheet.

Keep in mind that when these options are removed or changed in the workbook during the conversion to Pocket Excel, they are added back in when you convert it back to Excel. Therefore, if you decide to copy the same workbook back to your PC, you may want to place it in a different location so that you do not overwrite the original. Otherwise, you may find yourself forced to do a great deal of reformatting to make the workbook look like the original on your desktop computer.

Printing Worksheets

Unfortunately, on most handheld PCs you can't print a worksheet directly from your handheld PC. Check out the documentation that came with the handheld PC to determine whether your handheld PC can print documents.

Assuming that your handheld PC cannot print documents, you need to use the H/PC Explorer program on your desktop computer to print your worksheets. Connect your handheld PC to your desktop computer, highlight the desired worksheet in H/PC Explorer, and then choose File➪Print, as shown in Figure 7-28.

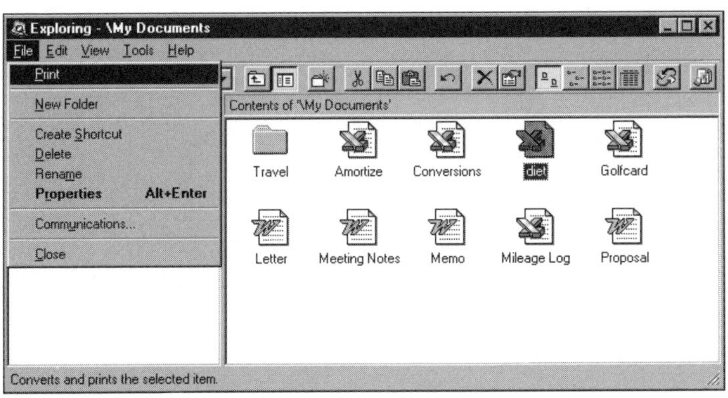

Figure 7-28: If you can't print a worksheet from your handheld PC, you can use H/PC Explorer to send it to the printer.

When you select the Print option, the H/PC Explorer program automatically performs the following steps on your desktop computer:

1. Temporarily copies the selected Pocket Excel worksheet to your computer. After you print, it removes the worksheet from your computer.

2. Converts the Pocket Excel worksheet to a Microsoft Excel worksheet.
3. Opens the converted worksheet within Microsoft Excel.
4. Sends the worksheet to the primary printer for your computer.
5. Closes Microsoft Excel.

For more information about working with the H/PC Explorer on your desktop computer, refer to the information in Part III.

Chapter 8
Managing Your Files

In This Chapter

- Locating files
- Determining file types
- Viewing file properties
- Creating new files and folders
- Removing and renaming files and folders
- Changing the location of a file
- Working with added storage on PC Cards
- Sharing files with another handheld PC or desktop computer

Figuring out how your handheld PC stores files is probably one of the most difficult things you must do in order to use your handheld PC. You know that horrible syndrome of the lost file. (I know, I was there yesterday.) Windows CE comes with its own type of file management that you can tailor to fit your likes and dislikes.

This chapter explains how to use the various file management features available with Windows CE. I discuss the basics of using Windows CE Explorer to perform file management tasks, such as viewing the contents of folders, creating new files, and moving and deleting files. I also talk about how to locate files and folders on PC storage cards and how to share files with other handheld PCs that are running Windows CE.

Locating Files

Imagine the ideally organized office in which all important, and even not so important, documents are filed in easy-to-find folders in a file cabinet. If you want a document, you just pull open the appropriate drawer in the file cabinet, open the appropriate folder, and remove the document. It may seem like I am describing an unrealistic dream scenario, but the file management system that Windows CE uses resembles the one in the ideally organized office.

The Windows CE "file cabinet" is called *Windows CE Explorer;* this program provides access to all the folders on your handheld PC. You can use two methods to open the main drawer of the Windows CE Explorer. The easiest method is to double-tap on the My Handheld PC icon that is located on your desktop. The My Handheld PC icon resembles a handheld PC with a stylus pointing at it. If you don't like that option or if you just like to be different, tap on the Explore option in the Start menu.

When you select an option that opens the Windows CE Explorer, the main folder is opened on your handheld PC (see Figure 8-1). This folder is named My Handheld PC, which explains where the name for the icon came from. (Or perhaps the icon name came first.) It contains all the folders and files on your handheld PC.

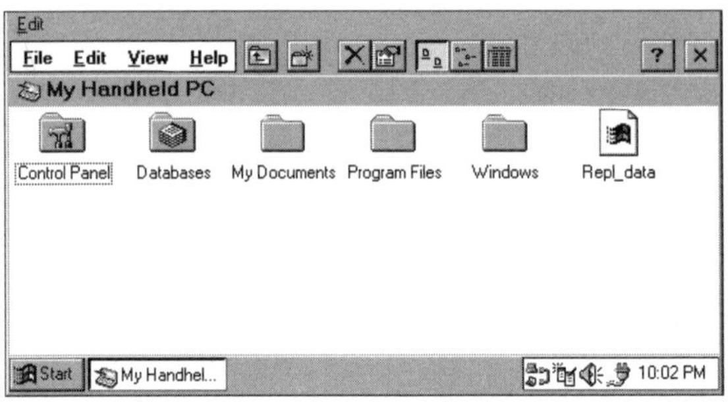

Figure 8-1: Windows CE Explorer enables you to view the contents of your handheld PC.

When you look inside the My Handheld PC folder, you will probably see at least five other folders. (You may see more if you have created some folders of your own.) Each of these folders contains a specific type of file, as outlined in Table 8-1.

Table 8-1 Figuring Out the My Handheld PC Folder

Folder	*Purpose*
 Control Panel	The Control Panel folder contains all the stuff you need to control the settings for your handheld PC. You also can open this folder by tapping on the Settings option in the Start menu. For information about the contents of the Control Panel folder, see Chapter 18.

Folder	*Purpose*
 Databases	The Databases folder maintains the database files used by the programs that run under Windows CE. A *database* is essentially a large file that keeps track of related pieces of information. Windows CE maintains a database in this folder that contains all the contacts you have set up by using the Contacts program. You should leave this folder alone; if you mess with one of the database files in this folder, your Windows CE programs may not work properly.
 My Documents	The My Documents folder is a generic folder that is the home for all your documents. Each time you create a document in a program, Windows CE stores the document in this folder. If all your documents are in one location, they should be easy for you to locate. If you use this folder for documents, you may want to create additional folders to sort the documents into groups.
 Program Files	The Program Files folder contains additional folders that hold all the programs on your handheld PC, with the exception of the system programs. When you add a new program to your handheld PC, Windows CE creates a folder for the program files used by the new program in the Program Files folder.
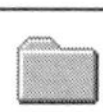 Windows	The Windows folder contains all of the files and programs that are required to make Windows CE work properly. Try to avoid making changes to the files in this folder; Windows CE uses them to keep your handheld PC running efficiently.

Changing the way you view folder contents

You can view the contents of a folder in Windows CE Explorer in many ways. You can change the way you view a folder's contents by using the View menu (shown in Figure 8-2) or by selecting one of the three buttons described in Table 8-2.

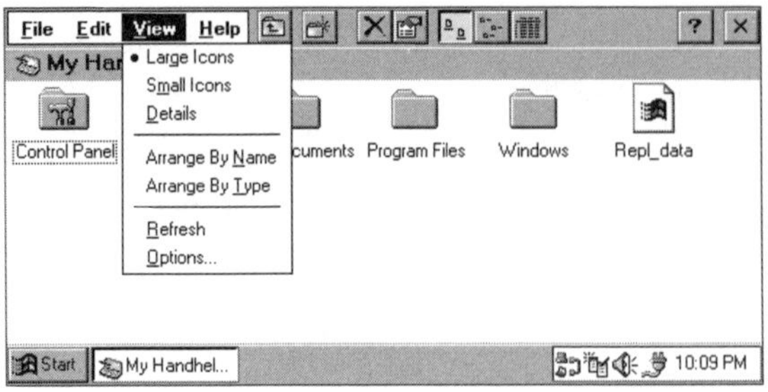

Figure 8-2: The View menu provides options for customizing the way you view the contents of a folder.

Table 8-2	**Windows CE Explorer View Options**
Select This Button	***If You Want To***
	View the contents of the folder by using large icons. You can quickly see what is in the folder, although you can't see everything on-screen at the same time if the folder contains several items.
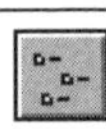	View the contents of the folder by using small icons. You can see more icons on-screen at the same time than you can if you use large icons.
	View the details about each item in the folder, including the name of the item, its size, type, and the date and time when it was last modified.

When you view the details of the folder, you may find that the columns that display the information are not wide enough. You can adjust the width of a column by touching the stylus to the separator line next to the column name, and then dragging the line to the size you want.

Keep in mind that Windows CE does not save your view settings within Windows CE Explorer. In other words, the folder's contents appear in large icons every time you run the Windows CE Explorer.

Within any view, you can sort the items either by name or by file type. To sort by name, choose View➪Arrange By Name. To sort by file type, choose View➪Arrange By Type.

If you have added an item to this folder since opening the Windows CE Explorer, you may need to refresh the screen before the new item appears in the list. To refresh the list, choose View➪Refresh.

Windows CE Explorer lets you hide certain system files so that you do not accidentally delete them. To hide system files, choose View➪Options to display the Options dialog box, as shown in Figure 8-3. Then select Hide Hidden files and files with the following extensions: DLL, CPL, and DRV. This option is automatically set for you as the default so that you don't get confused when you find a bunch of system files that Windows CE needs in order to run properly.

If you select the Hide file extensions check box, you will not see the three-character extensions that identify the file type to the system.

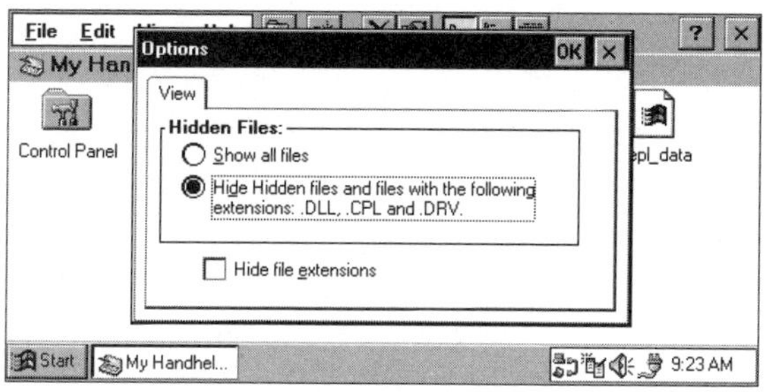

Figure 8-3: Use the Options dialog box to hide system files when you view information in Windows CE Explorer.

Looking inside a folder

You cannot look at an item in a folder in your file cabinet without locating and opening the folder. The same holds true on your handheld PC — you cannot run any of the programs or view any of the documents in a folder until you have opened the folder.

To open a folder in Windows CE Explorer, you simply double-tap on the folder's icon.

When you open a folder, the folder's name appears in the bar under the toolbar. This bar is commonly called a *banner.* For those of you who come from a DOS background, the banner basically contains the path. The *path* is just a computer nerd term that indicates the names of the folders that are currently open. For example, in Figure 8-4 the path bar says `\Program Files\Games`. Since `Games` is the last folder name listed, it is the folder that appears on the screen.

Keep in mind that after you open a folder that is within the My Handheld PC folder, the name of the main folder (My Handheld PC) does not appear in the path.

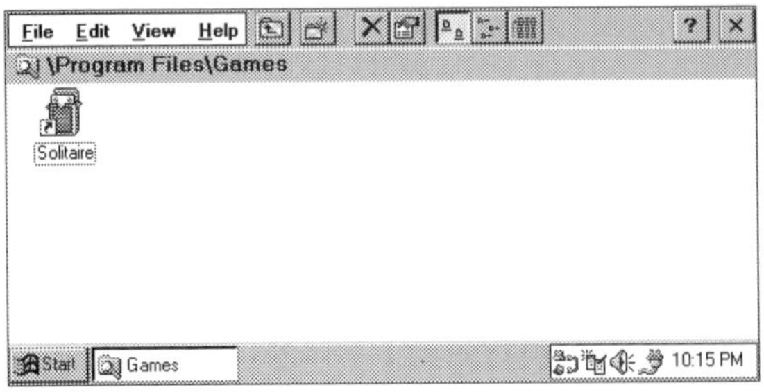

Figure 8-4: The path appears in the banner under the toolbar.

To close the current folder and view the contents of the previous folder, you can tap on the Previous Folder icon on the toolbar. The Previous Folder button resembles a folder with an arrow on it. You can keep closing folders and displaying the previous folder contents until you get back to the Desktop folder.

Working with Folders

In keeping with the office theme, Windows CE uses files and folders to deal with everything that is stored on your handheld PC. A *folder* is a place to store related files, just like you store related pieces of paper in a folder on your desk. For example, Windows CE comes with a folder called My Documents, in which you can place documents you create on your handheld PC.The word *file* is a general term that refers to each item on your handheld PC, such as programs, word processing documents, spreadsheets, and so on. You use the Windows CE Explorer to deal with the different files and folders that you have on your handheld PC.

If you are one of those old-timers who started using computers when DOS was the only operating system, you may be comforted to know that *folder* is just another name for *directory*.

When you see an icon that resembles a folder, tap on the icon, and the folder opens and reveals it contents — usually a bunch of files. A folder can also contain other folders. In fact, Windows CE lays out the entire storage area of your handheld PC by using a series of folders within folders. The main folder on your handheld PC is named My Handheld PC. This folder contains all other folders and files on your handheld PC.

The following sections describe several interesting things that you can do with folders and files.

Creating a new folder

Hopefully, you are not content using the folders that come with Windows CE. After all, you should organize your own stuff. The more folders you use to organize your files, the more easily you can locate your files later.

Creating a new folder under Windows CE is almost as easy as picking up a new folder and writing a name on it. To create a new folder, you can either select File⇨New Folder or tap on the New Folder button on the taskbar. The New Folder icon resembles a folder with a starburst behind it.

To create a new folder called Budget within the My Documents folder, follow these steps.

1. **Open the Start menu and tap on the Explore option to display Windows CE Explorer.**

   You can also tap on the My Handheld PC icon to display Windows CE Explorer.

2. **Double-tap on the My Documents icon to display the current contents of the My Documents folder.**

   Before you create a folder, you always need to open the folder where you want the new folder to reside.

3. **Tap on the New Folder icon or choose File⇨New Folder.**

   A new folder icon appears with the name New Folder highlighted (see Figure 8-5).

4. **Type a new name for the folder.**

   Because the name of the folder is highlighted, you can simply start typing to enter a name for the folder — for example, **Budget**.

5. **Press the Enter key.**

   You can double-tap on the folder to open it and begin adding files to it.

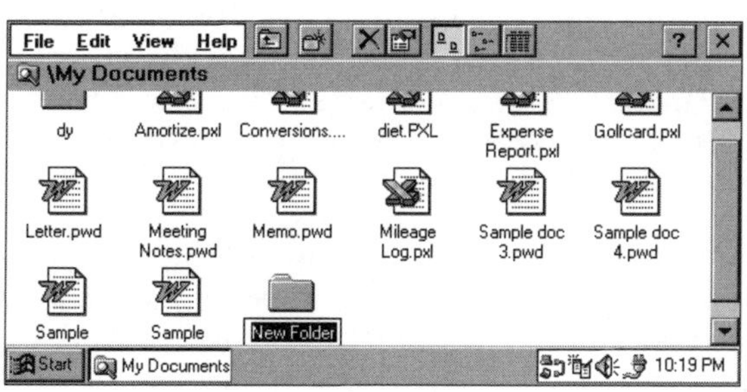

Figure 8-5: You can add new folders to organize the related files on your handheld PC.

Renaming a folder or file

With Windows CE Explorer, you can easily modify the names of files and folders on your handheld PC. Simply tap on the item to highlight it and then choose File⇨Rename. Explorer draws a box around the name and places the cursor at the end of the name. If you want to replace the entire name, start typing, and the new name appears in the box. If you want to modify only a portion of the name, use the arrow keys to move the cursor to the desired location in the name and then begin typing.

Use the Rename option to change the name of your personal document files only. Do not attempt to rename system or program files. If you avoid renaming any files in the Windows folder, where Windows CE stores the files it requires for the operating system, you should be okay. If you make changes to your system or program files, your handheld PC may not run properly.

Moving stuff around — cut, copy, and paste

Not too many of us are content to leave things where we first put them. You know how it is — the plant looks just fine in the corner until you buy new drapes. Then you need to move the plant into the kitchen.

Well, lucky for you, you have plenty of ways to move items around on your handheld PC. You can move a file, a folder full of files, or several files and folders all at the same time, as long as you move them to the same folder.

You can use the Cut, Copy, and Paste options on the Edit menu of Windows CE Explorer to move and copy any files and folders that are not read-only. For example, to move the January, February, and March budget spreadsheets inside your Budget folder, follow these steps:

1. **Locate and highlight the files you want to move.**

   If you select multiple files, as shown in Figure 8-6, you can move them at the same time. If the files are located next to each other, you can select them by tapping on the first file, holding down the Shift key, and then tapping on the last item. If the items are not next to each other, hold down the Ctrl key while you tap on the files you want to select.

2. **Choose Edit⇨Cut.**

   Explorer copies the files into the handheld PC's storage closet, commonly referred to as the Clipboard. The selected file icons appear grayed-out on-screen to remind you that you just cut them.

   If you select the Copy option rather than the Cut option, the items you select remain in the original folder.

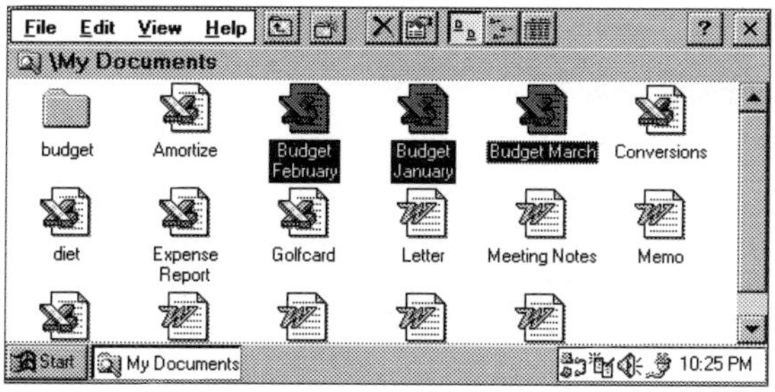

Figure 8-6: You can select multiple files.

3. **Open the folder where you want to put the files.**

   If you want to put the files in a folder that is in the current folder, simply double-tap on the folder icon to open it; otherwise, tap on the Previous Folder button and find the correct folder.

4. **Choose Edit⇨Paste.**

   Windows CE copies the stored items out of the Clipboard and into your folder.

TIP: You can use the drag-and-drop method to move items into a folder whose icon sits on the screen. Simply touch the stylus to the item you want to move and drag the item to the new folder.

Deleting a folder or file

With Windows CE Explorer, you can quickly remove unwanted folders or files. Simply tap on the item to highlight it and then tap on the Delete icon on the toolbar. The Delete icon resembles a big X. You can also delete a selected item by choosing File⇨Delete.

When you delete an item, Windows CE verifies your selection by displaying an alert box, as shown in Figure 8-7. This way, Windows CE makes sure that you really want to delete the item you selected. If you are sure that you want to delete the item, tap on the Yes button, and Windows CE moves the item to the Recycle Bin to await trash pickup. If you tap on the No button, the item remains unaffected in the same location.

REMEMBER: You can restore an item to its original location as long as you have not emptied the Recycle Bin. After you empty the Recycle Bin, however, its contents are gone forever. After all, you don't expect to be able to find something after it has been hauled to the city dump. Do you?

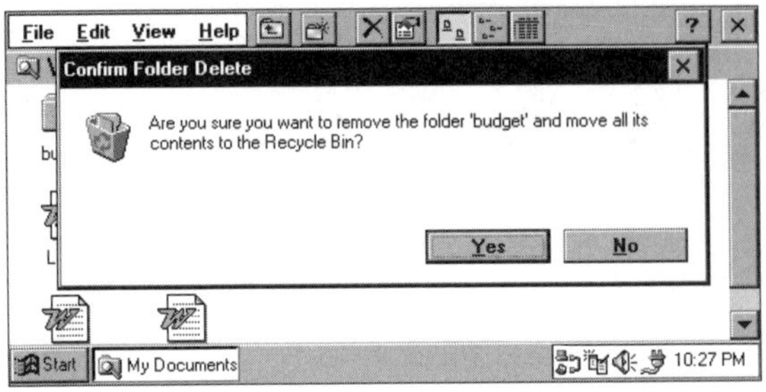

Figure 8-7: Before deleting an item, Windows CE verifies your selection.

If you delete a shortcut off the Windows CE desktop or from any location on your handheld PC, Windows CE deletes only the shortcut; the original program remains intact in the appropriate folder. Remember, you can tell a shortcut icon from the original program icon by the small arrow in the bottom-left corner of the shortcut icon. Almost all of the icons sitting on your desktop, with the exception of the My Handheld PC and the Recycle Bin, are shortcuts.

If you want to remove a program from your handheld PC, use the Remove Programs option from the Control Panel, as described in Chapter 18.

Do not delete files from the Windows folder. If you remove the wrong files, your handheld PC will not run properly.

Rescuing a deleted file

Before you pull out too much hair over that report you accidentally deleted, you should know that you can retrieve it if the file is still waiting in the Recycle Bin. Simply follow these steps:

1. **Open the Recycle Bin by double-tapping on the Recycle Bin icon on your desktop.**

   The Recycle Bin window appears (see Figure 8-8).

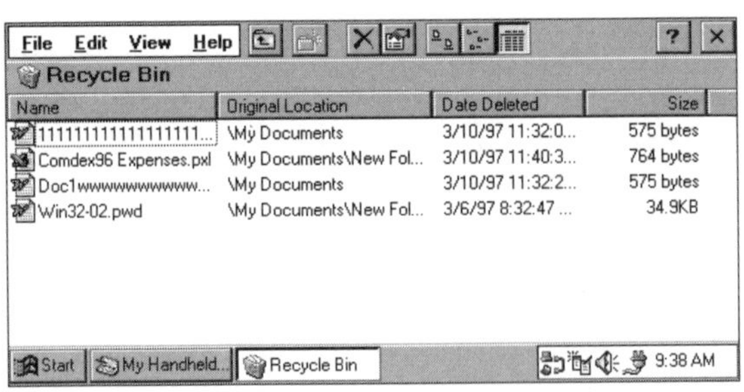

Figure 8-8: Double-tap on the Recycle Bin icon to see the contents of the Recycle Bin.

2. **Highlight the file you want to undelete.**
3. **Choose File⇨Restore.**

   The file is placed into its original folder location and is essentially as good as new.

To get the full scoop on the Recycle Bin, check out Chapter 2.

Determining file types

As I am sure you have already determined, your handheld PC contains many different types of files. Many of the types of files are just program files that are required to make a specific program work properly under Windows CE.

You may be able to determine a file's type by examining the file's icon or by viewing the file's properties.

Understanding file icons

All files have icons that represent them in Windows CE Explorer. Table 8-3 describes several standard icons that are used to indicate specific types of files.

Table 8-3 Common File Icons

Icon	*Always Indicates*
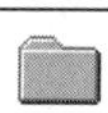	A folder that contains other files and possibly even other folders.
	A document that was created in Pocket Word and saved as a Pocket Word document.
	A document that was created in Pocket Excel and saved as a Pocket Excel workbook.
	A file that contains only text. If it was created in Pocket Word, it does not have any of the formatting options you may have used, such as bold, italics, or font size changes.
	A database file. These files are used with programs such as the Contacts program to maintain the data that you add to the program.
	A help file. These help files provide extra information about a specific topic.
	A bitmap graphics file. If this file is copied to your PC, it is converted to a .BMP file.
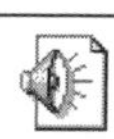	A sound file. These types of files contain the different sounds, such as the beep when it is time for an appointment, that you may hear on your handheld PC.

Files with .EXE extensions are program files. The .EXE extension is an abbreviation for *executable,* which refers to a file that is actually a program. If you double-tap on the icon for the EXE file, the specified program opens on your handheld PC.

Viewing file properties

Windows CE lets you gather more detailed information about each file on your handheld PC. The added information about a file appears in the Properties dialog box, as shown in Figure 8-9.

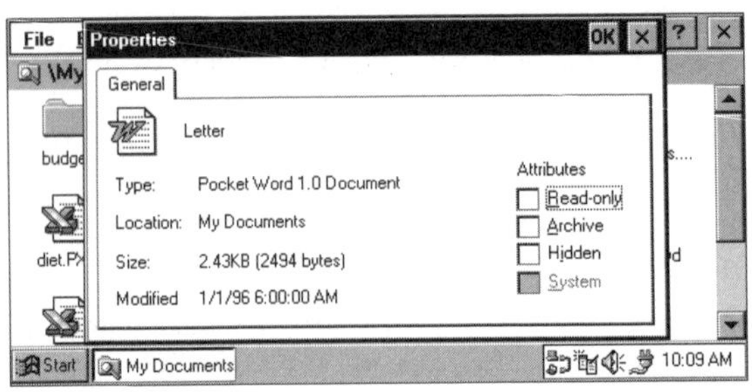

Figure 8-9: The Properties dialog box provides important information about each file.

The Properties dialog box provides some important information about each file, such as the file type, its location on your handheld PC (the name of the folder where it is located), the size of the file, and the date and time when the file was last modified.

The Properties dialog box also allows you to modify the attributes of the file. Just select the desired check box in the Attributes section of the window. For example, if you want to keep the file from being modified, select the Read-only check box. By setting a file as read-only, you can view the file but can't make any modifications to it.

If you select the Hidden attribute, the file still appears when you view the folder in Windows CE Explorer if you have the Show all files option selected in the Options window.

The System attribute can be selected only by Windows CE. It identifies files that are required by the Windows CE operating system. If you find a file with the System attribute selected, do not try to delete the file.

Working with Files on a PC Card

Most handheld PCs come with a slot in which you can add different types of PCMCIA cards, commonly referred to as PC Cards. You can use a PCMCIA slot to add features, such as a modem or a storage card, to your handheld PC. If you insert a storage card into your handheld PC, you see a folder called PC Card in the My Handheld PC folder when you open Windows CE Explorer (see Figure 8-10).

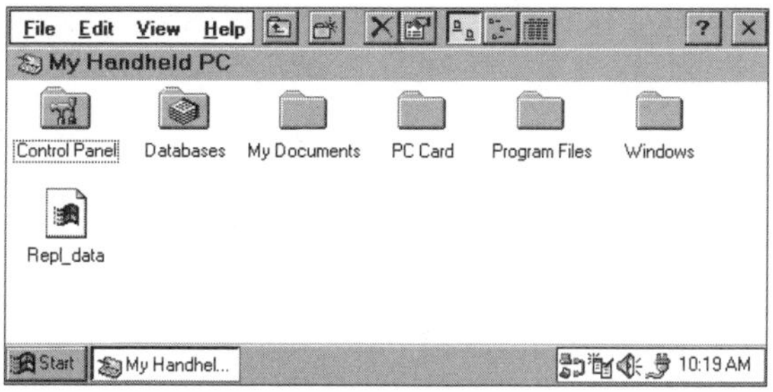

Figure 8-10: A folder is added so that you can manage the files on the card.

Although the storage card is not a permanent fixture in your handheld PC, Windows CE treats it as just another folder on the handheld PC. You may want to think of a storage card as essentially an expensive floppy disk for your handheld PC.

You can copy and move files between the card and your handheld PC. To copy files from either location, highlight the files in Windows CE Explorer and choose Edit⇨Copy. Then locate the new spot for the file and choose Edit⇨Paste. To move files, use the Cut option rather than the Copy option.

Even though Windows CE treats the storage card as a folder, you cannot copy or move folders between your handheld PC and the storage card. If you want a specific folder to exist on the storage card, you need to create the new folder on the card and then copy the files into it.

WARNING! Do not remove a storage card while your handheld PC is turned on. If you pull out a card with your handheld PC turned on, you may lose some of your data or even ruin the card (and believe me, they are not cheap enough to just throw away). Before removing a card, make sure that the files from the card are all closed within Windows CE. Then turn off the handheld PC and remove the card.

TIP: Because each handheld PC is designed differently, there is no exact science when it comes to removing the PC cards from a handheld PC. For information about removing the card from your handheld PC, refer to the hardware documentation that came with your handheld PC.

Sharing Files with Another Handheld PC

You can share files on your handheld PC with someone else who has a Windows CE handheld PC as long as both handheld PCs have an infrared port.

The infrared port looks sort of like a black mirror. To determine whether a handheld PC has an infrared port, refer to the hardware documentation that came with the handheld PC.

You can perform the following steps to transfer files between two handheld PCs:

1. **Make sure that both handheld PCs are turned on and Windows CE Explorer is running on each unit.**
2. **Place the handheld PCs so that the infrared ports are lined up.**

   The ports need to be within about three feet of each other, with nothing blocking the view. Because infrared ports use light beams to transfer data, they cannot transfer information if the ports do not have a good view of each other.
3. **On the first handheld PC (the one with the information), highlight the file you want to send to the other handheld PC.**

   Windows CE allows you to send only one file at a time using the infrared port. If you have multiple files that you want to copy to the other handheld PC, you need to repeat these steps for each file.
4. **Choose File⇨Send.**

   An alert box indicates that the handheld PC is looking for another handheld PC.
5. **On the other handheld PC, choose File⇨Receive.**

   When the handheld PCs make contact with each other, the file is transferred from the first handheld PC to the second handheld PC.

Some types of fluorescent lighting can interfere with the data transfer. If you have problems transferring data, try moving the handheld PCs to another location.

REMEMBER

The infrared ports use light beams to send information back and forth. You need to make sure that the infrared ports are not blocked by anything. If the ports cannot see each other, the handheld PCs cannot transfer data.

Part III

Interfacing with Your Desktop Computer

"OH, WELL SHOOT! MUST BE THAT NEW PAINT PROGRAM ON MY HANDHELD PC."

In this part . . .

You don't have to look too long at your handheld PC to realize that it's missing some common desktop computer features, such as a floppy drive, a CD-ROM drive, or other methods for loading new software programs. Fortunately, Windows CE does have a way of loading new software programs, backing up the contents of the handheld PC, and synchronizing appointments, tasks, and contacts with a desktop computer. In order to do these different tasks, you need to *interface,* or connect your handheld PC to a desktop computer.

This part covers everything you need to know to interface with a desktop computer and then tells you in a step-by-step fashion how to back up your handheld PC, load new software, and even synchronize all appointments, tasks, and contacts.

Chapter 9

Installing H/PC Explorer

In This Chapter

- Figuring out what is required to connect Windows CE to either Windows 95 or Windows NT 4.0
- Installing the desktop computer programs you need
- Connecting the interface cable

One of the biggest advantages of selecting a Windows CE handheld PC over other types of handheld devices (commonly referred to as PDAs) is the ability to easily interface with a desktop computer running either Windows 95 or Windows NT 4.0. Whew! Okay, I know that was a mouthful — so what exactly does that all mean?

To be as plain and simple as possible, you can connect your handheld PC to any desktop computer that is running Windows 95 or Windows NT 4.0. After you connect to the desktop computer, you have the ability to do all kinds of cool stuff. For example, you can copy a Microsoft Word document from your desktop computer and place it on your Windows CE handheld PC.

This chapter explains how to set up the connection between Windows CE and your desktop computer, including how to connect the serial cable between your handheld PC and your desktop computer and how to install the necessary software on your desktop computer.

Figuring Out when to Connect

By connecting your handheld PC to a desktop computer, you can move all kinds of information back and forth between the two machines. The desktop computer and handheld PC can become partners in the effort to make sure that you are able to accomplish your various tasks. Here is a list of the different things you can do when you interface your handheld PC with a desktop computer:

Different versions of H/PC Explorer

Many different versions of the H/PC Explorer setup program are available. Some of the CD-ROMs that are being packaged with the handheld PCs contain the original version of the H/PC Explorer program that only ran on Windows 95 and would only synchronize with Microsoft Schedule+. Other vendors are packaging a newer CD-ROM that contains the setup program for H/PC Explorer Version 1.1. This is the version of the CD that this chapter covers. This version is designed to work with both Windows 95 and Windows NT 4.0. It will also allow you to synchronize appointments, tasks, and contacts with either Microsoft Schedule+ or Microsoft Outlook.

The crazy part of this whole deal is that it is difficult for you to know which CD-ROM you have actually received with your handheld PC. The best way I know of is to do the following: Look at the actual CD-ROM — if the Microsoft logo states that it was designed for Windows 95/Windows NT, you have the current version; if the logo states designed for Windows 95 only, you probably want to locate the newer version.

You can contact your hardware vendor for a newer CD-ROM or download the setup program from the Internet. You can find the setup program at: `http://www.microsoft.com/windowsce/hpc/software/hpcexplorer.htm`.

- Install new programs on your handheld PC
- Back up your handheld PC in case something goes wrong
- Restore a backup after something has gone wrong on your handheld PC
- Copy files between the two machines
- Install new fonts on your handheld PC
- Make sure that appointments and tasks match on both machines

Understanding the Requirements for Connecting

Before you can interface your handheld PC with your desktop computer, you must complete a few tasks. Unfortunately, you're kind of stuck if you don't have a computer that is running either Windows 95 or Windows NT 4.0. The H/PC Explorer software (sometimes called Handheld PC Explorer) that comes with your handheld PC runs only on Windows 95 or Windows NT 4.0.

If you have a computer but are unsure whether your computer is running Windows 95 or Windows NT 4.0, the quickest way to find out is to look for the Start button at the bottom of the screen. If you do not have a Start button at the bottom of your screen, chances are you are running an older version of Windows. You can purchase a copy of Windows 95 or Windows NT 4.0 from any computer software store.

In order to interface your handheld PC with your desktop computer, you must install the H/PC Explorer program on your desktop computer. You need the *H/PC Explorer* to perform the interface tasks, such as backing up your handheld PC, or synchronizing appointments and tasks. If you have not already installed the program on your computer, see the "Running the H/PC Explorer Install Program" section in this chapter for step-by-step instructions on setting up the program.

Finally, you need a serial interface cable in order to connect your handheld PC to the desktop computer. If you did not receive one of these cables with your handheld PC, contact your handheld PC manufacturer for information about how to purchase one.

Connecting the Interface Cable

The only way to connect a Windows CE handheld PC to a desktop computer is to use the serial interface cable. When the cable is connected, you can copy data files and programs to and from your handheld PC.

This interface cable should have been packaged with your handheld PC when you purchased it. If you are not sure which cable it is, refer to the hardware documentation that came with your handheld PC. Some handheld PCs may not have been shipped with the cable; if this is the case with your handheld PC, you can obtain this cable by contacting your handheld PC's manufacturer.

You connect the cable to a serial port on the back of your computer. You can recognize the correct serial port because it has nine little pins poking out of it, as shown in Figure 9-1. If you only have a 25-pin serial port available on your computer, you need to locate an adapter to convert the cable so you can plug into a 25-pin port. You should be able to purchase a 9-pin to 25-pin adapter at any computer store.

You connect the other end of the interface cable to the *data interface port* on your handheld PC. This port may be covered with a small door, which you need to open in order to plug in the cable. This port is where data is sent from your handheld PC to the desktop computer. If you are using a docking station with your handheld PC, you probably need to plug the cable into the docking station. To determine the exact location for the cable, refer to the hardware documentation that came with your handheld PC.

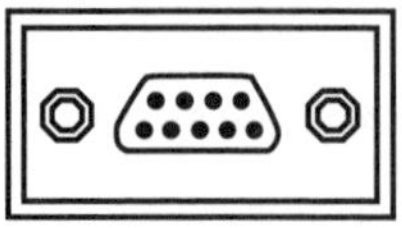

Figure 9-1: A nine-pin serial port.

You need to make sure that you properly attach the cable anytime you intend to interface your handheld PC with your desktop computer. If the cable is not properly connected, the two units can't interact.

Running the H/PC Explorer Install Program

Before you can interface with your desktop computer, you must install the H/PC Explorer program. You will probably only have to go through this process one time. Although if you decide to change and interface with another computer, you will need to repeat this installation process on that computer, too. For example, you may decide you want to interface with both a home and office computer.

The H/PC Explorer software comes with your handheld PC on a CD-ROM titled Desktop Software for Microsoft Windows CE. Remove the CD-ROM from the case and place it in the CD-ROM drive on the computer where you intend to create the interface with your handheld PC. Remember, the computer must be running Windows 95 or Windows NT 4.0, or the programs will not install properly. The H/PC Explorer CD-ROM setup program should appear automatically, as shown in Figure 9-2.

If the H/PC Explorer setup screen does not load automatically when you install the CD-ROM in your computer, you need to run the H/PC Explorer setup program manually. To do this, tap on the Run option in the Start menu to display the Run dialog box. Type **d:\setup** in the Open text box as shown in Figure 9-3 to run the setup program on the CD-ROM. If your CD-ROM drive has been assigned a different drive letter than D, such as drive E; type that drive letter instead of D.

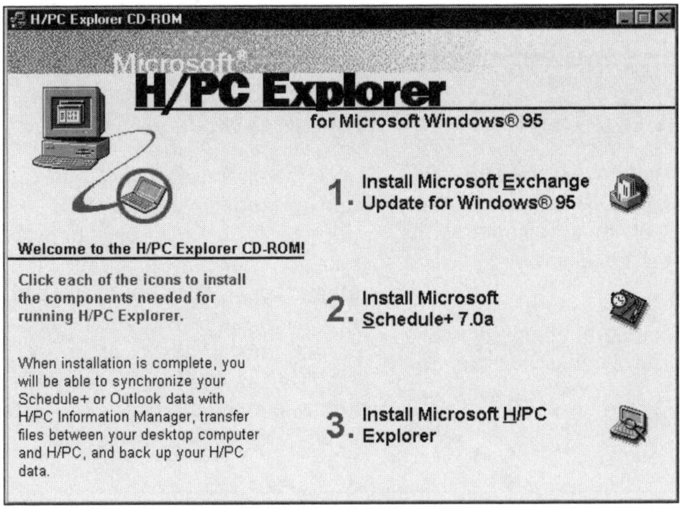

Figure 9-2: You can install the different options needed to run the H/PC Explorer program on your computer.

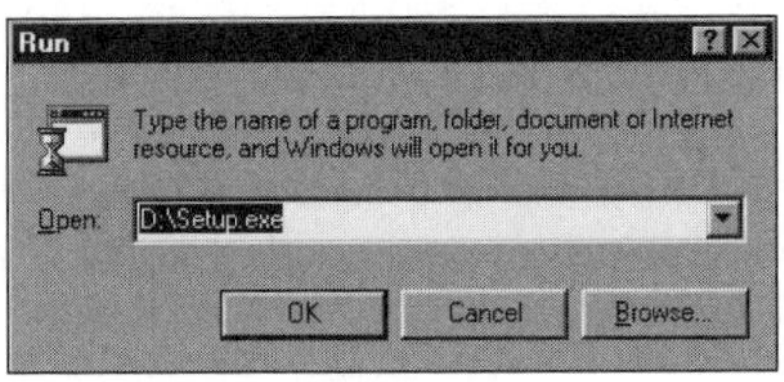

Figure 9-3: Type the name of the CD-ROM drive followed by a colon and the word SETUP and then click the OK button.

In the H/PC Explorer setup screen, you see three options under Windows 95 and two options under Windows NT 4.0. Each option loads programs that are related to the different options that are available using the H/PC Explorer program. Because of the requirements of each setup option, the setup program is designed to have you run each installation separately. When you run the H/PC Explorer setup program, it checks your screen to see if you need to install each option. If an option appears grayed out on the setup screen, you do not need to install that option on your desktop computer. Whether an option needs to be installed on your computer depends on the following criteria:

What if I don't have a CD-ROM drive?

Unfortunately, Microsoft has shipped the H/PC Explorer program on a CD-ROM only. You can still install H/PC Explorer on a computer without a CD-ROM, but the installation requires a little extra footwork.

First, you need to find another computer with a CD-ROM drive so that you can copy the installation files onto floppy diskettes. You need nine formatted 3.5-inch floppy diskettes for this copying process.

If you install the H/PC Explorer program from floppy diskettes, you also need to know more information about what exactly is being installed on your system because the floppy disk setup program does not check your computer for you. To determine what you need to look for on your desktop computer, read the Read.Me file on the CD-ROM. This file describes the specific steps for installing H/PC Explorer off of floppy diskettes.

- You only need to run the Exchange Update if you are running Windows 95, you have already installed Microsoft Exchange on your desktop computer, and the version number is 4.0.410.59. You can find the version number by running Microsoft Exchange and choosing Help⇨About. If you do not have Microsoft Exchange loaded or the version number is greater than 4.0.410.59, do not run this installation option. Also, if you are running a non-U.S. English version of Windows 95, do not run this installation option. Keep in mind that the installation program is checking for these conditions, as well. If you are running Windows NT 4.0, this option does not appear on the Handheld PC setup screen.
- The Schedule+ 7.0a installation option is available if you do not already have Version 7.0a of Microsoft Schedule+ installed on your desktop computer. If you are running Microsoft Outlook on your desktop computer, this option is grayed out on the H/PC setup screen.
- The H/PC Explorer option installs all the files required to run the H/PC Explorer program. If you want to use this program, you must run this installation option.

Installing the Microsoft Exchange messaging update

You must select the Microsoft Exchange Messaging Update option if you have been using Microsoft Exchange under Windows 95. This update changes some of the settings in the version of Exchange that came with Windows 95 so that you can use the H/PC Explorer properly. As noted in the previous section, if this option is grayed out, you don't need to install this option.

Also, keep in mind that this option is not needed for Windows NT 4.0, so the option does not appear on the H/PC Explorer setup screen.

Follow these steps to install the Microsoft Exchange Messaging Update on your desktop computer:

1. **Click the Install Microsoft Exchange Update for Windows 95 button.**

   This button is the first one on the H/PC Explorer setup screen; it resembles a letter sitting in front of a sketch of the world.

2. **In the Windows Messaging dialog box, click on the Yes button to continue the process.**

   This standard dialog box, shown in Figure 9-4, usually appears when you install new software on your computer. This dialog box provides some brief legal mumbo-jumbo to inform you that this program has all the legal rights of all other Microsoft programs. If you click on the No button, it means that you do not agree to the terms, and the installation process is canceled.

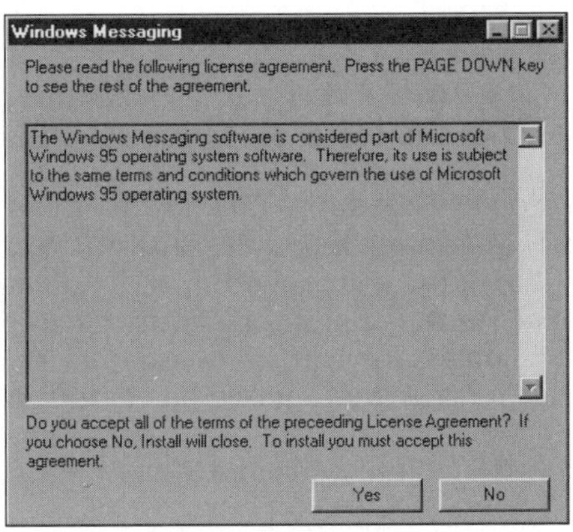

Figure 9-4: The licensing information for the update is rather brief. Click the Yes button to continue.

3. **In the Windows Messaging Setup dialog box, click on the Continue button to continue with the installation process.**

   This dialog box simply provides some more legal information about installing this program, like the fact that you should only install the program on one computer.

4. **Type the current name and organization information in the Name and Organization dialog box and then click on the OK button.**

5. **In the Confirm Name and Organization Information dialog box, make sure that you typed the correct information in each field. If the information is correct, click the OK button to continue.**

The dialog box that appears, shown in Figure 9-5, allows you to check that the name and organization information is correct before it is used to register to program. If you typed the wrong information in one of the fields, click on the Change button to return to the Name and Organization Information dialog box and then make the modifications you want.

When you click on the OK button, the installation process begins, and the required files are installed on your computer.

6. **When the installation is complete, click on the OK button to return to the H/PC Explorer Setup screen and continue with the next installation.**

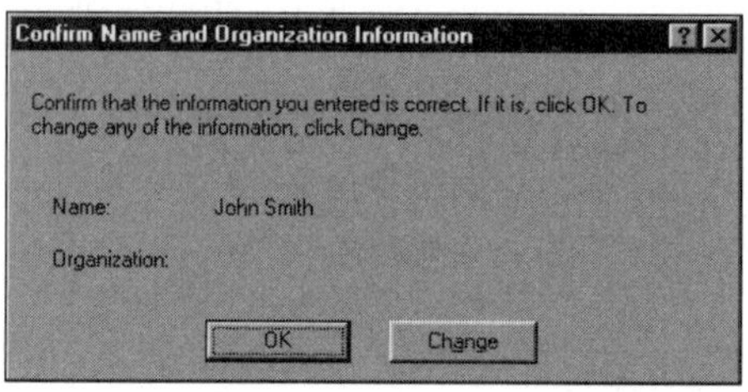

Figure 9-5: Verify the name and organization information.

Installing Microsoft Schedule+ 7.0a

You must select the Install Microsoft Schedule+ 7.0a option if you have not already installed Version 7.0a of Microsoft Schedule+ on your computer, and you are not using Microsoft Outlook for your scheduling. If you are not sure which version you have installed on the computer, simply click the button and the installation program will check for you. If you do not need to install this program, you get a message telling you to move on to the next option.

If you have Microsoft Outlook installed on your desktop computer, the Install Microsoft Schedule+ 7.0a option is grayed out.

The following steps illustrate the process of installing the Microsoft Schedule+ 7.0a on your desktop computer:

1. **Click on the Install Microsoft Schedule+ 7.0a icon.**

   This is the middle icon on the H/PC Explorer setup screen and resembles a clock and a compass sitting on a desktop.

2. **In the first dialog box of the Microsoft Schedule+ setup process, click on the Continue button to start the process.**

   The dialog box that appears provides some brief legal mumbo-jumbo, such as informing you that you should only install this program on one computer (see Figure 9-6).

Figure 9-6: You are reminded that you should not share this copy of Schedule+ with other users.

3. **Type the name and organization information on the Name and Organization dialog box, and then click on the OK button.**
4. **The Product ID number for the version of Schedule+ that you are installing on your machine appears. Click on the OK button to continue the setup process.**
5. **Next, the setup program indicates the folder where it intends to install Schedule+, as shown in Figure 9-7. If this location is okay, click on the OK button to continue the installation process.**

   You can specify another folder for the program by clicking on the Change Folder button. The Browse dialog box appears, and you can highlight a new folder location for the program.

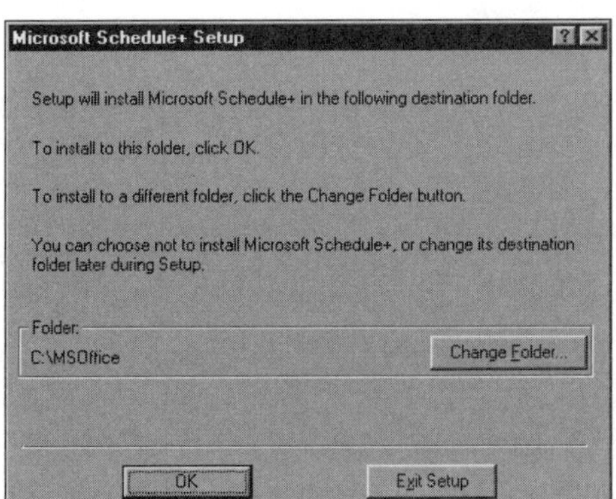

Figure 9-7: You can specify the folder location for the Schedule+ program.

6. **Click on the Typical button to begin the setup process.**

   When you click the Typical button, shown in Figure 9-8, the setup program automatically installs the files that are *typically* required to run Schedule+ efficiently on your computer.

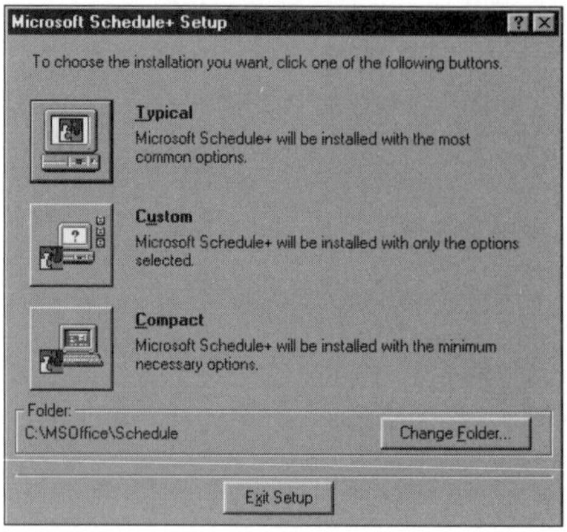

Figure 9-8: Click the Typical button in the setup program to select the files that should be installed.

7. **When the installation is complete, click on the OK button to return to the H/PC Explorer Setup screen and continue with the next installation.**

Depending on the current settings on your machine, you may be instructed to restart your computer before the installation can be completed. Do not be alarmed if this occurs; some types of program options require the computer to be rebooted before they can be installed properly. After you reboot your computer, you should see a setup complete message.

Installing Microsoft H/PC Explorer

The Install Microsoft H/PC Explorer option on the H/PC Explorer setup screen actually installs all of the H/PC Explorer program files on your desktop computer. If you don't install this program, your handheld PC can't interface with your desktop computer.

Follow these steps to install Microsoft H/PC Explorer on your desktop computer.

1. **Click the Install Microsoft H/PC Explorer icon.**

   This is the bottom button on the H/PC Explorer setup screen. It resembles a handheld PC with a magnifying glass over it.

2. **In the first dialog box of the Microsoft H/PC Explorer Setup, simply click the Next button to start the installation process.**

   This standard dialog box normally appears when you install any new software on your computer. It reminds you not to run any other programs on your computer while installing this program.

3. **In the Microsoft H/PC Explorer License Agreement dialog box, click on the Yes button to continue the setup process.**

   This dialog box contains the entire license agreement that Microsoft has created for the H/PC Explorer software, as shown in Figure 9-9. By selecting the Yes button, you are stating that you agree to adhere to the terms outlined in the license agreement.

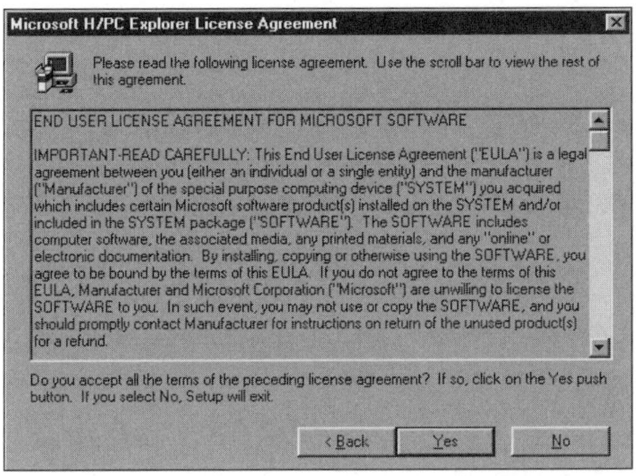

Figure 9-9: You must agree to the legal stuff before you can continue installing the H/PC Explorer program.

4. **Type your name in the Name text box and press the Tab key. Type your company name in the Company text box and then click the Next button (see Figure 9-10).**

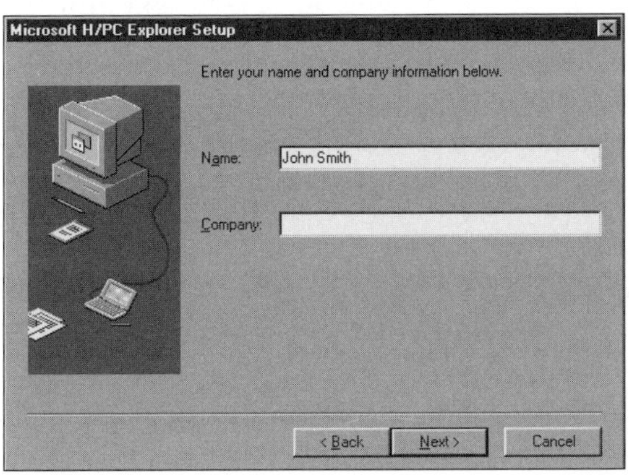

Figure 9-10: You must type a name in the Name field, but the Company field is optional.

5. **In the Select Components dialog box, make sure that the folder where the setup program wants to install the H/PC Explorer is okay. If so, click the Next button.**

   The Select Components dialog box (see Figure 9-11). This dialog box allows you to select the specific components you want to install. Go ahead and install all three components on your computer. The first two options are necessary to perform all of the options available with the H/PC Explorer program.

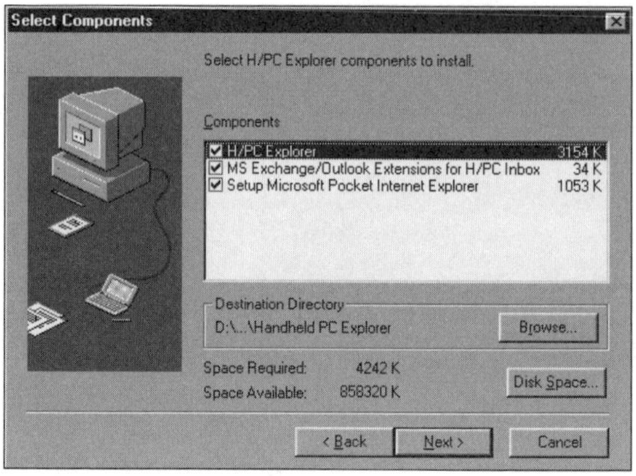

Figure 9-11: Install all three of the components listed for the H/PC Explorer to ensure that everything runs properly on your computer.

   The third option copies the installation file for the Pocket Internet Explorer onto your desktop computer, so you can install the files on your handheld PC. If your handheld PC came with the Pocket Internet Explorer program already installed, you do not need to select this option. For more information, see Chapter 15.

   If for some reason you do not like the location where the setup program intends to place H/PC Explorer, you can change the location by clicking the Browse button and then specifying a new location on the Choose Directory dialog box.

6. **In the Select Start Menu Location dialog box, click the Next button to select the name of the folder that will be used to add H/PC Explorer to your Start menu.**

   The setup program automatically tries to create a new folder called Handheld PC Explorer to make the program easy to locate on your Start menu, as shown in Figure 9-12. If you don't like the selected folder name, you can type a new name in the Program Folders field or highlight an existing folder name in the Existing Folders list.

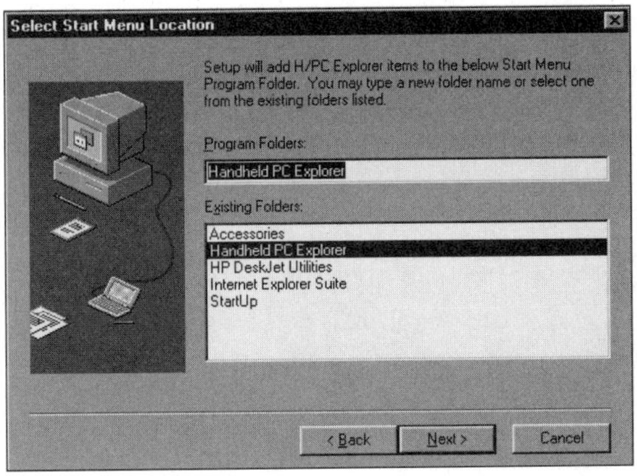

Figure 9-12: The specified folder name is created on your Start menu.

7. **On the Start Copying Files dialog box, if the setup options look okay, click the Next button to begin the installation process.**

   Before any files are copied to your desktop computer, the Microsoft H/PC Explorer Setup program makes sure you know what it is going to do, as shown in Figure 9-13. The installation program lets you know what components it is going to install, where it will install those components, and what it will call the place where it puts the components.

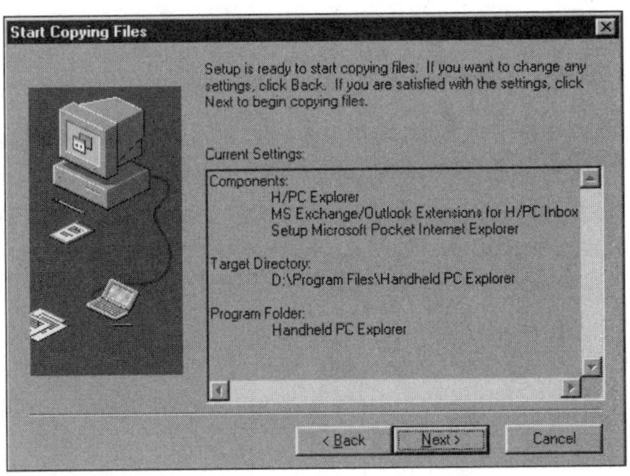

Figure 9-13: Verify the setup options because as soon as you select the Next button, the installation begins.

8. **On the Configure Synchronization dialog box, make sure that the appropriate option is selected and click the Next button.**

   If you have both Schedule+ and Outlook installed on your computer, you see the dialog box shown in Figure 9-14. The setup program automatically selects an option for you, based on your current system settings. To change the selection, click on the corresponding option.

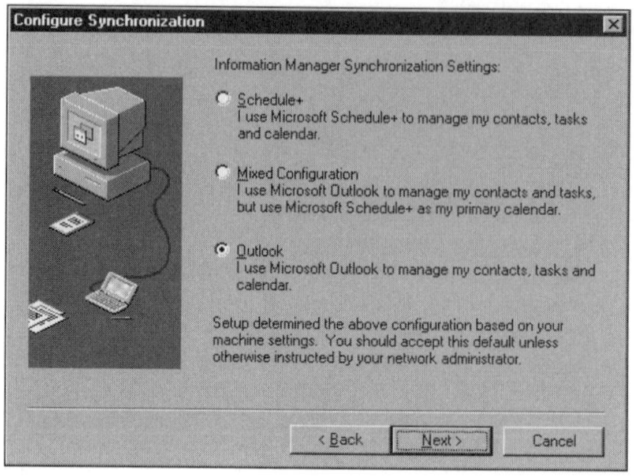

Figure 9-14: Make sure that the program you use for scheduling is selected.

9. **In the Select Start Menu Location dialog box, select the Start menu location for the Handheld Explorer option, and click on the Next button.**

   A menu option will be placed in the folder that you select on the Start menu. I recommend letting the setup program create the folder called Handheld PC Explorer, so that you can easily locate the program when you want to run it, but if you want a different folder, either type the name in the input field, or highlight the name of an existing folder.

10. **On the Start Copying Files dialog box, verify that the setup program is installing the options in the appropriate folder and then click on the Next button.**

    When you click on the Next button, the setup program installs the H/PC Explorer program files on your desktop computer.

11. **On the Setup Communications dialog box, verify that the interface cable is connected between the desktop computer and your handheld PC, and then click on the Next button.**

    After the program files are installed, the setup program verifies that all of the connections will work properly with H/PC Explorer. At this point the setup may request that you insert your installation disks or CD-ROM for Windows 95 or Windows NT 4.0, so make sure that you have it handy.

12. **In the Create Shortcuts dialog box, indicate where you want to put the shortcuts to the H/PC Explorer program and then click the Next button.**

    The Create Shortcuts dialog box allows you to place a shortcut in the desktop as well as place a shortcut in the StartUp folder. To select an option in this dialog box, click the check box next to the option.

13. **Click the Finish button to complete the installation of the H/PC Explorer program and connect to your handheld PC.**

    At this point, the setup program has completed copying all the required files to your handheld PC and is now ready to set up the communications between your handheld PC and desktop computer.

14. **On the Communications Properties dialog box, select the name of the port where you have connected the serial interface cable to your computer and then click on the OK button.**

    You use the Communications Properties dialog box, shown in Figure 9-15, to tell the H/PC Explorer program where to look for your serial interface cable. If you are unsure which port you connected the cable to, refer to the hardware documentation that came with your computer.

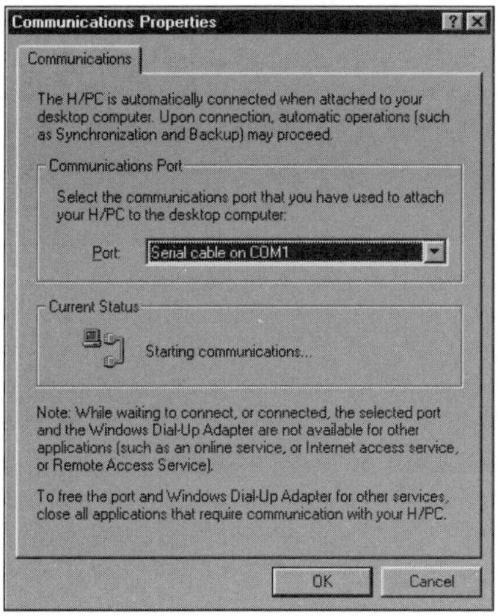

Figure 9-15: Select the port where the serial interface cable is connected to your desktop computer.

If you have followed all the instructions up to this point, H/PC Explorer should be properly set up and ready to communicate with your handheld PC. You can now copy files, print files, back up your handheld PC, and synchronize your calendar and tasks with Schedule+. For more information about performing each of these tasks, see Chapters 10, 11, 12, and 13.

Chapter 10

A Tour of H/PC Explorer

In This Chapter

- Running H/PC Explorer
- Viewing the stuff on your handheld PC
- Moving files between your desktop computer and your handheld PC
- Cutting, copying, and pasting
- Creating new folders
- Removing files and folders
- Renaming files and folders
- Printing files
- Setting file conversion properties

One tool that you will definitely want to master is H/PC Explorer. By using this program on your desktop computer, you can form an alliance between your desktop computer and your Windows CE handheld PC. By connecting the two units, you can move information between your desktop computer and your handheld PC.

This chapter explains how to use H/PC Explorer on your desktop computer to connect to your handheld PC and look for files, copy files, and even print files from your handheld PC. This can be especially valuable when you have a proposal you created on your handheld PC that you would like to give to a customer. Or you may have a monthly budget on your desktop computer that you need to copy to your handheld PC so that you can work on it after dinner.

Running H/PC Explorer

H/PC Explorer is (also called Handheld PC Explorer) the key to being able to transfer any type of information between your handheld PC and a desktop computer. This program comes on a CD with your handheld PC. H/PC Explorer must be installed on your desktop computer under Windows 95 or Windows NT 4.0; if you have not installed it yet, refer to Chapter 9.

Depending on how H/PC Explorer was installed on your computer, you will probably either find an icon for it sitting on your desktop or a shortcut option on the Start menu called H/PC Explorer. The H/PC Explorer icon is very similar to the My Handheld PC icon on your handheld PC — it looks like a Windows CE handheld PC with a magnifying glass over it.

TIP

Before you select the H/PC Explorer option on your desktop computer, make sure that your handheld PC is properly connected to the computer. Remember, the serial interface cable is used to connect your handheld PC to the computer. When the H/PC Explorer program starts, it immediately tries to establish a connection with your handheld PC. For more pointers on connecting your computer and handheld PC, refer to Chapter 9.

During the connection process, messages are displayed on both your computer screen and on your handheld PC, as shown in Figure 10-1, indicating the progress of the connection.

If a message does not appear on your handheld PC as shown in Figure 10-1, your handheld probably is not properly connected to the computer. Verify that the serial interface cable is properly connected to both the handheld PC and the computer.

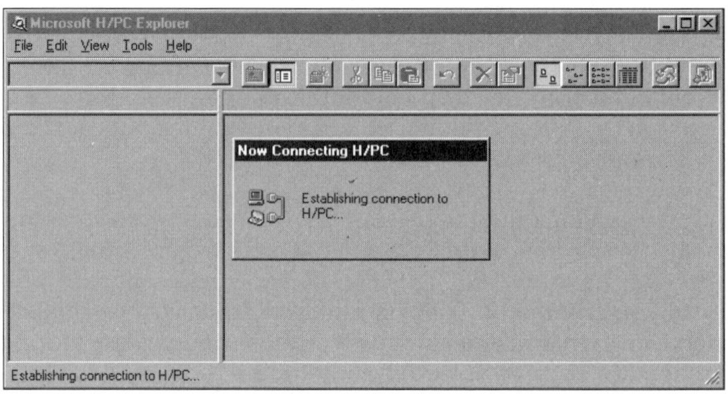

Figure 10-1: Messages are displayed on both your handheld PC and desktop computer during the connection process.

Exploring Your Handheld PC from Your Desktop Computer

If you are a veteran to the world of Microsoft Windows, you will soon recognize that H/PC Explorer very closely resembles the other Explorer programs that run on other versions of the Windows operating system, such as Windows 95 and Windows NT 4.0. In fact, with all the different Explorer programs, trying to keep track of which one you use when can be confusing.

As with other Windows Explorer programs, you can use H/PC Explorer to look at the files and folders on your handheld PC in several ways. For example, you can display a list of the folders on your handheld PC on the left side of the screen with the contents of the highlighted folder, the one with a black box around the name, displayed on the right side of the screen, as shown in Figure 10-2.

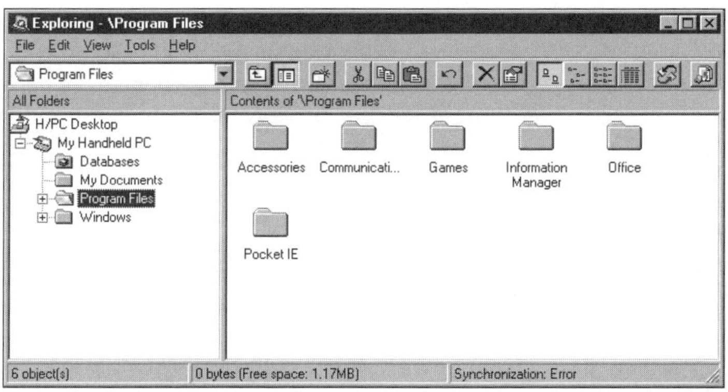

Figure 10-2: Use H/PC Explorer to view the folders and files within a folder.

Other view options are available on the View menu, shown in Figure 10-3. Or you can access the options by selecting one of the five buttons described in Table 10-1.

Table 10-1 H/PC Explorer Toolbar View Buttons

Click on This Button	*To Do This*
	Turn on or off the tree listing of folders on the left side of the screen. The tree listing provides a map of the way folders are stored on your handheld PC; you can quickly see all of the folders within a specific folder.

(continued)

Table 10-1 *(continued)*

Click on This Button	*To Do This*
	View the contents of the folder by using large icons. This way, you can quickly see what is in the folder; however, if you have several items, you will not be able to display everything on-screen at the same time and will need to use the scroll bars to look at the entire contents of the folder.
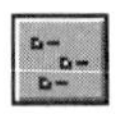	View the contents of the folder by using small icons. Small icons look just like large icons, but the icons are smaller so you can get more on-screen at one time. Although these icons are more difficult to see, small icons are a better solution if you have a folder that contains several items.
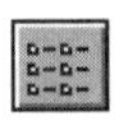	View a list of the files in the folder by using small icons and filenames.
	View the details about each item in the folder. This option displays information such as the name of the item, its size, its file type, and the date and time when it was last modified.

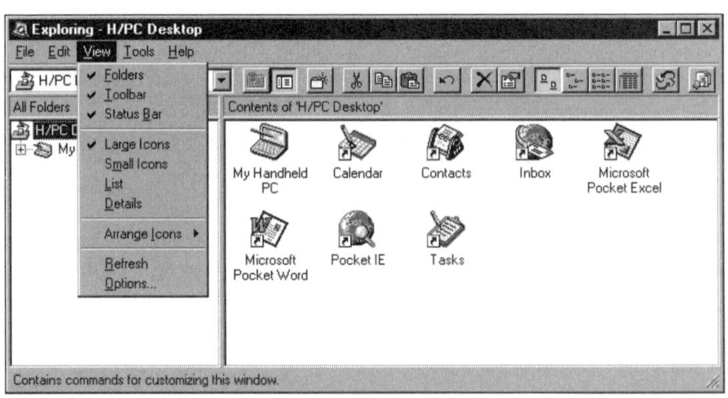

Figure 10-3: The View menu offers several options to customize the way you view things on your handheld PC.

After you decide how you want to view the information on your handheld PC, you can use the options on the View menu to arrange the order of the items in each folder:

- Within any view, you can sort items by name or file type. To sort by name, choose View➪Arrange By Name. To sort by file type, choose View➪Arrange By Type.
- If you have added an item to a particular folder since opening H/PC Explorer, you may need to refresh the screen before the new item appears in the list. To refresh the list, choose View➪Refresh.
- TIP: Like Windows CE Explorer, H/PC Explorer enables you to hide certain system files so that you do not accidentally delete them. To hide the system files, choose View➪Options to open the Options dialog box, shown in Figure 10-4. Then select Hide Hidden files and files with the following extensions: .dll, .cpl, and .drv.
- You can also indicate whether the path for the current folder is displayed in the title bar (at the top of the window) and indicate whether the two panes (the left and right sides of the screen) of information are labeled with the name of the open folder.

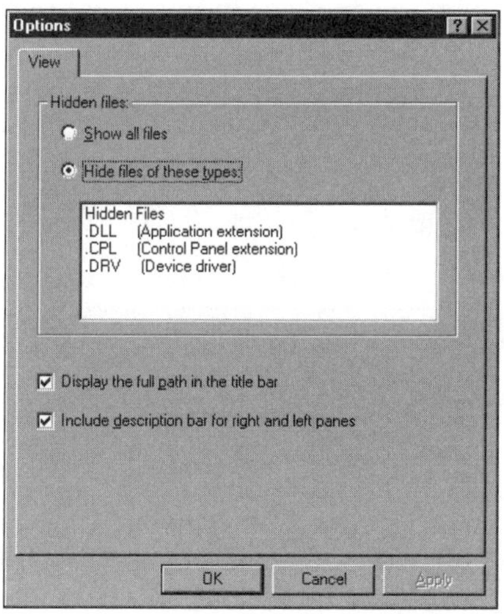

Figure 10-4: The Options dialog box.

Moving Stuff Between Your Computer and Handheld PC

One of the most useful features of H/PC Explorer is the capability to copy documents between a handheld PC and a desktop computer. If you have a proposal that you just wrote in Microsoft Word, for example, you may need to copy it to your handheld PC so that you can quickly haul the document to a meeting. With H/PC Explorer, moving files between your computer and your handheld PC is easy. You can either use the drag-and-drop method or the cut, copy, and paste method. Both methods enable you to quickly move stuff back and forth. You can find more information about these methods for moving documents back and forth in this section.

Dragging and dropping files and folders

One of the fastest and easiest ways to move files between your desktop computer and your handheld PC is to use the Windows 95 drag-and-drop method. In order to drag and drop the files, you need to have H/PC Explorer and Windows 95 Explorer open simultaneously on your desktop, as shown in Figure 10-5.

The following steps illustrate how you can easily move documents between your handheld PC and your desktop computer:

1. **Open the Windows 95 Explorer program.**

   To open this program, choose Programs⇨Windows Explorer from the Start menu.

2. **In Windows Explorer, locate the file you want to move to your handheld.**

   For this example, I selected my Proposal.doc file in the My Documents folder under Windows 95, as shown in Figure 10-6.

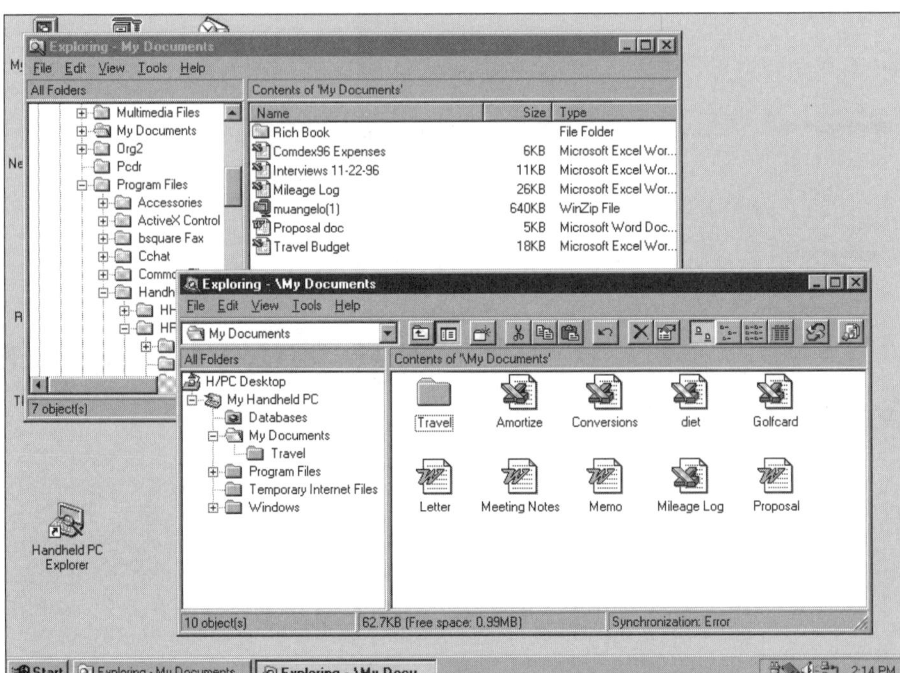

Figure 10-5: Open both Explorer programs so that you can drag files from one program and drop them on the other.

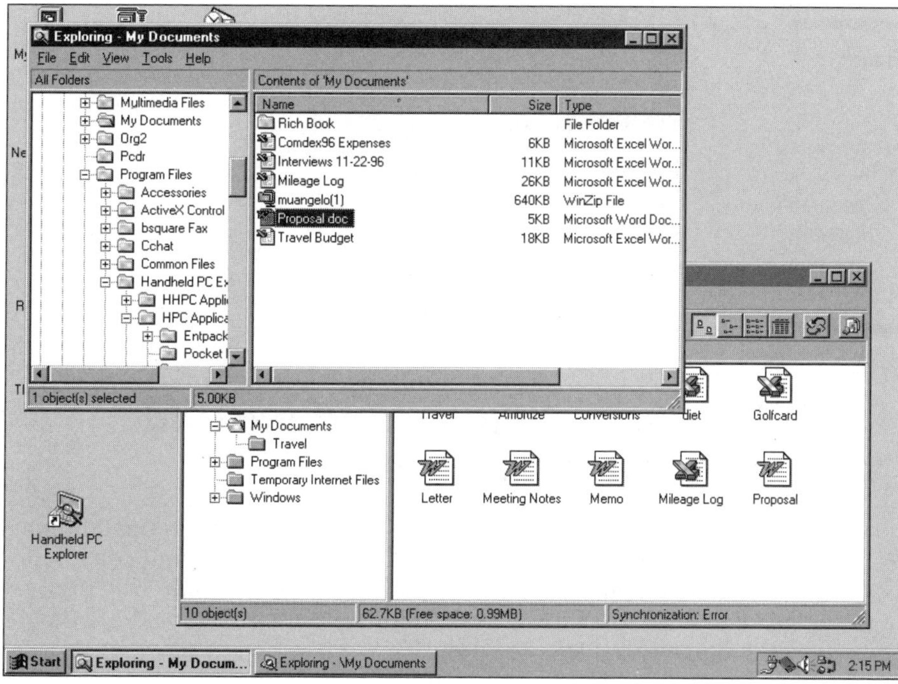

Figure 10-6: In the Windows Explorer program, locate the file that you want to copy.

3. **Open the H/PC Explorer program.**

   For more information, check out the "Running H/PC Explorer" section, earlier in this chapter.

4. **Open the folder containing the document you want to copy.**

   For example, to easily open the My Documents folder, click the My Documents folder on the left side of the screen with the mouse.

   Make sure that both Explorer windows are sized small enough so that you can move information between them. If you need to make one of the windows smaller, move the cursor to the bottom left corner of the window (the cursor should look like a double arrow), hold down the left mouse button, and drag the window to a smaller size.

5. **Drag the file from Windows Explorer to H/PC Explorer.**

   To copy the file, position the mouse cursor over the file's icon in Windows Explorer, press and hold the left mouse button, and drag the icon to the H/PC Explorer window. After the file is in the H/PC Explorer window, release the mouse button. A window appears, indicating that Windows is copying and converting the file (see Figure 10-7).

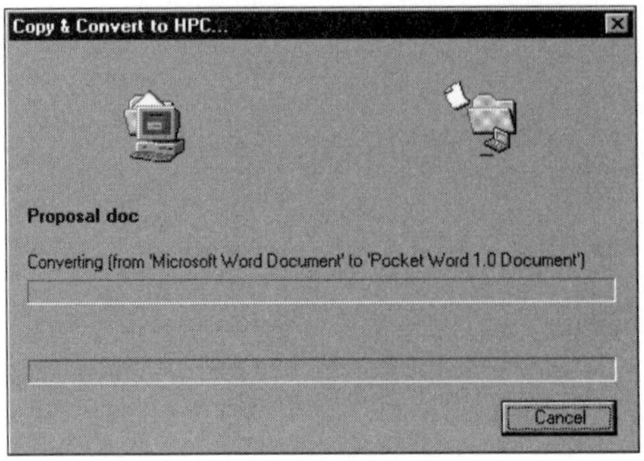

Figure 10-7: You can view the progress as the file is copied between the two machines.

Cutting, copying, and pasting files between locations

You can use the Cut, Copy, and Paste commands on the Edit menu of both H/PC Explorer and Windows 95 Explorer to move and copy items from one location to another. This method is good for anyone who prefers menu commands. H/PC Explorer also provides buttons for these functions on the toolbar, as outlined in Table 10-2.

Table 10-2 H/PC Explorer Toolbar Copy Icons

Click on This Button	*To Do This*
	Cut the existing file out of the existing folder. Remember, if you cut from your desktop computer and paste on your handheld PC, the file or folder remains on your desktop computer, too.
	Copy the selected file.
	Paste the last file that was either cut or copied into the current folder.

To copy a file from your handheld PC and paste it onto your desktop computer, follow these steps:

1. **Open H/PC Explorer on your desktop computer.**

   You should be able to locate an option for the program on the Programs menu of the Start menu.

2. **Open the folder that contains the file you want to copy and click on the file's icon.**

   Simply click on the icon with the mouse to select it. A black box appears around the name of the file, indicating that the file is selected, as shown in Figure 10-8.

3. **Click on the Copy icon on the toolbar.**

   The Copy icon looks like two identical sheets of paper sitting one on top of the other.

4. **Open Windows 95 Explorer (or Windows NT Explorer).**

5. **Locate the folder in which you want to place the file.**

6. **In Windows 95 Explorer, choose File⇨Paste.**

   The window shown in Figure 10-9 appears, indicating that the selected file is being copied to the specified folder and converted from a Pocket Word file format (.PWD) to a Microsoft Word file format (.DOC).

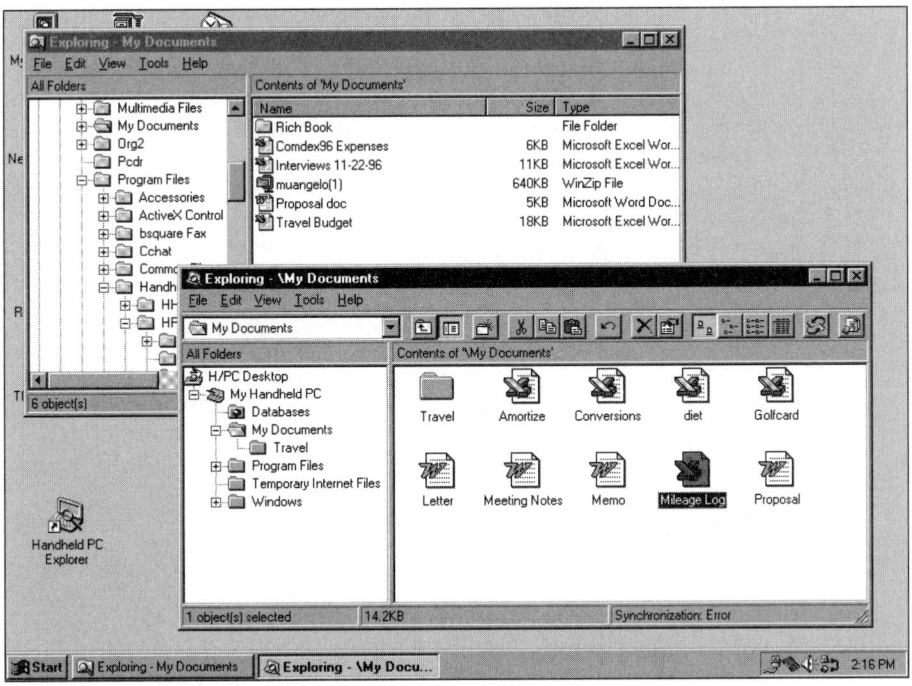

Figure 10-8: Highlight the icon that corresponds to the file you want to copy.

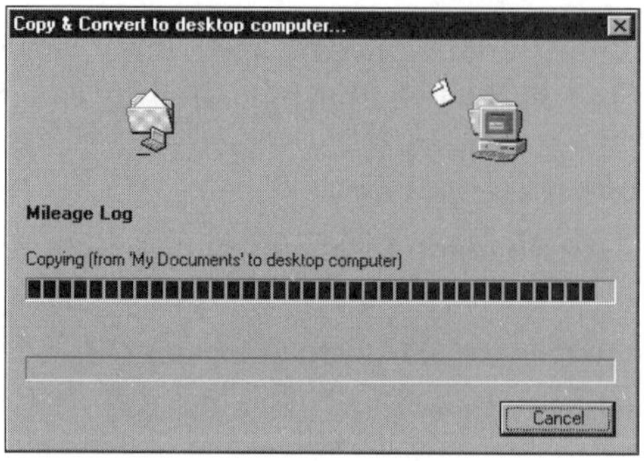

Figure 10-9: As long as you have automatic conversion selected, the file is quickly converted to the appropriate format as it is copied.

When you copy files between your handheld PC and your desktop computer, you can use either the Cut option or the Copy option — both perform the same function and simply copy the file, leaving the original file in its original folder. You can move the file without leaving a copy in the original location by using the Cut option only if you cut and paste on the same unit (either on the computer or the handheld PC). If you cut and paste between the two units, the file is copied and placed in the new location, but the original file will remain.

Dealing with Folders

Folders provide a sense of organization to your handheld PC by allowing common files to be grouped together in one location. With H/PC Explorer, you can work with existing folders and create new folders on your handheld PC. You can get the full scoop in the following sections.

Adding a new folder

To use H/PC Explorer to create a new folder, you can either choose File⇨New Folder or click the New Folder button on the toolbar. The New Folder icon resembles a folder with a starburst behind it. A folder named New Folder appears, as shown in Figure 10-10. Click the folder name and type a name for the folder.

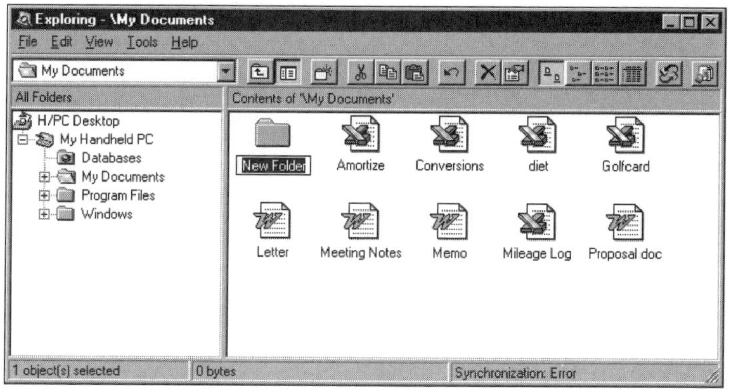

Figure 10-10: You can add new folders to organize the related files on your handheld PC.

Renaming a folder or file

Suppose that when you name a file, you mistype the filename. Or maybe you decide to store different files in the folder and want to change the folder name to reflect the contents of the folder more accurately. With H/PC Explorer, you can easily modify the names of files and folders on your handheld PC.

In H/PC Explorer, click on the file or folder you want to rename and then choose File⇨Rename. A box appears around the name, and the cursor moves to the end of the item name.

You can replace the entire name of the file or folder or change a portion of the name. If you want to replace the entire name of the item, simply start typing. The new name appears in the box. If you want to modify only a portion of the name, use the arrow keys to move the cursor within the name and start typing.

TIP

Another easy way to rename the file or folder is to click on the icon twice (but not as fast as a double-click). When the black box appears around the name, you can type the new name.

WARNING!

Use the Rename option to change the names of your personal document files only. Do not attempt to rename system or program files. Avoid renaming any files in the Windows directory — Windows CE stores the files it requires for the operating system there, and changes in this area can keep your handheld PC from running properly.

Printing Files

Unfortunately, you cannot print a document directly from most handheld PCs. Some units do have this capability, however, so check out the documentation that came with your handheld. For example, some handheld PCs come with the ability to use the infrared port to send information to the printer.

The easiest way to print a document from your handheld PC is to use your H/PC Explorer program on your desktop computer. Of course, doing so requires that the computer running H/PC Explorer be connected to a printer.

You can print any type of document or graphic file. Basically, anything that you can view or read can be printed. You cannot print a program or system file. Most types of files, such as Pocket Word files, are converted by H/PC Explorer to the corresponding file format under Windows 95 before they are sent to the printer.

To print a file from your Windows CE handheld PC, follow these steps:

1. **Open H/PC Explorer on your desktop computer.**
2. **Locate the file you want to print.**

   Remember, you can print a file from any folder on your handheld PC. The selected file should be highlighted on-screen, as shown in Figure 10-11.

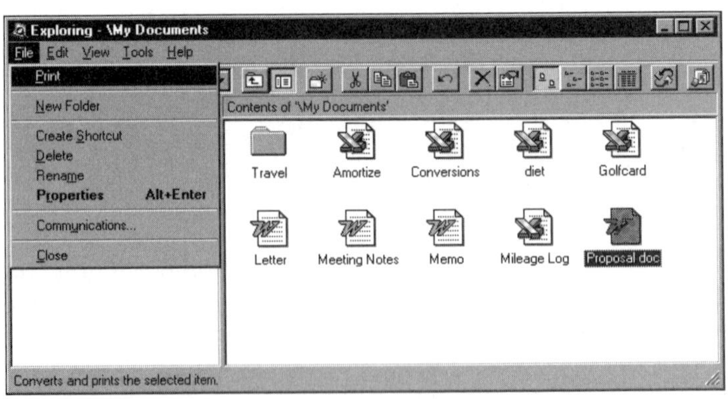

Figure 10-11: The selected file is temporarily copied to your desktop computer so that it can be printed.

3. **Choose File⇨Print.**

   The handheld temporarily converts the selected file and copies it to your computer. The file is opened up in a related program on your desktop computer long enough to send the file on to the printer. The actual program used to open and print the file depends on the file type. For example, a bitmap graphic file is opened in Microsoft Paint.

Setting File Conversion Properties

If you have copied files between your computer and your handheld PC, you have probably noticed that besides copying each file, H/PC Explorer also performs some type of data conversion. This conversion ensures that a file can be opened once it is copied to the desktop computer or handheld PC. For example, when you copy Microsoft Word documents (.doc files) to your handheld PC, the files are converted to Microsoft Pocket Word files (.pwd files).

To allow you to make some selections about the way files are converted, H/PC Explorer provides the File Conversion command, located on the Tools menu. When you select this option, the File Conversion Properties dialog box appears, as shown in Figure 10-12.

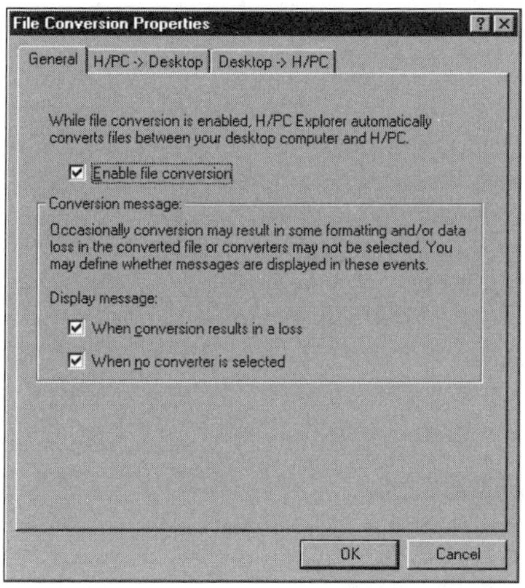

Figure 10-12: Specify whether files should be automatically converted when you copy them between your handheld PC and desktop computer.

The File Conversion Properties dialog box contains three tabs. You use the options on these tabs to customize your conversion options. To view a different set of options, click the tab.

Setting general conversion options

When the File Conversion Properties windows appears, the General tab is visible. Although this tab has only three little check boxes, each one has an important purpose.

The Enable file conversion option indicates that whenever a file is copied between your handheld PC and desktop computer, H/PC Explorer automatically converts the file based on the settings on the other two tabs. If this option is not selected, the file is copied onto the other unit but not converted. This option should only be turned off if you do not want any file conversion to occur when you copy files, but keep in mind that if the files are not converted, you cannot open them after they are copied.

You can also have H/PC Explorer display messages when specific conditions exist during the file conversion process. You can specify that a message appears when a data loss occurs during the file conversion process and also if a converter isn't specified for the type of file you are copying. The options to display these messages are selected in the Conversion message section.

Indicating settings for copying to the desktop computer

Although Windows CE has only a limited amount of file formats, I would imagine that you are aware that the number is limitless on the desktop computer. For example, Pocket Word can save documents in only two file formats (.pwd and .txt), yet Microsoft Word can save a file in several formats.

On the H/PC -> Desktop tab of the File Conversion Properties window, shown in Figure 10-13, you need to indicate how each of the Windows CE file types are converted when they are copied to your desktop computer.

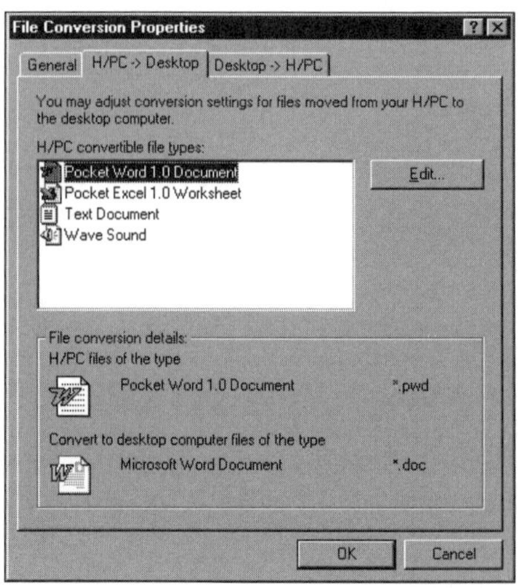

Figure 10-13: For each of the major file formats that you can copy from your handheld PC, you can specify how each format is converted.

The following steps illustrate how to specify that a Pocket Word document is to be converted to a rich text format (.RTF) so that the document can be read by any word processor.

1. **Highlight the Pocket Word 1.0 Document option in the H/PC Convertible file types list.**
2. **Click on the Edit button.**

   When you click on the Edit button, the Edit Conversion Settings window appears, as shown in Figure 10-14. The currently selected conversion type is specified in the Type field.

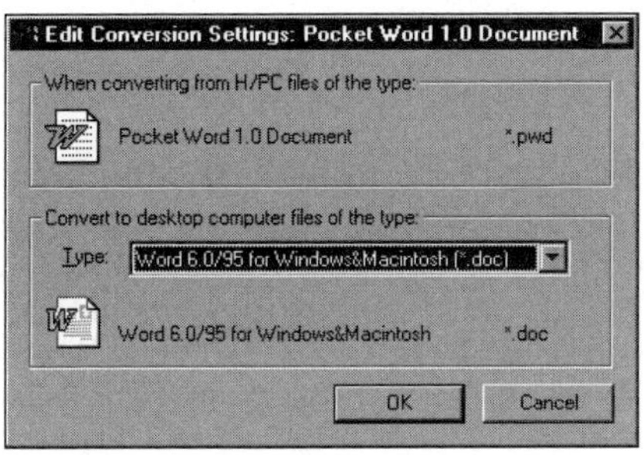

Figure 10-14: Select the Down Arrow button and highlight a file type for the conversion.

3. **Click on the Down Arrow button next to the Type field and highlight the Rich Text Format (*.rtf) option.**

   Obviously, you can select any format type that is listed, but remember that all files copied from your handheld PC will be converted to this format.

4. **Click on the OK button to select the new format.**

TIP: The format conversions can be modified at any time by simply choosing Tools⇨File Conversion from H/PC Explorer. When you change the conversion formats, it does not affect any files that you have already copied to your computer. The setting only corresponds to future files that are copied to your computer.

Indicating settings for copying to your handheld PC

You can convert several types of files from your desktop computer to be viewed on your Windows CE handheld PC. To specify how these file types are to be converted, select the Desktop⇨H/PC tab of the File Conversion Properties window, shown in Figure 10-15.

The file formats that can be converted for use on your handheld PC are listed in the Desktop computer convertible file types list. When you highlight one of these file types, the current conversion settings for the file format appear in the File conversion details section. You can change a format by highlighting it and then selecting the Edit button.

TIP: If you are using a word processor other than Microsoft Word on your desktop computer, you probably will not be able to save the documents as .doc files (Microsoft Word file format). In that case, try saving the document as an .rtf file, commonly referred to as *Rich Text Format.* The .rtf format is a standard file format that can be read by most word processing programs. By using this file format, the file conversion option in H/PC Explorer can then convert the .rtf file to a Pocket Word format of .pwd.

REMEMBER: Keep in mind that H/PC Explorer cannot convert a Microsoft Word or Microsoft Excel file that is password protected. If you want to convert these files for use on your handheld PC, you must first remove the password protection from the file on your desktop computer.

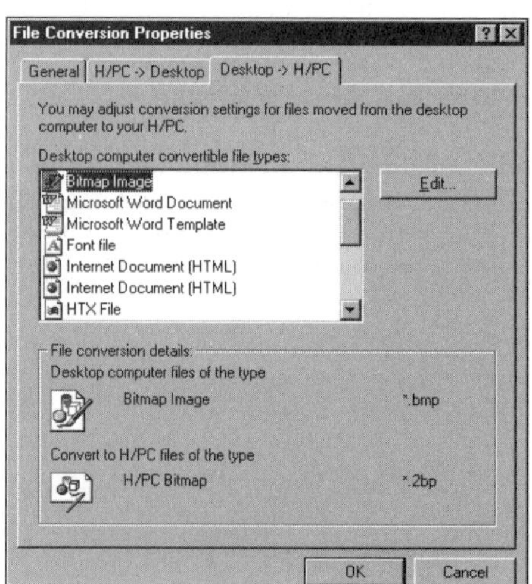

Figure 10-15: For each of the main file formats, you can indicate how the file formats are to be converted.

Chapter 11

Synchronizing Information

In This Chapter

- Understanding the synchronization process
- Performing a synchronization
- Setting the different synchronization options

Have you ever set up your appointments for the next day, only to go home from the office and forget exactly what time you are expected to be in the office in the morning? With a Windows CE handheld PC, you can copy all your appointments and your to-do list from either Microsoft Schedule+ or Microsoft Outlook to your Windows CE handheld PC and vice versa.

This chapter explains how to use H/PC Explorer on your desktop computer to synchronize the calendar and task information between your handheld PC and a desktop computer. I also discuss how to set the different synchronization options.

Understanding Synchronization

If you have looked at any of the information that came with your handheld PC, or even just seen ads for Windows CE handheld PCs, I am sure that you have heard mention of how easily you can synchronize with a desktop computer. Isn't it nice how companies always mention all these benefits but never really take the time to explain them?

Well, to be totally honest, the concept of *synchronizing* two devices is rather simple: Essentially, all of the information on each unit is combined so that each unit not only has its current information, but also the information that was originally only contained on the other unit.

For example, assume that I ask you to list the five best Mexican restaurants in your town. I also ask your neighbor to do the same thing. If I wanted to synchronize the two lists, I would take your list of five names and combine it with your neighbor's list. If the combined list had any duplicates, I would remove the second copy of the item, leaving me with a list of favorite Mexican restaurants for your neighborhood.

When H/PC Explorer synchronizes with your handheld PC, it performs the same steps I just described. The information on your handheld PC is combined with the information on your desktop computer. H/PC Explorer then copies the combined information to each unit. If any conflicts (such as two appointments scheduled at the same time) or duplicates are found, they are resolved using the current synchronization settings. For more information, check out the "Setting the Synchronization Options" section later in this chapter.

Ideally, synchronizing everything on your handheld PC would be great. Unfortunately, Windows CE only allows you to synchronize the information outlined in Table 11-1.

Table 11-1 Synchronization Options

This Windows CE Option	*Synchronizes with This Desktop Computer Option*
Calendar	All appointments and events are added to the calendar in Schedule+ or Outlook.
Tasks	All tasks become to-do items for Schedule+ or Outlook.
Contacts	All contact information is synchronized with the contacts in Schedule+ or Outlook.

Performing a Synchronization

You can synchronize task, calendar, and contact information between your handheld PC and desktop computer at any time by using H/PC Explorer. All you have to do is click on the Synchronize Now button on the toolbar.

To synchronize your handheld PC with your desktop computer, follow these steps:

1. **In H/PC Explorer, click on the Synchronize Now button, located on the toolbar.**

   The Synchronization in Progress dialog box appears, indicating that H/PC Explorer is merging all the contact, task, and calendar information from your Windows CE handheld PC with the same information on your desktop computer (see Figure 11-1).

Figure 11-1: The Synchronization in Progress window.

2. **Choose the Combine option from the Synchronization Manager dialog box.**

   The Synchronization Manager dialog box, shown in Figure 11-2, provides two synchronization options. The Combine option combines the information on your desktop computer with the information on your handheld PC, removes the duplicates, and makes sure that each unit has an identical list of items.

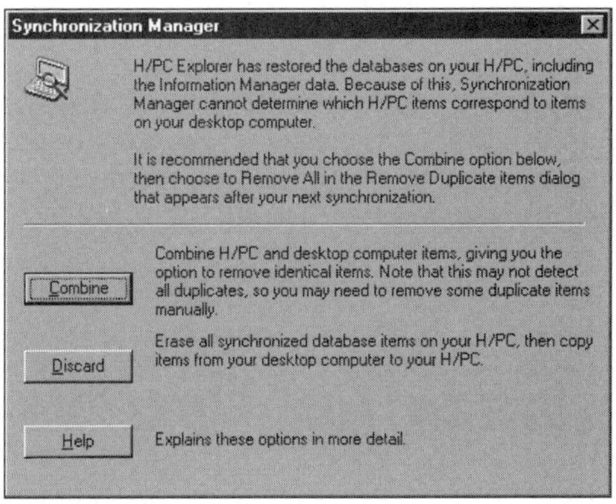

Figure 11-2: The Combine option ensures that the same information exists on your desktop computer and handheld PC.

If, for some reason, you do not want to retain the contact, task, and calendar information on your handheld PC, you can select the Discard option, and H/PC Explorer removes the information from your handheld PC and copies all the desktop computer contact, task, and calendar information to your handheld PC. This option is useful when the information on your desktop computer is more current than the information on your handheld PC.

If you synchronize your information frequently, duplicate items will probably exist on your handheld PC and your desktop computer. The duplicates occur because after you synchronize your data, H/PC Explorer does not keep track of where the appointment or task was originally created. So the next time you perform a synchronization, H/PC Explorer sees the appointment on both your handheld PC and the desktop computer and figures it is a duplicate. When H/PC Explorer finds duplicate items, it displays a dialog box that contains all of the duplicates, as shown in Figure 11-3.

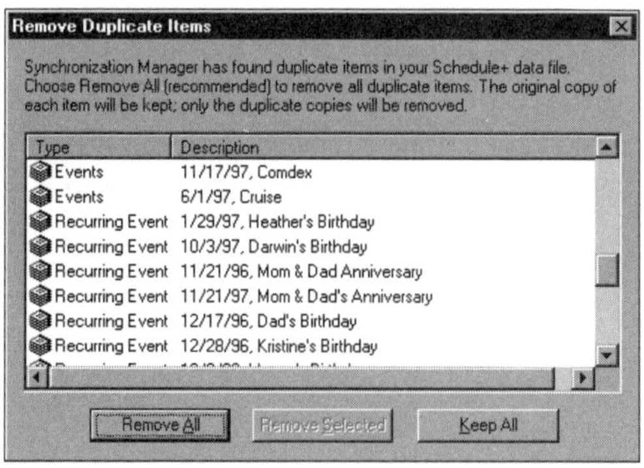

Figure 11-3: Make sure that you remove all duplicates from the list.

To resolve the duplicate item issue, tap on the Remove All button to remove all of the duplicates listed in the list. Handheld PC Explorer deletes only the duplicates; each list will still contain the original appointment, task, or contact. If you don't remove the duplicates, you will find both the original and the copy of the item on your handheld PC.

Setting the Synchronization Options

H/PC Explorer allows you to customize your synchronization options. For example, you may want to make sure that your handheld PC is synchronized with the desktop computer every time the two units are connected. You can also indicate how H/PC Explorer should resolve conflicts, such as two appointments scheduled at the same time.

The synchronization options are specified on the Synchronization Manager dialog box, as shown in Figure 11-4. This dialog box appears whenever you choose Tools⇨Synchronization Manager within H/PC Explorer.

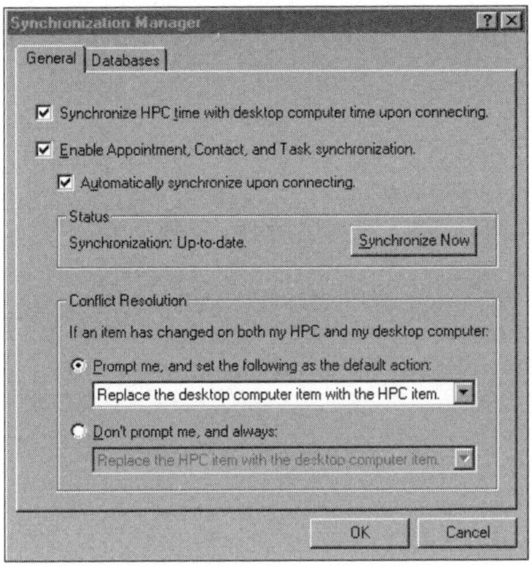

Figure 11-4: Use the Synchronization Manager dialog box to specify the settings for synchronizing your handheld PC with your desktop computer.

TIP: You can make sure that the time setting on your handheld PC matches that of the computer by selecting the Synchronize H/PC time with desktop computer time upon connecting setting on the Synchronization Manager dialog box. The option is selected if a check mark is in the check box next to the option. Of course, if you know that your computer does not keep the correct time, you probably want to make sure that this option is not selected.

TIP: The Status section of the dialog box indicates the synchronization status for the two units. If a problem arose with the last synchronization, for example, the status indicates that an error occurred. You can run a synchronization process again from the Synchronization Manager dialog box by clicking the Synchronization Now button.

Selecting automatic synchronization

If you are scheduling appointments and tasks on both your handheld PC and desktop computer, make sure that you synchronize the two units frequently to help ensure that you have not created conflicting appointments. The best way to make sure that your device gets synchronized frequently is to have H/PC Explorer automatically synchronize the appointment, task, and contact information on your handheld PC and desktop computer when you run the program. If you select this option, H/PC Explorer automatically synchronizes the two units immediately after establishing a connection between your handheld PC and desktop computer.

To specify that the synchronization should occur whenever the device and computer are connected, you need to make sure that the Automatically synchronize upon connecting option is selected on the Synchronization Manager dialog box.

TIP: With the automatic synchronization, you will have to wait for the synchronization process to finish before you can use H/PC Explorer to perform other tasks with your handheld PC. Of course, the more frequently you synchronize, the faster the process is.

Resolving scheduling conflicts

Have you ever had a situation where you accidentally scheduled yourself to be in two places at the same time? Conflicting appointments, tasks, and contacts can exist on your handheld PC and desktop computer. When you have an appointment, task, or contact record that was modified on both your handheld PC and desktop computer, and so the two records don't match, H/PC Explorer considers this situation a *conflict.*

The Conflict Resolution section of the Synchronization Manager dialog box allows you to specify how H/PC Explorer handles conflicts that are encountered during the synchronization process. You can have H/PC Explorer prompt you each time the synchronization encounters a conflict by selecting the Prompt me option. If you select this option, you also need to select one of the options in the drop-down list box to indicate the default action for the resolving the conflict, as outlined in Table 11-2.

If you want H/PC Explorer to automatically resolve all the conflicts that a synchronization encounters, select the Don't prompt me option. With this choice, you must select one of the options in the drop-down list box to indicate how H/PC Explorer should resolve all conflicts, as outlined in Table 11-2.

Table 11-2 Conflict Resolution Options

If You Want to Always	*Select This Drop-Down List Option*
Select the handheld PC item	Replace desktop computer item with H/PC item
Select the desktop computer item	Replace H/PC item with desktop computer item
Keep both items	Skip, don't replace either item

Chapter 12

Backing Up and Restoring Windows CE Information

In This Chapter

- Backing up your handheld PC
- Setting the options
- Restoring a backup

Have you ever had an important paper that you wanted to keep but someone in the family decided that the paper made a good gum wrapper? Perhaps you did some spring cleaning of your own and somehow managed to accidentally discard that important document. If you were wise enough to make a copy of the paper, then you could just get out the backup paper and be none the worse for wear.

Even on your handheld PC, documents and files can suddenly disappear. (At some point, you'll inevitably delete a document that you need to keep.) The possibility exists that something could go wrong with your handheld PC, and if the machine were to totally reset itself, you would lose all of the files that had been stored on it. The chances of that happening are slim, but if everything on your handheld PC is backed up, you can always restore the backup and continue working as if nothing happened.

This chapter explains how to use H/PC Explorer on your desktop computer to back up all the information stored on your handheld PC. I discuss the different options that can be selected to specify the type of backup you want to perform. Finally, I look at how you can quickly restore a backup file and replace the current information with a previous copy.

Performing a Backup

The H/PC Explorer program that runs on a desktop computer gives you the ability to back up your handheld PC on a regular basis. When you back up your handheld PC, the H/PC Explorer program copies all the stuff that you have placed on your handheld PC since you originally set it up. This backup file is stored on your desktop computer so that if anything ever goes wrong on your handheld PC, you can restore the backed-up copy. Of course, your handheld PC must be connected to your desktop computer in order to either create or restore a backup.

You can back up your handheld PC at any time, as long as the unit is connected to your desktop computer, by selecting the Back Up Now button on the toolbar of the H/PC Explorer program. (Don't forget that the H/PC Explorer program is on your desktop computer.) The Back Up Now button looks like a stack of papers with a red arrow on top of them.

REMEMBER

Before you start your backup, make sure that all programs on your handheld PC are closed. After you start the backup, take a break while H/PC Explorer completes the process. Doing so ensures that you have a complete backup file if you ever need to restore one.

To back up the contents of your handheld PC, follow these steps:

1. **Click on the Back Up Now button on the H/PC Explorer toolbar or choose Tools⇨Backup Now.**

   H/PC Explorer automatically selects a location for the backup file and displays the default location in the Confirm Backup dialog box, as shown in Figure 12-1. You can accept this default location or specify a different location for the backup file. ***Remember:*** The backup file needs to be stored on your desktop computer so that it can be copied on to your handheld PC if any type of problem occurs.

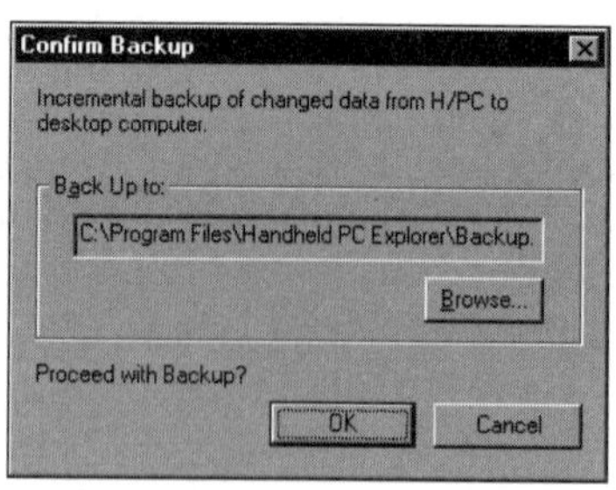

Figure 12-1: To perform a backup in the specified folder, click on the OK button.

When you click on the Back Up Now button, you get either an incremental or full backup of your handheld PC. The type of backup that is performed is determined by the settings you choose in the Backup/Restore Properties dialog box. The following section discusses this dialog box in detail.

2. **If you want to place the backup in a different folder, click on the Browse button to display the Select Backup Set dialog box, as shown in Figure 12-2. Specify the location for the backup file and then click on the Save button to use the specified location for the backup file.**

WARNING!

Do not use your handheld PC while the backup file is being created. If you are using files on your handheld PC, H/PC Explorer cannot make a backup copy of those files.

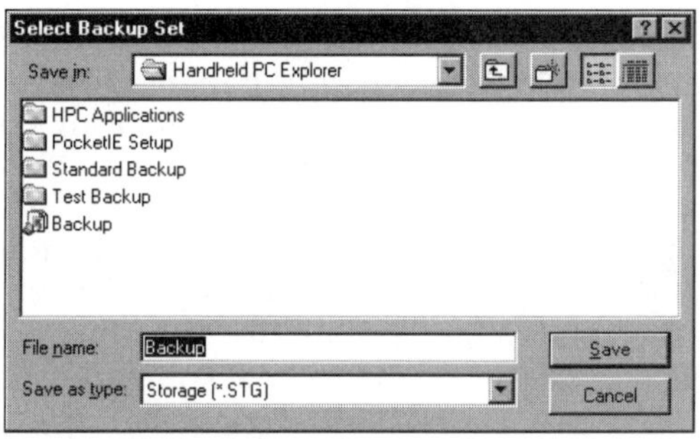

Figure 12-2: Indicate the name and location of the backup file on your desktop computer.

As the backup file is created, the Backup In Progress alert box shows you the status of the progress (see Figure 12-3). The length of time required to back up your device is based on the amount of stuff you have stored. If at any time you want to stop the backup process, simply click on the Cancel button. Keep in mind, however, that if you cancel the process, you do not have a complete backup file.

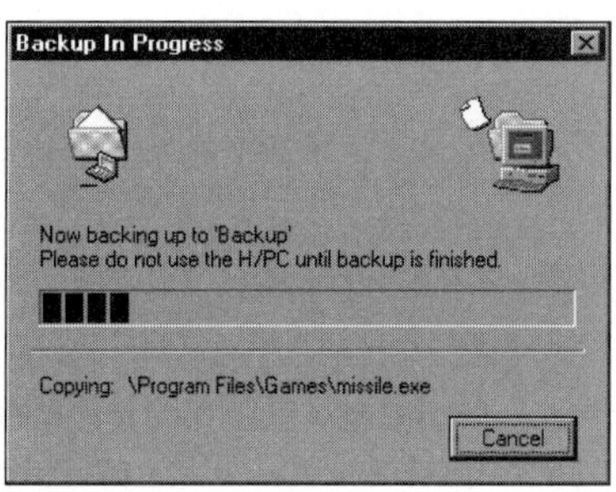

Figure 12-3: The Backup In Progress window.

3. **Click on the OK button on the Backup Complete alert box.**

   The Backup Complete alert box, shown in Figure 12-4, tells you that you can now safely use your handheld PC.

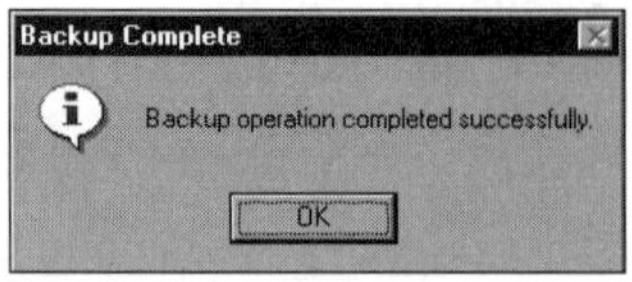

Figure 12-4: Click on the OK button to close the backup process.

Before you can back up your handheld PC, you must install the H/PC Explorer and establish a relationship between your handheld PC and the desktop computer that is running the H/PC Explorer program. For more information about setting up H/PC Explorer, refer to Chapter 9.

If something happens to the stuff you have stored on your handheld PC, you can restore only the stuff you last backed up. Anything you have done on your handheld PC since the last backup is lost. The more often you back up your handheld PC, the less likely you are to lose something important.

Setting the Backup Options

You can select specific options for each backup by choosing Tools⇨Backup/Restore. When you select the Backup/Restore option, the Backup/Restore Properties dialog box appears, as shown in Figure 12-5. The Backup tab allows you to do the following:

- Indicate the type of backup that is performed each time you request a backup
- Specify that the handheld PC is backed up every time you run the H/PC Explorer program
- Indicate the default location on your desktop computer for the backup file

To specify the type of backup, click on either the Full or Incremental option in the Back Up Now section of the Backup tab. The option you select determines the type of backup that is performed whenever you click on the Back Up Now button or choose Tools⇨Back Up Now:

- **Full:** When you make a full backup of your handheld PC, all the information on your handheld PC is copied into the backup file. The backup file is just another type of file that is created on your desktop computer. H/PC Explorer automatically creates this file when you do a backup of your handheld PC.
- **Incremental:** An incremental backup copies only the files that have changed since the last time you performed a full backup on your handheld PC. This type of backup is much quicker than a full backup because you only have to wait for the new stuff to be backed up. H/PC Explorer provides the option of having an incremental backup performed whenever you connect your handheld PC to the desktop computer. This can be a valuable option to use, because it eliminates the need for you to keep track of when you last backed up your handheld PC.

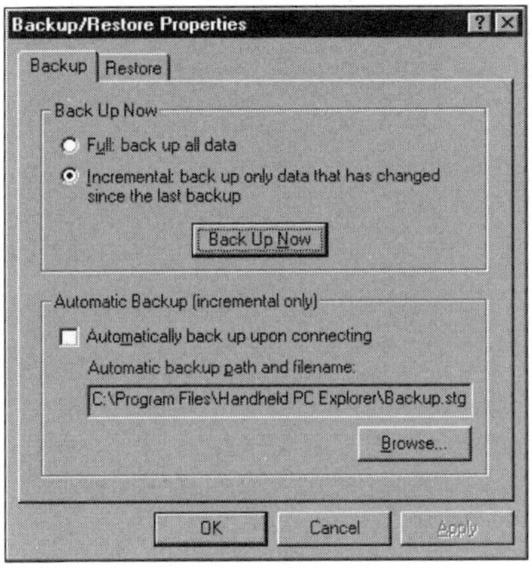

Figure 12-5: Specify the type of backup performed by H/PC Explorer.

TIP

To ensure that your handheld PC gets backed up on a regular basis, you can request that H/PC Explorer always back up the device when you connect to it. To have an automatic backup, you need to select the Automatically back up upon connecting option.

If you want the backups to be placed in a different folder on your computer, click on the Browse button to display the Select Backup Set window. Specify the folder location for the backup file. You can even change the name of the backup file, although I would recommend keeping a name that reminds you that the file contains a backup of your handheld PC.

Restoring a Backup

When you restore a backup, all the stuff currently on your handheld PC is replaced with the files in the backup that you restore. For this reason, make sure that you really want to restore the backup before you perform the following steps on your handheld PC. The only way to undo the process is to restore another backup, assuming that you have one for your current settings.

Make sure that you close all programs that are currently running on your handheld PC before restoring the backup file; the restore process will not run properly if a file is open on your handheld PC.

1. **In H/PC Explorer, choose Tools⇨Backup/Restore.**

   The Backup/Restore Properties dialog box appears.

2. **On the Restore tab of the Backup/Restore Properties dialog box, click on the Restore Now button (see Figure 12-6).**

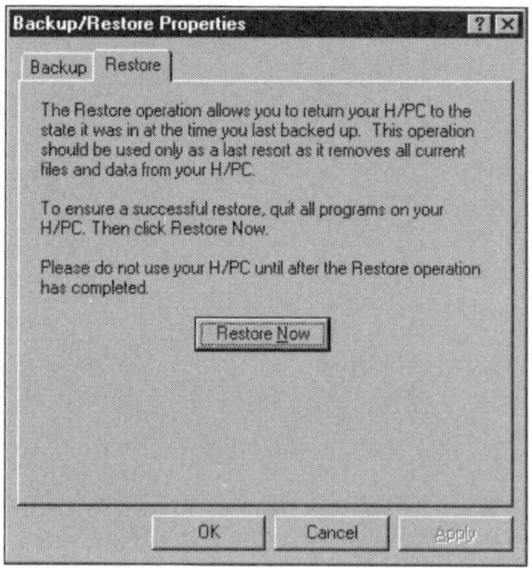

Figure 12-6: Click on the Restore Now button to begin restoring the last backup.

3. **Click on the OK button if you want to restore the specified file onto your device.**

   The Confirm Restore dialog box indicates which backup file will be restored onto your handheld PC, as shown in Figure 12-7. If this file is not the one you want to restore, you can select the Browse button to display the Select Backup Set window where you can specify the path of the backup file.

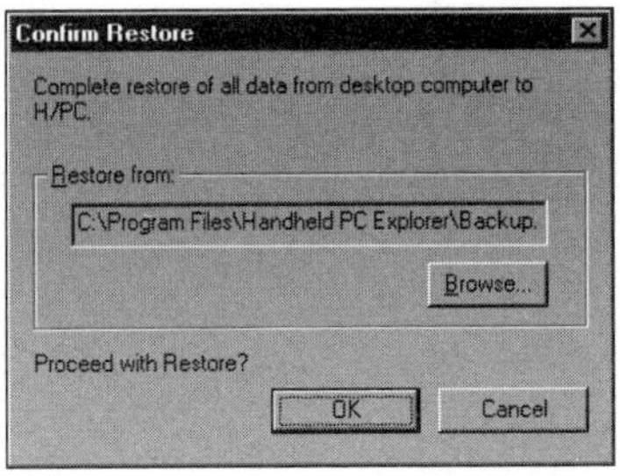

Figure 12-7: Verify that the specified path contains the backup you want to restore.

4. **Click on the OK button to start the restore process.**

   The Proceed with Restore? alert box appears, asking whether you really want to perform this restore, as shown in Figure 12-8. You have essentially reached the point of no return — when you select the Restore button, the process starts. Do not use your handheld PC while the information is being restored.

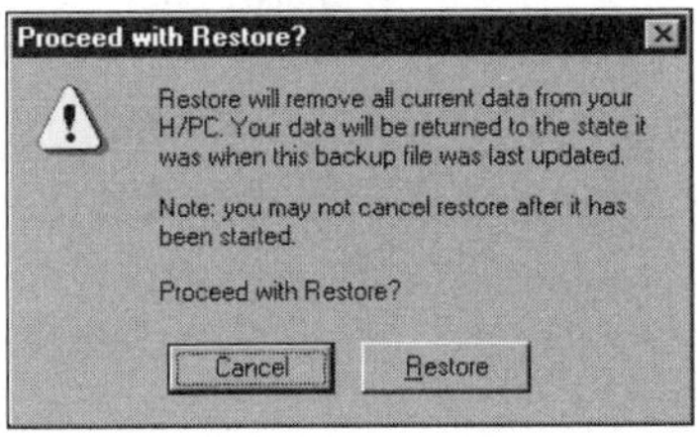

Figure 12-8: Select the Restore button to restore all the backed up information.

5. **If you get a message about open files on your handheld PC, close the specified programs on your handheld PC and click on the Retry All button.**

   If you have left any programs running on your handheld PC, the restore program will not be able to restore some files onto your handheld PC, as shown in Figure 12-9. To resolve the problem, close all running programs on your handheld PC and select the Retry All button. If you are not sure which programs are running, check for any programs listed in the status bar at the bottom of the screen. If you see any buttons, other than the Start button, the corresponding program is still open. You may also need to close a program sitting in the Status portion of the taskbar (the bottom-right corner of the screen); to close these programs, simply double-tap on the corresponding icon.

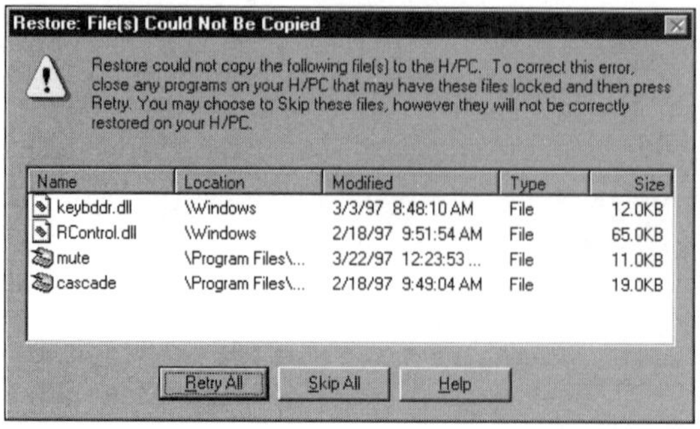

Figure 12-9: You must close the specified program files so that the files can be properly restored.

If you are not concerned about restoring the specified files, you can select the Skip All button and the restore process will continue without attempting to restore the specified files.

6. **When you see the Restore Complete alert box, click on the OK button, disconnect your handheld PC from your desktop computer, and press the Reset button.**

   You must reset your handheld PC before the restored settings take effect. If you are not sure where the Reset button is located on your handheld PC, refer to the hardware documentation that came with your handheld.

REMEMBER

In order to properly restore all the files onto your handheld PC, you must make sure that all programs are closed before running the restore process.

Chapter 13

Adding New Software to Your Handheld PC

In This Chapter

- Installing new software on your handheld PC
- Locating software for your handheld PC
- Getting rid of unwanted stuff

One of the biggest selling features for a Windows CE handheld PC, when compared to other handheld devices on the market, is that with Windows CE, you can easily add new programs to your handheld PC. This capability turns your handheld PC into a literal pocket laptop computer. This chapter explains how to locate and install new Windows CE programs on your handheld PC. It also illustrates how simply you can remove anything that you have added to your handheld PC to allow storage space for something new.

Locating Windows CE Programs

Because Windows CE is still fairly new to the market, locating software to add to your handheld PC can be tricky. But believe it or not, several programs have already been created for Windows CE.

Although you can locate some software at computer stores, one of the best sources for locating programs available for your handheld PC is the Internet. For example, check out `http://www.mobilesoft.com`, shown in Figure 13-1.

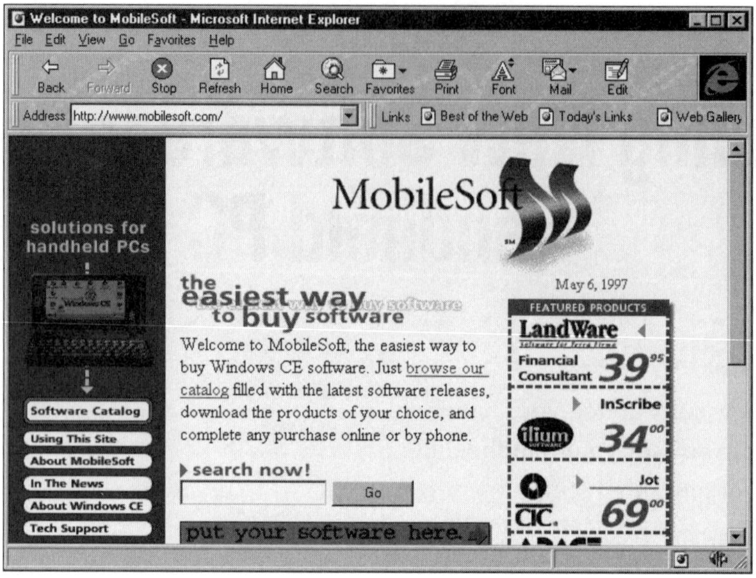

Figure 13-1: A great deal of information about Windows CE is available on the Internet.

TIP

Because most programs have to be installed onto your handheld PC from your desktop computer, use a desktop computer to search for software for your handheld PC. Download the software to the desktop computer, not your handheld PC. New sites that contain information about Windows CE programs are constantly being added to the Internet, so the best thing to do is to use one of the search engines and look for all references to Windows CE.

WARNING!

Before you download or purchase anything, make sure that the program is specifically designed to run on Windows CE. You can often get away with placing a Windows 95 program on Windows NT, and almost all Windows 3.1 programs run on Windows 95. But that is not the case with Windows CE — the program must be specifically created for Windows CE, or you will not be able to use that program on your handheld PC.

The other thing that you must keep in mind is the type of processor that you have in your handheld PC. The processor (often referred to as the CPU in computer lingo) is the heart of your handheld PC, and it controls everything that occurs on your handheld PC. The processors that are available for handheld PCs are almost as varied as the handheld PC manufacturers. Essentially, the software developer is required to make a different version of the program for each processor, so check to see if the program will work with the processor on your handheld PC before you purchase the program.

Installing a New Program

Common knowledge says that no two things are exactly alike, and this analogy definitely holds true when it comes to talking about how you install new software programs onto your handheld PC: No two installation programs are the same. Software developers create their own unique installation program for their specific program. Although the installation programs are all different, you do find some consistency as to how the programs are actually installed on your handheld PC.

Keep in mind that you cannot install any software on your handheld PC if you have not connected it to a desktop computer. The computer needs to have H/PC Explorer set up on it. (For more information, refer to Chapter 9.) Depending on the software developers' installation instructions, though you may not have to have H/PC Explorer running before you run the installation program.

You can add programs to your Windows CE handheld PC in two ways. Both methods require using a desktop computer connection.

- **Copy required files:** You add some programs by simply copying a file from your desktop computer to the folder on your handheld PC. To do so, you click on the program icon in Windows Explorer (on your desktop computer) and drag the program icon into the H/PC Explorer window.
- **Run install program:** Most software developers create an installation program that you run on your desktop computer to install the necessary files on your handheld PC. This method is probably the easiest way to install new software because typically, the installation program requires very little input from you.

Copying the program file to your handheld PC

You can copy most Windows CE programs to your handheld PC in the same manner that you would copy a file to your handheld PC. You usually use this method if only one file is required to run the program on your handheld PC, and the program does not require any changes to the system settings for Windows CE. The following steps illustrate how to copy a program file to your handheld PC:

1. **Make sure that you have a connection established between your Windows CE handheld PC and the desktop computer.**

   Usually, all you need to do is to connect your handheld to the computer with the serial interface cable and then run the H/PC Explorer program on your desktop computer. H/PC Explorer automatically establishes the connection with your handheld PC. For additional information about establishing a connection, refer to Chapter 9.

2. **In H/PC Explorer, open the Windows CE folder where you want to place the new program.**

   The easiest way to open the folder is to click on the appropriate folder in the folder list on the left side of the window, as shown in Figure 13-2. The right side of the H/PC Explorer window indicates the contents of the selected folder.

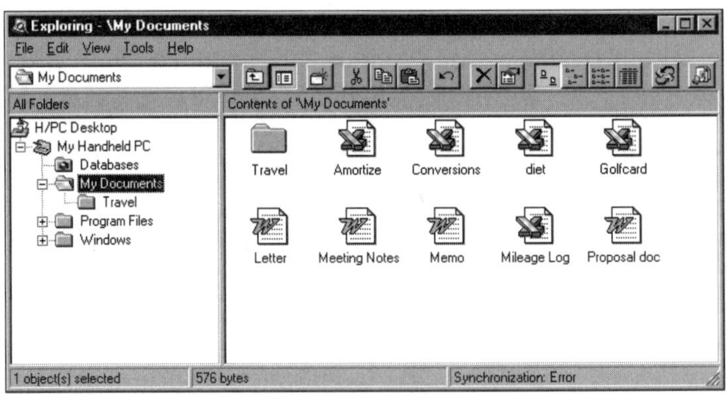

Figure 13-2: To open a folder, click on its icon on the left side of the window.

3. **Open Windows 95 Explorer and locate the file that you intend to copy.**

4. **Click on the program file and drag it into the H/PC Explorer window.**

   Remember that to drag and drop you need to position the mouse pointer on the item, hold down the left mouse button as you drag the item to the appropriate location, and then release the mouse button when the item is in the new location. When you release the mouse button, the Copy & Convert to H/PC window appears on your desktop computer to display the progress as the program is copied to your handheld PC.

5. **To run the program, simply double-tap on the program icon.**

   Remember that you need to use the Windows CE Explorer to locate the program icon in the folder where you copied it. If you need some pointers on using the Windows CE Explorer, refer to Chapter 2.

Running an installation program

Quite often, the software developer creates an installation program that you run to install the new program on your handheld PC. These installation programs are almost always designed to be run from the computer that is connected to the handheld PC. The installation programs are probably the easiest way to install a program on your handheld PC, because the program does all of the work of copying the required files to your handheld PC and placing the files in the appropriate directories. The following steps illustrate how to install the Microsoft PowerToys programs, which is actually a collection of different small programs, desktop wallpaper, and sound files that can be added to your handheld PC. I selected this program as an example because it contains some useful tools you may want to add to your handheld PC, and better yet, it is free.

TIP: Just in case you are wondering, I originally located the PowerToys installation program on the Internet, and that location is probably your best source if you would like to install the program on your handheld PC. You can find the PowerToys program on the Microsoft Windows CE Web site at `http://www.microsoft.com/windowsce/hpc/software/powerr.htm`. PowerToys may eventually be available in stores, but you can currently get the program for free if you are willing to download it yourself off the Internet.

1. **Make sure that you have a connection established between your Windows CE handheld PC and the desktop computer.**

   Some installation programs automatically run H/PC Explorer and establish the connection with your handheld PC. But to ensure that you have a good connection, I suggest connecting to your handheld PC before starting the installation program. For most models, all you need to do is to connect your handheld PC to the computer with the serial interface cable and then run H/PC Explorer.

2. **Run the PowerToys installation program on your desktop computer.**

   The easiest way to locate the installation program is to use Windows 95 Explorer. After you find the program, double-click on the program icon or name to start it. A setup screen similar to the one shown in Figure 13-3 appears.

3. **Click on the Next button to continue with the installation process.**

4. **Click the Yes button to agree to the license agreement for the program.**

   If you do not agree to the terms in a license agreement, the setup program will not install the new program.

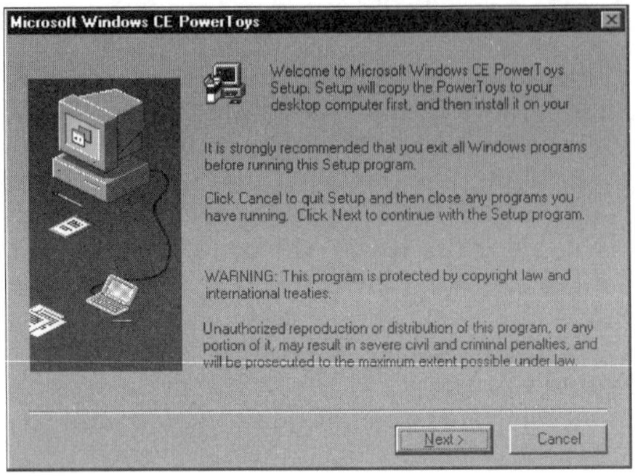

Figure 13-3: All setup programs have some type of start-up screen to remind you that you are about to install a new program.

5. **Type your name in the Name field, press the Tab key, type your company name in the Company field, and then select the Next button.**

   For consistency, you should use the name that you used when you originally set up your handheld PC. You can also type the name of your organization, such as your company name, in the Company field, although this field is optional and can be left blank.

6. **Verify the location where the setup program plans to install software on your desktop computer and then click on the Next button to continue.**

   The PowerToys programs come with some software that is installed on your computer to allow you to interact with your desktop computer. If you do not want the software installed in the specified directory, click on the Browse button to display the Choose Directory dialog box, shown in Figure 13-4, where you can select a new location for the files.

7. **Select the options you want to install and then click on the Next button.**

   As shown in Figure 13-5, the PowerToys setup comes with several *components,* or options, that you can select. A component is selected if a check mark is placed in the check box next to it. To select or unselect a component during an installation, click on the corresponding check box.

8. **Click on the Finish button to copy the selected options onto your handheld PC.**

   At this point in the installation, your handheld PC must be connected to the computer so that the setup program can connect to it and copy the requested files.

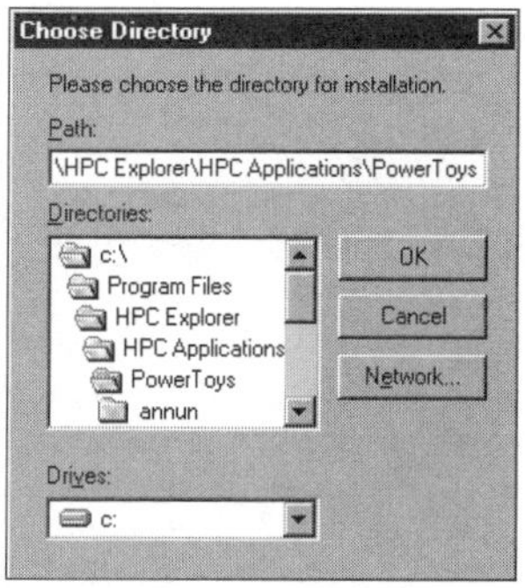

Figure 13-4: To select a new folder, click on the folder in the Directories section.

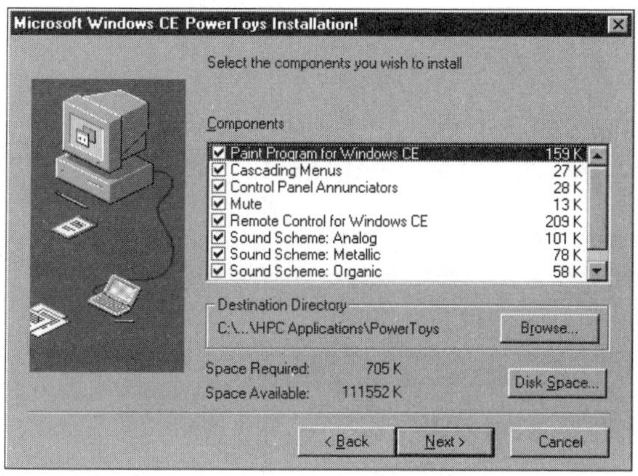

Figure 13-5: Some setup programs allow you to specify the options that you want to install on your handheld PC.

9. **Wait while the files are copied to your handheld PC.**

   The setup program normally provides you some type of status information as files are copied onto your handheld PC. When the setup is complete, you get a message indicating that you can now run the new programs on your Windows CE handheld PC.

Removing a Program from Your Handheld PC

On your Windows CE handheld PC, you only have a limited amount of storage space. To ensure that you do not run out of space for the things you want, you will probably want to eliminate those programs that you no longer use.

The easiest way to remove a program is to select the Remove Programs icon in the Control Panel folder. The Remove Programs icon looks like an Explorer Window with an X through a program icon.

When you click on the Remove Programs icon on your handheld PC, the Remove Program Properties window appears, as shown in Figure 13-6. To remove a program in the list from your handheld PC, tap on the selected program to highlight it and then tap on the Remove button. You will see a message verifying that you want to delete the program, as shown in Figure 13-7. To continue the process, click on the Yes button.

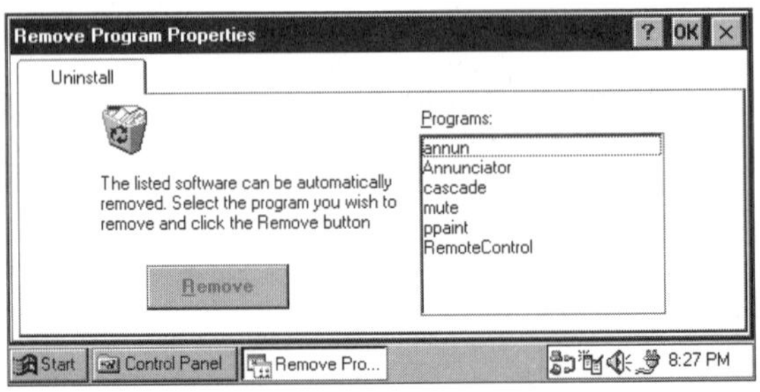

Figure 13-6: The Remove Program Properties window.

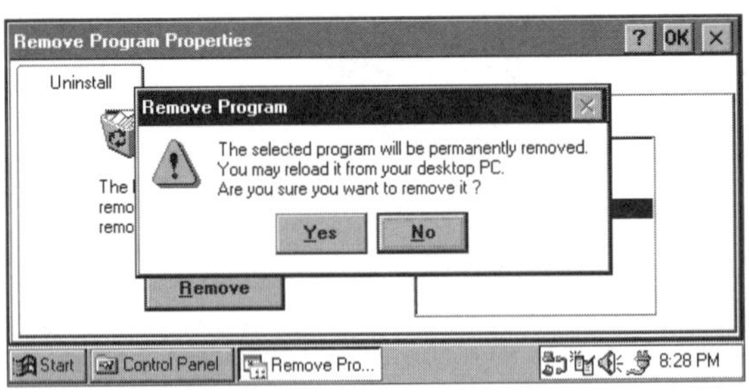

Figure 13-7: Windows CE verifies that you want to remove a program.

TIP

If you do not see the program you want to remove listed on the Remove Programs Properties window, the program was probably installed by copying the appropriate file onto your handheld PC, as discussed earlier in this chapter. To remove any programs not listed on this window, simply locate the program file by using Windows CE Explorer, highlight the program file icon, and tap on the Delete button.

Part IV

Getting Online with Windows CE

The 5th Wave By Rich Tennant

"OKAY, SO MAYBE COMDEX WASN'T READY FOR OUR MICROWAVE SLOW-COOKER THIS YEAR, BUT I STILL THINK WE SHOULD GO AHEAD WITH THE TRACKBALL GARAGE DOOR OPENER.

In this part . . .

In this electronic age, sending e-mail messages and connecting to the Internet are probably the most commonly performed tasks of the mobile professional. With Windows CE and your handheld PC, you now have the ability to send and receive e-mail from any location, all in the palm of your hand. Imagine being able to surf the net while watching Monday Night Football! You find all the secrets for dealing with modems, e-mail accounts, and the Internet within the pages of this part.

Chapter 14

Connecting to a Remote Location

In This Chapter

- Setting up remote connections
- Changing the configuration setting
- Connecting to a computer at another location

One of the most widely mentioned capabilities of Windows CE handheld PCs is that they enable you to use a modem and connect to other sites, such as a company network or even to the Internet. In order to connect to a remote site, you need to create a remote connection on your handheld PC for that site.

This chapter explains how to connect to another location from your handheld PC. It outlines the basic requirements for creating a remote connection and takes you step by step through the process of creating a remote connection.

Creating a Remote Connection

Windows CE comes with the built-in capability to connect to a remote location with your handheld PC. You can use your handheld PC and a modem to connect to a computer network or even to an Internet Service Provider. In order to connect to a computer network at your work or another location, the network computer must:

- **Be set up as a remote access server.** A remote access server is basically just a computer that is responsible for handling the connections made to the network using modems.
- **Be using *PPP (point-to-point protocol).*** PPP is how your handheld PC will communicate with the remote computer; because this is the only protocol supported by your Windows CE handheld PC, you need to make sure that it is supported by the network you are connecting to. (*PPP* is just another nerdy computerese term that describes the way the machines communicate across modems, but the system administrator at the location where you want to connect will be able to verify whether the machine is using PPP.)

Before you can connect to a remote location, you need to create a remote connection specifically for that location, as explained in the following steps:

1. **Select the Remote Networking folder icon in the Communications folder.**

   The Remote Networking folder icon looks just like a normal folder except that it has a picture of a computer and handheld PC connected on the front. You can find the Communications folder by tapping on the Start menu, tapping on the Programs option, and then tapping on the Communications folder. When you open the Remote Networking folder, you see the Make New Connection icon and icons for any existing remote connections on your handheld PC, as shown in Figure 14-1.

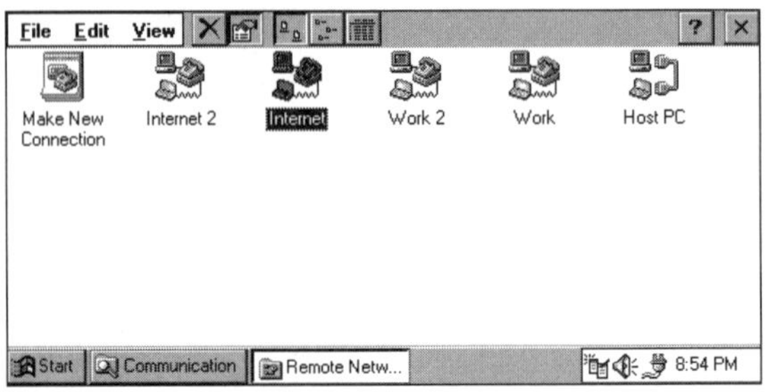

Figure14-1: The Remote Networking folder.

2. **Tap on the Make New Connection option.**

   When you select the Make New Connection option, the Make New Connection dialog box appears, as shown in Figure 14-2. You use this dialog box to name your new remote connection and to specify the connection type. You can actually create two different types of connections from this dialog box:

   - **Dial-Up Connection:** Select this remote connection type to create a connection that you will use your modem to connect to.
   - **Direct Connection:** Use this type to create a connection where the handheld PC is connected to a computer by using the serial interface cable. You will only select this connection type when you are setting up a connection between your handheld PC and a desktop computer.

3. **Type the name of your new remote connection.**

   REMEMBER

   Type a name that is different from any other connections that you have on your handheld PC. Remote connections are just like files — you cannot have two with the same name on your handheld PC.

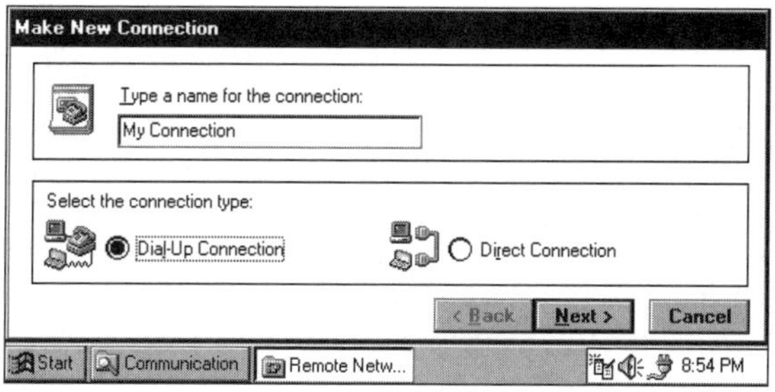

Figure 14-2: Type a unique name for your new remote connection.

4. **Tap on the Dial-Up Connection options.**

   Doing so allows you to create a remote connection for your modem. You will probably select this option most often because the direct connection between your computer and handheld PC is created when you set up the H/PC Explorer software on your computer. So the only time you select the Direct Connection option is if you need to create a connection to a different desktop computer.

5. **Select the Next button.**

   When you select the Next button, the Make a New Dial-Up Connection dialog box appears, as shown in Figure 14-3.

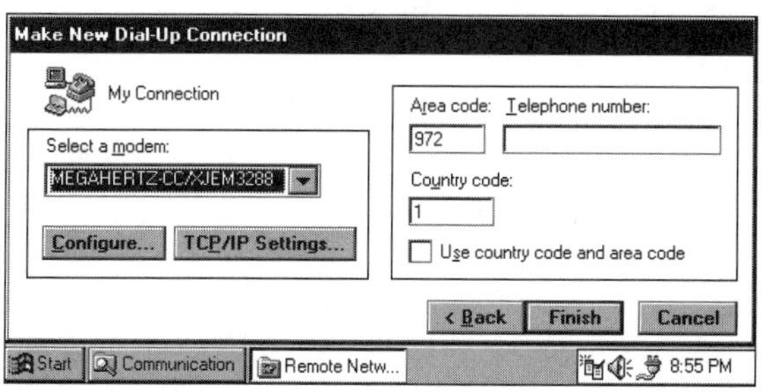

Figure 14-3: The Make a New Dial-Up Connection dialog box.

6. **Make sure that the Select a modem drop-down list box contains the name of your modem.**

   If your modem is not listed, select the Down Arrow button and highlight the name of your modem. If your modem is not listed in the drop-down list, it may not be properly connected to your device. You need to make sure that the modem was connected to your handheld PC properly, based on the installation instructions that came with the modem.

7. **Type the area code for the remote connection in the Area code field.**

8. **Type the phone number for the remote connection in the Telephone number field.**

9. **Type the country code for the remote connection in the Country code field.**

   The country code is only necessary if you are dialing from one country to another. If you are calling a location within your country, the Country code field contains the long-distance access for your country. For example, in the United States, this code is 1. You can find out the area code for most cities and country codes in the World Clock program on your handheld PC. The quickest way to run this program is to double-tap on the time display in the bottom-right corner of the desktop. (For more information, see Chapter 18.)

10. **Select the Use country code and area code option if necessary.**

    If the phone number for your remote connection is a long-distance number, you need to make sure that the check box next to this option contains a check mark. This step is especially important to remember if the connection number shares the same area code as you do, but the phone call is still considered long distance.

11. **Select the Finish button to save the new remote connection.**

Before you save the connection, you can configure the connection by selecting the Configure button or selecting the TCP/IP Settings button to change the TCP/IP settings for your remote connection. If you are not sure of these settings right now, you can set or modify them at any time after the remote connection has been created. You can find more information about entering the proper information when you select each of these buttons in the following sections.

Configuring a connection

You may need to change the configuration settings for the remote connection. This step is necessary if you need to change the connection settings for the modem, make sure that the terminal window appears during the connection, or even indicate how long Windows CE should allow the phone to ring before a connection is made. To modify the connection settings, you need to select the Configure button on the Dial-Up Connection screen to display the Device Properties dialog box, as shown in Figure 14-4.

Port settings

You use the options on the Port Settings tab of the Device Properties dialog box to specify how the modem actually connects to the remote location.

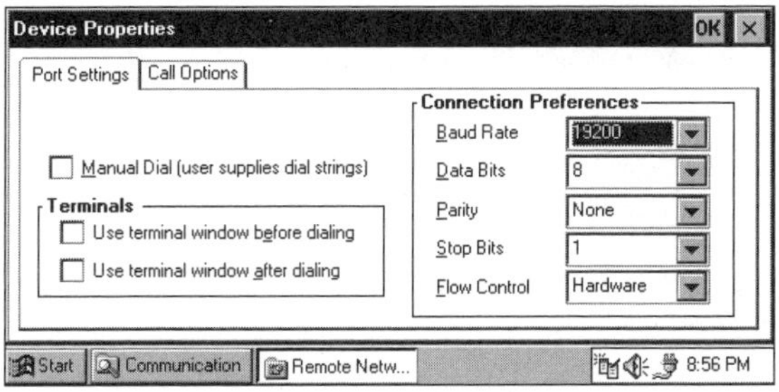

Figure 14-4: Indicate how the modem should connect to the remote connection.

Some types of remote connections may require you to manually log into the machine. Manually logging in is normally done by using a *terminal window,* which means that you basically get a blank screen where you type in the information required to connect to the network. For most Internet connections, manual login is not required, although if you know or have been informed by a system administrator that the connection you are making requires a manual connection, you will probably need to select one of the Terminal options.

The Connection Preferences section contains different preferences that can be selected to inform the modem how to connect to the remote location. The fields in this section automatically contain a default set of values. If you need to change any of the values in those fields, tap on the Down Arrow button next to the appropriate field and tap the value you want to input for the field. Again, you should change these fields only if you have been informed that you need to connect with a different set of values. Use only the values you are provided for each of these fields. Each of these fields affect the way your handheld PC makes the connection.

Call options

The options on the Call Options tab of the Device Properties screen, as shown in Figure 14-5, allow you to indicate how much time should elapse between certain events during the call.

You can indicate a specific amount of time that the modem should wait for a connection before hanging up. You do so by selecting the check box next to the Cancel the call if not connected within field and then typing the appropriate number of seconds in the seconds field.

To ensure that the modem does not start dialing without a dial tone, you can select the check box next to the Wait for dial tone before Dialing option. Of course, if you are going to make a credit card call, you want to wait for a dial tone, so specify the amount of time that your modem should wait for a dial tone in the field next to the Wait for credit card tone option.

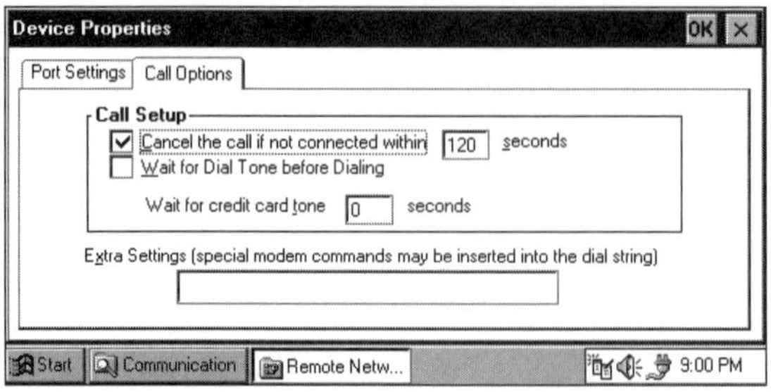

Figure14-5: Indicate the amount of time that the modem should wait for different events to transpire.

You may want, or even need, to add some special strings of characters to the characters that the modem dials to connect to your remote connection. These characters can be used to indicate that you are placing a credit card call, insert a pause when attempting to access an outside line, or wait for a second dial tone. You specify these special characters in the Extra Settings field. Check out the following sidebar for more information about the different dialing pattern characters that you can use.

Modifying the TCP/IP settings

When you create a remote connection under Windows CE, another button you can select is the TCP/IP Settings button. These settings are required for most types of remote connections.

TCP/IP deals with the communication between different types of computers. It was a standard communications protocol that was developed so that computers with different operating systems could talk to each other. TCP/IP is used as the standard communications protocol on the Internet. In case you are really curious, TCP/IP stands for Transmission Control Protocol/ Internet Protocol. (Test that one out on your friends.)

Quite often, the remote connection that you want to use requires you to specify certain addresses so that your device will connect properly. These address settings are specified by selecting the TCP/IP Settings button on the Dial-Up Connection dialog box. When you select this button, the TCP/IP Settings dialog box appears, as shown in Figure 14-6.

Dialing patterns

You may need to use different dialing methods with your modem when you are connecting from different locations. For example, if you are making a connection from a pay phone, you will probably want to use a calling card, so you need to tell the modem to wait for the calling card tone and then dial the calling card number.

A standard list of characters can be used under Windows CE to send added instructions to your modem. These extra characters are normally typed in the Extra Settings field on the Call Options tab option of the Device Properties screen. The characters can be any combination of the characters listed in the following table.

Character	Purpose
0-9	Indicates a numeric character that is part of the dialing string.
E	Dials the country code that is indicated by the program that is dialing the modem.
F	Dials the area code that is indicated by the program that is dialing the modem.
G	Dials the local number that is indicated by the program that is dialing the modem.
P	Indicates that the digits that follow should be pulse dialed.
T	Indicates that the digits that follow should be tone dialed.
W	Waits for a second dial tone. You will normally want to use this code after entering a credit card number to wait for the next dial tone.
$	Waits for the credit card tone.
,	Inserts a pause in the dialing string. The length of the pause is determined by the specific modem, but it is usually about 2 seconds.
!	Transfers to another extension.
@	Waits for a quiet answer, no noise on the other end of the line. This quiet answer normally indicates that the modem has made a connection.
A,B,C,D,*, #	Used on some tone systems for special control characters. The purpose of these characters varies. You will probably rarely use these characters.

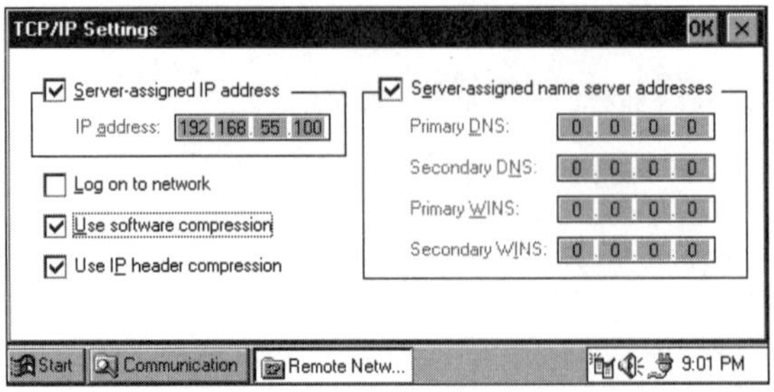

Figure 14-6: Indicate the server addresses for your remote connection.

You need to specify one of three basic address types for your remote connection. Each address type is discussed in Table 14-1. Before you type any values in these fields, check with your systems administrator, if connecting to an internal company network, or with your Internet Service Provider to get the required values for each field.

Table 14-1 TCP/IP Settings

Setting	*Description*
IP address	This address tells the Internet where to send information you request while connected to an Internet Service Provider. If you have a *static IP address,* you need to remove the check mark from the Server-assigned IP address check box and type the address in the IP address field. A static IP address means that the address for your handheld PC connection on the Internet is always the same. This type of situation normally only occurs if you have a machine that is constantly connected to the Internet. Normally, with most Internet Service Providers, the IP address is assigned to you each time you connect to the Internet, so you will want to keep a check mark in the Server-assigned IP address field.
DNS address	This is the address of a machine, called the *Domain Name Server,* that is responsible for converting the name you request to a physical IP address on the Internet. For example, if you type `www.microsoft.com`, the DNS server converts it to the physical address of `207.68.156.73`. You may need to specify the location of the DNS server that you need to use. If so, remove the check mark from the Server assigned name server addresses check box and type the address in the Primary DNS field. Some Internet Service Providers have more than one DNS address for converting IP addresses; if you receive more than one address, type the second one in the Secondary DNS field.

Setting	*Description*
WINS address	This is the address of a Windows NT server, running the Windows Internet Naming Service, that is responsible for resolving the IP addresses for Internet sites that you request. The server will also normally assign IP addresses to computers within the internal computer network of the company. You may need to specify the location of the WINS server that you need to use. If so, remove the check mark from the Server assigned name server addresses check box and type the address in the Primary WINS field. Again, some Internet Service Providers have more than one DNS address for converting IP addresses, if you receive more than one address, type the second one in the Secondary WINS field.

Changing the settings for a remote connection

Doesn't it seem that as soon as you get something set up, it needs to be modified for one reason or another? Windows CE has planned for just such an occurrence. You can change most of the information for a remote connection by locating the desired connection in the Remote Networking folder and selecting the Properties icon on the toolbar. The Properties icon resembles a list with a hand at the top of it. (Or you can choose File⇨Properties from the Remote Networking folder.)

When you tap the Properties icon, the Dial-Up Connection dialog box appears with the information for the selected remote connection, as shown in Figure 14-7. In this dialog box, you can modify the phone number settings, configure the connection, or change the TCP/IP settings for the connection.

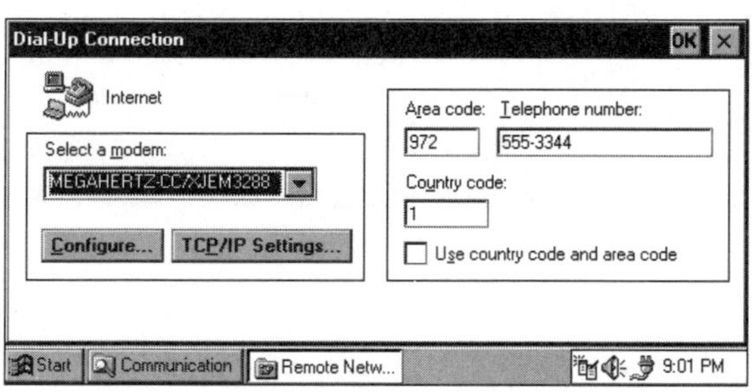

Figure 14-7: Make modifications to a remote connection on the Dial-Up Connection screen.

TIP

To modify the way the modem actually connects to the remote location, select the Configure button. Doing so displays the Device Properties dialog box which you can use to adjust your settings.

Connecting a modem to your handheld PC

In order to connect to a remote location, your handheld PC must have access to a modem. Some handheld PCs come with an internal modem. If that is the case with your handheld PC, then you don't have to worry about how to connect to a modem. For handheld PCs without modems, the current modem options for your handheld PC fall into basically two categories: analog and wireless.

An *analog modem* connects to a regular phone line and allows the modem to dial out in basically the same way that you dial the phone when you place a phone call. This type of modem is probably the most versatile because it can be used to connect to any location. The easiest way to connect your device to one of these modems is to find a small modem card that you can plug into the PC-Card slot on your handheld PC.

You can also connect to an external modem. To do so, you need to purchase a null-modem cable and a 9-pin to 25-pin adapter. (Your local computer store can help you with these items.) A *null-modem cable* resembles a normal computer cable; the only difference is that a couple of wires have been crossed on the inside of it. You don't need to know the specifics of it, just remember to ask for one. The *9-pin to 25-pin adapter* converts the null-modem cable so that it will plug into the back of your modem properly.

Connect one end of the null-modem cable to the end of the serial interface cable that normally connects to the computer, attach the 9-pin to 25-pin adapter to the other end of the null-modem cable, and then pull the adapter into the external modem.

The new breed of modems is the *wireless modem.* These modems eliminate the need to connect your handheld PC to a phone line. Just like a cellular phone, you can use the modem from any location. The main drawback with wireless modems is the fact that they require you to have a subscription with a service, similar to a cellular contract, which means that you pay extra for the ability to connect.

No matter what type of modem you select, keep in mind that a modem causes a big power drain on your handheld PC. If at all possible, you need to make sure that your unit is plugged in to an outlet while using the modem. Some types of modems will not even work on a handheld PC that is only using battery power. If you need to be able to use your modem when your handheld PC is running on battery power, locate a modem that runs on low power.

Connecting to a Remote Location

After you create a remote connection on your handheld PC, you can quickly connect to the remote site at any time. The following steps tell you how to connect to the remote site:

1. **Locate the icon for your remote connection.**

   The remote connection icons are normally located in the Remote Networking folder, as shown in Figure 14-8. This folder can be found within the Communications folder located in the Programs folder. So tap the Programs option on the Start menu, tap on the Communications folder, and then tap on the Remote Networking folder.

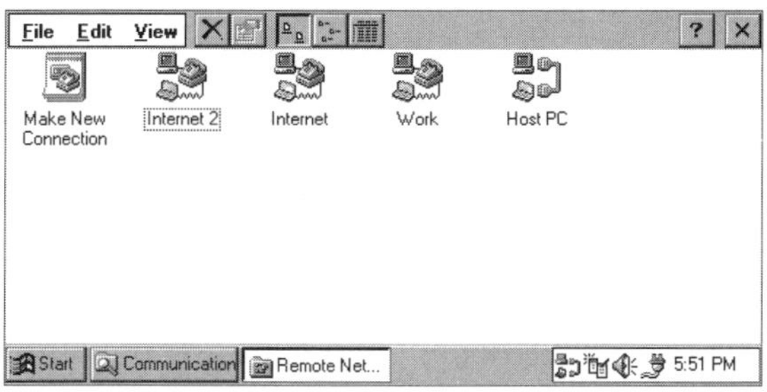

Figure 14-8: Double-tap on the appropriate remote connection icon.

2. **Double-tap on the selected remote connection icon.**

   When you double-tap on the icon, the Connect To dialog box appears, allowing you to type the connection information for your account, as shown in Figure 14-9.

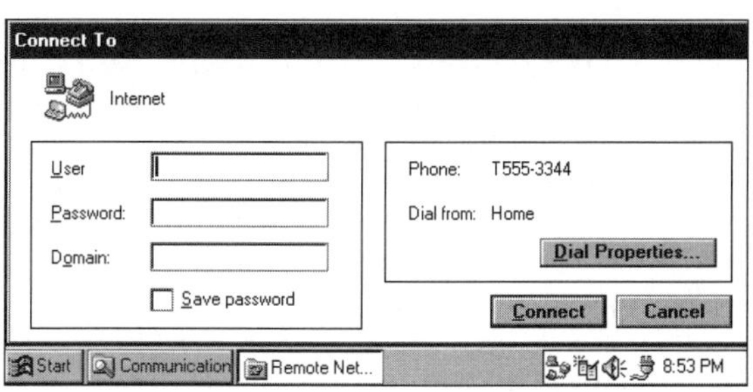

Figure 14-9: Connect your modem to the phone line before tapping on the Connect button.

3. **Type your user name in the User field.**

   Use the user name that was assigned to you by the remote site you're attempting to connect to. This user name is the one that you received when you set up your remote login account; if you are connecting to a machine at work, quite often this is the same user name that you connect with at work.

4. **Type your password in the Password field.**

5. **If required, type a domain name in the Domain field.**

   This field is normally not needed for Internet connections. The Domain field is normally used when connecting to an internal network at a company. If you need to type a value in this field, you should receive that information when you set up your account with either the Internet Service Provider or systems administrator.

6. **Select the check box next to the Save password field.**

   By having your handheld PC remember your password and user name information, you don't have to type the information each time you want to connect to the Internet. However, if you share the handheld PC with someone else, you may not want to select this check box.

7. **Select the Connect button.**

   The modem dials the phone number and connects to your remote site.

TIP

By using the Save password option, you don't have to worry about forgetting or mistyping your user name, password, or even the domain name. Your device automatically remembers this information, and if someone does look at the screen, she won't be able to figure out your password because Windows CE substitutes asterisks for each character in your password.

Turning off call waiting

If you are lucky enough to have access to that ever-popular calling feature called call waiting, you will soon find that it is not much of a blessing when it comes to using a modem. Those little beeps indicating that someone else is on the line can cause your modem to hang up. To eliminate this problem, you can either cancel your call waiting service, which is probably not the answer you want to hear, or you can have your handheld PC disable call waiting when you are using your modem.

In order to temporarily disable call waiting, you need to get the code that disables it from your local phone company. Each phone company has its own code that can be typed before placing a phone call to temporarily disable the call waiting service during that call. For example, some phone companies have you type the code *70 before dialing a phone number to disable the call waiting feature.

After you know the code for disabling call waiting, tap on the Dial Properties button in the Connect To dialog box to display the Communications Properties dialog box, shown in Figure 14-10. Or you can double-tap on the Communications icon in the Control Panel folder.

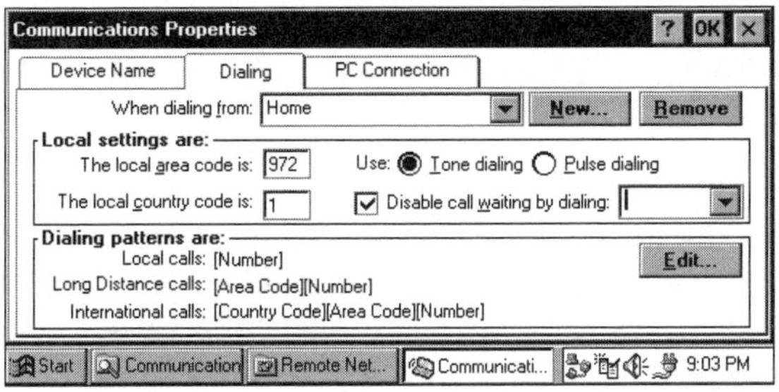

Figure 14-10: Select the Disable call waiting by dialing option and specify the disable code.

Select the check box next to the Disable call waiting by dialing option. In the drop-down list box next to the option, select the code that your phone company uses to disable call waiting. If you do not see the correct code in the list, type the code in the field next to the Down Arrow button.

TIP: Don't worry about turning your call waiting back on. With most phone companies, the call waiting option is only disabled during one phone call. As soon as you hang up the phone, call waiting will start working again.

Connecting from a different location

Because your handheld PC is so mobile, you'll probably use it in all kinds of places. For example, you may be on vacation in Florida and want to check your e-mail messages at work (not that anyone would do that on vacation, but it's a good example). You can set up different locations on your handheld PC from which to dial, thus allowing you to dial into the office from Florida without altering the settings for your home location.

To set up a new dialing location, you need to use the Dialing tab option on the Communications Properties dialog box. This dialog box appears when you select the Dial Properties button on the Connect To dialog box. The When dialing from field at the top of the dialog option indicates the name of the current dialing from location. To create a new location, select the New button and type the name of the new location in the window, as shown in Figure 14-11.

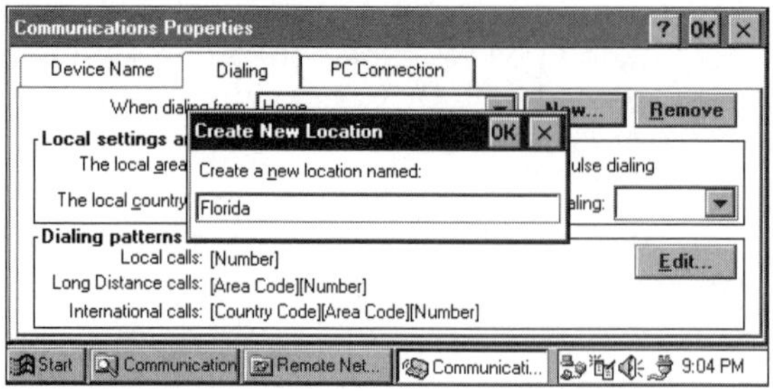

Figure 14-11: Type a unique name for the dialing location and tap on the OK button.

Remember to specify the local area code for the new location and the local country code. If you are unsure of the area code, check the World Clock program — it contains area codes for several different locations.

After you create a location, you can select it by simply tapping the Down Arrow button next to the When dialing from field and highlighting the appropriate location in the drop-down list.

You can remove dialing locations from the list by selecting a location from the drop-down list and then tapping the Remove button.

Chapter 15

Connecting to the Internet

In This Chapter

- Setting up your handheld PC to connect to the Internet
- Locating information on the Internet
- Customizing the way you view information on the Internet

Connecting to the Internet has gone from being a casual pastime to a way of life for many people. Now with Windows CE, you can connect to the Internet from any location.

This chapter explains how to locate and install Pocket Internet Explorer on your handheld PC and identifies the basic requirements for connecting to the Internet. I also explain how to connect to the Internet and locate the information you want — all from the comfort of your handheld PC.

Installing Pocket Internet Explorer

Before you can browse the Internet, you need to have a program, commonly referred to as a *browser,* that allows you to look at the different sites on the Internet. Currently, the most popular browser for Windows CE is Pocket Internet Explorer. (The fact that it comes with your handheld PC may have something to do with the program's popularity.)

Before you can use Pocket Internet Explorer on your handheld PC, you need to make sure that the program is installed. On some Windows CE models, this program comes installed on the handheld PC. If the program is already installed on your handheld PC, you don't have to waste your time trying to install it again. You can figure out whether Pocket Internet Explorer is already installed on your handheld PC by looking for the Pocket Internet Explorer icon. (This icon resembles a world with a magnifying glass over the top of it.)

Internet basics

In case you haven't heard, the Internet is the latest craze to sweep the nation — or should I say the world. You can hardly turn around without hearing something about the Net. The big question: What exactly is the Internet?

The Internet is essentially a worldwide network of computers that allows people to communicate with each other, gather information about different topics, and even order new products.

Your Windows CE handheld PC comes with all of the software you need to get on and surf the Net. The Inbox program allows you to send and receive e-mail messages via the Internet, and Pocket Internet Explorer, which comes either on your handheld PC or on a separate CD you can install, allows you to get out and look for all information available on the Internet.

Unfortunately, Internet software won't do you much good if you lack two basic items: an Internet account with an Internet Service Provider and a modem to allow your handheld PC to call the provider. An Internet Service Provider (ISP) is a company that is constantly connected to the Internet and provides you an account so you can log on to their network with your handheld PC and have access to the Internet.

So if you have an Internet account, a modem, and the right software, you have the essential elements you need to surf the Net from your Windows CE handheld PC.

Copying the Pocket Internet Explorer files to your desktop computer

Before you can install the Microsoft Pocket Internet Explorer program on your Windows CE, you must copy the setup files from the Desktop Software for Microsoft Windows CE CD-ROM that came with your handheld PC. Unfortunately, Microsoft has made these setup files a little difficult to locate on the CD-ROM. In fact, it's almost as if the dear folks at Microsoft intentionally hid the darn things. These files are actually loaded onto your desktop computer when you click on the Install H/PC Explorer icon. For more information, refer to Chapter 9.

When you run the setup, make sure that you select the Setup Microsoft Pocket Internet Explorer check box on the Select Components dialog box, as shown in Figure 15-1. This option copies the setup files to your computer.

If you originally installed the H/PC Explorer program but did not select the Setup Microsoft Pocket Internet Explorer check box, the setup files were not copied to your computer. You need to rerun the setup program for H/PC Explorer. When you rerun the setup, the Modify Current Installation dialog box appears (see Figure 15-2). Be sure to select the Change button in this dialog box so that you can make sure that the Setup Microsoft Pocket Internet Explorer check box gets selected.

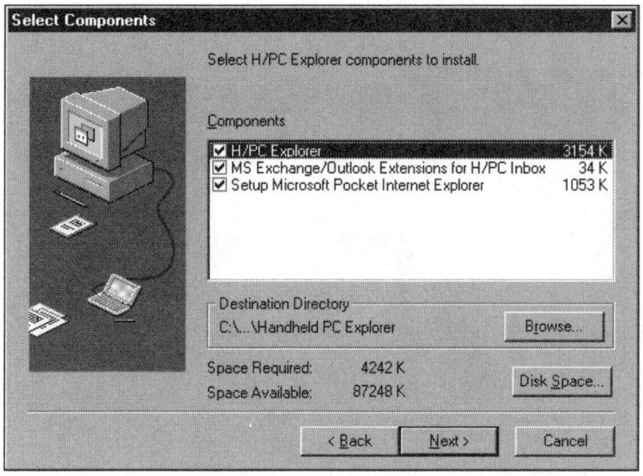

Figure 15-1: When you run the setup, make sure that the check box is selected for Pocket Internet Explorer.

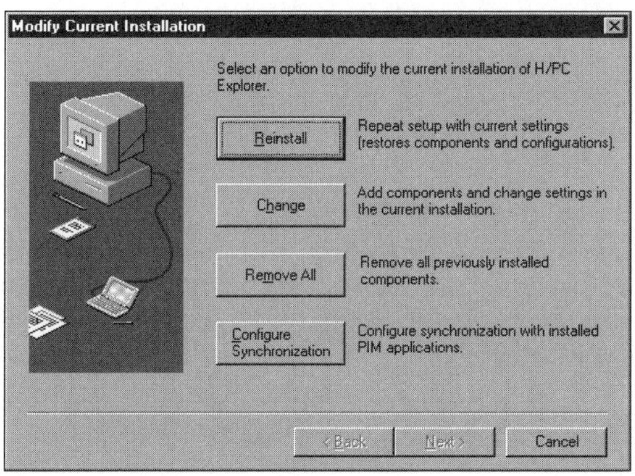

Figure 15-2: The Modify Current Installation dialog box.

Loading Pocket Internet Explorer on your handheld PC

After you install the Pocket Internet Explorer setup files onto your desktop computer, you are halfway there. (I know this setup stuff is rather boring and tedious, but unfortunately it is a necessary evil if you want to connect to the Internet from your handheld PC.) Your next step is to install the Pocket Internet Explorer files from your desktop computer onto your handheld PC. If you haven't already copied the files to your desktop computer, refer to the preceding section.

1. **Click on the Setup Microsoft Pocket Internet Explorer option.**

   Depending on what options you selected when you installed the setup files, you should be able to choose Programs➪Handheld PC Explorer➪Setup Microsoft Pocket Internet Explorer, as shown in Figure 15-3.

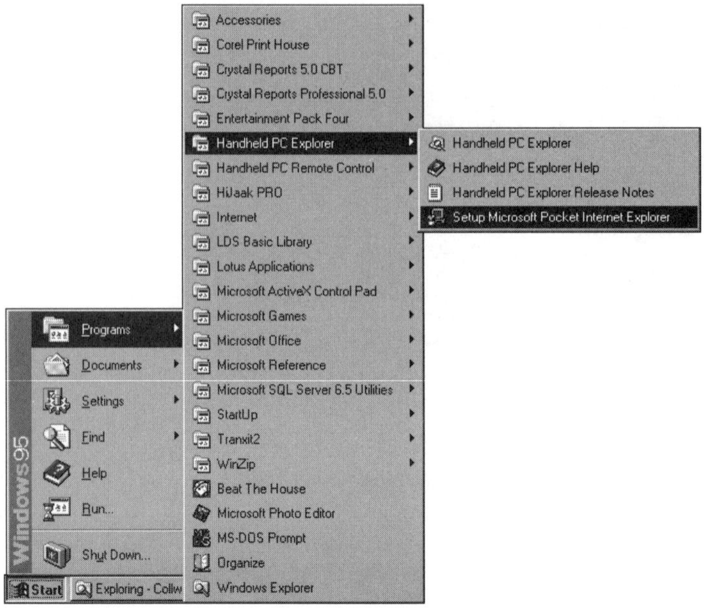

Figure 15-3: The easiest place to look for the Pocket Internet Explorer setup program is on the Start menu.

If the Setup Microsoft Pocket Explorer option is not on the Start menu, use the Explorer program on your desktop computer and locate the Setup program in the Pocket IE Setup folder, which should be in the Handheld PC Explorer folder.

2. **In the Microsoft Pocket Internet Explorer setup dialog box, click on the Next button to start the setup process.**

3. **In the Software License Agreement dialog box, click on the Yes button to continue the setup.**

   Remember, this means you promise to only use this program as it was intended — for connecting to the Internet.

4. **In the Name and Company dialog box, type your name in the Name text box and press the Tab key. Type your company name in the Company field and then click on the Next button.**

5. **In the Install Pocket Internet Security dialog box, select the check box if you want to be able to connect to secure sites on the Internet and then click on the Next button.**

   You will want to select this check box option, as shown in Figure 15-4, if you want to purchase anything over the Internet. Most Internet sites that deal with personal information, such as credit card numbers, use secure methods to ensure that no one else can get your personal information. Keep in mind that if you do load this extra feature, it does use up extra memory on your handheld PC, but it is definitely worth it.

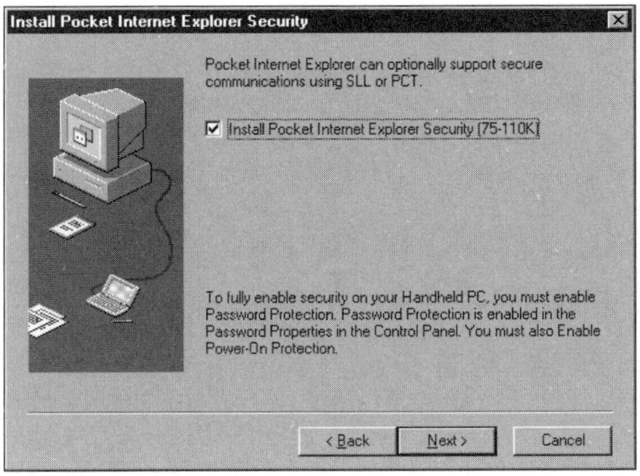

Figure 15-4: To ensure secure communications on the Internet, select the check box.

6. **On the Select Destination Directory on the Desktop dialog box, specify the location on your computer where you want the related files to be installed and then tap on the Next button.**

   The setup program needs to install some files on your desktop computer before placing files on your handheld PC. It automatically defaults to a folder where other Windows CE program information is stored on your computer, as shown in Figure 15-5.

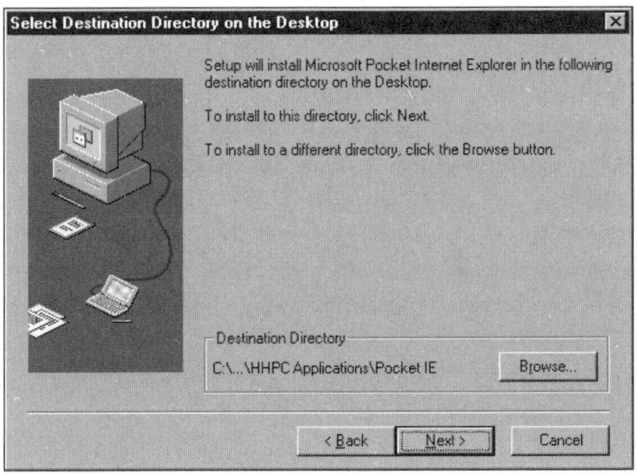

Figure 15-5: The setup program places all Windows CE program stuff in one common location on your desktop computer.

7. **When you see the H/PC Downloading dialog box, make sure you have properly connected your handheld PC to your computer and click on the Finish button to copy the program onto your handheld PC.**

8. **Tap on the OK button to close the setup program.**

   When you see the Setup Complete message, all of the required files have been copied to your handheld PC. You are now ready to jump onto the Internet from your Windows CE handheld PC.

Upgrading to other versions of Pocket Internet Explorer

Due to the Internet's popularity, it seems that Internet Web browsers are the most frequently updated programs around. About the time you load a browser onto your computer or Windows CE handheld PC, it seems another version of the program becomes available. Luckily, the updates are usually free. But these updates still require you to find the new version on the Internet, copy it to a computer, and then install it onto your handheld PC. What a hassle.

The best way to determine if a new version of a browser is available for Pocket Internet Explorer is to check the Microsoft Windows CE Web page at `http://www.microsoft.com/windowsce/default.asp`. If a new version exists, you can download it to your desktop computer and then follow the instructions the Microsoft folks provide to install it onto your handheld PC.

Setting Up Your Internet Connection

After you load Pocket Internet Explorer onto your Windows CE handheld PC, you are almost ready to start surfing the Internet. Before you can start your surfing, you need to figure out how you are going to connect to the Internet. Unfortunately, nothing these days is ever really free, and the same goes for connecting to the Internet. If you are lucky enough to have access to an Internet connection through your work, then I guess you may be able to connect for free and let your boss pick up the tab. But for the rest of us, getting on the Internet is similar to subscribing to cable television.

If you don't currently have Internet access, you need to locate an Internet Service Provider (commonly referred to by Internet geeks as an ISP). You can find an ISP by looking in the Yellow Pages or on billboards or even by checking with your local computer store. Internet Service Providers normally charge a monthly access fee for you to use their Internet connection so that you can send e-mail messages and explore the Web. This monthly charge is usually either for a set number of hours a month or a flat fee for unlimited usage. The ISP market is competitive and so are the rates. Base the type of service that you choose on your own personal needs. If you plan to spend a lot of time on the Internet, for example, you will probably find an ISP that provides you an unlimited number of connection hours more economical.

After you establish an Internet account with a provider, you're ready to connect to the Internet. To do so, you need to create a remote connection for your Internet Service Provider's site by using the Remote Networking options, which I cover in Chapter 14. To create the remote connection, you need to know the phone number that your modem dials to connect to your ISP.

TIP

Keep in mind that most ISPs will tell you that their service doesn't support your Windows CE handheld PC. This assertion is more a result of ignorance than fact. Many ISPs just don't have a clear understanding about the capabilities of handheld PCs. All handheld PCs can connect to the Internet through a Internet Service Provider. I suggest that you set up an Internet connection on your desktop computer along with your Windows CE connection. That way if you do have a problem connecting to the Internet on your handheld PC, you can test things with your desktop computer before calling your ISP's support department. Based on my own experience, most ISPs aren't going to be much help when you're having trouble connecting with your handheld PC, for the simple fact that they can't visualize what you are actually doing. Of course, as Windows CE becomes more widely used, this will become less of a problem.

Manually connecting to the Internet

After you create a remote connection on your handheld PC to your Internet Service Provider, you can quickly connect to the Internet at any time. Remember, you must have a modem that is connected both to your handheld PC and to a phone line; otherwise, your efforts to connect to the Internet will be in vain. The following steps illustrate the process of manually connecting to the Internet:

1. **Double-tap on the remote connection icon for your Internet Service Provider.**

   When you tap on the icon, the Connect To dialog box appears and allows you to type the connection information for your account, as shown in Figure 15-6. You can find the icon in the Remote Networking folder — choose Programs➪Communications➪Remote Networking from the Start menu.

2. **Type your user name in the User text box.**

   Type the user name that your ISP assigned you.

3. **Type your password in the Password text box.**

4. **If required, type a domain name in the Domain text box.**

   Most Internet connections don't require this field. Normally, you use the Domain text box only when you are connecting from an internal network at a company. If you need to type a value in this field, you'll receive that information when you set up your Internet account.

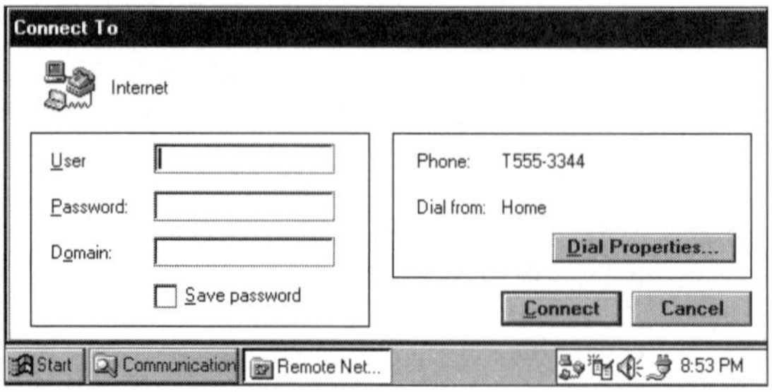

Figure 15-6: Connect your modem to your handheld PC before tapping the Connect button.

5. **Select the Save password check box.**

   By using the Save password option, you don't have to worry about forgetting or mistyping your user name or password. Your handheld PC automatically remembers this information for you. If someone looks at this screen, don't worry — they can't figure out your password because Windows CE substitutes asterisks for each character in your password. If you share your handheld PC with someone else, however, you may not want to select this check box.

6. **Tap on the Connect button**.

   The modem dials the phone number and connects to your Internet Service Provider.

7. **Double-tap on the Pocket Internet Explorer icon.**

   This icon is located on your desktop. If you can't find it, look in the choose Program Files⇨Pocket IE. When you double-tap on the Pocket Explorer icon, you get your default Web page loaded within the Pocket Explorer. You are now ready to start browsing the Web.

Setting the automatic dialing option

With Windows CE, you can set up Pocket Internet Explorer to automatically dial out to your ISP whenever you want to view a site on the Internet. This is a handy feature to use because it eliminates the need for you to go and locate your Internet connection. Whenever you request to look at a Web site, the Connect To dialog box automatically appears and allows you to quickly connect to the Internet.

You can also specify the amount of time that you want your handheld PC to remain connected to the Internet if you are not using it. This eliminates the risk of you forgetting to disconnect when you finish surfing. This option is especially valuable if you have to pay an hourly rate for your Internet service.

To set up the automatic dialing options for your Internet connection, follow these steps:

1. **Choose View⇨Options.**

   The Options dialog box appears.

2. **Tap on the Auto Dial tab (see Figure 15-7).**

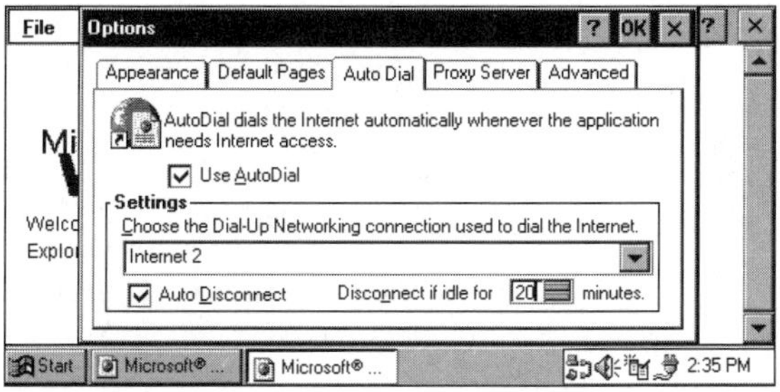

Figure 15-7: The Auto Dial option automatically connects you to the Internet.

3. **Select the Use AutoDial check box.**

   Remember, you simply need to tap the check box with the stylus to select or unselect an option.

4. **Select the remote connection that you want to use to connect to your Internet Service Provider.**

   To select a connection, tap on the Down Arrow button and highlight the appropriate connection in the drop-down list box.

5. **Select the Auto Disconnect check box.**

   This selection is optional. By using it, you ensure that your handheld PC will always disconnect after specified amount of time has passed since you used it.

6. **Specify the amount of time the handheld PC should sit idle before hanging up.**

Browsing the Internet

Well, if you are reading this section, you have probably jumped through all of the proper hoops and are ready to start exploring the Internet. If you have never experienced the Internet, you are in for quite an adventure.

Surfing the Internet essentially means looking at different locations on the Internet that both companies and individuals have developed. These Internet locations are commonly referred to as *Web sites*.

Working with proxy servers

Quite often, companies set up proxy servers for their employees to use when connecting to the Internet. A proxy server essentially provides a security barrier between your company's internal network and the Internet so that the internal network isn't accessible to people on the Internet.

If you are attempting to connect to the Internet by using an Internet connection at your company, you may find it necessary to use a proxy server. If you're unsure whether this is required, check with your network administrator. If you need to use a proxy server, get the proxy server address information from your network administrator.

To set up the proxy server information, choose View⇨Options. When the Options dialog box appears, tap on the Proxy Server tab, as shown in the figure.

Select the Use Proxy Server check box. Then type the proxy server address in the Proxy Server field and the port information in the Port text box.

Keep in mind that Pocket Internet Explorer works only with Proxy servers that comply with the CERN proxy server standard. I know this sounds like Greek, but essentially, before attempting to set up the proxy server information, double-check to see if the proxy server is compliant with this standard to avoid any additional headaches. If the proxy server is not compliant with this standard, you need to find another method for connecting your handheld PC to the Internet.

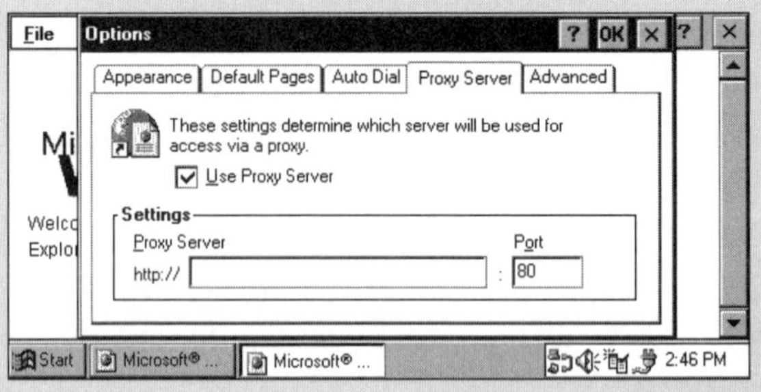

Using the Pocket Internet Explorer toolbar

Pocket Internet Explorer provides several buttons on the toolbar at the top of the screen. The only drawback to using the toolbar buttons is trying to figure out what each button does. Unfortunately, the buttons are not labeled. So to help ease the frustration of tapping on the wrong button, you can find a description of each button in Table 15-1.

Table 15-1 Pocket Internet Explorer Toolbar Buttons

Button	*Description*
	Opens a specific Web page on the Internet. You still need to type the address of the Web site.
	Views a Web site from a list of favorite Web site addresses that you have saved.
	Adds the current Web page to your list of favorite Web sites. By adding a Web site to the list, you can quickly locate that site when you want to view it again.
	Scrolls back to the previous Web page.
	Scrolls forward to the next Web page.
	Stops a process. You use this if you want to cancel a Web page you requested or to stop a search.
	Reloads the Web page that you are viewing, commonly referred to as *refreshing the page*.
	Displays your home page, which is whatever page you specify as your default start page.
	Displays your default search page. This page helps you look for specific information on the Internet.
	Provides help information for Pocket Internet Explorer. (Of course, it won't be as helpful as this book, but nothing is perfect.)

TIP: Keep in mind that all of the toolbar buttons are also listed in the menus. So if you don't want to decipher little pictures, go ahead and use the menus. But after you use the buttons a few times, I'm sure you'll realize that it is much faster to select a button than to find a menu option.

Jumping to a new location

Nowadays, it seems everyone has an Internet address. How often have you heard someone say "Come visit us on the Web at WWW," and then proceed to list a long string of characters? Well, those long character strings are commonly referred to as *Internet addresses* or, if you want to sound really technical, *URLs* (Uniform Resource Locators). You use these addresses to locate information on the Internet. Each person, business, organization, school, and so on, on the Internet has their own unique address. For example, if you wanted to visit the Microsoft Web site, you simply type the address `http://www.microsoft.com`.

To make it simple to jump to an address, Pocket Internet Explorer comes with a dialog box where you can type the desired address, as shown in Figure 15-8. To display the Open Internet Address dialog box, either tap on the Open button on the toolbar or choose File⇨Open.

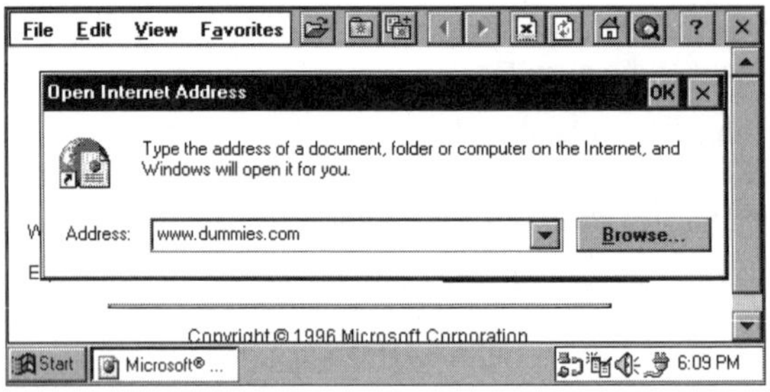

Figure 15-8: Type the exact address of the location you want to explore.

Typing an Internet address is a lot like dialing a phone number: If you don't type the characters exactly right, you are going to end up getting a wrong number. To view the desired Web site, type the correct address in the Address field. If you have visited this Web site before, it may be listed in the Address drop-down list box. Tap on the Down Arrow button to see which addresses Windows CE has saved.

TIP

You can also open up a document on your handheld PC by clicking on the Browse button and then locating the desired document. This option is useful for people who have created HTML documents on their handheld PC, but don't remember the name of the document.

Searching for a specific site on the Internet

You have no way of knowing the address of every Web site that you may want to look at, and luckily you don't have to. Several programs, commonly referred to as *search engines,* keep track of different Web sites. If you are looking for information on a specific topic, you simply type the topic on the search engine page, and you get a list of several Web sites that discuss your topic. For example, you can use a search engine to locate all the sites that discuss scuba diving, as shown in Figure 15-9.

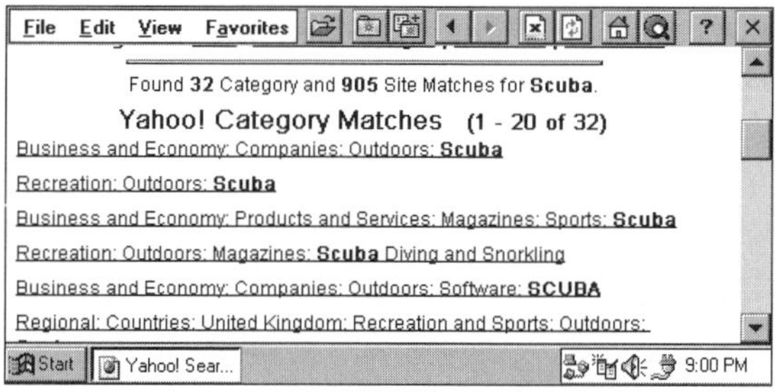

Figure 15-9: You can locate all of the sites that discuss scuba diving by using a search engine.

Your Pocket Internet Explorer program comes set up to use a default search site whenever you request a search. To display the search site, you can either tap on the Search button or choose View➪Search Page. Because search engines look at Web sites all around the world to find your specified topic, the Search button resembles a world with a magnifying glass over it. When you tap on the Search button, your default search page appears, as shown in Figure 15-10. This page has links to several different search engines available on the Internet.

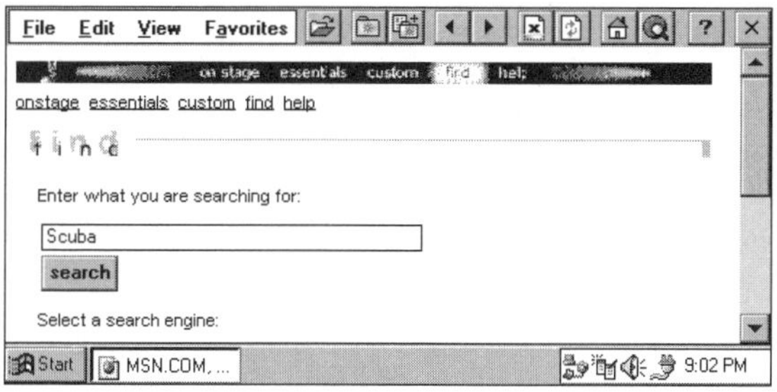

Figure 15-10: Type the keyword for the information you want to locate on the Internet and then tap on the Search button.

TIP

If you don't find the information you are looking for with the first search, try selecting a different search engine. Your search page comes with the ability to search the Internet by using any one of seven different search engines, and each one is bound to locate different Web sites. To select a search engine, simply tap on its radio button. If you cannot see the radio buttons for the search engines, tap on the scroll bar to scroll down the page until the radio buttons are visible.

Deja View: Returning to a page you've previously viewed

Viewing Web sites on the Internet is similar to reading a book: At any time during the process, you may decide you want to go back and read the information on a previous page again. To make it easy to return to a previously viewed Web site, Pocket Internet Explorer comes with a couple of different options.

The easiest way to jump back to a previously viewed page is to tap on the Back button on the toolbar. This button allows you to scroll back through the different Web sites you have visited during your current Internet session. The only drawback is that you have to wait for each site to reload while you look for the one you want to see.

To move forward through the previously viewed Web sites, tap on the Next button on the toolbar. This button allows you to scroll forward until you get to the last new page that you viewed.

TIP

Another way to locate a previously viewed Web page is to look at your viewing history. Pocket Internet Explorer keeps a list of the Web sites that you have visited and calls it your history. To view the history list, choose View⇨History to display the History window, as shown in Figure 15-11. On the History window, select the page you want to go back to and then tap on the OK button. Pocket Explorer displays the selected page without forcing you to scroll through all of the previously viewed pages.

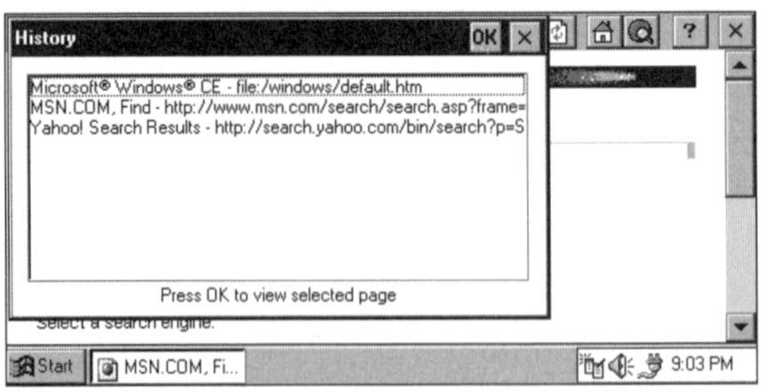

Figure 15-11: Highlight the Web site to select it, and then tap on the OK button.

Saving Your Favorite Sites

You can keep track of Web sites that you may want to visit again by storing their addresses in your list of favorites. Storing a favorite site is as easy as setting a bookmark in a favorite book. To store the address of the Web site that you are currently viewing, tap the Add to Favorites button on the toolbar. The Add to Favorites button looks like a folder sitting in front of a page. When you tap on the Add to Favorites button, the Add to Favorites dialog box appears, as shown in Figure 15-12.

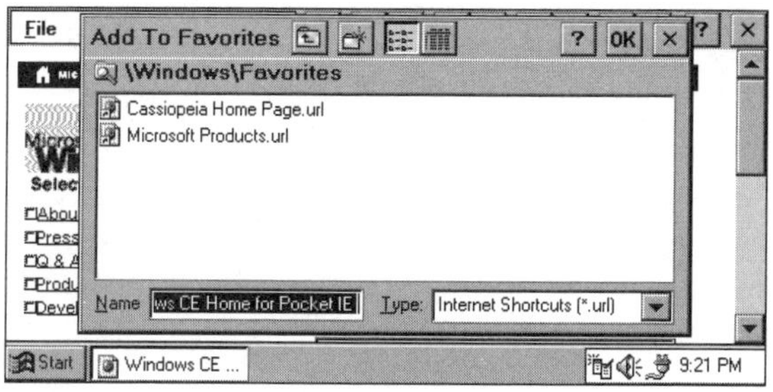

Figure 15-12: Tap on the OK button to add the current Web page to your list of favorites.

The Name field provides the name of the Web site that you are currently viewing. This is the name that is stored when you tap on the OK button. If you want to use a different name to refer to this Web page, type that name in the Name field. You can call the page anything you want — when you select the name you assign, Pocket Internet Explorer will jump to the page you want to view.

In the Add to Favorites dialog box, you can also create different folders to store related favorite Web sites. For example, you could create a Windows CE folder where you could place all of the Web sites that relate to Windows CE. To create a new folder, simply tap on the New Folder button in the Add to Favorites dialog box. Remember, the New Folder button looks the same in all Windows CE programs (it resembles a folder with a star behind it). When you tap the New Folder button, a folder is added with the words New Folder highlighted. Simply type the desired name for the folder you are creating.

TIP

You can also display the Add to Favorites dialog box by choosing Favorites⇨Add to Favorites or pressing Ctrl+T.

Jumping to a favorite Web site

If you have created bookmarks for your favorite Web sites, you can display them any time you want to review the information they contain. To view your list of favorite Web sites, tap on the Open Favorites button on the toolbar. This button looks like a folder with a star on the front of it. When you tap on the Open Favorites button, the Open Favorites dialog box appears, as shown in Figure 15-13.

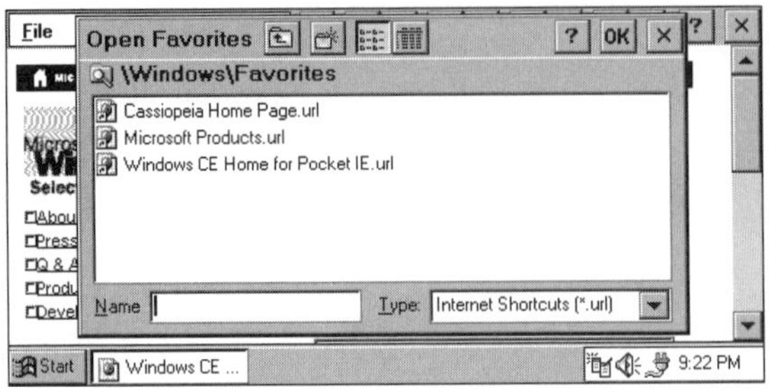

Figure 15-13: Select the Web site you want to view.

Select the Web site that you want to view and tap on the OK button. If you are not currently connected to the Internet but you have set up the AutoDial option, Windows CE attempts to connect to the Internet. If Windows CE connects, it then displays the Web site you selected.

You can also view the Open Favorites dialog box by choosing Favorites⇨Open Favorite Folder. And you can always use the keyboard method and press Ctrl+Shift+T.

Creating shortcuts on the desktop

If you have a Web site that you visit often, you may want to create a shortcut for that Web site on your desktop. For example, you may regularly check a particular Web site to see the latest stock prices. If you have a shortcut for that site on your desktop, you can load Pocket Internet Explorer, and it will connect to the Internet and quickly locate the Web site you selected. Creating the desktop shortcut saves you the trouble of manually opening Pocket Internet Explorer and then locating the desired Web site in your favorites list.

All right, that all sounds nice. But you want to know how to accomplish this astounding feat — right? To create a desktop shortcut for a Web site, you need to make sure that the Web site is displayed on the screen in Pocket Internet Explorer. Then choose File⇨Desktop Shortcut. An icon is added to your Windows CE desktop with the name of the current Web site, as shown in Figure 15-14.

Don't add too many different Web site shortcuts to your desktop, or it will become cluttered and locating information will be a hassle. If you want to remove a Web site shortcut from your desktop, drag-and-drop it into the Recycle Bin.

Figure 15-14: You can easily add icons for your most frequently visited Web sites to your desktop.

Customizing Your Browser

Although Pocket Internet Explorer comes with several standard settings, you can customize the browser to fit your own specific needs. For example, you can have a specific page loaded whenever you run Pocket Internet Explorer.

You can accomplish most of your Pocket Internet Explorer customizing tasks by using the Options dialog box. This dialog box appears when you choose View⇨Options.

Specifying a different start page

Your start page is the page that is always loaded first when you run Pocket Internet Explorer on your handheld PC. It is also the page that is loaded when you tap on the Home button. The Home button is easy to spot because it looks just like a little house.

When you install Pocket Internet Explorer on your handheld PC, a default start page is also loaded onto your handheld PC. The default page that is loaded when you run Pocket Internet Explorer is called default.htm.

You may decide that you want to use a different page for your start page whenever you run Pocket Internet Explorer. For example, you may want to use a company page as a start page or even a favorite Web site.

TIP

Keep in mind that if you set your start page as a page that is not loaded on your handheld PC, you will be prompted to connect to the Internet immediately when you run Pocket Internet Explorer.

To set your start page, choose View⇨Options and tap on the Default Pages tab, as shown in Figure 15-15.

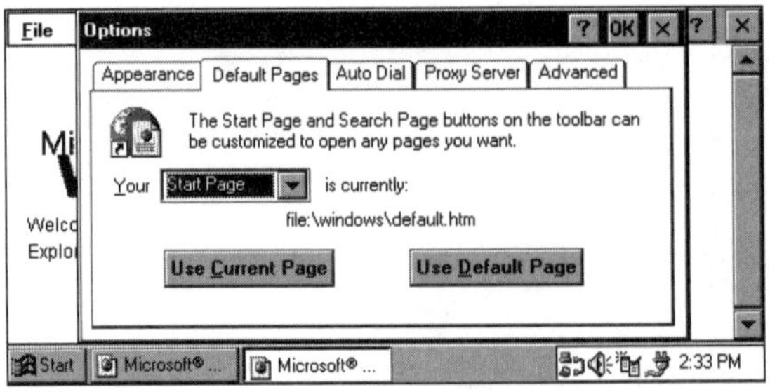

Figure 15-15: You can quickly select a new start page for Pocket Internet Explorer.

To set a Web page you are currently viewing in Pocket Internet Explorer as your new start page, follow these steps:

1. **Make sure the drop-down list box has the value Start Page selected.**

   If you do not see the words *Start Page* in the field next to the word *Your,* tap the Down Arrow button and select the Start Page option.

2. **Tap the Use Current Page button.**

   The address of the Web site you are currently viewing in Pocket Internet Explorer appears above the Use Current Page button as the address of your start page.

TIP: To switch back to the default start page that came with Pocket Internet Explorer, tap on the Use Default Page button in the Default Pages tab of the Options dialog box.

Specifying a different search page

Your search page is similar to the appendix in a book: You tell it a certain word or phrase that relates to the information you are looking for, and it provides you a list of the closest matches to that word. You can load the search page when you tap the Search button on the toolbar. The Search button looks just like a word with a magnifying glass sitting on top of it.

When you install Pocket Internet Explorer on your handheld PC, you already have a default search page. The default search page is a Web site that Microsoft established to give you access to several of the major search engines on the Internet. Search engines are actually just programs that run on the Internet and locate the information that you are looking for.

You may decide that you want to use a different page for your search page within Pocket Internet Explorer. To set your search page, choose View➪Options to display the Options dialog box. In the Options dialog box, tap on the Default Pages tab, as shown in Figure 15-16.

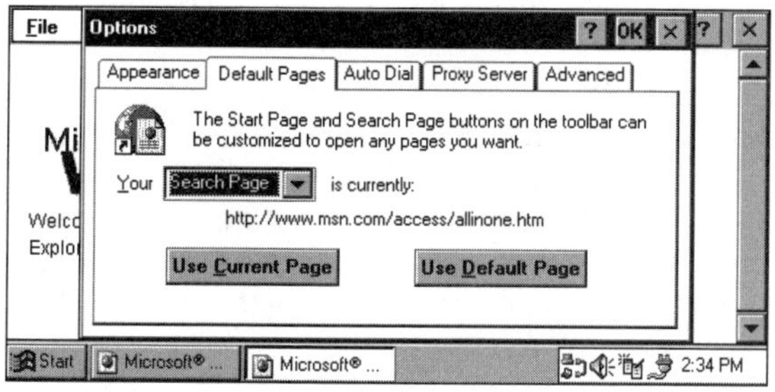

Figure 15-16: You can quickly select a new search page for Pocket Internet Explorer.

To set the Web page you are currently viewing in Pocket Internet Explorer as your new search page, follow these steps

1. **Make sure that the drop-down list box has the value Search Page selected.**

   If you do not see the words Search Page in the field next to the word *Your,* tap on the Down Arrow button and then select the Search Page option.

2. **Tap the Use Current Page button.**

   The address of the Web site you are currently viewing in Pocket Internet Explorer appears above the Use Current Page button as the address of your search page.

To switch back to the default search page that came with Pocket Internet Explorer, tap on the Use Default Page button in the Default Pages tab in the Options dialog box.

Changing the appearance of Web pages

Unfortunately, with a smaller screen than your desktop computer, Web pages aren't as easy to view as they are on your desktop computer. You may even find that certain added features, such as pictures and sounds, slow down your handheld PC's ability to display Web pages adequately.

To change the way Web pages appear on your handheld PC, choose View⇨Options and tap on the Appearance tab, as shown in Figure 15-17.

You can use three options to specify how you want different Web pages to appear on your handheld PC. To select one of these options on the Appearance tab, simply tap on the check box next to the desired option to add or remove the check mark. Table 15-2 provides a description of the effect that each one of these options causes on your Web pages.

Table 15-2 Web-Page Appearance Options

Option	*Description*
Show Pictures	Displays all the Web page's pictures. If you turn off this option, the site loads without taking the time to download the different pictures that normally appear on the Web site. You can still see the location where the pictures normally appear.
Play Sounds	Plays all the Web site's sounds. If you turn off this option, Web sites with sounds load faster because the sound files don't have to download.
Make page fit window	Adjusts the sizing of the Web page to make sure that the entire page appears within the width of your screen. If you select this option, you may find that some tables and images are too small and difficult to see; to resolve the problem, unselect this option.

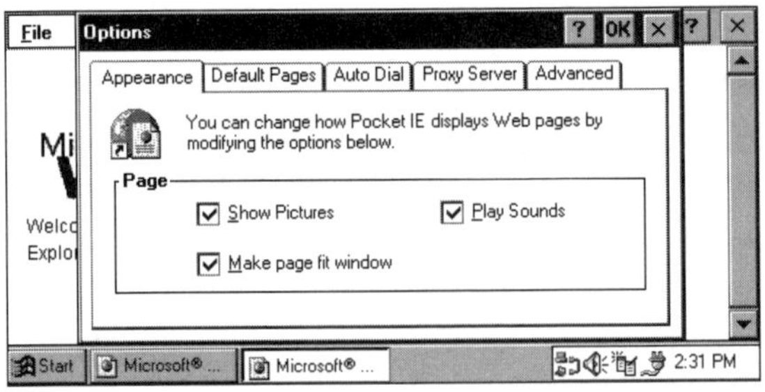

Figure 15-17: You can modify the way a Web page displays on your handheld PC.

Chapter 16

Sending and Receiving E-Mail

In This Chapter

- Using e-mail
- Customizing your mailbox
- Sending and receiving mail
- Figuring out a person's address

These days, e-mail is a way of life in the workplace. Quite often, whole meetings transpire solely through the use of e-mail. Windows CE affords you the luxury of maintaining constant contact via e-mail from any location, either at your company, on the Internet, or both.

This chapter explains how to send and receive e-mail messages by using Windows CE. I also discuss customizing your e-mail environment by doing such things as creating folders for related mail messages.

Connecting to a Mail Server

In order to send e-mail messages, you must connect to a mail server. The *mail server* is a machine at the remote connection that is responsible for sending your messages to the appropriate addresses and delivering messages that you receive into your mailbox, or *e-mail account.*

Most people compose the messages they want to send and then connect to the mail server to send the messages, which is commonly called *working offline.* You can connect to the server and then create your messages while online, but if you are charged for connect time to your Internet Service Provider, you probably want to remain connected for the minimum amount of time necessary.

Before you connect to a mail server, you need to set up your e-mail account information by using the Inbox program on your handheld PC. The following sections describe how to locate the Inbox program, create an e-mail account, and use your handheld's modem to send and receive messages.

Locating the Inbox program

Before you can send e-mail messages from your Windows CE handheld PC, you need to locate the Inbox program. The icon for the Inbox program sits on the left side of your desktop (unless you have reorganized your desktop). The Inbox icon looks like a world with a message being sent around it. After you locate the icon, double-tap on it to display the Inbox program.

If you cannot find the Inbox program icon sitting on your desktop, don't despair; you should be able to locate it by following these simple steps:

1. **Use your stylus to tap the Start button (in the bottom-left corner of the screen).**
2. **Open the Start menu and tap on the Programs option.**

   Windows CE Explorer opens the Programs folder on your handheld PC.
3. **Tap the Communication folder.**

   You should be able to locate the Inbox program icon in the Communication folder, as shown in Figure 16-1.

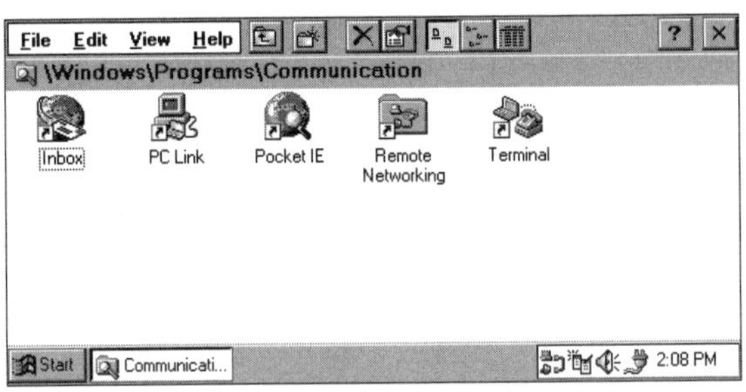

Figure 16-1: The Inbox program icon can also be found in the Communication folder.

4. **Double-tap the Inbox icon in the folder to display the Inbox program, shown in Figure 16-2.**

   Here is where you can send and receive e-mail messages by using a company e-mail system or the Internet. You can also transfer messages between your handheld PC and your desktop computer.

Before you can send or receive e-mail messages, you need to set up your e-mail account information in the Inbox program, as described in the next section.

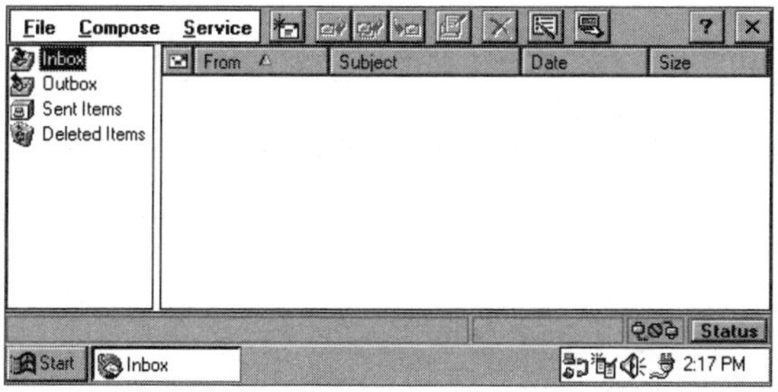

Figure 16-2: The Inbox program allows you to check e-mail messages from any location.

Specifying your e-mail address

Before you can send or receive e-mail messages, you need to tell the Inbox program some information about the e-mail account that you want to connect to. In essence, the Inbox program needs to know where you want it to look for your e-mail messages as well as the location of the mail server (which is similar to a post office) where it should transfer the messages you send so that they can be routed to the appropriate location.

The following steps illustrate how to set up the e-mail account information on your handheld PC:

1. **Tap on the Options button on the toolbar. (The Options button resembles a list with a stylus on top of it.)**

   The Options dialog box appears, sporting four tabs full of options.

2. **Tap on the Services tab.**

   The Services tab, shown in Figure 16-3, is where you create and modify the e-mail account information for your handheld PC.

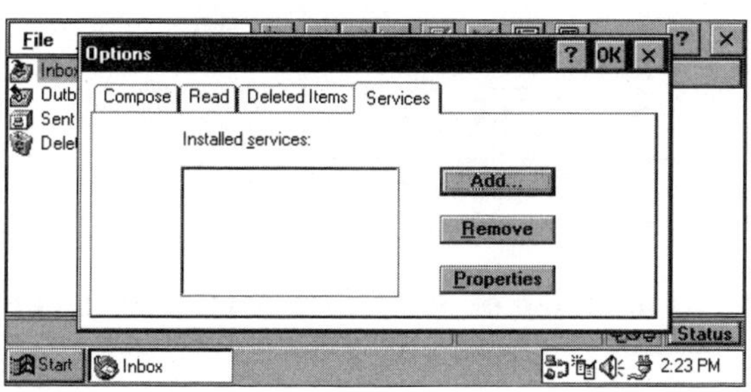

Figure 16-3: The Services tab of the Options dialog box.

3. **Tap on the Add button.**

   The Services dialog box displays the types of e-mail accounts that you can create.

4. **Tap on the Internet Mail option and then tap on the OK button.**

   The Service Name dialog box appears, as shown in Figure 16-4.

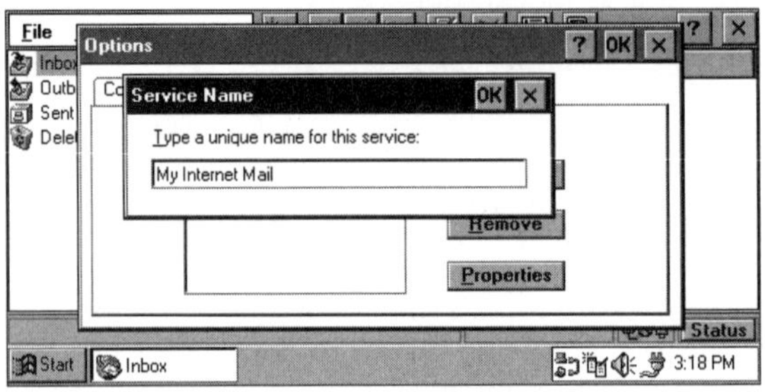

Figure 16-4: The Service Name dialog box.

5. **Type** My Internet Mail **in the field and then tap on the OK button.**

   You need to assign a unique name in the field on the Service Name window. For ease of use, you may want to use the name of your access provider as the name. This name is displayed when you select the e-mail account to connect to. When you tap on the OK button, the Service Definition screen appears, as shown in Figure 16-5. Here you actually indicate your e-mail address, the remote connection to use to locate your e-mail, and Logon information.

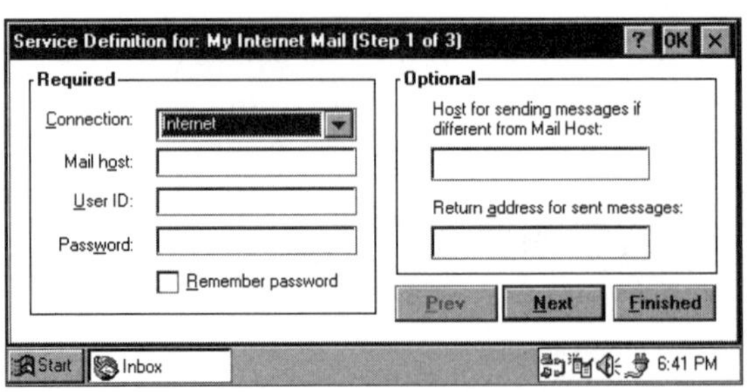

Figure 16-5: Specify the e-mail account information on this screen.

6. **In the Connection field, tap on the Down Arrow button and then tap on the remote connection to use for your e-mail.**

   All of the remote connections you have created on your handheld PC are listed in the drop-down list. If you do not find the connection you want, you need to go to the Remote Networking folder and create the connection before you can select it on this screen.

7. **Type the address of the mail server in the Mail host field.**

8. **Type your e-mail user ID in the User ID field.**

   The User ID is the part of the e-mail address before the at symbol (@). Therefore, if your mail address is `john@xyzinc.com`, you simply type characters that precede the @, which is **john** in this example, in the User ID field. Most e-mail addresses have all lowercase characters.

9. **Type the password for your e-mail account in the Password field.**

   Depending on how your account was set up, this password may be the same as the password that you use to connect to your Internet Service Provider. If you want to avoid the drudgery of always typing your password, select the check box next to the Remember Password field to have your handheld PC remember your password. If you are concerned about someone using your handheld PC to make a remote connection when you are not around, however, you may want to avoid selecting this field so that the password will be requested each time.

10. **If your Internet Service Provider uses a different server to send outgoing messages, type the address in the first field in the Optional section.**

    Some Internet Service Providers use a different machine to handle mail messages that people are sending out to reduce the demand on the mail server that is receiving your mail from other locations. Not all providers exercise this option, so leave the field blank if the information is not applicable.

11. **Type your return address in the second field in the Optional section.**

    Indicate the address you want used when someone selects the reply option for your message. You will probably just want to place your Internet mail address here, although you may have occasion to have mail returned to another address, such as a company Internet account. If so, type that address in the field.

12. **Tap on the Next button to continue the setup process.**

    You get the second set of steps for setting up your e-mail service, as shown in Figure 16-6.

13. **Specify the connection settings.**

    In the Connection settings section, indicate whether you want the modem to hang up after sending and receiving messages, how often to check for messages, and finally how you want to be notified when you receive a message.

    If your Internet Service Provider charges you a fee based on the number of minutes that you are connected to the Internet, select the Automatically disconnect session after actions are performed option.

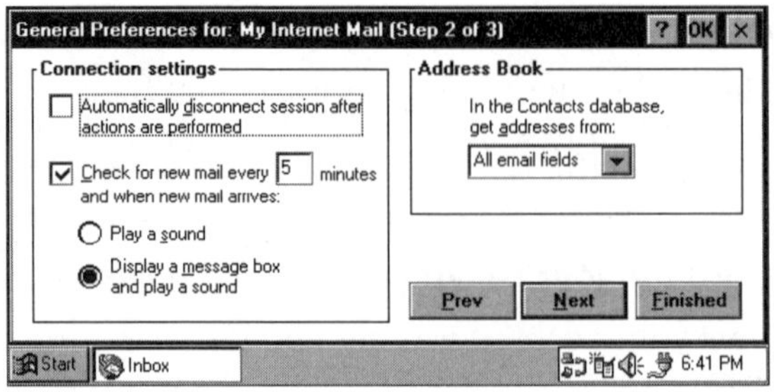

Figure 16-6: This dialog box contains the second set of steps for setting up your e-mail service.

14. **In the Address section, indicate which e-mail addresses you want to display when you select the Address Book button while creating a message and then tap the Next button.**

    You get the final set of steps for setting up your e-mail service, as shown in Figure 16-7.

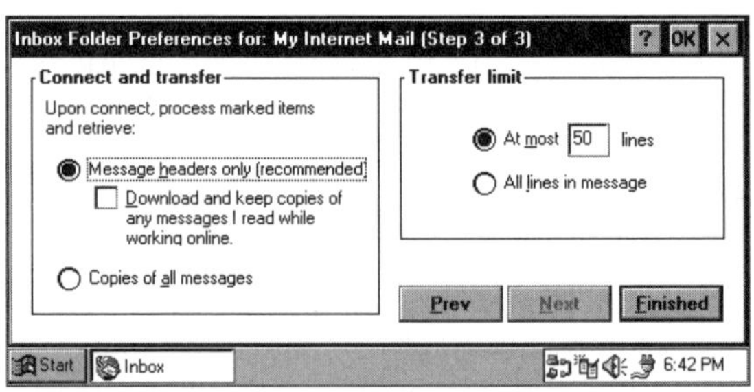

Figure 16-7: This dialog box contains the final set of steps for setting up your e-mail service.

15. **In the Connect and Transfer section, indicate whether you want to see just the message headers or the entire message.**

    I recommend that you download just the message headers, because you have a limited amount of memory on your handheld PC. If you decide to read a message, additional lines of the message are downloaded when you double-tap on the message.

16. **In the Transfer limit section, indicate the maximum number of lines that you want to download for a message.**

    I recommend setting this field to about 50 lines, which is more than enough lines for most messages.

17. Tap on the Finished button to save the new e-mail service.

You are now ready to connect to the Internet Service Provider and get your e-mail messages.

These steps only set up the e-mail portion of your Internet or other remote connection account. You must also establish a remote connection that you can use to access this account. For more information on creating remote connections, refer to Chapter 14.

You may only have the ability to set up an e-mail service for an Internet e-mail account. This option comes standard on all handheld PCs. As you add other types of software and services to your handheld PC, you can set up e-mail for other types of services. For example, a popular add-on to Windows CE handheld PCs is a paging card, which provides you with the ability to set up an e-mail server for paging messages.

Making the connection

To connect to your e-mail service, tap on the Connect button on the toolbar of the Inbox program. The Connect button is the last one on the toolbar; it resembles a hand holding up a computer monitor. (You may have to think deep thoughts to find the correlation there.)

If you have set up multiple e-mail services, Windows CE connects to the last e-mail service that you selected. The current e-mail services for your handheld PC are listed on the Service menu between the Connect option and the Retrieve a Copy option, as shown in Figure 16-8. A small dot appears next to the currently selected service. To select another service, simply tap on the one you want.

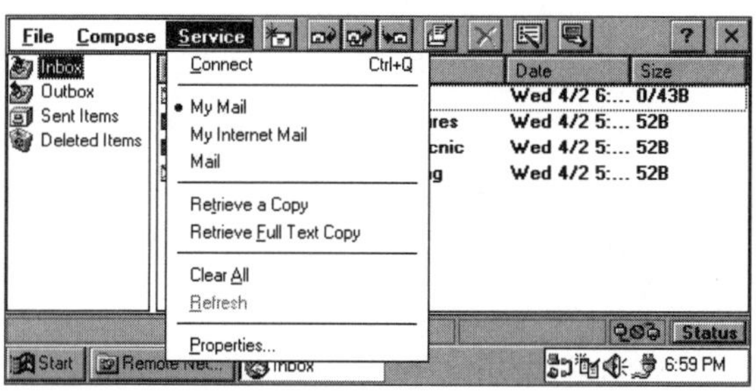

Figure 16-8: You can switch between different e-mail services on the Service menu.

When you select the Connect button, the Connect To screen appears if you are not already connected to the remote location, verifying that you desire to make a connection. When you select the Connect button, you are connected to the remote location. After you are connected to the location, Windows CE connects to the appropriate mail server and sends and receives your messages.

Handling E-Mail

The Inbox program on your handheld PC provides the ability to quickly send and receive e-mail messages from any location. You can send a message to anyone who has an e-mail account. After you receive a message, you have the option of sending a response back to the person who sent the message. You can find more information about sending and receiving e-mail in the following sections in this chapter.

Creating an e-mail message

When most people use an e-mail program for the first time, the first thing they want to do is figure out how to write a message. To send an e-mail message, all you need is the recipient's e-mail address.

Creating an e-mail message is easy. Simply tap on the New Message button — it's the first button on the toolbar — and a window in which you can compose your new e-mail message appears, as shown in Figure 16-9.

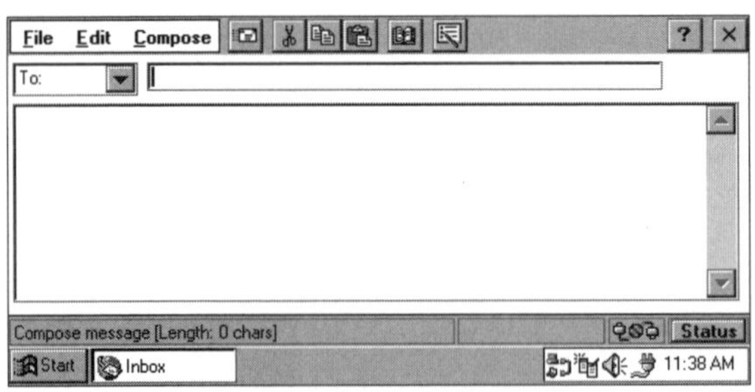

Figure 16-9: Composing a new e-mail message.

In the window where you create your e-mail messages, you have basically three different fields or areas for information:

- The top two fields on the window are used for specifying the heading information for the message.
- The bottom section contains the actual message that you are sending.

Typing the message

You type the message that you are trying to send in the bottom portion of the window (the big section). The message section is free-form, similar to a word processor, which means that you can type information on any line of the section.

TIP: You can use the Copy, Cut, and Paste buttons on the toolbar to copy and move information around in your message. If you are like me, you probably don't always like the way the message sounds when you first type it. By using these toolbar options, you can move information around in the message without retyping any of it.

Specifying the message headings

The top two fields are used for specifying the heading information for your message, such as the address where the message should be sent, the address where you would like to send a copy of the message, the subject of the message, and so on. The To field is the only field that must have a value when sending a message. It needs to contain the address where the message should be sent.

To check the values assigned to the different message header fields for your message, tap on the Down Arrow button to view a drop-down list, as shown in Figure 16-10. If any of the fields contain values, the values are listed next to the fields. For all the heading fields, you can simply type the information in the text box on the right side of the screen.

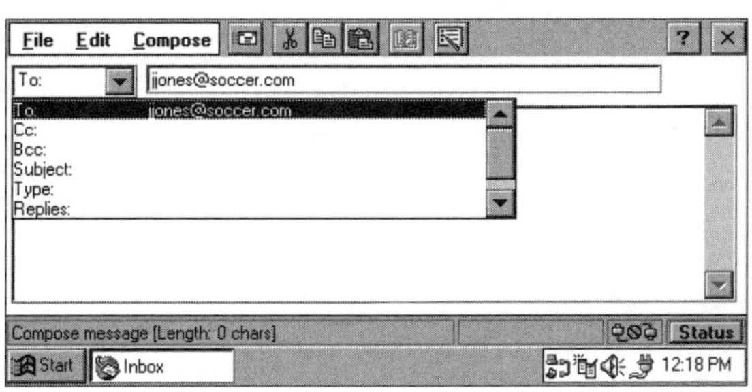

Figure 16-10: Checking the values assigned to the message header fields.

To make typing an e-mail address even easier, the Inbox program is linked to the Contacts program, allowing you to add an e-mail address from your contacts database. To find an e-mail address from your contacts database, tap on the Address button on the toolbar. This button looks like an open address book.

When you select the Address button, the Choose Address dialog box displays a list of the different e-mail addresses that you have added to the Contacts program and the name that corresponds with each address, as shown in Figure 16-11. You can tap on the Address button to select addresses for the To, Cc, and Bcc heading fields. When you select an address, it is added to whichever heading field you selected.

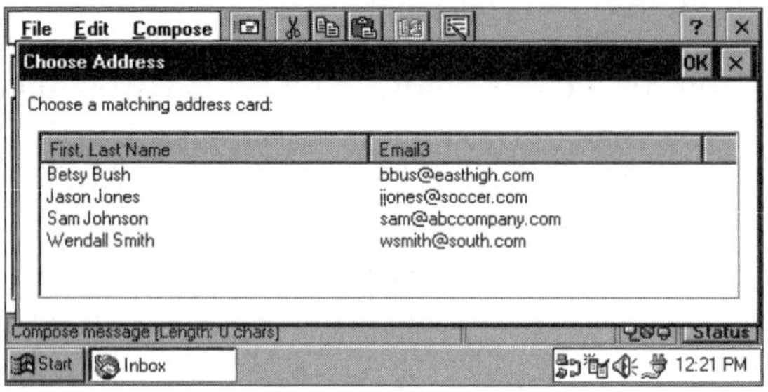

Figure 16-11: Tap on an e-mail address and tap the OK button.

The e-mail addresses that are actually displayed on the Choose Address dialog box are determined by the value you assigned the Address Book section when you set up your e-mail service. For example, if you requested that only Email2 addresses be displayed, you do not see any of the Email1 addresses that you may have added to the Contacts program on the Choose Address dialog box.

Reading a message

After you receive messages, you can open them and read them. To open a message, simply double-tap the message with the stylus. The selected message opens in a window, as shown in Figure 16-12.

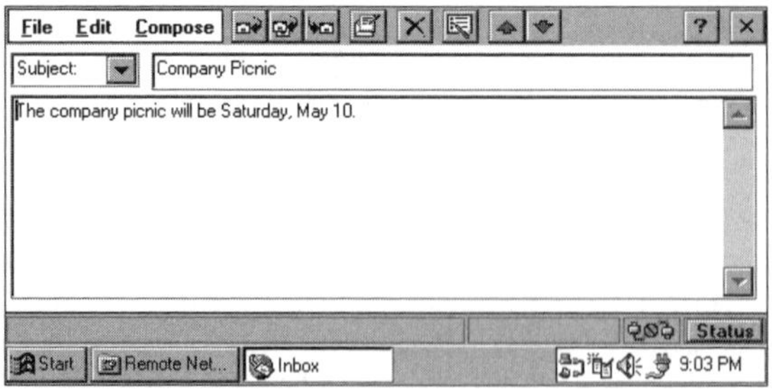

Figure 16-12: Double-tap on a message in the Inbox to view the message text.

You can use the up- and down-arrow keys to scroll through the messages in your Inbox. Tapping on the Up Arrow button displays a previous message and tapping on the Down Arrow button displays the next message in the Inbox.

Retrieving a copy of a message

Windows CE always tries to help by adding only a minimal amount of stuff to the memory on your handheld PC. The amount of each message that is copied to your handheld PC is determined by the settings you specified when you set up the e-mail service. Normally, you only get the headers to the messages copied to your handheld PC, and then you can copy the messages you select to your handheld PC. By only copying the messages that you want to read, you do not fill your storage memory with messages you are not interested in.

To copy the text of a message to your handheld PC, select the server message that you want to copy and choose Service➪Retrieve Full Text Copy.

Replying to a message you received

You can reply to the message while it is listed in the Inbox or reply to a message you are currently viewing. Windows CE provides options that enable you to respond to a message in three ways, as described in Table 16-1. You can also find these options in the Edit menu.

Table 16-1 Replying to a Message

Tap on This Button	*To Do This*
	Send a response to the person who sent the message
	Send a response to everyone who received the original message
	Forward a copy of the message to someone else

When you select one of the reply options, a copy of the message appears onscreen, as shown in Figure 16-13. You can add additional information to the message and select the Send button to send the message out.

If you cannot connect to your e-mail service when you create the reply, the outgoing messages sit in your Outbox folder until you connect again. Basically, the Outbox is just like putting mail in the mailbox at home — it sits there until the letter carrier picks it up.

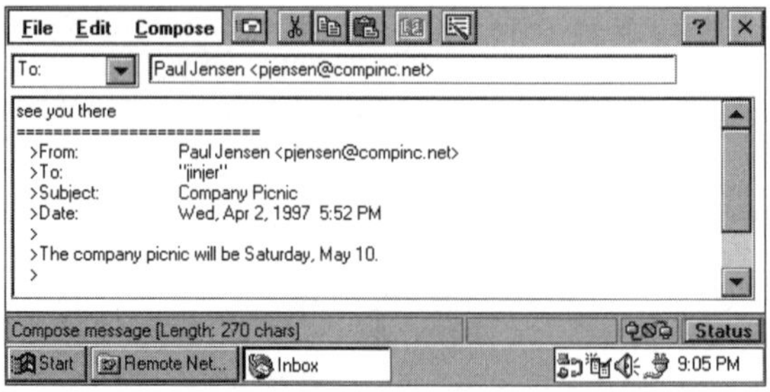

Figure 16-13: Type the text and select the Send button.

Organizing Your E-Mail

The Inbox program provides options for organizing your messages. For example, you can create new folders and move the messages you want to keep into these folders. You can also delete any unnecessary messages as soon as possible to ensure that you have plenty of storage space for other things on your handheld PC.

You can read about all the cool tools for organizing e-mail in the following sections. You will even find out how to move messages from your handheld PC onto your desktop computer.

Finding new places to store messages

You may find that you want to keep a copy of certain messages that you have either received or sent. The best way to store messages is to create a folder to place them in. By creating a folder, you can separate the old messages that you want to keep from the new messages in your Inbox. Doing so helps to eliminate the possibility of accidentally deleting a message that you want to keep.

The following steps illustrate how to create a new folder called Work on your handheld PC and then use the drag and drop options to move a message from your boss into that folder.

1. **On the left side of the screen, tap on the Inbox folder to select it.**
2. **Choose File⇨New Folder.**

   The New Folder dialog box appears, as shown in Figure 16-14.
3. **Type** Work **in the Folder name field and tap on the OK button.**

   The new folder is added to the list of folders on the left side of the Inbox screen, as shown in Figure 16-15. The Inbox program always lists the four main folders first, and then your personal folders in the order that you created them. In other words, the list is not alphabetized in any fashion.

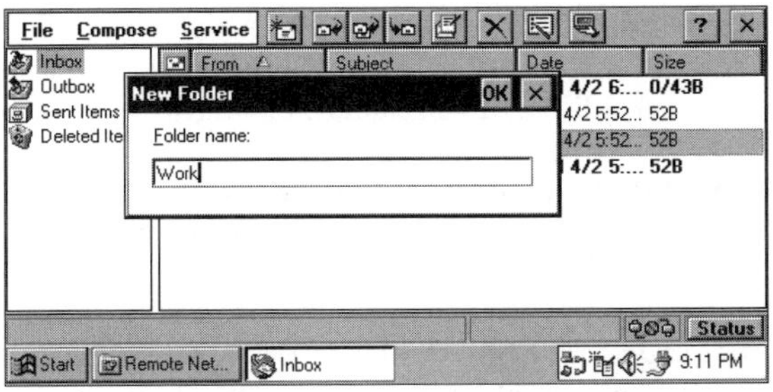

Figure 16-14: The New Folder dialog box.

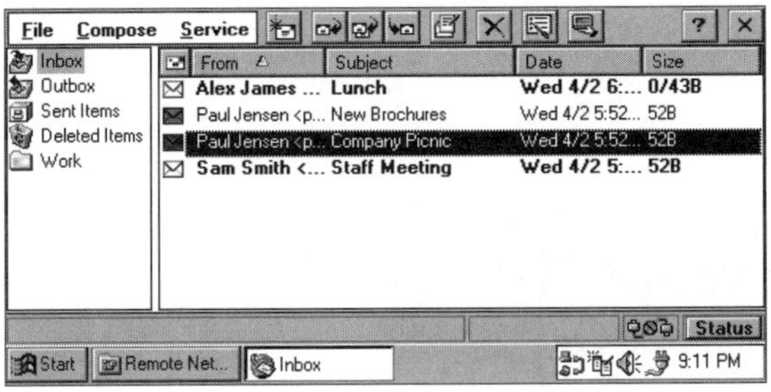

Figure 16-15: Your new Work folder.

4. **Tap on the message you are moving, drag it across the screen, and drop it on the new folder.**

   The message is moved from the Inbox folder to the Work folder.

TIP: Only messages that exist on your handheld PC can be moved into new folders. If you try to move a message of which only the message heading has been copied to your handheld PC, it will be marked to move, but it will not actually be moved until you connect to the server where the message is located.

WARNING! If you move a message to a folder on your Windows CE handheld PC, the message is removed from the server and any attachments to the message are lost. Because Windows CE does not support attachments, you want to keep the message on the server so that you can read it from your desktop computer and retrieve any attachments.

Copying and moving messages

Windows CE gives you the ability to move messages between folders by using the Move to and Copy to commands on the Edit menu. Both of these commands work almost the same. The only difference is the Move to command moves the actual message, whereas the Copy to command places a copy of the message in the specified folder. So in deciding which command to use, you need to decide just exactly how attached you are to that message. In other words, do you like that message enough to keep two copies?

Each message you save takes up some of your storage space. You may decide you want to keep a copy of a message in a separate folder for backup purposes.

When you select a message and choose either the Move to or Copy to command, a window appears, as shown in Figure 16-16. In this window, you can select the folder where you want the message to go. Keep in mind that dragging and dropping a message between folders produces exactly the same results as the Move to option.

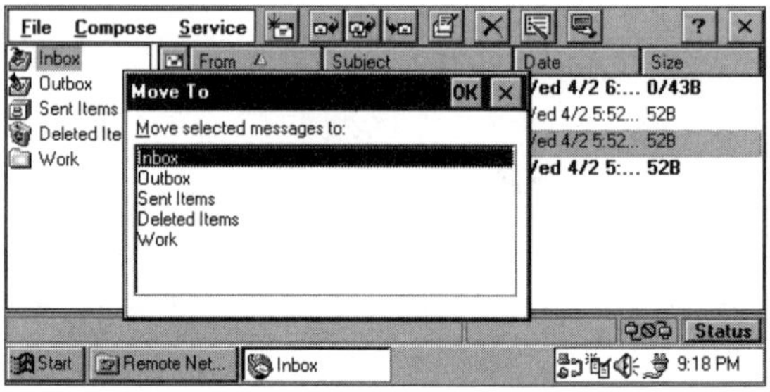

Figure 16-16: Highlight the folder where you want to place the message and tap on the OK button.

Deleting unwanted mail

Everyone needs to do a little bit of housecleaning from time to time. Doing so is especially important when you are dealing with your e-mail. Each message that you keep takes up valuable memory on your handheld PC.

To delete an item, select the item you want to delete and then tap on the Delete button on the toolbar. Remember, this button looks like a giant X. The confusion comes after the message is deleted. You see, Windows CE tries to be helpful by coming up with all sorts of ways to determine when to actually delete the message. Some messages are moved to the Deleted Items folder, and others are immediately deleted.

You can have some say in how Windows CE handles the messages you choose to delete, and I would suggest that you make a few changes. The settings for deleted messages are determined based on the options that are selected on the Deleted Items tab option in the Options dialog box, as shown in Figure 16-17.

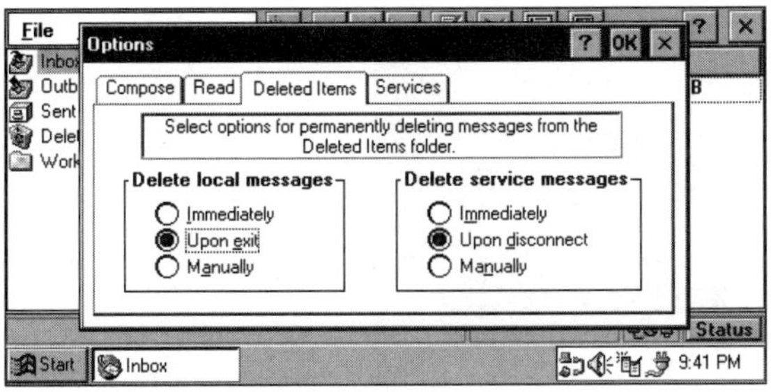

Figure 16-17: Set deleted message options on the Options dialog box.

TIP: By making sure that the *local messages* you delete (the ones that are sitting on your handheld PC) are not deleted until you exit the Inbox program, you can restore a deleted message from the Deleted Items folder if you want. This feature helps to ensure that you do not accidentally remove something that you intended to save. Also, make sure that the messages that are sitting on the server are only deleted when you disconnect from the server. These two steps will save some heartache in the future.

Transferring messages between your handheld PC and desktop computer

One feature that may prove to be of some use is the ability to copy messages between your handheld PC and desktop computer. This feature can be useful, especially if you have messages on your handheld PC that you want to keep for an extended period of time. You can move them to your desktop computer and save them with other related messages.

Transferring messages can be accomplished using either the Inbox program or the Outlook program under Windows 95 or Windows NT 4.0 on your desktop computer. In either program, simply choose Tools⇨HPC Inbox Transfer. The HPC Inbox Transfer dialog box appears on your desktop computer, as shown in Figure 16-18. Of course, you have to have a connection between your desktop computer and your Windows CE handheld PC in order to make this transfer possible.

If you want to transfer messages from your computer to your handheld PC, you need to highlight the messages before selecting this option and then specify the name of the folder that contains the selected messages in the Transfer messages to your HPC section. To make sure that the messages are not too large, I recommend that you only transfer the first 50 lines of each message.

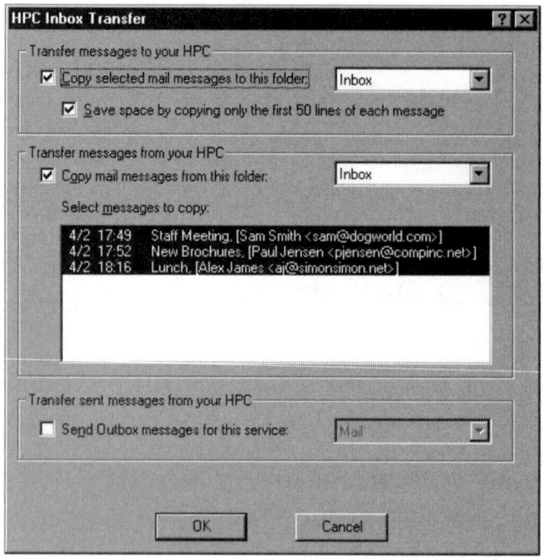

Figure 16-18: You can copy messages between your computer and handheld PC.

If you want to copy messages from your handheld PC and place them on your computer, select the folder on your handheld PC that contains the messages and then highlight each message that you want. When you tap on the OK button, a dialog box appears so that you can indicate where you want to place these messages on your computer, as shown in Figure 16-19. Simply highlight the folder name and then tap on the OK button.

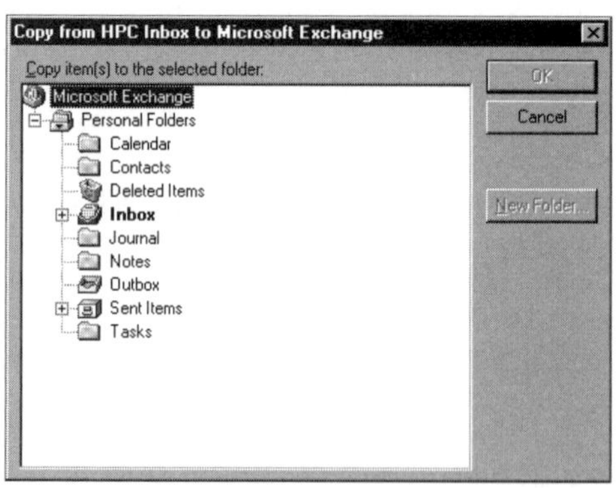

Figure 16-19: Select the location for the messages that you are copying from your handheld PC.

If you did not get all of the messages sent from your handheld PC, you can have your desktop computer send them by selecting the check box in the Transfer sent messages from your HPC section. Remember to select the service that you want to use to send the messages.

TIP

When you transfer messages from your handheld PC to Windows 95, the date on the message is changed to the date you transferred the message, which can be confusing when trying to determine exactly when you received the message.

TIP

If for some reason you cannot locate the HPC Inbox Transfer option when you run the Inbox program or Outlook program on your computer, you probably did not install all of the options with H/PC Explorer. The Inbox program update is one of the options that you can select when installing H/PC Explorer on your computer — the install program just isn't clear as to what is actually occurring. You need to rerun the installation for H/PC Explorer in order to get the proper stuff installed on your computer. For more information about the installation of H/PC Explorer, refer to Chapter 9.

Part V
Personalizing Your Handheld PC

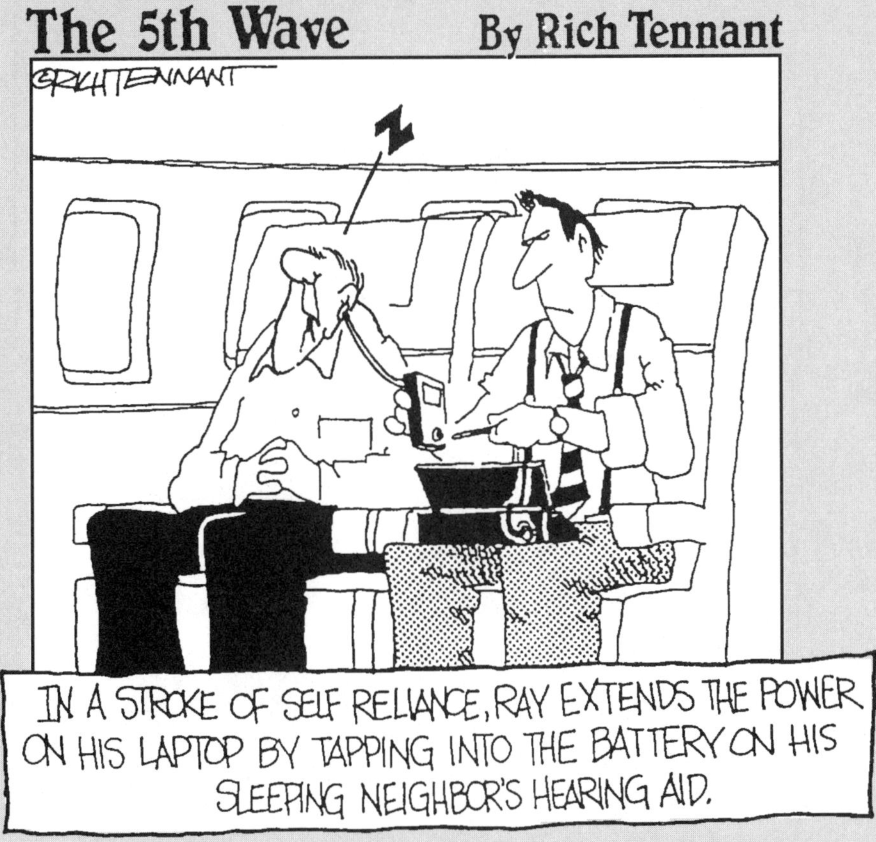

In this part . . .

Whether you don't like the wallpaper, need to turn down the volume, or want to set a password for your handheld PC, you can find options to perform all of these tasks and more in the Control Panel folder on your handheld PC. The chapters in this part look at various ways you can personalize your handheld PC to fit your own unique tastes.

Chapter 17

Protecting Vital Information

In This Chapter

- Changing your personal information
- Password-protecting your handheld PC

I'm betting that at an early age you were taught the importance of labeling your personal belongings so that others would know that your stuff belonged to *you*. With that same theory in mind, Windows CE allows you to equip your handheld PC with your own personal information. To make your handheld PC more secure, you also have the ability to set a password on your handheld PC to keep confidential information totally and completely confidential.

This chapter explains how to go about setting up your personal information and then takes things one step further and tells you how to protect your handheld PC by using a personal password.

Labeling Your Handheld PC With Your Personal Information

Nothing is equal to the frustration of finally getting all of your pertinent stuff entered into your Windows CE handheld PC and then realizing you don't have a clue as to where you put your handheld PC. Now, if you label your handheld PC and someone finds it, that person will know where to return your handheld PC. Makes sense, doesn't it? (Of course, I can't guarantee that the person who finds it will return it — so don't lose it.)

Anyhow, Windows CE provides the ability to display your name, address, and phone number on the first screen that appears when you turn on your handheld PC. So all anyone has to do is turn on your handheld PC and they will immediately know who owns it. This initial screen is known as the Owner Identification screen, and it provides a way to display personal information, as shown in Figure 17-1.

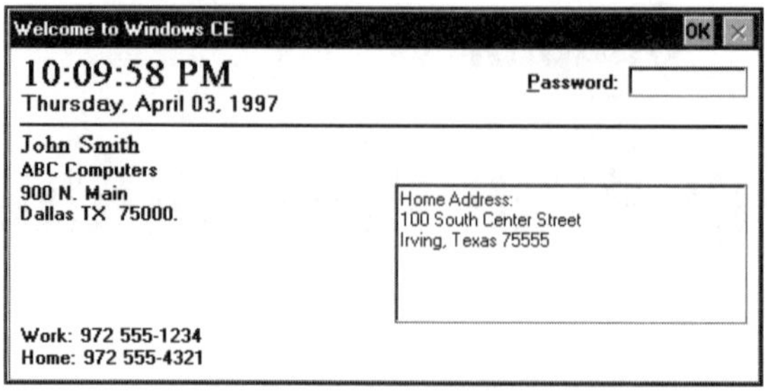

Figure 17-1: The Owner Indent-ification screen.

To set or modify the Owner Identification screen, you need to select the Owner icon in the Control Panel folder. The Owner icon illustrates its purpose by looking like a couple of luggage tags.

The following steps describe how to set up your personal information to display whenever someone turns on your handheld PC.

1. **Tap on the Owner icon in the Control Panel folder.**

   The easiest way to get to the Control Panel folder is to select the Settings option in the Start menu. When you tap on the Owner icon, the Owner Properties dialog box appears, as shown in Figure 17-2. This dialog box is where you type all your personal information.

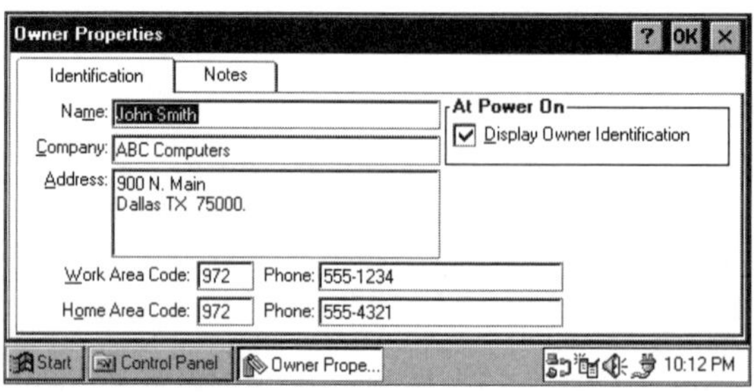

Figure 17-2: Anyone who turns on your handheld PC will see this information.

2. **Type the appropriate information in the Name, Company, Address, and phone number text boxes.**

   Remember, whatever you enter in this dialog box appears when someone turns on your handheld PC. You do not have to type information in all of these fields. If you are really worried about other people learning your home phone number, you may not want to put it in this screen.

3. **Select the Display Owner Identification check box.**

   You must select this check box if you want the information to appear whenever your handheld PC is turned on.

4. **In the Notes tab, type any additional information you want to appear.**

   The Notes tab provides a text box where you can type additional information that you may want to appear in the Owner Identification window, as shown in Figure 17-3.

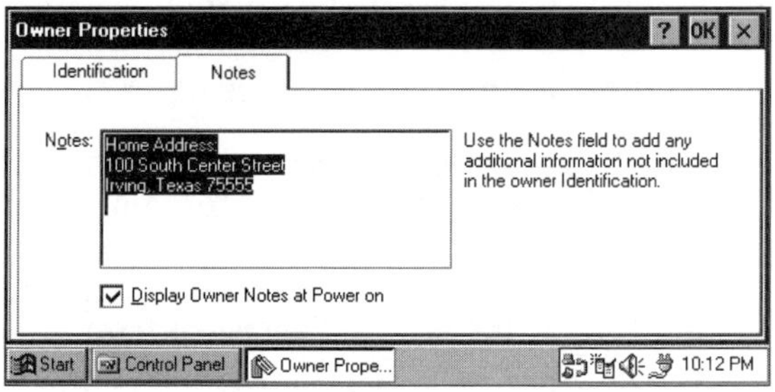

Figure 17-3: Put extra information, such as a home address, in the Notes tab.

5. **Select the Display Owner Notes at Power On check box.**

   Select this option so that anything you type in this tab appears in the Owner Identification text box.

6. **Tap on the OK button to save the changes to the Owner Properties screen.**

You may find that this information is already set up on your handheld PC. When you turn on your handheld PC for the first time, you can set up all of this information. The Owner option allows you to make modifications to the information at any time.

Password-Protecting the Contents of Your Handheld PC

If you work for a large company, you probably have heard how important it is to protect your computer by using a password. You may have even seen videos illustrating how easily someone can copy sensitive information from your computer if you don't take precautions to make sure that it is locked with a password whenever you walk away from it.

Well, the information contained on your Windows CE handheld PC is every bit as vulnerable as the information on your desktop computer. All someone has to do is turn on your handheld PC and they instantly have access to all the stuff that you think you have hidden. To help protect your sensitive information, Windows CE allows you to password-protect your handheld PC. If you password-protect your handheld, the first screen that appears when someone turns on your handheld PC will require a valid password before any other information can be viewed. This screen also contains owner information, if you select that option.

Whether or not you decide to password-protect your handheld PC is up to your own discretion. If you want to set a password for your handheld, simply perform the following steps:

1. **In the Control Panel folder, tap on the Password icon.**

   Don't forget, the easiest way to find the Control Panel folder is to simply tap on the Settings option in the Start menu. The Password icon looks like a couple of keys.

2. **Type your password in the Password text box.**

   Don't be concerned if you are unable to see what you type in the Password field. The field is encrypted, meaning that Windows CE substitutes an asterisk for each character typed (see Figure 17-4). This ensures that someone cannot find out your password by looking at the Password Properties screen.

Figure 17-4: Windows CE displays asterisks when you type in the Password and Confirm Password text boxes.

3. **Type your password again in the Confirm Password text box.**

   Make sure that you type exactly the same password as you typed in the Password text box.

4. **Select the Enable Password Protection check box.**

   This ensures that your handheld PC will request your password whenever someone turns it on. If the person does not know the password, they will not be able to get beyond the initial screen.

5. **Tap the OK button to save the password settings.**

One thing to remember: If you have a password on your handheld PC and you plan to interface your handheld PC with your desktop computer, you need to type in your handheld PC's password on your computer before you can access your handheld PC. This step helps ensure that someone cannot bypass your password security and access your handheld PC by using your desktop computer.

Make sure that you select a password that is easy for you to remember. If for some reason you forget your password, the only way to reset the password is to totally reset your handheld PC. Totally resetting your handheld PC also erases everything that you have stored on it, and your handheld PC will appear as if you have never used it before. If you are really worried about forgetting your password, make sure that you write your password down in a safe place so that you can find it should you ever forget it. The despair of forgetting your password will be nothing compared to the shock of losing everything on your handheld PC.

Chapter 18

Personalizing Your Desktop

In This Chapter

- Hanging new wallpaper on your desktop
- Adding new sounds
- Adjusting the volume
- Modifying the time settings
- Changing the keyboard settings

Okay, get ready to do some redecorating. Everyone got his or her paint cans ready? Oops, I guess I got the wrong book. But Windows CE does let you personalize the look and feel of the operating system by changing the wallpaper on your desktop, changing sounds, and adjusting the volume. The great thing about these adjustments is that they don't require all the work needed to redecorate your office.

This chapter explains how to use some of the options in the Control Panel folder to change the look of your Windows CE desktop, modify the sounds you hear and the volume at which you hear them, adjust the keyboard settings, and change the time and date settings.

Locating the Control Panel Options

The Windows CE Control Panel folder is full of options that you can use to customize the settings on your handheld PC. If the sounds coming from your Windows CE handheld PC are attracting too much attention in the company meeting, for example, you can adjust the Volume and Sounds setting to make the sounds softer or even turn the sounds off.

The easiest way to open the Control Panel folder is to tap on the Start button and then tap on Settings⇨Control Panel. In the Control Panel folder, you see several icons for adjusting the settings on your handheld PC, as shown in Figure 18-1.

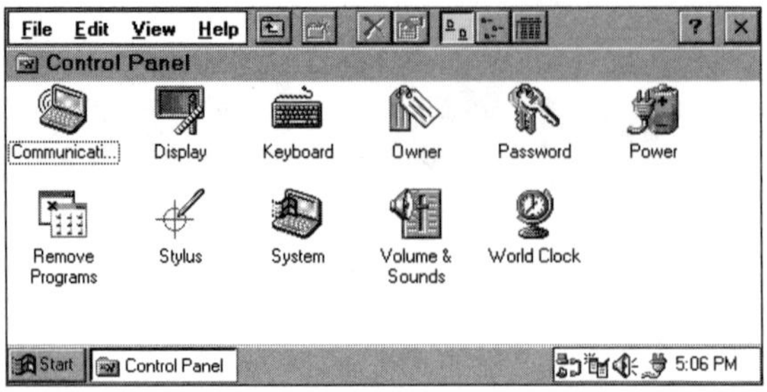

Figure 18-1: You use the icons in the Control Panel folder to customize the settings for your handheld PC.

You use the options in the Control Panel folder to control everything from how your desktop looks to the way your stylus selects items. Table 18-1 provides a brief description of when to select each icon.

Table 18-1 Control Panel Options

Double-Tap on This Icon	*To Do This*
	Set the communication properties for your handheld PC. This icon controls how the handheld PC connects to your desktop computer as well as how it connects to a remote location, such as the Internet. For more information about setting communication properties for your remote connection, refer to Chapter 14.
	Specify what your desktop looks like as well as adjust the contrast settings (determine how bright things look on-screen) for the display.
	Tell Windows CE how fast to type repeating characters by using the keyboard. In other words, if you hold down a key on the keyboard for too long, the character repeats on the screen. This option lets you specify how fasssssssst that happens.
	Create the identification information that appears when you turn on your handheld PC. Check out Chapter 17 for more information.
	Set a password for your handheld PC. Chapter 17 has more information on setting passwords.
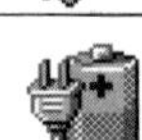	Check the battery level for the main and backup batteries on your handheld PC. Refer to Chapter 1 for more information on using this option.

Double-Tap on This Icon	*To Do This*
	Get rid of programs that you don't want to keep on your handheld PC. Keep in mind that you cannot remove the standard Windows CE programs that were originally installed on your handheld PC, such as Pocket Excel and Pocket Word. Refer to Chapter 13 for more information about removing programs.
	Recalibrate your stylus. If your stylus is not selecting the items you want, use this option. Refer to Chapter 1 for more information on using this option.
	Adjust the memory settings for your handheld PC. Refer to Chapter 1 for more information on using this option.
	Change the sounds that you hear from your handheld PC. You can also adjust the volume for all sounds with this option.
	Set the date and time for your handheld PC.

TIP

You can also display some of these options by tapping on the icons that are pictured in the status bar (the bottom-right corner of the screen). If you double-tap on the time, for example, the World Clock dialog box appears.

Changing the Look of Your Desktop

You probably have already noticed that Microsoft has been nice enough to remind you that Windows CE is loaded on your desktop by painting it across your desktop. For those of you who are a little bored with that look, you can change the *wallpaper* (a generic term used to refer to the background of your desktop) on your desktop.

To modify the wallpaper for your desktop, double-tap on the Display icon in the Control Panel folder. The Display icon looks like a miniature computer monitor. The Display Properties dialog box appears, as shown in Figure 18-2. In this dialog box, you can change the background settings for your desktop and adjust the contrast settings for your display.

To select an image for the background of your desktop, tap on the Down Arrow button next to the Image drop-down list box and tap on the picture you want to display on your desktop. Whatever you select appears on the sample display in the center of the screen.

Figure 18-2: You use the Display Properties dialog box to modify the wallpaper for your desktop and adjust the contrast settings for your display.

If the image you select is quite small, you may want to have that image repeated across the desktop. This process of duplicating the same image all over your desktop is called *tiling*. To tile the selected image, tap on the check box next to the Tile image on background field.

TIP

If you want to use a picture for the desktop background that does not appear in the drop-down list, tap on the Browse button to display the Browse dialog box, shown in Figure 18-3. You'll probably need to use the Previous Folder button (which looks like a folder with an arrow pointing up on the front of it) to navigate through the folders and find the filename for the picture you want. When you find it, select the filename and tap on the OK button.

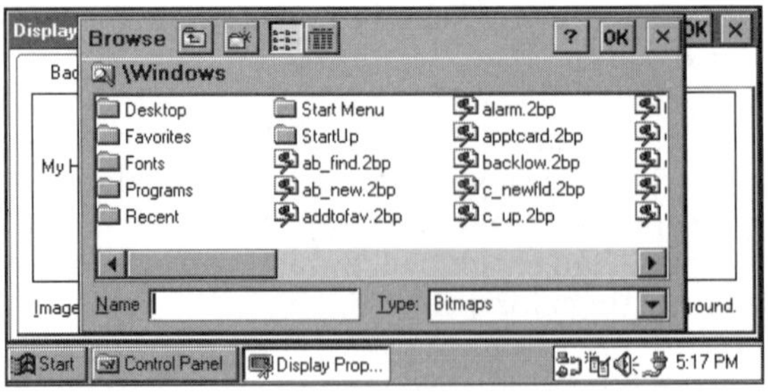

Figure 18-3: You can select any picture on your handheld PC as the background for your desktop.

You can use just about any bitmap image as the background on your Windows CE handheld PC, as long as the image is in the Windows CE bitmap format of .2bp. If you have a bitmap image on your desktop computer that you want to transfer to your handheld PC, make sure that the image is converted from a .bmp image to a .2bp image as it is copied to your handheld PC.

The Display Properties dialog box has another tab, called *Contrast* (see Figure 18-4). The options on this tab give you some images to look at while you are adjusting the contrast button on your handheld PC. The advantage of using this option to adjust the contrast is that it provides a range of shades to view as you adjust the contrast.

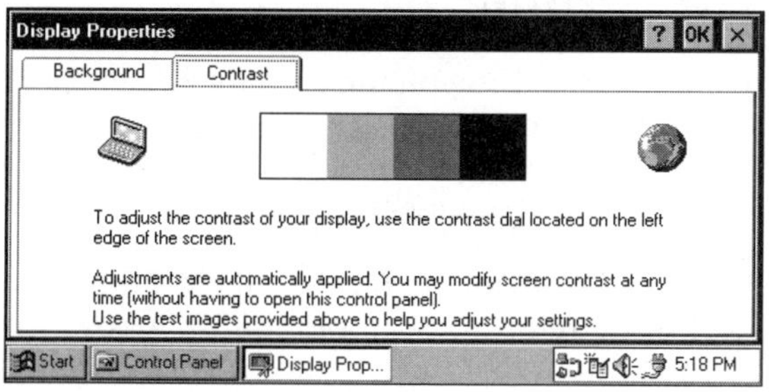

Figure 18-4: The Contrast tab of the Display Properties dialog box.

Making Things Sound Differently

You have probably noticed by now that your Windows CE handheld PC makes different sounds depending on what is happening or even which option you have selected. On some handheld PCs, these sounds may seem a little too loud, especially if you use your handheld PC in meetings where other people can be easily distracted.

Luckily, you can adjust the volume of the sounds that come out of your handheld PC and change or eliminate any sounds that you don't care for by double-tapping on the Volume and Sounds icon in the Control Panel folder. This icon looks like a loudspeaker sitting on top of an adjustment control.

When you tap on the Volume and Sounds icon, the Volume and Sounds Properties dialog box appears (see Figure 18-5). This dialog box provides two tab options: one for setting the volume of your handheld PC, and the other for indicating the specific sounds that occur for different events on your handheld PC.

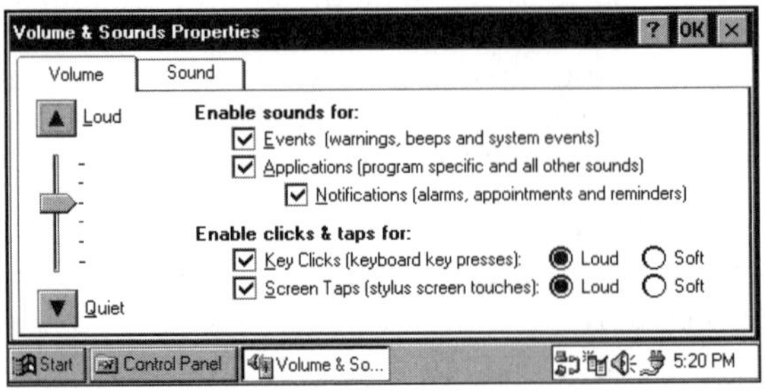

Figure 18-5: Indicate how loud you want the sounds to be on your handheld PC.

Adjusting the volume

The options on the Volume tab in the Volume and Sounds Properties dialog box allow you to specify how loud sounds are on your handheld PC and whether or not sounds occur for specific events or programs or when you press certain keys or tap on the screen with the stylus.

You can adjust the volume of sounds on your handheld PC by using the slider on the left side of the screen. You can tap the Up Arrow button or the Down Arrow button to make sounds louder or softer, or you can drag the slider itself up and down.

The check boxes on the right side of the screen indicate whether or not sounds occur for different events on your handheld PC. If you do not want to be interrupted with sounds as you work, simply remove the check marks from all the check boxes.

TIP

Sounds are a great way to confirm that the action you just performed (typing or tapping) was recognized by your handheld PC. I recommend keeping these options selected. You may decide that you want to select the Soft radio buttons next to each option so that the sound will not be quite so loud, however.

Selecting new sounds

You can use the options on the Sound tab of the Volume and Sounds Properties dialog box to specify the exact sound you hear when different things happen under Windows CE. For example, you can select which sound you hear every time Windows CE starts.

As shown in Figure 18-6, the Event Name list box indicates all the Windows CE events that currently have an associated sound. The events with a sound have the little speaker icon next to the event name.

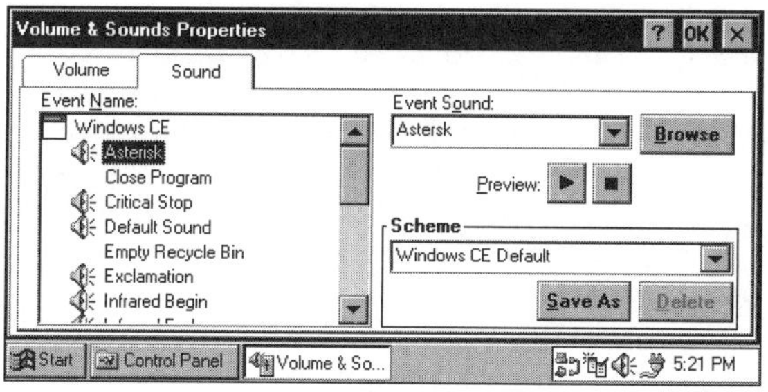

Figure 18-6: The Event Name list box indicates which events currently have an associated sound.

To listen to the sound that plays whenever a specific event occurs, tap on the sound in the Event Name list box and then tap on the Right Arrow button. The Event Sound list box contains the name of the selected sound.

If you want to change the sound, tap on the Down Arrow button next to the Event Sound drop-down list box, and highlight the sound you want to use for that event. If you don't want a sound for that event, make sure that you select the (None) option.

TIP

You may want to use different sounds on your handheld PC depending on your location. At home, for example, you may want to use sounds for every event, and at the office, you may want to use only a few sounds. The good news is that you do not need to manually switch the sounds each time; you can create what is referred to as a *scheme,* which is basically a group of selected sounds. The scheme information is shown in the Scheme drop-down list box. If you have never created or switched schemes, you probably see the Windows CE Default scheme in the list box. To create a new scheme, simply type a name for the scheme in the list box and then tap on the Save As button. When you change the sounds for a scheme, make sure that the scheme name is displayed in the drop-down list box and then tap on the Save As button.

If you have used the options on the Volume tab to turn off the volume or indicate that you do not want certain types of sounds, you may not hear the sounds you select on the Sound tab. If you are having problems with the sounds you have selected, recheck the settings on the Volume tab.

Changing the World Clock Options

You have probably noticed by now that the current time always appears in the bottom-right corner of your handheld PC screen. If you double-tap on the time display, you see the World Clock window, which contains a calendar indicating today's date and clocks for the current time in both your home and visiting locations (see Figure 18-7).

You can also display the World Clock window by double-tapping on the World Clock icon in the Control Panel folder. The icon looks like a globe with a clock in the center of it.

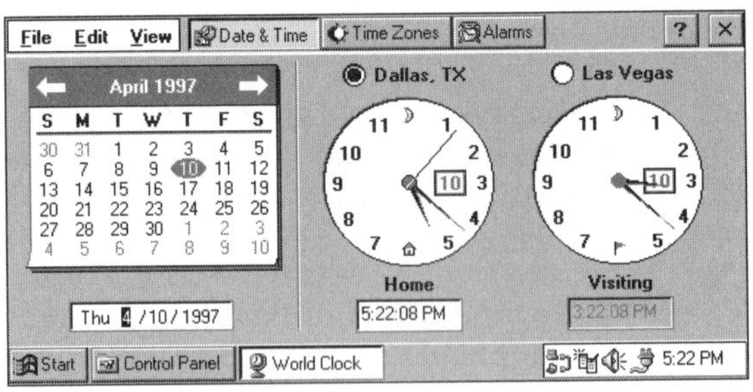

Figure 18-7: Set your date and time information on the World Clock window.

You can view the World Clock window in three ways, depending on the button you select at the top of the screen. You can set date and time information, check the time zone, and set different alarms for your handheld PC.

Windows CE is able to keep track of date and time information for two locations simultaneously. You set one location as your Home location and the other as your Visiting location. For example, if you live and work in Dallas, Texas, but you frequently visit your company's headquarters in Los Angeles, California, you can set Dallas as your Home location and Los Angeles as your Visiting location. For the full scoop, see the next section.

Setting date and time information

When you tap on the Date & Time button at the top of the World Clock program, you are presented with options for setting the date and time in two locations. The Home clock should be labeled with the name of the location where you live (or at least the closest city within your time zone). The Visiting clock is normally used to keep track of the time in another city that you visit frequently. To change either the Home or Visiting city, you need to select the city you want on the Time Zones screen, as described in the next section.

To change the current date, simply tap on the correct date on the calendar. If you need to select another month, tap on the left and right arrows at the top of the calendar to move through the months of the year.

To change the time on either clock, you can either drag the hands of the clock to the appropriate location or type the correct time in the time field under the clock. Note that when you change the minutes on one clock, the minutes automatically change to match on the other clock as well.

The clock that is currently selected is the time that is used for different events on your handheld PC. For example, the Calendar program uses this time to determine when it should notify you of a meeting or appointment. If you are in the Visiting location, be sure to select the radio button for that clock.

Modifying the time zone

When you select the Time Zones button in the World Clock program, you are presented with options that enable you to select the specific Home and Visiting city locations. This screen provides added information about the selected cities, such as the area code, current time, and even the sunrise and sunset times for the current date, as shown in Figure 18-8.

The Home and Visiting buttons on the left side of the screen provide the option to switch between the settings for the home city and the settings for the visiting city. To see the information for one of the cities, simply tap on the appropriate button.

If you want to change one of the cities, simply tap on the Down Arrow button next to the City drop-down list box and select the appropriate city in the list. If you really want to have fun, try tapping on the world map and the desired location; the information shown on-screen changes to the city you selected.

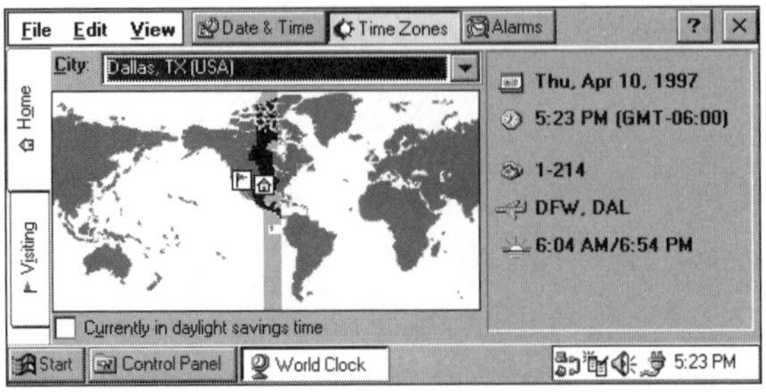

Figure 18-8: The Time Zones portion of the World Clock window.

If you cannot find the city you want, you can create a new city by performing these steps.

1. **Select Edit⇨Add City.**

   When you select the Add City option, the Choose Nearby City dialog box appears, as shown in Figure 18-9.

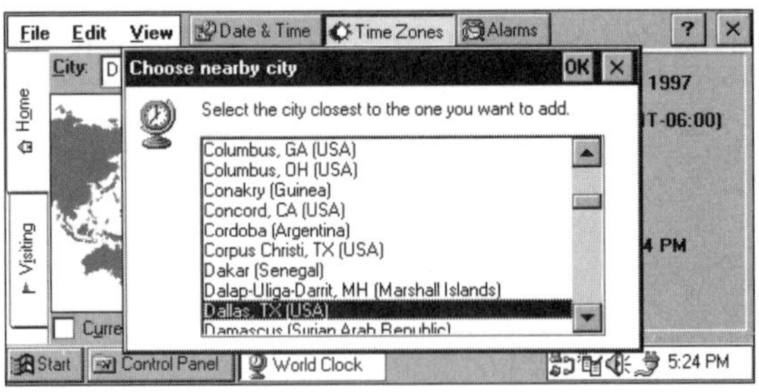

Figure 18-9: The Choose Nearby City dialog box.

2. **Tap on the appropriate city in the list box and then tap on the OK button.**

3. **In the Add City dialog box, type the name of the city in the City Name field.**

   The Add City dialog box copies most of the information it displays from the city that you selected in the Choose Nearby City dialog box. If you know any of the other information, simply type the information in the appropriate fields and then tap on the OK button (see Figure 18-10).

You cannot modify the information for any of the cities that are already set up within Windows CE. If some of the information changes for these cities, such as a new area code, you have to create another city with the same name and modify the appropriate information.

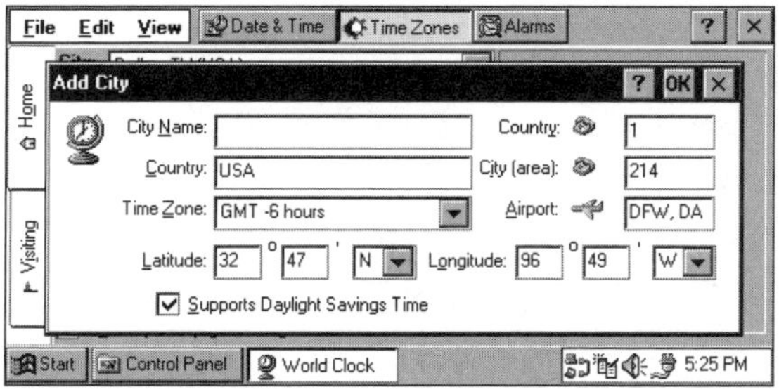

Figure 18-10: Type the information for the new city and tap on the OK button.

Setting alarms

When you select the Alarms button in the World Clock program, you are presented with options that enable you to set alarms for every day at a specific time (see Figure 18-11). For example, you may want to set an alarm to ring every morning at 10:00 to remind you to take your medication.

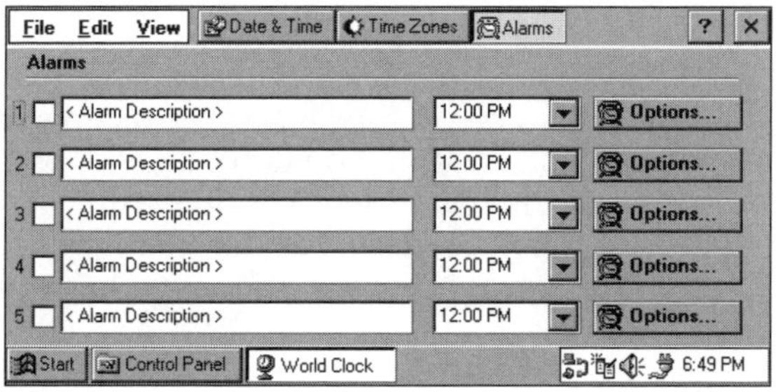

Figure 18-11: Create an alarm to ring daily at the specified time of day.

You can create up to five alarms. The alarms are turned on if a check mark is in the check box next to the alarm. You can type a description for an alarm in the fields that say Alarm Description. Make sure that the time field contains the appropriate time; you can either type a time or tap on the Down Arrow button and highlight the appropriate time for the alarm.

TIP

You can specify the type of alarm that will occur by tapping on the Options button next to the alarm. When you tap on the Options button, the Notifications Options dialog box appears, as shown in Figure 18-12. Select the alarm type and then tap on the OK button.

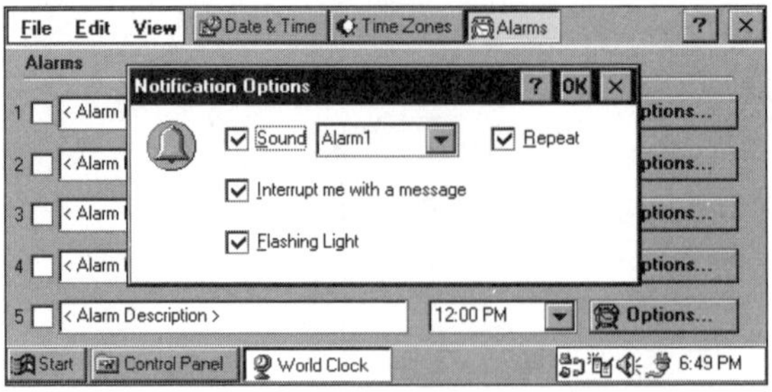

Figure 18-12: Select the type of alarm you want for the specified time.

Adjusting the Keyboard Settings

You cannot change the location or size of the keyboard on your handheld PC, but you can adjust the key repeat settings. The key repeat settings indicate the amount of time a key needs to be held down before the keyboard assumes that you want to repeat the character. It also indicates how quickly the keyboard repeats the character on-screen, once it actually starts to repeat that character.

You can totally eliminate the ability to have a key repeat when you hold it down, but you may find the capability to repeat a keystroke by simply holding down the key — which means that you don't have to press it down several times — useful. Most people find that the repeat rate set on the handheld PC is adequate, but if you find that you are getting a lot of duplicate characters when you type on your handheld PC, you will probably want to adjust these settings.

To set the repeat properties for the keyboard on your handheld PC, you use the Keyboard Properties dialog box, shown in Figure 18-13. To open this dialog box, choose Settings⇨Control Panel from the Start menu and then double-tap on the Keyboard Properties icon in the Control Panel folder. The Keyboard Properties icon resembles a miniature keyboard. You also can open this dialog box by pressing the Windows key+K.

A check mark in the box next to the Enable Character Repeat field indicates that a key will repeat when you hold it down on the keyboard. Remove the check mark from the box only if you do not want keys to repeat.

The Delay before first repeat field indicates the amount of time that should elapse before the key that is held down on the keyboard is repeated. To adjust the setting, tap on either the Long or the Short arrow until the pointer is in the location you want. After you adjust this setting, test it to make sure that you like the new adjustment.

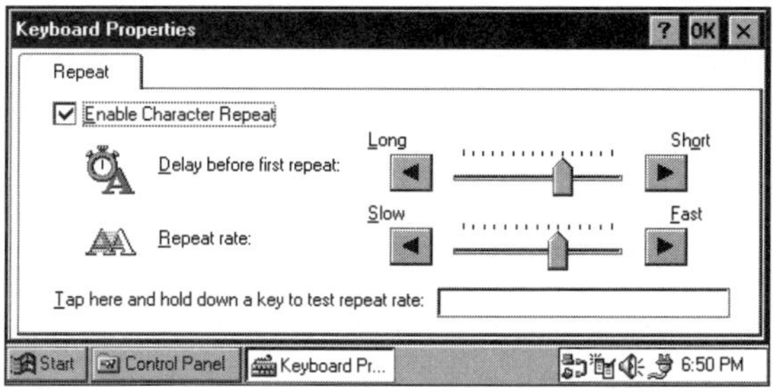

Figure 18-13: You can modify the repeat settings for keys pressed on the keyboard in the Keyboard Properties dialog box.

The Repeat rate field indicates how quickly the key repeats after specified delay has elapsed. To adjust the setting, simply tap either the Long or the Short arrow until the pointer is in the location you want.

You can test the repeat rate by using the text box at the bottom of the dialog box called Tap here and hold down a key field to test the repeat rate. If you want to use this feature, tap in the field with your stylus so that the cursor is displayed in the field and then hold down a key to see the repeat rate. The selected key is repeated in the field. Although this field provides you an immediate test, you will probably need to use the keyboard more to determine whether the setting is exactly what you want.

If you decide to change these settings, you will probably have to make a few adjustments before you find the setting that works best for you.

Part VI
The Part of Tens

The 5th Wave **By Rich Tennant**

"GATHER AROUND, KIDS. YOUR MOTHER'S WINDOWING!"

In this part . . .

You have stumbled across the much-acclaimed Part of Tens found in all *...For Dummies* books. If you are a person who likes to make lists, this part is for you. You will find lists containing approximately ten related items, all dealing with Windows CE.

In this part, you can find out about each of the top Windows CE devices, figure out what else you can get for your handheld PC, and find answers to some of the most common problems with Windows CE.

Chapter 19

Top Ten Windows CE Handheld PCs

In This Chapter

- Cassiopeia
- PC Companion
- Velo 1
- MobilePro
- Palmtop PC
- LG Handheld PC
- Hitachi Handheld PC
- TouchPhone

The market for Windows CE hardware is constantly growing. Although today the hardware is mostly found only on small handheld devices, referred to as *Handheld PCs,* it is also being integrated into hardware such as telephones, DVD players (digital video disks — a new technology that brings movies into your home on disks that resemble the CDs you place in your computer or listen to music on), and other entertainment equipment. This section gives you a peek at the top Windows CE handheld PCs that are currently on the market or about to make an appearance.

One thing that you may quickly notice is the fact that most of the current handheld PCs use the same computer chip for the CPU (Central Processing Unit), which basically means that the computer brains on these units is exactly the same. You should be most concerned with the actual features that come with each unit, and whether those features are beneficial in meeting your own expectations for the handheld PC.

Casio Cassiopeia

The Cassiopeia was the first Windows CE handheld PC to hit the market, making it probably the most widely available handheld PC. The handheld PC comes in two models: The A-10 comes with 2MB of RAM (random-access memory) and the A-11 with 4MB of RAM. Other than the memory differences, both models are identical. Casio has also released several different add-ons that can be purchased and used with both units.

The following features are standard on the Cassiopeia:

- 4MB of ROM used to store the system programs
- Either 2 or 4MB of RAM for storage of files and additional programs
- 480 x 240 display size with everything displayed in 4 shades of gray
- PCMCIA card slot used to add additional hardware options, such as modems and storage cards
- Hitachi SH3 CPU (Central Processing Unit) — the brains
- Infrared port for communicating with other Windows CE handheld PCs
- RS-232C port for communicating with your desktop computer
- Serial interface cable to connect handheld PC to a desktop computer
- Backlight to allow you to see the handheld PC screen in dimly lit locations

The Cassiopeia comes with all of the standard features necessary to run Windows CE efficiently. If you are mainly looking to keep track of appointments and contacts and don't anticipate the need to add much additional software, the 2MB A-10 model will probably be more than adequate to suit your needs. However, the added memory on the A-11 is definitely worth the extra expense; it gives you the ability to store twice as much stuff as the A-10 handheld PC. Keep in mind, though, that memory upgrades are available for both units, so if after purchasing either unit, you find you want to increase the onboard storage, you can boost up your storage. With the PCMCIA card slot, you can add an unlimited amount of options, such as a modem, extra storage, and even paging cards (which turn your handheld PC into a pager).

Compaq PC Companion

You don't have to look too close to see that the Compaq PC Companion looks exactly like the Cassiopeia handheld PCs from Casio. The Compaq PC Companion handheld PCs were actually built by Casio; however, Compaq offers three options, as opposed to the two distributed by Casio. The C120 comes with 2MB of RAM, and the C140 comes with 4MB of RAM. The C120+ is exactly the same as the C120, but it includes a 14.4 Kbps PC-Card modem and an AC adapter so that you can plug the unit into an outlet.

The following features are standard on the PC Companion:

- 4MB of ROM used to store the system programs
- Either 2 or 4MB of RAM for storage of files and additional programs
- 480 x 240 display size with everything displayed in 4 shades of gray
- PCMCIA card slot for adding additional hardware options such as modems and extra storage
- Hitachi SH3 CPU (the brains of the handheld PC)
- Infrared port for communicating with other Windows CE handheld PCs
- RS-232C port for communicating with your desktop computer
- Serial interface cable to connect handheld PC to a desktop computer
- Backlight to allow you to see the handheld PC screen in dimly lit locations

All three models of the PC Companion come with all of the standard features required to run Windows CE efficiently. Although the C120+ comes with a modem, it only has 2MB of RAM, and it actually retails for more than the C140 with 4MB of RAM. Before buying the C120+, check to see if you could possibly buy the C140 (with the extra memory) and a separate PC-Card modem for about the same price. If you go that route, however, don't forget to also purchase an AC adapter.

Because the PC Companion handheld PCs are identical to the Cassiopeia handheld PCs, most of the accessories for the two handheld PCs are interchangeable. You may want to compare prices when you look at the different accessories.

Philips Velo 1

The Velo 1 is one of the newest Windows CE handheld PCs to come to market. This handheld PC not only comes with the standard features found on most of the other handheld PCs, but it also adds some unique features such as a built-in modem as well as a built-in microphone and recording software that allows you to record messages to be listened to at a later date. The Velo 1 is available in both 2MB and 4MB versions.

The following features come standard with the Velo 1:

- 8MB of ROM containing the operating system and programs that come preinstalled on the handheld PC
- Built-in 19.2 Kbps modem
- Either 2 or 4MB of RAM for storage of files and additional programs
- Built-in microphone for recording messages
- 480 x 240 display size with everything displayed in 4 shades of gray
- MIPS R3910 CPU (the brains of the handheld PC)
- Two miniature card slots for adding more hardware options such as extra storage cards
- A proprietary V-module for additional hardware expandability
- Infrared port for communicating with other Windows CE handheld PCs
- Jack for communicating with your desktop computer
- Serial interface cable to connect handheld PC to a desktop computer
- Backlight to allow you to see the handheld PC screen in dimly lit locations
- AC adapter to allow to plug the unit into an electrical outlet
- Velo dock where your Velo 1 sits while you connect to the desktop computer and recharge the battery

The Velo 1 is the perfect handheld PC for those individuals who are looking for a lot of expandability in a handheld PC. The built-in modem provides the ability to have a modem and external storage plugged into your handheld PC simultaneously. In fact, with the two miniature card slots and the V-module expansion, you can potentially add several extra options simultaneously. The CPU is actually one of the fastest available in a Windows CE handheld PC. If you have a PCMCIA card that you want to add to the Velo 1, you need to use the V-Module connection.

Other neat features of the Velo 1 are the additional software programs that come installed on it. The Velo 1 comes with two programs not found on other handheld PCs, a database program that allows you to create simple databases and a voice memo program where you can record messages to be played back later from your handheld PC. One other thing that you are bound to find useful is the shortcut keys found on your keyboard. You can instantly run any of the ten programs that come preinstalled on your handheld PC by pressing the appropriate key sequence on the handheld PC.

NEC MobilePro

The NEC MobilePro comes in two different versions: The MobilePro 200 comes with 2MB of RAM, and the MobilePro 400 has 4MB of RAM and comes with a docking station and AC adapter. By using the docking station, you can connect the MobilePro to an electrical outlet and connect to the desktop computer simultaneously.

The following features are standard on the MobilePro:

- 4MB of ROM used to store the system programs
- Either 2 or 4MB of RAM for storage of files and additional programs
- 480 x 240 display size with everything displayed in 4 shades of gray
- PCMCIA card slot for adding additional hardware options, such as modems and storage cards
- NEC V4101 CPU (the brains)
- Infrared port for communicating with other Windows CE handheld PCs
- Port for communicating with your desktop computer
- Serial interface cable to connect handheld PC to a desktop computer

The serial interface cable that comes with the MobilePro 400 does not connect directly to the handheld PC. In order to interface with your desktop computer, you need to make sure that the handheld PC is sitting in the docking station; the 9-pin cable must also be connected to the docking station. The MobilePro 200 comes with a different serial interface cable that attaches directly to the handheld PC. Several other accessories are available from NEC, such as rechargeable battery packs and modem cables.

Hewlett Packard Palmtop PC

The new Palmtop PCs from Hewlett Packard (HP) bring some new and exciting features to the world of Windows CE handheld PCs. Hewlett Packard offers two different models: the HP300LX with 2MB of RAM, and the HP320LX with a backlight, 4MB of RAM, docking station, and compact Flashcard slot for adding smaller cards. Both of these models come with the widest display currently available on a Windows CE handheld PC, giving you a display of 640 x 240 (which is claimed to be 28 percent wider than most of the standard Windows CE handheld PCs).

Hewlett Packard has added the ability to print from your handheld PC as well. You can print from Microsoft Pocket Word by using the infrared port on your handheld PC to hook to any printer with an infrared port. If your printer does not have an infrared port, you can print to it by using a serial cable.

The following features are standard on the HP Palmtop PC:

- 5MB of ROM used to store the system programs
- Either 2 or 4MB of RAM for storage of files and additional programs
- 640 x 240 display size with everything displayed in 4 shades of gray
- PCMCIA card slot for adding hardware options such as modems and additional storage
- Compact Flash RAM slot on the HP320LX for adding more storage
- Hitachi SH3 CPU (brains of the handheld PC)
- Infrared port for communicating with other Windows CE handheld PCs and printing to HP printers with infrared ports
- RS-232C port for communicating with your desktop computer
- Backlight to allow you to see the handheld PC screen in dimly lit locations (available only on the HP320LX)
- Serial nterface cable to connect handheld PC to a desktop computer

The HP Palmtop PCs definitely offer some features worth looking at. If you intend to use Pocket Excel a great deal, then you will definitely benefit from the wider screen size. If you have several documents that you want to send from Pocket Word to the printer, you will definitely appreciate the ability to print directly from your Windows CE handheld PC. (This feature is only available in Pocket Word. You will have to use the standard method of copying the files to a desktop computer for other Windows CE programs.)

LG Electronics Handheld PC

LG Electronics brings two different model options to the handheld PC market: a 2MB RAM model and a 4MB RAM model. An optional 28.8 Kbps modem can be added without taking up the PC-Card slot.

The following features are standard on the LG handheld PC:

- 4MB of ROM used to store the system programs
- Either 2 or 4MB of RAM for storage of files and additional programs
- 480 x 240 display size with everything displayed in 4 shades of gray
- PCMCIA card slot for adding hardware options, such as modems and extra storage
- Hitachi SH3 CPU (brains of the handheld PC)
- Infrared port for communicating with other Windows CE handheld PCs
- RS-232C port for communicating with your desktop computer
- Serial interface cable to connect handheld PC to a desktop computer

The built-in 28.8 Kbps modem is a feature you should consider when looking for a Windows CE handheld PC, especially if you want to be able to use your handheld PC for e-mail and connecting to the Internet. With the built-in modem, your PC-Card slot is free to add other types of PCMCIA cards such as added storage memory.

Hitachi Handheld PC

Hitachi has also entered the handheld PC market with three model options: a 2MB RAM model, a 4MB RAM model, and a 4MB RAM model with a built-in 28.8 Kbps modem. Hitachi's handheld PCs also provide a larger screen than most of the other handheld PCs on the market: Its handheld PCs have a 5.6 inch diagonal screen instead of the standard 5.1 inch diagonal.

The following features are standard on the Hitachi handheld PC:

- 4MB of ROM used to store the system programs
- Either 2 or 4MB of RAM for storage of files and additional programs
- 480 x 240 display size with everything displayed in 4 shades of gray
- PCMCIA card slot for adding hardware options such as modems and additional storage
- Hitachi SH3 CPU (brains of the handheld PC)
- Infrared port for communicating with other Windows CE handheld PCs
- RS-232C port for communicating with your desktop computer
- Rechargeable NiMH (Nickel Metal Hydride) main battery
- AC adapter and battery charger
- Serial interface cable to connect handheld PC to a desktop computer

The built-in 28.8 Kbps modem and larger screen size may be some features you want to consider when looking for a Windows CE handheld PC. With the built-in modem, your PC-Card slot is free to add other types of PCMCIA cards such as added storage memory.

Navitel TouchPhone

The TouchPhone by Navitel is the first of a new breed of Windows CE handheld PCs. The TouchPhone brings telephones to a whole new platform by not only offering sought after features of Caller ID and voice mail, but also by adding the sophistication of Windows CE. You can also explore the Internet, send e-mail, and use all of the other standard Windows CE applications.

The TouchPhone comes in two models: the TouchPhone 100 with a 320 x 240 display and a 14.4 Kbps modem, and the TouchPhone 200 with a 640 x 480 display and a 28.8 Kbps modem. Both models come with the ability to use two different phone lines.

The following features are standard on the TouchPhone:

- 8MB of ROM used to store the system programs
- 4MB of RAM for storage of files and additional programs
- Either a 320 x 240 display on the TouchPhone 100 or a 640 x 480 display on the TouchPhone 200
- PCMCIA card slot on the TouchPhone 200 for adding additional hardware options
- RC3000 CPU (brains of the phone)
- Full Windows CE-type keyboard available with a retractable drawer to hide keyboard when not in use
- Normal 12-button telephone keypad
- Serial port for communicating with your desktop computer

Chapter 20

Ten Ways to Spend Money on Your Handheld PC

In This Chapter

- Spend some more bucks to become connected
- Purchase more memory
- Save money on battery purchases — by spending some money
- Pick up a stylus to match your attire

Surely when you bought that Windows CE handheld PC you did not think you were finished spending money. After all, what good is buying a handheld PC with so much expansion capability if you never expand? Every day more and more items are available that can be added onto your handheld PC; I'm just including some of the major ones in this chapter.

Modem

Okay, the box said that your handheld PC can connect to the Internet; what it may not have mentioned is that in order to do so, you must have a modem connected to your device. Some of the Windows CE devices do come with a built-in modem; if this is the case with your device, you probably don't need to worry as long as you don't want to add a faster modem or even a wireless one.

If your handheld PC does not have a modem, you definitely need to acquire one before you can connect your handheld PC to another remote location. If you run down to your local computer store to purchase a modem, you are going to quickly find that modems come in all shapes and sizes, and the salesperson is going to immediately start asking you how fast you want the modem to be, internal or external, and have you considered a wireless modem? Enough to make your head spin yet?

You should consider three types of modems for your Windows CE handheld PC:

- A **PC-Card modem** (also called a PCMCIA card) is a modem that is about the size of a credit card. The modem is inserted into your handheld PC in a PC-Card slot. Most of the handheld PCs come with a PC Card slot. This slot is designed to accept any of the standard PCMCIA cards. If you purchase a PCMCIA modem for your handheld PC, be sure to look for one with a low power rating.
- You can also use an **external modem** with your handheld PC. An external modem is a good option if you already own a modem and don't want to purchase a PCMCIA modem. The only drawback is the fact that an external modem is more bulky to haul around. The only requirement for using an external modem is that you need to purchase a null-modem cable and a 9-pin to 25-pin adapter. (Your local computer store can help you with these items — don't worry about knowing what they are; just ask for them by name.) To use the external modem, connect one end of the null modem cable to the end of your serial interface cable that normally connects to your computer, attach the 9-pin to 25-pin adapter to the other end of the null-modem cable, and then plug the adapter into the external modem.
- A **wireless modem** is one of the newest breed of modems available. This type of modem is similar to a cellular phone in that you do not need to plug the modem into a telephone line like other modems. A wireless modem transmits a signal through the air by using a small antenna. Probably one of the only drawbacks with the wireless modem is that it requires some type of monthly contract to pay for your wireless service. But if you are looking for freedom to use the modem when you are away from home, this solution is definitely one to consider.

TIP

If you do not want the expense of purchasing a wireless modem, but you own a cellular phone, then you do have another option to consider. Some modem cards come with the option of plugging into a cellular phone. If you're interested in this capability, be sure to read the modem box carefully to see if it comes with this option before purchasing the modem card.

TIP

When using a modem with your handheld PC, use an electrical adapter if at all possible. A modem causes an extreme power drain on your handheld PC. In fact, some modems will not even work without using the electrical adapter.

Memory Card

No matter how much memory you have available on your handheld PC, sooner or later, you'll inevitably run out. At that point, you can remove all of the old files from your handheld PC. But if you are like I am, you prefer to hold on to everything. Before you run out and plop more money for the latest handheld PC with double the amount of storage space, you do have another option.

You can purchase a *PCMCIA storage card.* This card fits in the PC-Card slot on your handheld PC. By adding one of these cards, you can move all of the files onto the card and use your handheld PC's memory (RAM) for storing programs.

These storage cards come in an array of different sizes. Keep in mind that you can only use them for file storage — most programs will not run off of a storage card.

TIP: Before you run out and purchase a PCMCIA card, you need to make sure that your handheld PC has a slot for these types of cards. If you own a Velo 1, for example, you may want to consider purchasing the miniature memory cards used by that device. You can use PCMCIA cards if you own a V-Module, however.

Docking Station

Docking stations are one of those things that may or may not have some importance to your handheld PC. If you decide to purchase one, you must purchase one designed specifically for your unit. For example, a NEC docking station will not work with a Cassiopeia.

Some handheld PCs come with docking stations, while they are add-on options for other devices. On most devices, the docking station serves as a method for plugging the unit into the power adapter and connecting to your desktop computer.

Refer to the hardware documentation that came with your device to determine if acquiring a docking station would be useful for you.

Storage Case

If you are going to be carrying around your Windows CE handheld PC (which is probably a dumb statement, because I'm sure that is why you bought it), you may want to consider purchasing a storage case for it. Several types of storage cases are available for handheld PCs. You can get ones that just carry your handheld PC, and others give you the ability to carry everything but your desk. A storage case ultimately helps protect your handheld PC, and after spending all that money, I'm sure that you'd like to protect your investment.

Rechargeable Battery

If your handheld PC did not come with a power adapter, you have probably purchased enough batteries to own stock in a certain battery company. To eliminate the need to constantly buy new batteries, most Windows CE handheld PCs have a rechargeable battery available that can be used to replace the main batteries in your device.

Make sure that you follow the instructions for recharging the battery. Some types of rechargeable batteries do not hold a full charge if they are not drained before recharging. Always make sure that you recharge the batteries immediately when you get a low battery message; otherwise, you drain the backup battery.

AC Adapter

As convenient as owning a device that can be carried everywhere is, you will find occasions when you will want to plug it into an outlet. For example, when you use a modem with your handheld PC, you should plug in the handheld, if at all possible, in order to reduce the battery drain caused by the modem.

Unfortunately, not all Windows CE device manufacturers have packaged AC adapters with handheld PCs. If your handheld did not come with one, you should definitely look into purchasing one.

Stylus

Okay, so that little plastic stylus is just not your style. Don't despair: Many types of styluses are available on the market, designed to fit anyone's taste buds.

TIP

Whatever type of stylus you purchase will probably not fit in the stylus holder on your handheld PC, so you may want to go ahead and keep the stylus that came with your handheld PC stored there. That way, if you forget your new, fancy one, you will still have a stylus to use with your handheld PC.

Additional RAM

When you first got your handheld PC, that 2 or 4MB of RAM probably seemed more than adequate. After all, you only wanted to put so many programs on that little handheld PC. But by now, you may be sorry you didn't pick up a handheld PC that had more memory.

Luckily, most Windows CE device manufacturers kept that in mind when designing the handheld PCs. Most of these devices can be expanded to have more memory. Although the memory expansion may not be cheap, it is definitely cheaper than purchasing a new handheld PC.

For more information about increasing the RAM on your device, contact the technical support group for the company that developed your specific handheld PC. Most of the upgrades are done by taking your handheld PC into a service center.

Paging Equipment

If you are the type of mobile professional who is lucky enough to be able to carry a pager, you will definitely be interested in the paging equipment available for your handheld PC. You can purchase paging equipment that allows you to receive a message on your Windows CE handheld PC.

To take things one step further, you can even acquire two-way paging units that allow you to send and receive pages by using your Windows CE handheld PC. Imagine being able to type in a response to a page. These paging units even allow you to send e-mail messages to Internet accounts, and all of this is done through your pager, not a modem.

GPS

This gadget is one that you may want to consider adding to your Windows CE device, especially if you are a gadget nut or if you tend to get lost easily. Commonly referred to as a *global positioning device,* its sole purpose is to determine your exact location on earth by using satellite signals.

These types of devices are being added to automobiles, and now you can carry one with you wherever you go.

Chapter 21

Ten Common Problems You May Encounter with Your Handheld PC

In This Chapter

- Figuring out why your battery bill has gone up
- Fixing a blank screen
- The horrors of forgetting your password
- Why doesn't my handheld PC connect to the outside world?
- Determining why desktop computer files won't work on a handheld PC

Sometimes it seems like no matter what you do, something seems to always go wrong. Nearly everything that occurs with your handheld PC can be resolved, although you may not always get the resolution that you are looking for. This chapter provides a look at some of the common problems that you may encounter when using your handheld PC with a few suggestions about how to resolve the problem.

The Batteries Run Down Too Quickly

The box your handheld PC came in said that you would get 20 hours of battery life, yet you're getting a low battery message after using the device for a considerably less amount of time. This problem is actually a common one. Unfortunately, when the manufacturers determine battery life, they base it on optimal conditions, such as using the handheld PC without additional PC Cards, a backlight, or an internal modem. When you use any of these additional features, your batteries are used up at a much faster rate.

To help conserve your batteries, always use an AC adapter when you use a modem. Modems tend to use a great deal of extra power. Even the modems that claim to use low power will cause your handheld PC to use more battery power than when you are not using the modem. The backlight causes a considerable drain on the batteries, so try to reduce the use of this feature; if at all possible, move to a location where the backlight is not required.

In earlier models of handheld PCs from Casio or Compaq, a battery problem existed when the device was in Suspend mode. Evidently the device was not shutting off all programs, and therefore, battery power was used even when the handheld PC was turned off. A program fix is available on the Internet for these handheld PCs. The Internet address that discusses this problem and its resolution is at `http://www.microsoft.com/windowsce/hpc/support/bug.htm`. You may want to check with your hardware vendor to make sure that your specific handheld PC is one that requires this update. Also, if you don't have Internet access, they can probably provide you with the update. If you don't have a Casio or Compaq handheld PC, you do not need to worry about this fix.

The Handheld PC Won't Turn On

You have tried in vain to turn on your handheld PC, and now you are probably sure that you made a mistake spending all that money on it. Take a deep breath before you go throwing it against the wall. You can perform a very easy step that will probably solve the problem.

Try tapping the Reset button with your stylus. The Reset button is located in a different spot on each handheld PC, so if you don't know where it is, you will probably have to check your hardware documentation. On most handheld PCs, the button is either on top, near the display, or on the bottom of the device.

When you shut down your device, it remembers exactly where you were and what you were doing so that the next time you turn it on, you can continue at that location. Occasionally, all of this information just seems to jumble up its brains and the device does not want to turn on. By pressing the Reset button, you are telling the device to forget about what you had open and start as if all the programs were closed.

If you had a file open that you had not saved before shutting down your handheld PC, you may lose the contents of that file when you reset. Always save before shutting down the handheld PC to eliminate the possibility of losing important information.

I Can't Remember My Password

OOPS!!! This mistake is probably the worst one that you can make with your Windows CE handheld PC. I'm sure that is exactly what you wanted to hear at this time — right? Unfortunately, you are probably not going to like the steps required to resolve this dilemma.

Windows CE does a fantastic job of protecting your handheld PC when you have password-protected it. If someone does not know your password, that person cannot view any information you may have stored on the handheld PC, no matter what steps he or she takes.

The only way to get around a password is to totally reset the handheld PC. This type of resetting is different than pressing the Reset button, which just restarts your handheld PC. When you totally reset your handheld, everything you have stored on the device is erased. In fact, when you turn on your handheld PC, it appears as if you have never used it before. If at all possible, try to figure out your password first — once you reset your handheld PC, you cannot undo the results.

If you have a backup of your handheld PC before you forgot your password, you can restore that backup once you reset your handheld PC. For more information on restoring a backup, refer to Chapter 12.

For information about how to totally reset your specific handheld PC, refer to the hardware documentation that came with the device. For some handheld PCs, totally resetting the device is simply a matter of removing the main and backup batteries for a certain amount of time.

In the future, keep your password written down in a safe place. That way, if you ever forget it again, you will know where to look for it. Just make sure that you can remember where that safe place is.

I Can't Install Windows 95 Programs

If you have used other versions of Microsoft Windows, such as Windows 95, Windows 3.1, or even Windows NT, you have probably figured out that when you install a new version of a Windows operating system, you can almost always copy the programs from the previous version and use them with the newly installed version of the operating system. So because Windows CE is a new Windows operating system, you should naturally be able to copy all of your Windows 95 programs onto any device running Windows CE. Right?

Well, here is where Microsoft has thrown you a curve ball. Although Windows CE very closely resembles Windows 95, only Windows CE programs can be installed on your Windows CE handheld PC.

TIP: If you have a favorite program that you run on your desktop computer, chances are that a version may be available for your Windows CE handheld PC. Check with the software developer to see if they have developed a Windows CE version.

The Device Can't Locate My Desktop Computer

If you are having problems getting your handheld PC and desktop computer to communicate, you can try a couple of things. Before doing anything else, you need to make sure that the serial interface cable is properly connected between your handheld PC and the desktop computer. Without the cable, the two units will not be able to communicate.

TIP: If the two units are turned on with the cable connected, your desktop computer immediately tries to make a connection to the Windows CE handheld PC, but for some unknown reason, it does not always make the connection. To remedy the situation, try running the PC Link option on your Windows CE handheld PC at the same time your desktop computer is attempting to connect, or at least after it has failed the connection. Sometimes when the desktop computer is still booting up and attempting to connect to the handheld simultaneously, it cannot successfully connect to the handheld PC.

TIP: If you are still having problems, and the cable is definitely connected correctly, you may have a *hardware conflict* on your desktop computer. This means that another item inside your computer is trying to use the same serial port where you plugged in the cable. If you have another serial port, try it; otherwise, you may have to break down and ask one of the nerdy computer people to look at your desktop computer and determine why you cannot use that serial port.

To find the serial port on your desktop computer, look for a small port with either 9 or 24 small pins poking out of it. Serial ports are normally used to connect hardware devices such as a modem or a mouse.

H/PC Explorer Can't Convert Microsoft Word Files

If you recently installed Microsoft Office 97, you may find that suddenly the H/PC Explorer program is unable to properly convert your Microsoft Word files to the Pocket Word format. To resolve this problem, reinstall the H/PC Explorer software on your desktop machine.

My Microsoft Word File Won't Open in Windows CE

Okay, you just copied a Microsoft Word or Microsoft Excel file to your Windows CE device, but when you try to open the file on your handheld PC, you get a bunch of funny characters all over the screen. Don't start jumping up and down on your handheld PC; the problem probably has a very simple fix.

When you copy either a Microsoft Word or Microsoft Excel file to your handheld PC that you want to be able to open on your handheld PC, you must convert the file to the appropriate Windows CE format. For Microsoft Word documents, the .doc and .rtf file formats are converted to .pwd file formats — the file format recognized by Pocket Word.

To make sure that the H/PC Explorer program is properly converting the file as it is copied to your device, perform the following steps:

1. **Choose Tools⇨File Conversion.**

   The H/PC Explorer program runs on your desktop computer. When you select the File Conversion option, the File Conversion Properties dialog box appears. Make sure that the check box next to the Enable file conversion option is selected.

2. **Choose Desktop⇨H/PC tab option and highlight the Microsoft Word Document option in the list box.**

   You should see that all .doc files are converted to .pwd files in the File conversion details section at the bottom of the screen.

3. **If the appropriate file conversion type is not selected, click on the Edit button and make the appropriate selection in the Edit Conversion Settings dialog box.**

I Want to Send E-Mail to Several People at Once

You have an e-mail message that you want to send to several different people simultaneously from the Inbox. If you have used other e-mail programs in the past, you may have accomplished this feat before. The easiest way to send a message to more than one address is to type a semicolon between each address in the To field.

If you have a standard group of people that you need to e-mail frequently, such as the people in your department, here is another trick you can try. Create a contact in the Contacts program for the desired group (you may call the group *Coworkers,* for example). In the e-mail field, type each of the e-mail addresses for the different people and place a semicolon between each address. To send to that group, simply select the Address book option in the Inbox program and highlight the Coworkers option.

Need Storage Space for a New Program

You have probably figured out by now that each Windows CE handheld PC comes with a limited amount of storage space. In fact, the maximum amount of memory space that comes standard on current Windows CE devices is 4MB. This memory, though, is actually divided into two different types of memory, storage memory and program memory. The *storage memory* is where Windows CE keeps all of the files and programs that you add to your handheld PC, and the *program memory* is memory that Windows CE uses to move stuff around so that programs run properly.

You may get an error message if your handheld PC is set up so that most of the memory is available for program memory. To change the memory settings, double-tap on the System icon in the Control Panel folder. On the Memory tab option, slide the little slider so that it indicates that more memory is available for storage. Keep in mind that you want to make sure that plenty of memory is still available for running programs.

If you still do not have enough memory available for the program you want to add, you can try adding some additional storage, such as a PC storage card. Remember that you will probably have to move your files to the card and keep all of the programs in the regular memory on your handheld PC.

The Device Turns Off by Itself

If your handheld PC is running on battery power, Windows CE is designed to shut it down automatically if the machine sits idle for a specified amount of time. This option is designed to help conserve your batteries when the handheld PC is not in use. The default time that the handheld PC will sit before shutting down is about 3 minutes, but you can modify this time if you want.

TIP

To change the amount of time that your device waits before shutting down, select the Power icon in the Control Panel folder and change the number of minutes on the Power Off tab option.

WARNING!

If your handheld PC is connected to the desktop computer, whether or not it is running on batteries, the machine will remain on and not shut down. Don't forget and leave the handheld PC connected too long, or you may end up running down your batteries.

Glossary

The Windows CE online help is not as robust as the online help systems for other Windows operating systems. You soon find that the Windows CE online help does not even provide the ability to search for specific words. Anyhow, since Windows CE does not provide a glossary, I provide one here with most of the terms that you may come across as you work with Windows CE.

25-pin: Believe it or not, this term means exactly what it says. 25-pin refers to a connector of some type that has 25 little pins sticking out of it. When dealing with your Windows CE handheld PC, 25-pin is normally the type of port on your handheld PC where you need to plug in the serial interface cable from your desktop computer.

2BP: To be or not to be — oops, wrong book. Actually, 2BP is the file format for pictures you store on your handheld PC. If you have the Windows CE Explorer program show you the full name of each file, you see the characters 2BP at the end of each filename for your pictures. These graphic files are commonly referred to as bitmap images. However, you must convert the graphic files, by using H/PC Explorer, for the files to be actually used as a bitmap on any other operating system.

32-bit: Another nerdy computer term that refers to the size of computer-like instructions that your handheld PC can handle at one time. Other 32-bit operating systems are Windows 95 and Windows NT. Older versions of Windows were only 16-bit operating systems.

bitmap: A form of a graphic image or picture used on a computer or Windows CE handheld PC. The term bitmap simply refers to the way the picture was saved when it was created. The name bitmap comes from the fact that a bunch of tiny little dots, or bits, compose the image. Under Windows CE, bitmap images have the file extension of .2BP.

Clipboard: An invisible storage location where everything you cut or copy in a Windows CE program gets stored so that you can paste it in another location. The Clipboard can store only one block of information at a time; therefore, if you copy one paragraph and then jump down and copy another paragraph, the Clipboard remembers only the second paragraph.

cursor: Your marker on the screen that indicates where the next thing you type will appear. The cursor normally looks like a short, vertical blinking line on the screen.

default: In Windows CE, quite often you must make some type of decision, such as whether or not to save a file. The default is an answer that the computer selects for you, unless you specify otherwise. To accept default values, you can usually just press the Enter key.

desktop: The place where your shortcuts for desired program options sit. You can liven up your desktop by adding wallpaper.

DNS: This crazy acronym stands for Domain Naming System. DNS is a type of program that usually runs on the machines you connect to at your Internet Service Provider. DNS is responsible for converting the numeric IP addresses (such as 205.80.51.140) into host names such as `http://www.dummies.com`. Essentially, the DNS program remembers all of the numbers — you just have to figure out the name of the Web site you want.

document: A common way to refer to a file that contains information that you can normally view and modify on your handheld PC using a specific program. An example is a Pocket Word document.

double-tap: Tapping on or touching a specific button or location on the screen twice in fairly quick succession. You normally double-tap when you want to run a specific program.

drag: The common Windows CE process of touching the desired item with the stylus and then dragging the item across the screen to another location before releasing it.

drop: This term indicates that you release an item after you drag it across your screen. You drop an item by lifting up the stylus from the screen.

e-mail: The process of sending a message from one computer or handheld PC to another. You send the text in an electronic format, so the process got the name e-mail (electronic mail). To send and receive electronic mail, you need to have a connection to a network of some type. You normally make the connection with a modem.

e-mail address: No matter what kind of e-mail system you use (the Internet or a corporate system), you must have a unique address where people can send the mail. Usually, an Internet e-mail address has three parts: a unique name identifying the user, such as `jsmith`; an @ character; and finally the name of the mail server, such as `abccorp.com`. The whole address looks like this: `jsmith@abccorp.com`.

file: A related chunk of information stored in a format that your handheld PC or computer can interpret.

folder: The storage location for different files. On older computers, you normally refer to this storage location as a directory. You may even store other folders within a folder. Under Windows CE, folders look like miniature file folders. You can view folders' contents by double-tapping on the folders.

highlighted: Any item or text that you select. Normally, highlighted items have a dark gray box around them.

HTML: An Internet acronym that refers to a format for most Internet files. If you want to impress someone, HTML stands for HyperText Markup Language, although no one ever says it that way. Most of the Web sites that you look at were created with HTML. HTML is basically just plain text with some codes put in to describe how the text should look.

hyperlink: A predefined link to another object. For example, in the Windows CE online help, you see hyperlinks as bold and underlined. When you tap on a hyperlink, you see information related to the words you tapped on.

icon: A small picture used to represent an option that you can select. An option is normally either a program to run or a specific task that you can perform in a program. For example, tapping on an icon that depicts a pair of scissors cuts (or deletes) selected stuff from the screen.

infrared: The process of sending and receiving information using a beam of light. Your Windows CE handheld PC comes with an infrared port that you can use to communicate with other Windows CE units. On some handheld computers, you may even have the option of printing to a printer using the infrared port.

Internet: The Internet is a series of computers linked together around the world. When you connect to the Internet, you can search for information on a specific topic and send messages to other people.

Internet Service Provider: A company that provides people access to the Internet. The computers at this provider company have a constant Internet connection, so when your modem connects to their computers, you also have access to the Internet.

IP: This acronym stands for Internet Protocol. The protocol used on the Internet that is responsible for routing a message to the appropriate location.

IR: An acronym for infrared. See *infrared.*

ISP: An acronym for Internet Service Provider. See *Internet Service Provider.*

maximize: The process of opening a program window back up after it has been minimized. When you minimize a program, a button still remains for it on the taskbar. To maximize a program, you simply tap on the associated button on the taskbar.

memory: Memory is where your handheld PC not only stores the operating system, programs, and files, but also performs calculations. Your handheld PC comes with at least two types of memory, ROM and RAM. The first, ROM (read-only memory), is where the basic Windows CE operating system and programs are stored. You cannot modify anything stored in ROM. On the other hand, RAM (random access memory) is where you add extra programs and store your files. The handheld PCs use RAM to run the programs you select. You may also add other types of memory, such as memory cards, to increase the amount of storage space you have on your handheld PC.

minimize: The process of shrinking a program so you can perform a different task. When you minimize a program, a button still remains for it on the taskbar. To minimize a program, you simply tap on the associated button on the taskbar. When you want to work in the program, tap on the button.

multitasking: This means doing multiple tasks at once. For example, if you chew gum and drive a car, you are multitasking. Your Windows CE handheld PC multitasks when it runs multiple programs simultaneously.

network: A series of computers that are connected.

operating system: This is just another software program with enormous responsibilities. On your handheld PC, Windows CE is the operating system. Windows CE is responsible for controlling everything that occurs on your handheld PC. For example, it keeps track of the date and time, monitors the battery levels, keeps track of the programs you are running, and makes sure all of the behind-the-scenes stuff goes on properly.

program: Something that you use on your handheld PC to perform a certain task. For example, you use the program Pocket Word to create and view different documents.

RAM: An acronym for Random Access Memory, the nerdy computer term for where you store new programs and files on your handheld PC.

recurring: Refers to an event that occurs more than once. A recurring event may be a weekly piano lesson or Sunday dinner at Mom's. Therefore, if you create a recurring appointment on your handheld PC, such as a Monday morning staff meeting, Windows CE reminds you of the appointment every Monday morning.

Recycle Bin: The place where you keep all your deleted files until you empty the bin. If you accidentally delete the wrong item, you can go to the Recycle Bin to rescue the item. Keep in mind that deleted messages in the Inbox program are not placed in the Recycle Bin.

ROM: An acronym for Read-Only Memory, the nerdy computer term that refers to the place where the Windows CE operating system and all included programs are stored. You cannot change anything stored in ROM on your handheld PC.

search engine: A program that you can run on the Internet that searches for all Web sites that contain the information you specify. For example, to find all of the Web sites that talk about cruises, you type the word `cruise` into a search engine and let it search for the appropriate matches.

serial port: A connection on the back of your computer where you can plug in other items such as modems, printers, and even the cable from your Windows CE handheld PC. Each serial port has either 9 or 25 pins sticking out of it.

shortcut: A little picture (icon) on your Windows CE desktop that allows you to quickly run a program on your handheld PC. The term actually refers to a program stored in some other location on your handheld PC. A shortcut icon has a little arrow on the bottom of it to indicate that it is a shortcut.

shut down: The process of turning off your handheld unit. For a Windows CE handheld PC, shutting down either refers to pressing the appropriate button on the keyboard to turn off the handheld PC or selecting the Suspend option on the Start menu.

Start menu: This is basically your road map to your Windows CE handheld PC. The Start menu appears anytime you tap on the Start button on the taskbar. The menu gives you the ability to locate different files, find programs, change system settings, find information about Windows CE, and shut down your handheld PC.

Suspend: This option on the Start menu shuts off your handheld PC but remembers exactly what was running on your handheld PC. When you turn on your handheld PC again, you can start up exactly where you left off. With most handheld PCs, pressing the off button on the keyboard activates the Suspend option.

tap: The process of touching an item on the screen with the stylus.

taskbar: The bar across the bottom of your screen. This is where the Start button resides, along with buttons for any open programs and status information such as the current time.

TCP/IP: A communications protocol used specifically over the Internet to connect different types of machines together. If you want to really impress some of those computer nerds, TCP/IP stands for Transmission Control Protocol/Internet Protocol.

toolbar: The bar at the top of all your Windows CE programs that has different menu options and buttons. The actual menu options and buttons on the toolbar vary with each program.

URL: Another way to refer to the address where you can locate something over the Internet. For example, the URL (Uniform Resource Locator) for the main page at IDG Books is `http://www.idgbooks.com`.

wallpaper: The different pictures that display on the background of your desktop. You can change the desktop wallpaper to any bitmap graphic on your handheld PC using the Display option in the Control Panel folder.

Web site: A specific location, or server, on the Internet that contains specific information. For example, `http://www.microsoft.com` is the Web site that contains basically all the information you ever wanted to know about Microsoft. (Okay, well, *almost* everything.)

window: A term that Microsoft coined to identify the on-screen box in which each program runs. Messages and other information also display in windows on your handheld PC.

Index

• Numbers •

• A •

• B •

• C •

• D •

• E •

• F •

• G •

• H •

• I •

• N •

• O •

• P •

• S •

• T •

• X •

DUMMIES PRESS™

Title	Author	ISBN	Price
The Internet For Macs® For Dummies® 2nd Edition	by Charles Seiter	ISBN: 1-56884-371-2	$19.99 USA/$26.99 Canada
The Internet For Macs® For Dummies® Starter Kit	by Charles Seiter	ISBN: 1-56884-244-9	$29.99 USA/$39.99 Canada
The Internet For Macs® For Dummies® Starter Kit Bestseller Edition	by Charles Seiter	ISBN: 1-56884-245-7	$39.99 USA/$54.99 Canada
The Internet For Windows® For Dummies® Starter Kit	by John R. Levine & Margaret Levine Young	ISBN: 1-56884-237-6	$34.99 USA/$44.99 Canada
The Internet For Windows® For Dummies® Starter Kit, Bestseller Edition	by John R. Levine & Margaret Levine Young	ISBN: 1-56884-246-5	$39.99 USA/$54.99 Canada
MACINTOSH			
Mac® Programming For Dummies®	by Dan Parks Sydow	ISBN: 1-56884-173-6	$19.95 USA/$26.95 Canad
Macintosh® System 7.5 For Dummies®	by Bob LeVitus	ISBN: 1-56884-197-3	$19.95 USA/$26.95 Canad
MORE Macs® For Dummies®	by David Pogue	ISBN: 1-56884-087-X	$19.95 USA/$26.95 Canad
PageMaker 5 For Macs® For Dummies®	by Galen Gruman & Deke McClelland	ISBN: 1-56884-178-7	$19.95 USA/$26.95 Canad
QuarkXPress 3.3 For Dummies®	by Galen Gruman & Barbara Assadi	ISBN: 1-56884-217-1	$19.99 USA/$26.99 Canad
Upgrading and Fixing Macs® For Dummies®	by Kearney Rietmann & Frank Higgins	ISBN: 1-56884-189-2	$19.95 USA/$26.95 Canad
MULTIMEDIA			
Multimedia & CD-ROMs For Dummies® 2nd Edition	by Andy Rathbone	ISBN: 1-56884-907-9	$19.99 USA/$26.99 Canad
Multimedia & CD-ROMs For Dummies® Interactive Multimedia Value Pack, 2nd Edition	by Andy Rathbone	ISBN: 1-56884-909-5	$29.99 USA/$39.99 Canad
OPERATING SYSTEMS:			
DOS			
MORE DOS For Dummies®	by Dan Gookin	ISBN: 1-56884-046-2	$19.95 USA/$26.95 Canad
OS/2® Warp For Dummies® 2nd Edition	by Andy Rathbone	ISBN: 1-56884-205-8	$19.99 USA/$26.99 Canad
UNIX			
MORE UNIX® For Dummies®	by John R. Levine & Margaret Levine Young	ISBN: 1-56884-361-5	$19.99 USA/$26.99 Canad
UNIX® For Dummies®	by John R. Levine & Margaret Levine Young	ISBN: 1-878058-58-4	$19.95 USA/$26.95 Canad
WINDOWS			
MORE Windows® For Dummies® 2nd Edition	by Andy Rathbone	ISBN: 1-56884-048-9	$19.95 USA/$26.95 Canad
Windows® 95 For Dummies®	by Andy Rathbone	ISBN: 1-56884-240-6	$19.99 USA/$26.99 Canad
PCS/HARDWARE			
Illustrated Computer Dictionary For Dummies® 2nd Edition	by Dan Gookin & Wallace Wang	ISBN: 1-56884-218-X	$12.95 USA/$16.95 Canad
Upgrading and Fixing PCs For Dummies® 2nd Edition	by Andy Rathbone	ISBN: 1-56884-903-6	$19.99 USA/$26.99 Canad
PRESENTATION/AUTOCAD			
AutoCAD For Dummies®	by Bud Smith	ISBN: 1-56884-191-4	$19.95 USA/$26.95 Canac
PowerPoint 4 For Windows® For Dummies®	by Doug Lowe	ISBN: 1-56884-161-2	$16.99 USA/$22.99 Canac
PROGRAMMING			
Borland C++ For Dummies®	by Michael Hyman	ISBN: 1-56884-162-0	$19.95 USA/$26.95 Canac
C For Dummies® Volume 1	by Dan Gookin	ISBN: 1-878058-78-9	$19.95 USA/$26.95 Canac
C++ For Dummies®	by Stephen R. Davis	ISBN: 1-56884-163-9	$19.95 USA/$26.95 Canac
Delphi Programming For Dummies®	by Neil Rubenking	ISBN: 1-56884-200-7	$19.99 USA/$26.99 Canac
Mac® Programming For Dummies®	by Dan Parks Sydow	ISBN: 1-56884-173-6	$19.95 USA/$26.95 Canac
PowerBuilder 4 Programming For Dummies®	by Ted Coombs & Jason Coombs	ISBN: 1-56884-325-9	$19.99 USA/$26.99 Canac
QBasic Programming For Dummies®	by Douglas Hergert	ISBN: 1-56884-093-4	$19.95 USA/$26.95 Canac
Visual Basic 3 For Dummies®	by Wallace Wang	ISBN: 1-56884-076-4	$19.95 USA/$26.95 Canac
Visual Basic "X" For Dummies®	by Wallace Wang	ISBN: 1-56884-230-9	$19.99 USA/$26.99 Canac
Visual C++ 2 For Dummies®	by Michael Hyman & Bob Arnson	ISBN: 1-56884-328-3	$19.99 USA/$26.99 Canac
Windows® 95 Programming For Dummies®	by S. Randy Davis	ISBN: 1-56884-327-5	$19.99 USA/$26.99 Canac
SPREADSHEET			
1-2-3 For Dummies®	by Greg Harvey	ISBN: 1-878058-60-6	$16.95 USA/$22.95 Canac
1-2-3 For Windows® 5 For Dummies® 2nd Edition	by John Walkenbach	ISBN: 1-56884-216-3	$16.95 USA/$22.95 Canac
Excel 5 For Macs® For Dummies®	by Greg Harvey	ISBN: 1-56884-186-8	$19.95 USA/$26.95 Canac
Excel For Dummies® 2nd Edition	by Greg Harvey	ISBN: 1-56884-050-0	$16.95 USA/$22.95 Cana
MORE 1-2-3 For DOS For Dummies®	by John Weingarten	ISBN: 1-56884-224-4	$19.99 USA/$26.99 Cana
MORE Excel 5 For Windows® For Dummies®	by Greg Harvey	ISBN: 1-56884-207-4	$19.95 USA/$26.95 Cana
Quattro Pro 6 For Windows® For Dummies®	by John Walkenbach	ISBN: 1-56884-174-4	$19.95 USA/$26.95 Cana
Quattro Pro For DOS For Dummies®	by John Walkenbach	ISBN: 1-56884-023-3	$16.95 USA/$22.95 Cana
UTILITIES			
Norton Utilities 8 For Dummies®	by Beth Slick	ISBN: 1-56884-166-3	$19.95 USA/$26.95 Cana
VCRS/CAMCORDERS			
VCRs & Camcorders For Dummies™	by Gordon McComb & Andy Rathbone	ISBN: 1-56884-229-5	$14.99 USA/$20.99 Cana
WORD PROCESSING			
Ami Pro For Dummies®	by Jim Meade	ISBN: 1-56884-049-7	$19.95 USA/$26.95 Cana
MORE Word For Windows® 6 For Dummies®	by Doug Lowe	ISBN: 1-56884-165-5	$19.95 USA/$26.95 Cana
MORE WordPerfect® 6 For Windows® For Dummies®	by Margaret Levine Young & David C. Kay	ISBN: 1-56884-206-6	$19.95 USA/$26.95 Cana
MORE WordPerfect® 6 For DOS For Dummies®	by Wallace Wang, edited by Dan Gookin	ISBN: 1-56884-047-0	$19.95 USA/$26.95 Cana
Word 6 For Macs® For Dummies®	by Dan Gookin	ISBN: 1-56884-190-6	$19.95 USA/$26.95 Cana
Word For Windows® 6 For Dummies®	by Dan Gookin	ISBN: 1-56884-075-6	$16.95 USA/$22.95 Cana
Word For Windows® For Dummies®	by Dan Gookin & Ray Werner	ISBN: 1-878058-86-X	$16.95 USA/$22.95 Cana
WordPerfect® 6 For DOS For Dummies®	by Dan Gookin	ISBN: 1-878058-77-0	$16.95 USA/$22.95 Cana
WordPerfect® 6.1 For Windows® For Dummies® 2nd Edition	by Margaret Levine Young & David Kay	ISBN: 1-56884-243-0	$16.95 USA/$22.95 Cana
WordPerfect® For Dummies®	by Dan Gookin	ISBN: 1-878058-52-5	$16.95 USA/$22.95 Can

For scholastic requests & educational orders please call Educational Sales at 1. 800. 434. 2086

FOR MORE INFO OR TO ORDER, PLEASE CALL ▸ 800. 762. 2974

For volume discounts & special orders Corporate Sales, at 415. 655. 3000

DUMMIES PRESS™ QUICK REFERENCES

FOR DUMMIES BOOK SERIES FROM IDG

IDG BOOKS WORLDWIDE

Fun, Fast, & Cheap!™

7/29/96

NEW!

he Internet For Macs® For ummies® Quick Reference

y Charles Seiter

SBN:1-56884-967-2
9.99 USA/$12.99 Canada

NEW!

Windows® 95 For Dummies® Quick Reference

by Greg Harvey

ISBN: 1-56884-964-8
$9.99 USA/$12.99 Canada

SUPER STAR

Photoshop 3 For Macs® For Dummies® Quick Reference

by Deke McClelland

ISBN: 1-56884-968-0
$9.99 USA/$12.99 Canada

SUPER STAR

WordPerfect® For DOS For Dummies® Quick Reference

by Greg Harvey

ISBN: 1-56884-009-8
$8.95 USA/$12.95 Canada

Title	Author	ISBN	Price
ATABASE			
Access 2 For Dummies® Quick Reference	by Stuart J. Stuple	ISBN: 1-56884-167-1	$8.95 USA/$11.95 Canada
dBASE 5 For DOS For Dummies® Quick Reference	by Barrie Sosinsky	ISBN: 1-56884-954-0	$9.99 USA/$12.99 Canada
dBASE 5 For Windows® For Dummies® Quick Reference	by Stuart J. Stuple	ISBN: 1-56884-953-2	$9.99 USA/$12.99 Canada
Paradox 5 For Windows® For Dummies® Quick Reference	by Scott Palmer	ISBN: 1-56884-960-5	$9.99 USA/$12.99 Canada
ESKTOP PUBLISHING/ILLUSTRATION/GRAPHICS			
CorelDRAW! 5 For Dummies® Quick Reference	by Raymond E. Werner	ISBN: 1-56884-952-4	$9.99 USA/$12.99 Canada
Harvard Graphics For Windows® For Dummies® Quick Reference	by Raymond E. Werner	ISBN: 1-56884-962-1	$9.99 USA/$12.99 Canada
Photoshop 3 For Macs® For Dummies® Quick Reference	by Deke McClelland	ISBN: 1-56884-968-0	$9.99 USA/$12.99 Canada
INANCE/PERSONAL FINANCE			
Quicken 4 For Windows® For Dummies® Quick Reference	by Stephen L. Nelson	ISBN: 1-56884-950-8	$9.95 USA/$12.95 Canada
ROUPWARE/INTEGRATED			
Microsoft® Office 4 For Windows® For Dummies® Quick Reference	by Doug Lowe	ISBN: 1-56884-958-3	$9.99 USA/$12.99 Canada
Microsoft® Works 3 For Windows® For Dummies® Quick Reference	by Michael Partington	ISBN: 1-56884-959-1	$9.99 USA/$12.99 Canada
NTERNET/COMMUNICATIONS/NETWORKING			
The Internet For Dummies® Quick Reference	by John R. Levine & Margaret Levine Young	ISBN: 1-56884-168-X	$8.95 USA/$11.95 Canada
ACINTOSH			
Macintosh® System 7.5 For Dummies® Quick Reference	by Stuart J. Stuple	ISBN: 1-56884-956-7	$9.99 USA/$12.99 Canada
PERATING SYSTEMS:			
OS			
DOS For Dummies® Quick Reference	by Greg Harvey	ISBN: 1-56884-007-1	$8.95 USA/$11.95 Canada
NIX			
UNIX® For Dummies® Quick Reference	by John R. Levine & Margaret Levine Young	ISBN: 1-56884-094-2	$8.95 USA/$11.95 Canada
INDOWS			
Windows® 3.1 For Dummies® Quick Reference, 2nd Edition	by Greg Harvey	ISBN: 1-56884-951-6	$8.95 USA/$11.95 Canada
Cs/HARDWARE			
Memory Management For Dummies® Quick Reference	by Doug Lowe	ISBN: 1-56884-362-3	$9.99 USA/$12.99 Canada
RESENTATION/AUTOCAD			
AutoCAD For Dummies® Quick Reference	by Ellen Finkelstein	ISBN: 1-56884-198-1	$9.95 USA/$12.95 Canada
PREADSHEET			
1-2-3 For Dummies® Quick Reference	by John Walkenbach	ISBN: 1-56884-027-6	$8.95 USA/$11.95 Canada
1-2-3 For Windows® 5 For Dummies® Quick Reference	by John Walkenbach	ISBN: 1-56884-957-5	$9.95 USA/$12.95 Canada
Excel For Windows® For Dummies® Quick Reference, 2nd Edition	by John Walkenbach	ISBN: 1-56884-096-9	$8.95 USA/$11.95 Canada
Quattro Pro 6 For Windows® For Dummies® Quick Reference	by Stuart J. Stuple	ISBN: 1-56884-172-8	$9.95 USA/$12.95 Canada
ORD PROCESSING			
Word For Windows® 6 For Dummies® Quick Reference	by George Lynch	ISBN: 1-56884-095-0	$8.95 USA/$11.95 Canada
Word For Windows® For Dummies® Quick Reference	by George Lynch	ISBN: 1-56884-029-2	$8.95 USA/$11.95 Canada
WordPerfect® 6.1 For Windows® For Dummies® Quick Reference, 2nd Edition	by Greg Harvey	ISBN: 1-56884-966-4	$9.99 USA/$12.99/Canada

lastic requests & educational orders please ational Sales at 1. 800. 434. 2086

FOR MORE INFO OR TO ORDER, PLEASE CALL ▸ 800. 762. 2974

For volume discounts & special orders please call Corporate Sales, at 415. 655. 3000

IDG BOOKS WORLDWIDE

7/29/96

"A lot easier to use than the book Excel gives you!"

Lisa Schmeckpeper, New Berlin, WI, on PC World Excel 5 For Windows Handbook

Official Hayes Modem Communications Companion
by Caroline M. Halliday

SBN: 1-56884-072-1
29.95 USA/$39.95 Canada
ncludes software.

1,001 Komputer Answers from Kim Komando
by Kim Komando

ISBN: 1-56884-460-3
$29.99 USA/$39.99 Canada
Includes software.

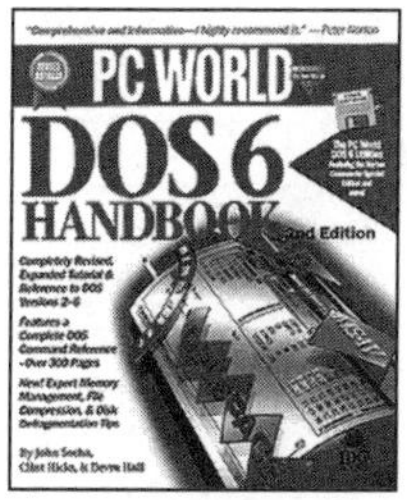

BESTSELLER!

PC World DOS 6 Handbook, 2nd Edition
by John Socha, Clint Hicks, & Devra Hall

ISBN: 1-878058-79-7
$34.95 USA/$44.95 Canada
Includes software.

PC World Word For Windows® 6 Handbook
by Brent Heslop & David Angell

ISBN: 1-56884-054-3
$34.95 USA/$44.95 Canada
Includes software.

BESTSELLER!

C World Microsoft® ccess 2 Bible, nd Edition
y Cary N. Prague & Michael R. Irwin

BN: 1-56884-086-1
39.95 USA/$52.95 Canada
cludes software.

PC World Excel 5 For Windows® Handbook, 2nd Edition
by John Walkenbach & Dave Maguiness

ISBN: 1-56884-056-X
$34.95 USA/$44.95 Canada
Includes software.

PC World WordPerfect® 6 Handbook
by Greg Harvey

ISBN: 1-878058-80-0
$34.95 USA/$44.95 Canada
Includes software.

QuarkXPress For Windows® Designer Handbook
by Barbara Assadi & Galen Gruman

ISBN: 1-878058-45-2
$29.95 USA/$39.95 Canada

NATIONAL BESTSELLER!

fficial XTree mpanion, 3rd Edition
Beth Slick

N: 1-878058-57-6
.95 USA/$26.95 Canada

NATIONAL BESTSELLER!

PC World DOS 6 Command Reference and Problem Solver
by John Socha & Devra Hall

ISBN: 1-56884-055-1
$24.95 USA/$32.95 Canada

SUPER STAR

Client/Server Strategies™: A Survival Guide for Corporate Reengineers
by David Vaskevitch

ISBN: 1-56884-064-0
$29.95 USA/$39.95 Canada

"PC World Word For Windows 6 Handbook is very easy to follow with lots of 'hands on' examples. The 'Task at a Glance' is very helpful!"

Jacqueline Martens, Tacoma, WA

"Thanks for publishing this book! It's the best money I've spent this year!"

Robert D. Templeton, Ft. Worth, TX, on MORE Windows 3.1 SECRETS

astic requests & educational orders please ational Sales at 1. 800. 434. 2086

FOR MORE INFO OR TO ORDER, PLEASE CALL 800. 762. 2974

For volume discounts & special orders please call Corporate Sales, at 415. 655. 3000

ORDER FORM

IDG BOOKS WORLDWIDE™

Order Center: **(800) 762-2974** *(24 hours a day, seven days a week)*

Quantity	ISBN	Title	Price	Total

Shipping & Handling Charges

	Description	First book	Each additional book	Total
Domestic	Normal	$4.50	$1.50	$
	Two Day Air	$8.50	$2.50	$
	Overnight	$18.00	$3.00	$
International	Surface	$8.00	$8.00	$
	Airmail	$16.00	$16.00	$
	DHL Air	$17.00	$17.00	$

*For large quantities call for shipping & handling charges.
**Prices are subject to change without notice.

Ship to:

Name ______________________

Company ______________________

Address ______________________

City/State/Zip ______________________

Daytime Phone ______________________

Payment: ☐ Check to IDG Books Worldwide (US Funds Only)

☐ VISA ☐ MasterCard ☐ American Express

Card # ______________________ Expires ____________

Signature ______________________

Subtotal ____________

CA residents add applicable sales tax ____________

IN, MA, and MD residents add 5% sales tax ____________

IL residents add 6.25% sales tax ____________

RI residents add 7% sales tax ____________

TX residents add 8.25% sales tax ____________

Shipping ____________

Total ____________

Please send this order form to:

IDG Books Worldwide, Inc.
Attn: Order Entry Dept.
7260 Shadeland Station, Suite 100
Indianapolis, IN 46256

Allow up to 3 weeks for delivery. Thank you!

IDG BOOKS WORLDWIDE REGISTRATION CARD

Visit our Web site at http://www.idgbooks.com

Title of this book: **Windows® CE For Dummies®**

My overall rating of this book: ❑ Very good [1] ❑ Good [2] ❑ Satisfactory [3] ❑ Fair [4] ❑ Poor [5]

How I first heard about this book:

❑ Found in bookstore; name: [6] ❑ Book review: [7]

❑ Advertisement: [8] ❑ Catalog: [9]

❑ Word of mouth; heard about book from friend, co-worker, etc.: [10] ❑ Other: [11]

What I liked most about this book:

What I would change, add, delete, etc., in future editions of this book:

Other comments:

Number of computer books I purchase in a year: ❑ 1 [12] ❑ 2-5 [13] ❑ 6-10 [14] ❑ More than 10 [15]

I would characterize my computer skills as: ❑ Beginner [16] ❑ Intermediate [17] ❑ Advanced [18] ❑ Professional [19]

I use ❑ DOS [20] ❑ Windows [21] ❑ OS/2 [22] ❑ Unix [23] ❑ Macintosh [24] ❑ Other: [25]____________ (please specify)

I would be interested in new books on the following subjects:
(please check all that apply, and use the spaces provided to identify specific software)

❑ Word processing: [26] ❑ Spreadsheets: [27]

❑ Data bases: [28] ❑ Desktop publishing: [29]

❑ File Utilities: [30] ❑ Money management: [31]

❑ Networking: [32] ❑ Programming languages: [33]

❑ Other: [34]

I use a PC at (please check all that apply): ❑ home [35] ❑ work [36] ❑ school [37] ❑ other: [38] ____________

The disks I prefer to use are ❑ 5.25 [39] ❑ 3.5 [40] ❑ other: [41]____________

I have a CD ROM: ❑ yes [42] ❑ no [43]

I plan to buy or upgrade computer hardware this year: ❑ yes [44] ❑ no [45]

I plan to buy or upgrade computer software this year: ❑ yes [46] ❑ no [47]

Name: Business title: [48] Type of Business: [49]

Address (❑ home [50] ❑ work [51]/Company name:)

Street/Suite#

City [52]/State [53]/Zipcode [54]: Country [55]

❑ **I liked this book!** You may quote me by name in future IDG Books Worldwide promotional materials.

My daytime phone number is ____________

IDG BOOKS WORLDWIDE
THE WORLD OF COMPUTER KNOWLEDGE®